The GIANT Encyclopedia of Preschool Activities for Three-Year-Olds

Dedication

This book is dedicated to all the wonderful, curious, and enthusiastic three-year-olds and the wonderful, curious, and enthusiastic adults who teach them.

The
GIANT
Encyclopedia of
Preschool Activities
for
Three-Year-Olds

Edited by Kathy Charner
and Maureen Murphy

gryphon house®, inc.
Beltsville, Maryland

Disclaimer

The publisher and the authors cannot be held responsible for injury, mishap, or damages incurred during the use of or because of the activities in this book. The authors recommend appropriate and reasonable supervision at all times based on the age and capability of each child.

Bulk Purchase

Gryphon House books are available at special discount for special premiums and sales promotions as well as for fund-raising use. Special editions or book excerpts also can be created to specification. For details, contact the Director of Sales at Gryphon House.

Copyright

Illustrations: K. Whelan Dery
Cover art: Beverly Hightshoe

Library of Congress Cataloging-in-Publication Data

The giant encyclopedia of preschool activities for three-year-olds / Kathy Charner and Maureen Murphy, editors ; illustrations, K. Whelan Dery.
    p. cm.
Rev. ed. of: It's great to be three. c2002.
  ISBN 0-87659-237-X
  1. Education, Preschool--Activity programs. 2. Creative activities and seat work. 3. Toddlers--Recreation. I. Charner, Kathy. II. Murphy, Maureen. III. It's great to be three.
  LB1140.35.C74I83 2004
  372.5--dc22

200301945

Table of Contents

Blocks

Books

Circle Time

Dramatic Play

Fine Motor

Fingerplays, Songs, & Poems

Games

General Tips

Gross Motor

Holidays and Special Days

Language

Literacy

Manipulatives

Math

Morning Greeting

Music & Movement

Outdoor Play

Rest & Nap Time

Sand & Water

Science & Nature

Snack & Cooking

Social Development

Transitions

Indexes

Introduction

Working with three-year-olds has its rewards and its challenges. Children in this age group are observant and love to imitate their teachers. They are mastering the physical skills of running, jumping, walking, and climbing. They are able to follow simple directions and help with straightforward, everyday tasks. Threes are also developing a strong interest in their peers and are engaging in cooperative play, which may be elaborate.

In addition, three-year-olds are developing literacy and language skills, including the ability to listen to stories, sing songs, and repeat simple rhymes. Their expressive language continues to develop, and some threes may speak in lengthy sentences. In short, they are busy individuals!

To keep up with children during this period of intense growth and development, teachers must have a variety of tools and tricks, as well as a tremendous amount of energy! *The GIANT Encyclopedia of Preschool Activities for Three-Year-Olds* provides the tools and tricks—excellent activities that address the needs and interests of three-year-olds. Many activities, especially those in the Books, Language, and Literacy chapters, support growing language and literacy skills that are so important for future readers. Most activities throughout the book include suggestions for related books, as well.

When selecting activities for three-year-olds, consider the following milestones.

In the area of physical development, threes are learning to:
- toilet with some help
- pedal a tricycle
- eat independently
- dress self with some help
- climb up and down stairs
- kick a ball
- hop on one foot

In the area of emotional/social development, threes are learning to:
- enjoy helping with simple tasks
- play for short periods of time with others
- enjoy fantasy play and may not distinguish between fantasy and reality

- enjoy playing "house"
- engage in cooperative play for short periods of time
- follow simple directions

In the area of intellectual/language development, threes are learning to:
- speak so that strangers can understand most of their speech
- pronounce words
- recognize shapes, such as a circle and a square
- recognize and distinguish common colors
- play with playdough
- listen to short stories and books
- sing simple songs
- count up to three
- put together a simple puzzle
- ask who, what, where, and why questions

How to Use This Book

We asked teachers to send us their great activities for three-year-olds. We selected the very best entries, and the result is this book of more than 600 child-friendly, teacher-approved activities. The contributing teachers have successfully used these activities with the children they teach. We trust that you and your children will benefit from the years of experience reflected in these pages. In addition to the sections listed below, this book has two indexes. One is an index of the children's books used in the activities, and the other one is an index of the materials used in the activities.

Each activity in this book contains some or all of the following sections:

Materials

Each activity includes a list of readily available materials. Investigate all possible sources of free materials in your community, including donations from paper stores, framing shops, woodworking shops, lumberyards, and, of course, parents.

What to do

The directions are presented in a step-by-step format. Patterns and illustrations are included where necessary.

More to do

Additional ideas for extending the activity are included in this section. Many activities include suggestions for integrating the activity into other areas of the curriculum such as math, dramatic play, circle time, blocks, language, and snack and cooking.

Related books

Under this heading are titles and authors of popular children's books that can be used to support the activity.

Related songs and poems

Familiar songs related to the original activity and original songs and poems written by teachers are in this section.

Have fun with the activities. Participate with the children. Laugh and giggle. Try to remember what it was like to be three. Use the ideas on these pages as a springboard for your own creativity. Most of all, share the love of learning and discovery with the children you teach.

Teaching Colors

Materials

Red, blue, and yellow fingerpaint
Fingerpaint paper
Spray bottle filled with water

What to do

1. Give each child a sheet of fingerpaint paper and a spray bottled filled with water. Ask the children to spray some water onto the glossy side of the paper.
2. Give each child two primary colors of his choice and encourage him to fingerpaint on the wet paper.
3. Discuss what is happening. Talk about the colors in the pictures and ask the children what colors they used to make the new color.

More to do

Use corn syrup and food colors instead of water and paint.

Related book

Mouse Paint by Ellen Stoll Walsh

❖❖ Phyllis Esch, Export, PA

Paint Pallets

Materials

Hot glue gun (adult only)
Plastic bottle caps
Large, plastic-coated paper plates, one for each child
Spoons
Tempera paint, several colors
Small brushes
Manila paper, white construction paper, or newsprint
Plastic containers of clean water, one for each child

What to do

1. Use a hot glue gun to glue three or four plastic bottle caps onto each paper plate (adult only).
2. Put a spoonful of different colored paint into each cap. (It's a good idea to start with the primary colors: blue, yellow, and red.)
3. Give one plate, a brush, and a piece of paper to each child. Show the children how to wash their brushes before changing colors (but don't be concerned if they skip this step).
4. Demonstrate how to take a small amount of one color, put it into the center of the paper plate (the "pallet"), and then blend it with a small amount of another color to make a third color. Then paint on the piece of paper.
5. Encourage all efforts and experiments. There is no wrong way for children to do this exploratory activity. The learning comes from exploring. Some children may not even apply the paint to the paper, and that's okay too!
6. Repeat this activity many times over the year and watch the children's skill and knowledge increase.

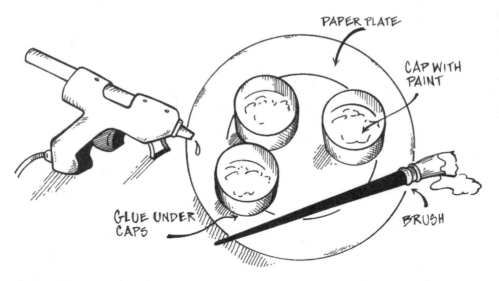

More to do

General Tips: Use these pallets when children are painting while sitting (or sprawling) on the floor. There's little chance of spilled paint, and very little paint to spill. Cover the floor with plastic tarps or shower curtains for quick and easy cleanup.

Related book

Color Dance by Ann Jonas

❖❖Barbara Backer, Charleston, SC

Smelly Paints

Materials

Clean, empty baby food jars
Fingerpaints in various colors
Different scented oils, such as peppermint and vanilla (found in the food section
   of grocery stores)
Spoons

What to do

1. Help the children pour different colored paint into several baby food jars.
2. Next, show them how to add about four drops of scented oil to each jar and
   mix with a spoon.
3. Cover and use as long as it lasts!

◆◆Lisa Chichester, Parkersburg, WV

Blotto Surprises

Materials

Tempera paints in several colors
Plastic containers
Plastic spoons
Scissors
Brown paper grocery bags
Damp sponge

What to do

1. Pour tempera paint into plastic containers and put a plastic spoon into each
   one.
2. Cut out 8" (22 cm) squares from brown paper grocery bags and give one
   square to each child.
3. Ask the children to rub a damp sponge on their squares to moisten them.
4. Challenge the children to twist the moistened paper, open them back up, and
   then crumple them into a ball. Repeat this a few more times.

5. Ask the children to place their wrinkled pieces of paper on the table in front of them. Encourage them to dip a spoon into one color of paint and drip the paint onto one area of the paper. Ask them to repeat this step using two other colors.

6. Encourage the children to crumple their paper again with the paint inside. The paint will run into the wrinkles, and in some places, it will mix with the other colors to form new colors.

7. When the children open up their paper, they will see the "Blotto Surprise!"

8. Place the painted papers on a flat surface to dry.

◆◆Barbara Backer, Charleston, SC

Q-Tip Painting

Materials

Paint
Empty egg carton containers
Tray
Q-Tips
Paper

What to do

1. Pour a small amount of paint into each section of an empty egg carton.
2. Place Q-Tips on a tray, along with the egg carton.
3. Give each child a piece of paper. Encourage the children to create their own designs using the Q-Tips as brushes.

◆◆Sue M. Myhre, Bremerton, WA

Rain Paintings

Materials

Large fingerpaint paper (coated paper is best for this activity)
Watercolors or tempera paints
Large trays or cookie sheets
A rainy day

What to do

1. Give each child a piece of large fingerpaint paper.
2. Encourage the children to fingerpaint freely with tempera paints or watercolors.
3. After the children have finished painting, place the paintings on a large tray.
4. Bring the trays outside into the rain. Watch as the rain falls on the paintings and talk about what is happening. Ask the children questions such as "What is happening when the raindrops hit the paper?" or "Why is the paint splattering?"
5. Leave the paintings in the rain for two or three minutes, and then bring them back inside and allow them to dry.
6. After the paintings have dried, ask the children to describe how the rain affected their paintings. Record their answers and display them along with the rain paintings.

More to do

Instead of painting, sprinkle dry tempera powder on the paper and place it on a tray. Put it outside in the rain and leave it out until it is soaked through. Bring it back inside and let it dry.

Music: Sing rain songs (see below) while watching the rain "paint" the paper.

Original songs

Rain, Rain, Come Today (Tune: "Rain, Rain, Go Away")

Rain, rain, come today.
Come to where our paintings lay.
Come and splatter all around
And on our paintings on the ground.

The Rain Is Falling Down (Tune: "The Farmer in the Dell")

The rain is falling down.
The rain is falling down.
It splatters on my painting that is
Lying on the ground.

The rain is falling down.
The rain is falling down.
I like to watch it splatter
On my painting on the ground.

Related books

In the Rain with Baby Duck by Amy Hest
It's a Shame about the Rain by Barbara Shook Hazen
Listen to the Rain by Bill Martin Jr., John Archambault
Mushroom in the Rain by Mirra Ginsburg
One Hot Summer Day by Nina Crews
One Stormy Night by Ruth Brown
One Stormy Night by Joy Cowley
The Rain Door by Russell Hoban
The Rainbabies by Laura Krauss Melmed
That Sky, That Rain by Carolyn Otto
The Umbrella Day by Nancy Evans Cooney

◆◆Virginia Jean Herrod, Columbia, SC

Golf Ball Painting

Materials

Vinyl tablecloth or newspaper
Paint smocks
9" x 12" (22 cm x 30 cm) construction paper
Gift boxes
Tempera paints
Plates or shallow containers
Several golf balls
Tongs

What to do

1. This activity can be a little messy, so make sure to cover the work area with newspaper or a vinyl tablecloth. Also make sure the children wear paint smocks.
2. Place construction paper inside the top or bottom part of a few gift boxes.
3. Pour a small amount of paint into several shallow containers or plates.
4. Give each child a golf ball.
5. Show the children how to place the golf ball into the paint and use tongs to roll it around so that it is completely covered with paint.
6. Then put the golf ball on the paper inside the box top or bottom.
7. Show the children how to hold one end of the box at a time to move the golf ball around on the paper. Remind the children to keep the box close to the

table when lifting to prevent the golf ball from moving around too fast or falling out of the box.

8. For a rainbow effect, use different colored paints.
9. Hang the papers to dry.
10. To prevent paint from getting onto carpets and so on, try doing this activity outdoors.

More to do

This is a good activity to do during a sports unit or in conjunction with a field day event.

◆◆Tina R. Durham-Woehler, Lebanon, TN

"Glad" to Paint

Materials

Gladiola flowers, cat o' nine tails, and dandelions
Scissors
Pipe cleaners
Newspaper
Paint cups or containers
Paint
Easel paper and easels

What to do

1. Cut the gladiola flowers into two shorter pieces and cut the stems of the cat o' nine tails to about 1' (30 cm).
2. Twist pipe cleaners around the stems of the dandelions to make them sturdier.
3. Put the flowers on a newspaper-covered table, along with containers of paint.
4. Put paper onto the easels.
5. Encourage the children to choose flowers to use as paintbrushes. They can make any designs they desire.

More to do

Play music and encourage the children to paint to the rhythm.

◆◆Ann Gudowski, Johnstown, PA

Mud Painting

Materials

Easels
Drop cloths or newspaper
Easel paper
Dirt
Water
Small buckets
Paintbrushes, all sizes

What to do

1. Place drop cloths or newspaper underneath the easels and put easel paper on each easel.
2. With the children's help, make mud. Pour dirt and water into the small buckets and mix.
3. Put three different-sized brushes into each bucket.
4. Place the buckets on the drop cloths next to the easels.
5. Encourage the children to create mud designs.

Related books

Dirt Is Delightful by Janelle Cherrington
The Piggy in the Puddle by Charlotte Pomerantz

◆◆Ann Gudowski, Johnstown, PA

Rubber Band Paintbrush

Materials

6 rubber bands
Scissors
Transparent tape
Pencil with eraser
Hot glue gun, optional (adult only)

What to do

1. Cut the rubber bands in half and then bunch them together.
2. Wrap a piece of tape around the middle of the rubber bands. Tape the center of the rubber bands to the end of the eraser. If desired, secure it using a hot glue gun (adult only).
3. Give each child a rubber band brush to use for painting.

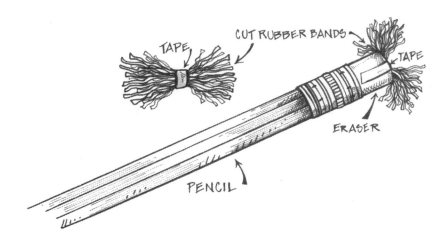

More to do

Make different sizes of brushes with different widths of rubber bands.

◆Jean Potter, Charleston, WV

Spoon and Roll Painting

Materials

Tempera paint
Spoons
Paper
Rolling pins

What to do

1. Pour tempera paint into containers and add spoons to each one.
2. Give each child two pieces of paper.
3. Ask the children to spoon some paint onto one piece of their paper.

4. Ask them to put the second sheet of paper on top.
5. Demonstrate how to use a rolling pin to roll over the top sheet. Separate the papers to see your creation!

More to do

Use wax paper as the top sheet.

◆◆Jean Potter, Charleston, WV

Feather Duster Painting

Materials

Paint
Pie pans or dishes
Paint shirts or smocks
Feather dusters, one for each child
Paper

What to do

1. Pour paint into pie pans or dishes, just enough to cover the bottom. Keep the extra paint close by so you can add more as needed.
2. Help the children put on paint shirts or smocks. (Some children will splatter a bit.)
3. Give each child a feather duster and a piece of paper.
4. Show the children how to press the feather duster into the paint and, in an up and down motion, press it onto the paper. Encourage them to explore what happens when using the feather duster. Some children will want to use it as a brush; however, it works better using a blotting method.
5. When the children are finished, rinse the feather dusters in a sink. The paint will wash out, but the feathers may remain stained the paint color. Be careful not to twist or pull on the feathers. Hang them up or lay them on a rack to dry.

TIP: Add a bit of liquid soap to the paint. It helps with cleanup and when washing the paint out of clothing.

More to do

Make a group mural using feather dusters. This painting makes a great background for bulletin boards.

◆◆Sandra Nagel, White Lake, MI

Cotton Ball Painting

Materials

Paint
Paper
Cotton balls
Marker

What to do

1. Give each child a piece of paper and a cotton ball.
2. Pour a bit of paint on the top corner of each child's paper.
3. Show the children how to dip the cotton ball into the paint and dab it on the paper. Demonstrate how to make a few lines, dabs, circles, or other designs.
4. While the children are painting, talk about other things that they could do with cotton balls.

◆◆A. Gail Whitney, Dameron, MD

Gadget Painting

Materials

Smocks or aprons
Paper plate or foam meat tray
Damp paper towels
Paint
Things to use as painting instruments, such as hair rollers, bolts and nuts, bristle
  blocks, building blocks, vegetable mashers, plastic parts, liquid detergent lids,
  combs, plastic forks, and fruit baskets
Paper

What to do

1. Help the children put on their painting smocks or aprons.
2. Cover the paper plates or meat trays with damp paper towels and pour paint onto the paper towels.
3. Encourage the children to create exciting art by dipping various gadgets into the paint and stamping them onto paper.

Hint: To be economical, try using brown paper grocery bags, newspaper, or old handouts for paper.

4. After the children finish, help them label each gadget print on their paper. This will help them review what they did, extend their vocabulary, and tie writing skills into this activity.
5. Continue adding various items to the painting area throughout the year.

More to do

Discuss sizes by showing the children the same shapes in various sizes.

◆◆Bev Schumacher, Dayton, OH

Twig Painting

Materials

Newspaper
Paint
Paint cups
Bark paper
Scissors
Twigs

What to do

1. Cover the table with newspaper. Pour paint into the cups and put them on the table.
2. Cut the bark paper into a variety of sizes, from 3" x 5" (7 cm x 12 cm) to 8" x 10" (20 cm x 22 cm), and place them on the table along with the twigs.
3. Have a discussion about twigs. Ask the children if they know where twigs come from.

4. Encourage the children to feel the texture of the paper. It's usually smooth and may surprise the children!

5. Explain to the children that they will use twigs to paint on the bark paper.

6. When the children are finished painting, transition to the next activity by singing the following to the tune of "The Ants Go Marching."

    When (child's name) is finished painting then,
    Hurrah! Hurrah!
    He'll wash his hands and go to (place),
    Hurrah! Hurrah!

More to do

Use twigs from different seasons. For example, use new green twigs in the spring, twigs with flowers on them in the summer, and so on.

◆◆A. Gail Whitney, Dameron, MD

Magic Painting Bags

Materials

Zipper-closure plastic bags (gallon size), one per child
Liquid laundry starch
Powdered tempera paint
Measuring cup and spoons
Construction paper in a variety of colors

What to do

1. This activity lets you enjoy the paint without the mess!

2. Into each bag, pour ¼ cup (60 ml) liquid starch and 3 tablespoons (45 g) tempera paint. Squeeze out all the air and seal it tightly.

3. Give one bag to each child. Demonstrate how to blend the paint and starch by gently squeezing the bags with the fingers.

4. Encourage the children to place their bags flat on a table and create designs using their hands and fingers. They can "erase" their designs by lifting up the bag and smoothing it out again.

5. The children can change the effect by placing different colors of paper under their bags.

More to do

Tie this activity into a unit about colors.

Related books

A Color of His Own by Leo Lionni
Liang and the Magic Paintbrush by Demi

◆◆Susan A. Sharkey, La Mesa, CA

Pots and Pans

Materials

Newspaper
Tempera paint in a variety of colors
Paintbrushes
Variety of old pots and pans
Very large piece of butcher paper

What to do

1. Cover the work surface or floor with newspaper and place a large sheet of butcher paper on it. Several children can make prints on this sheet of paper. Or, if desired, give each child a small piece of paper for individual projects.
2. Ask the children to paint the bottom of a pot or pan and then use it to make one or more prints on the paper. Encourage them to use the same pot or pan more than once, either using up the paint on the bottom or adding a new color before making more prints.
3. Encourage the children to make as many prints as desired, using more than one pot or pan. Put out new paper as needed.

More to do

Show the children how to clean the pots and pans in the sink using soap and a sponge. Use the pots and pans for a cooking activity or use them as a target or basket for a ball toss game.

◆◆Barbara Reynolds, Galloway Township, NJ

Print Painting

Materials

Yarn or twine
Recycled plastic bottles
Hot glue gun (adult only) or glue sticks
Water
Paint
Styrofoam plates
Paper

What to do

1. Encourage the children to wrap yarn around plastic bottles in various shapes and designs. Use a hot glue yarn to attach the yarn (adult only). Or, the children can use glue sticks to attach the yarn.
2. Fill the bottles with water and glue on the top. The water will help the bottle roll.
3. Pour paint onto Styrofoam plates.
4. Give each child a piece of paper. Encourage the children to roll their bottle in the paint to coat the yarn, and then roll the bottle on their paper to make prints.

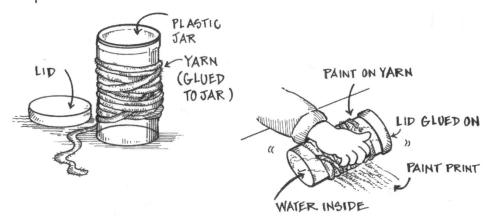

More to do

The children can use the same bottle in the sand and water table (filled with sand) to make prints in the sand. Or they can make prints in the sandbox outside.

◆◆ Nicole Sparks, Miami, FL

Spider Web Designs

Materials

Plastic paper plate holder (the kind with web-like designs on it)
Black paint
Sponges
White and black paper
Glue

What to do

1. Turn the plate holder over so that the bottom is facing up.
2. Show the children how to cover the bottom of the holder with black paint using sponges.
3. Demonstrate how to press the paint-covered bottom onto a piece of white paper. Lift it to reveal a "web-like" print.
4. Cut out circles and thin strips of black construction paper.
5. Encourage the children to make spiders out of the black circles and strips. Then, they can glue the spiders onto their "webs."
6. If desired, the children can make more than one print and overlap them.

More to do

Use a variety of colors instead of just black.
Berry baskets also make great prints. Just dip them into paint and print! After making berry basket prints, eat the berries that came in the baskets and read *Jamberry* by Bruce Degen.

Related books

The Itsy Bitsy Spider by Iza Trapani
The Very Busy Spider by Eric Carle

◆◆Audrey F. Kanoff, Allentown, PA

Night Glitter Skies

Materials

Black construction paper
Small paintbrushes
Glow-in-the-dark paint
Glitter glue or paint
Star stickers of various sizes
Moon stickers

What to do

1. Give the children black construction paper and encourage them to make nighttime skies using the paint and glue.
2. Encourage them to place star and moon stickers on their paper, too.
3. Allow the paintings to dry.
4. Write each child's name on his paper using white chalk or glittery paint or glue.

More to do

Have a PJ Day! Ask the parents to dress their children in pajamas and slippers and bring their favorite blankets. Pop popcorn or make s'mores for snack. Encourage the children to read books while resting in sleeping bags.

Related books

Goodnight Moon by Margaret Wise Brown
Good Night, Gorilla by Peggy Rathmann
Night Noises by Mem Fox
The Sky Is Full of Stars by Franklyn Branley

◆◆Tina R. Durham-Woehler, Lebanon, TN

Melted Crayon Art

Materials

Scraps of old crayons
Egg carton or sectioned container
Small food processor
Wax paper
Cup warmer or hot plate (with adult supervision)

What to do

1. With the children, peel the paper from old crayons.
2. Sort the colors into a sectioned container or egg carton sections.
3. Grind each color separately in a food processor and dump the shavings back into their section.
4. Place a piece of wax paper onto a cup warmer or hot plate. (If using a cup warmer, a small piece of wax paper about the same size as the warmer section works best.) Ask a child to place a pinch at a time of shavings onto the wax paper to make a design.
5. When the child is finished, cover his design with another piece of wax paper, turn on the cup warmer or hot plate, and watch the beautiful design that is created as the crayon melts.
6. Hang the melted crayon art in the windows of the room. Or the children can give them as presents.

More to do

Place rings of paper or doilies around the edge of the crayon designs.
Cut out various shapes from the crayon designs according to your current theme, such as numbers, shapes, animals, and so on.

Related book

Harold and the Purple Crayon by Crockett Johnson

◆◆Shirley R. Salach, Northwood, NH

Red, White, and Blue Crayon Rubbings

Materials

Plastic canvas
Scissors
Tape (double sided or regular)
White copy paper
Unwrapped red and blue jumbo crayons

What to do

1. Ahead of time, cut plastic canvas into stars of varying sizes.
2. Tape the stars to the work surface, using double-sided tape or rolled regular tape. Make sure the tape is completely underneath the stars.
3. Ask the children to choose partners to help hold their papers still when rubbing.
4. Place a sheet of copy paper over some of the stars and demonstrate how to rub over them using the side of an unwrapped red crayon. Then, move the paper on top of another star and rub over it with a blue crayon. Explain how to feel the shape of the star during the rubbing.
5. Demonstrate how to hold the paper still when the partner is working.
6. Encourage the partners to take turns experimenting with crayon rubbings.
7. If desired, cut out the star rubbings and mount them onto red and blue paper.

More to do

More Art: Sponge paint using cookie cutters shaped like stars.
Math: Ask the children to look at the stars on the flag and see how many they can count.
Snack: Serve slices of star fruit.
Special Day: Have a red, white, and blue day, and ask the children to dress in the colors of our flag.

❖❖Susan Oldham Hill, Lakeland, FL

Glue Webs

Materials

Wax paper
Glue, in squeeze bottles
Glitter and food coloring, optional
String
Black paper or string, optional

What to do

1. Three-year-olds love to use glue, and they use lots of it. Why not turn using glue into an art project?
2. Give each child a large piece of wax paper.
3. Encourage the children to squeeze glue all over their wax paper to make a web design. Explain to them that it is a good idea to use thick lines of glue and to leave a few spaces in the middle of their glue globs.
4. If desired, add glitter or food coloring to the glue.
5. Allow the glue to dry completely.
6. Peel the dried form off the wax paper.
7. If desired, the children can glue their webs onto black paper or hang them from the ceiling with string.

More to do

Literacy: Read *The Very Busy Spider* by Eric Carle.
Music and Movement: Sing "The Itsy, Bitsy Spider."
Outdoors: Go outside with the children and look for a spider's web.

❖❖Michelle Barnea, Milburn, NJ

Glue Bags

Materials

White glue
Zipper-closure plastic bags
Tempera paint
Paper
Scissors

What to do

1. Pour some glue into plastic bags.
2. Add tempera paint to the glue and seal the bag.
3. Give a bag of glue to each child. Show them how to use their fingers to knead the glue until it is colored.
4. Cut a small hole in one end of each bag (adult only).
5. Encourage the children to squeeze a little bit of glue onto their paper to make designs.

More to do

Put two colors of paint into the same plastic bag. Encourage the child to squish the paints in the bag to form a different color.

◆◆Jean Potter, Charleston, WV

Sparkly String Ornaments

Materials

Shallow dishes
White glue
Cotton string
Wax paper
Glitter, in gold, silver, red, green, or diamond colors
Scissors, optional
Hole punch

What to do

1. Pour glue into shallow dishes.
2. Give the children string and wax paper.
3. Show the children how to dip their string into the glue and make a design on the wax paper.
4. Encourage the children to sprinkle glitter onto their glue design.
5. Let dry overnight.
6. Help the children cut out the design, if desired.
7. Punch a hole with a paper punch into the top of the design. Tie a string through the hole to make an ornament.

More to do

Omit the string and make designs using glue in squeeze bottles. Sprinkle with glitter and let them dry. (Drying time takes longer than when using a string.)

◆◆Mary Jo Shannon, Roanoke, VA

Sprayed Leaves

Materials

Stiff paper or acetate (A good idea is to use old x-ray film from a local hospital—
it's free and works just as well as acetate.)
Scissors
Empty spray bottle
All the Colors of the Earth by Shelia Homanaka (or any other book that has
pictures of leaves)
Paper
Easels, one for each child
Newspaper
Spray bottle
Paint

What to do

1. Beforehand, cut out a large leaf shape from a piece of stiff paper or acetate. This will be your stencil.
2. Read the children *All the Colors of the Earth* by Shelia Homanaka or any other book that has pictures of leaves.
3. Get the children's attention by spraying an empty bottle around the room. Ask them what they would spray with a bottle.
4. Then show them a page in the book. Say, "I wonder how all those colors got on that page. I am going to try to spray paint on paper. Maybe that is how the illustrator got the paint to look that way. Would you like to try to spray paint on some paper?"
5. Put paper onto each easel and tape the leaf stencil on top of the paper. Make sure to put newspaper underneath the easels.
6. Give each child a spray bottle half filled with paint. Encourage them to spray over the leaf stencil. (You may have to help them work the sprayer at first.)
7. As the children finish, ask them how they liked painting with a sprayer instead of a brush. Ask them to think of any other ways to paint a picture.

8. This activity helps children use fine and gross motor muscles while painting. It also helps them to become more aware of different colors.

More to do

Use a different color of paint or size of spray bottle. You can even change the shape of the leaf to show how leaves are different.

❖❖A. Gail Whitney, Dameron, MD

Jazzy Jewelry

Materials

Scissors
Decorative fabric
Metallic wrapping paper
Hole punch
Pipe cleaners

What to do

1. Cut the fabric into small squares (or other shapes) and snip a hole into the center of each piece.
2. Cut the wrapping paper into small squares and punch holes in the center of each piece.

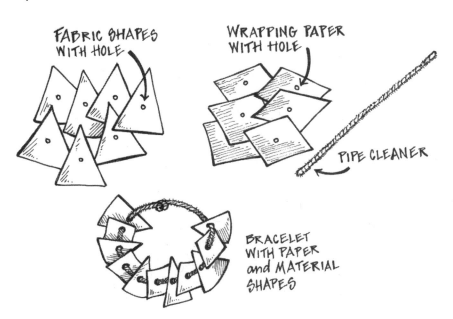

FABRIC SHAPES WITH HOLE

WRAPPING PAPER WITH HOLE

PIPE CLEANER

BRACELET WITH PAPER and MATERIAL SHAPES

3. Place the fabric and wrapping paper squares and pipe cleaners in the middle of the art table.

4. Encourage the children to string the squares onto the pipe cleaners. Show them how to twist together the ends when they are finished so they can wear their creation on their wrist or ankle. (Two pipe cleaners twisted together make the perfect length for a necklace.)

◆◆Ann Gudowski, Johnstown, PA

Straw Bracelets

Materials

Brightly colored plastic straws
String or pipe cleaners
Scissors
Tape

What to do

1. Precut straws into ½" to 1" (1 cm to 2 cm) lengths and precut string or pipe cleaners into 8" (20 cm) lengths. (If using string, wrap a piece of tape around one end to make it easier for sewing through the straw pieces.)

2. When using string, tape the untaped end to the table to prevent the straw pieces from falling off of it. When using pipe cleaners, roll the end back to keep the straws from sliding off.

3. Show the children how to slide the straw pieces onto the string or pipe cleaner. When the strings or pipe cleaners are almost full, help the children tie or twist the ends together to complete the circle.

4. If desired, put a small piece of tape with the child's name on it around one of the straws on the bracelet.

More to do

For holiday themes, use colored straws that reflect the holiday. For example, orange and black for Halloween, red and green for Christmas, and so on.
Math: If the children are working on simple patterns, give them straws in two different colors and encourage them to put them on the string in an ABAB pattern. For example, red, blue, red, blue, and so on.

◆◆Sandra Nagel, White Lake, MI

Dots Some More

Materials

Colored dots in various sizes
White construction paper
Pens or markers, optional

What to do

1. Give each child a few sheets of dots of varying colors and sizes.
2. Encourage the children to put the dots onto paper to create designs
3. If desired, the children can use pens or markers to draw on and between the dots.

❖❖Barbara Saul, Eureka, CA

Stamp Shapes

Materials

Pencils
Champagne corks
Exacto knife (adult only)
Paint or stamp pads
Paper

What to do

1. Trace different shapes onto the flat end of champagne corks.
2. Cut away the excess cork with an Exacto knife (adult only).
3. Create different shapes for different holidays, themes, or units.
4. Show the children how to make designs by pressing the cork into washable stamp pads or tempera or acrylic paints and then pressing it onto a piece of paper.
5. Corks are great to use because the children can get a good grip on the wide end, they also are easy to wash, and they last a long time.

❖❖Eileen Bayer, Tempe, AZ

Band-Aid Art

Materials

Large sheet of butcher paper or long roll of white paper
Masking tape
Band-aids in a variety of sizes and shapes
Markers or crayons
Yarn, wallpaper or fabric scraps, and glue, optional

What to do

1. Three-year-olds have a fascination with Band-aids and "owies," real or imaginary. Allowing them to explore the sticky qualities of Band-aids while attending to their hurts and boo-boos makes this a favorite, focused activity.
2. Tape a sheet of paper that is bigger than the child to the floor.
3. Ask the child to lie down on the paper and spread his legs and arms a little. Trace around the child's entire body, including his clothes, hair, and fingers.
4. Encourage the child to peel open Band-aids and stick them to the body tracing. (If the child needs helps getting started, peel open the Band-aid wrappers slightly.)
5. The children can also use crayons or markers to add features, boo-boos, or simple scribbling.
6. If desired, encourage the children to glue on yarn for hair and fabric or wallpaper scraps for clothes.

More to do

Instead of Band-aids, use address labels. You can decorate them with a few dots in the center to resemble a Band-aid.
Cut out a smaller body shape from a sheet of paper. A simple gingerbread man shape works nicely to decorate with Band-aids.

◆◆MaryAnn F. Kohl, Bellingham, WA

Thumbprint People

Materials

Ink pad with washable ink or jar lids filled with tempera paint
White drawing paper
Soap, water, and towels or handi-wipes
Fine-point black pens

What to do

1. Demonstrate how to press your thumb into the ink or paint and make thumbprints on white paper.
2. Give each child a sheet of paper. Encourage the children to take turns printing.
3. Keep soap, water, and towels close by for easy clean up.
4. Let the prints dry.
5. Encourage the children to use fine-point black pens to make faces on the fingerprints.
6. If desired, the children can make animals, flowers, and so on with the thumbprints.

More to do

Encourage the children to use all their fingers to make prints. They can also make handprints (or footprints!).

Related books

I'm Terrific by Marjorie Sharmat
It Takes a Village by J. C. Fletcher
The Relatives Came by Cynthia Rylant

◆◆Barbara Saul, Eureka, CA

Stained Glass Windows

Materials

Cellophane paper in a variety of colors
Scissors
Glue
Wax paper
Popsicle sticks or craft sticks
Yarn

What to do

1. Cut the cellophane into different shapes.
2. Encourage the children to glue the shapes onto sheets of wax paper, overlapping the edges of the cellophane.
3. Help the children make frames using Popsicle sticks and glue.
4. Demonstrate how to glue the collages onto the frames.
5. Attach yarn and hang them in the window.

◆◆Judy Perry, Fayetteville, NC

Drip Drip Dropper

Materials

Thinned tempera paint or watercolors
Paint cups
Eyedroppers
Paint paper

What to do

1. Pour different colors of thin paint (thinned tempera or watercolors) into four or five paint cups.
2. Place an eyedropper into each cup and place the cups in the middle of a worktable.
3. Give each child a large piece of absorbent art paper. (Do not use fingerpaint paper or paper with a high gloss.)

4. Encourage the children to create works of art by dropping colors onto the paper with the eyedroppers.
5. Ask the children to notice and discuss how mixing two of the colors creates a third color.
6. Hang the masterpieces to dry.

More to do

Encourage the children to drop colors onto coffee filters. Let them dry. Help the children cut out green strips of paper to represent a flower's stalk and leaves. Add the coffee filter "flower" to the top.

More Art: Use an old phonograph turntable to create "eyedropper spin art." Tape some absorbent paper to the turntable and turn it to the fastest speed. Ask the children to drop the color onto the paper as it spins. **Note:** The paint will spin out and off the paper. This activity is best done outside on a bright sunny day. Make sure your little artists wear aprons that cover the front completely.

Related books

Art Lesson (La Clase de Dibujo) by Tomie dePaola
Hattie and the Wild Waves by Barbara Cooney
The Painter by Peter Catalanotto

❖❖Virginia Jean Herrod, Columbia, SC

Presto Change-o Colors

Materials

Little Blue and Little Yellow by Leo Lionni
Muffin tin
Water
Red, blue, and yellow food coloring
Eyedroppers
Coffee filters (folded paper towels can be substituted)

What to do

1. Before beginning this activity, read the children *Little Blue and Little Yellow*. Help the children recognize that Little Blue and Little Yellow changed to become green when they hugged in the story.

2. Pour some water into each section of a muffin tin. Add plenty of red, blue, or yellow food coloring to each section to make bold colors.
3. Insert an eyedropper into each section.
4. Many three-year-olds have limited experience with eyedroppers. Model how to place the dropper into the water, squeeze it, pull it out, and squeeze the dropper again to release the liquid onto the coffee filter. As you model using the eyedropper, use simple language to describe what you are doing ("in squeeze; out squeeze").
5. Encourage the children to discover what happens as the different colors blend onto the coffee filter. Can they create "Little Green" as in the story, as well as the other color combinations, such as orange, purple, and even brown when all the colors mix?
6. Encourage the children to discover the difference when they squeeze a little bit of color and a lot of color. This activity encourages control of the children's fine finger muscles because a more colorful result occurs with less colored water.

More to do

Outdoors: Take a color walk and look for "a little blue" and "a little yellow."

◆◆Ann Wenger, Harrisonburg, VA

Playdough

Materials

1 cup (125 g) flour
½ cup (125 g) salt
1 cup (240 ml) water
1 tablespoon (15 ml) vegetable oil
1 teaspoon (5 g) cream of tartar
Food coloring, optional
Bowl
Measuring cup and spoons
Heavy large spoon
Saucepan
Stove or hot plate (adult only)
Plastic airtight container

What to do

1. Making playdough is a great fine motor and sensory experience.
2. Help the children measure flour, salt, water, vegetable oil, and cream of tartar and add them to the bowl. Show them how to mix it all together using the large spoon. If adding color, mix the food coloring with the water before mixing it in.
3. Pour the mixture into a sauce pan and cook it over medium heat until it thickens (adult only). Or, you can microwave the mixture in a plastic or glass container until it is warm. When it is thickened, remove it from the heat.
4. While the playdough is still warm, give each child some of it. Encourage the children to mix it with their hands, sprinkling in flour as they knead it. (You may want to sprinkle the table with flour, too.)
5. Enjoy and have fun!
6. Store the dough in a plastic container with a tight lid in the refrigerator.

More to do

Add plain unsweetened Kool-Aid to the playdough for color and scent.

◆◆Sandra Nagel, White Lake, MI

Baggie Playdough

Materials

Sturdy zipper-closure plastic bags
Flour
Salt
Water
Oil
Measuring cups and spoons

What to do

1. Pour 1 cup (125 g) flour and ½ cup (125 g) salt into each plastic baggie. Then add ½ cup (120 ml) water and 1 tablespoon (15 ml) oil.
2. Zip the bags closed, pressing out most of the air.
3. Encourage the children to squish by hand until it makes a nice dough.
4. Ask the children to unzip their bags and remove the dough.

5. Show the children how to knead the dough.
6. Encourage them to explore as with any playdough. Store the dough in the same baggie.

◆◆MaryAnn F. Kohl, Bellingham, WA

It's Silly Putty

Materials

Paint shirts or smocks
White glue
Liquid starch
Measuring cup
Bowl
Heavy large spoon
Gloves, optional
Shallow tub
Old scissors, optional
Zipper-closure plastic bag or plastic container

What to do

1. Help the children put on their paint smocks or aprons.
2. Help the children measure 1 cup (240 ml) each of white glue and liquid starch and pour them into a bowl. Mix them together using a large spoon.
3. Encourage the children to mix the ingredients together using their hands. It is very gooey, so it's a good idea to wear gloves.
4. As the children mix, point out how the ingredients are changing. Sometimes it will solidify, yet have some extra liquid. If this happens, hold onto the solid part and pour out the liquid.
5. Once the mixture is solid, place it in a shallow tub for the children to touch and explore.
6. As the silly putty is used, it begins to dry out. When it dries out, it can be pulled hard and it will snap. When it is in this stage, it is fun to cut it into chunks using old scissors.
7. Store the silly putty in a plastic container with a tight lid or a zipper-closure plastic bag.
8. This is great fine motor and sensory experience. It is almost magical how the two liquids react together and change.

NOTE: If the silly putty sticks to something, Goo Gone® products are useful in removing it. Or remove it as you would remove gum.

◆◆Sandra Nagel, White Lake, MI

"Do-It-Yourself" Art Box

Materials

Shallow box
Paper scraps, newspaper, and magazines
Glue sticks
Child scissors and zigzag scissors
String, optional

What to do

1. Put a variety of materials (see above list) into a shallow box so that the children can create their own masterpiece.
2. You may want to attach the scissors to the box with string so that the children can find the scissors when they need them.
3. Give the children plenty of unstructured art opportunities so they can practice their skills and use their imaginations.

More to do

Add the theme of the week to the box. For example, if you are working on a transportation unit, ask the children to look for pictures of vehicles and street signs or draw them.

◆◆Sandy L. Scott, Vancouver, WA

"To Do" Boxes

Materials

Small boxes, such as papier-mâché boxes (found in arts and craft stores) or jewelry boxes
Small decorative items, such as beads, trinkets, and puzzle pieces
Small photos of each child
Glue
Paint, optional
Small slips of paper
Marker or pen

What to do

1. Give each child a small box and encourage him to glue small decorative items and a photo of himself onto it as desired. (If desired, add paint to the glue so that if the child doesn't stick many items onto the box, it will still look nice.)

2. On small slips of paper, write some ideas that are nice for the child and his parents to do together. For example:
   - Look at photo albums together.
   - Find a cozy corner and read a book.
   - Dance to music together while waving scarves.
   - Make homemade playdough and play with it.
   - Bake cookies.
   - Take a nature walk.

3. Fold each slip of paper in half and put about 15 into each box.

4. Explain to the parents that they can use the ideas whenever they would like to spend some special time with their child. They can pull out one strip of paper at a time and save the rest for another day.

5. These boxes are a great Mother's Day or Father's Day gift. Parents love them!

❖❖ Audrey F. Kanoff, Allentown, PA

Sticker Box

Materials

Small box, such as a cigar or shoebox
Construction paper
Glue
Markers
Old, leftover stickers

What to do

1. Make a "sticker box" for the Art Center. Cover a small box with construction paper and decorate it using markers.
2. Add leftover stickers to the "sticker box" throughout the year. For example, when the children do a project with stickers and there are one or two stickers left on a page, put them in the box. Or, if you clean out your desk and find a few, add them to the box, too.
3. Explain to the children that they are free to use these stickers as they desire for art projects. They seem to enjoy sticking them into "blank books" (folded and stapled paper).
4. Make sure they know that the stickers are for sticking on paper only, not on tables or chairs. Also, ask them to throw away empty sticker pages.

More to do

Language: Ask the children to tell you a story about the picture or book they have made.

◆◆Linda N. Ford, Sacramento, CA

Memory Collage

Materials

Photos
Magazines, catalogs, or old calendars
Scissors
Small box, such as a shoebox
Poster board, matte board, or cardboard
Glue sticks
Markers, optional

What to do

1. Have you ever wondered what to do with duplicate photos, or the photos with red eyes, closed eyes, or the ones that are blurry and out of focus? Use them to make a memory collage! Put the photos into a small box.

2. Cut out pictures from magazines, catalogs, or old calendars and add them to the box for variety.

3. Spread out the photos and pictures on a low table and encourage the children to walk around and select favorites for their collage.

4. Give each child a poster board or piece of cardboard. Encourage them to rub glue sticks onto their poster board to make it sticky.

5. Show the children how to press their pictures onto the sticky poster board.

6. Encourage the children to continue adding more glue and more pictures until they are satisfied with their collage.

7. Allow them to dry.

8. When the collages are thoroughly dry, the children can draw over them with markers, if desired.

Author note: Three-year-olds relate best to photos of faces or familiar events, and love pictures of toys cut out from children's magazines and toy- or school-supply catalogs. Three-year-olds also tend to fill the entire collage board with random abandon, covering up some pictures, and leaving spaces between others. Raw edges are common. Others will stick on only one picture and call it finished!

More to do

Add other art materials such as pieces of ribbon, stickers, labels, or glitter-glue for additional decoration and design.

Language: Discuss the completed collages with the children. Encourage them to point out and name familiar faces and things.

◆◆MaryAnn F. Kohl, Bellingham, WA

Sun Catcher Earth

Materials

Glue
Cup
Blue food coloring
Spoon
Margarine tub lid
Brown and green permanent markers
Yarn or string

What to do

1. Fill a cup about ⅓ full of white glue and add about 5 to 8 drops of blue food coloring. Use a spoon to mix well.
2. Pour some of the glue into a margarine tub lid and let it dry completely. This may take several days, depending upon the humidity.
3. When the glue is completely dry, peel the blue circle from the lid.
4. With a permanent marker, draw landforms on the blue circle.
5. Now you have a sun catcher! It will usually stick to a glass window, but if it doesn't, punch a hole in the top and thread a piece of yarn or ribbon through it to hang.

More to do

Use different shades of food coloring to make a variety of sun catchers.

◆◆Jean Potter, Charleston, WV

Spring Flower Pots

Materials

Small clay pot and saucer
Newspaper
Acrylic paint
Small paintbrushes
Clear resin spray can (found at hobby stores)
Flower seeds or small flowering plants
Moist potting soil

What to do

1. Give each child a small clay pot and saucer.
2. Ask the children to place their pots upside down on newspaper and paint designs on them. (It's nice to write the date on the bottom.)
3. Leave the pots on the newspaper and allow them to dry thoroughly.
4. When the pots are dry, keep them on the newspaper and spray them generously with clear resin spray (adult only). Let them dry overnight.
5. When the pots are completely dry (not tacky), fill them with moist potting soil and place the saucers under each pot.
6. Help the children plant either the seeds or small flowers and water them lightly.
7. Place the pots in a warm, sunny window until they are ready to give as a gift.

More to do

Books: Read books about flowers and how they grow.
Field Trip: Visit a botanical garden or large nursery.
Holidays: Talk about Mother's Day and what it means.

❖❖Christina I. Waugh, Littleton, CO

Clothespin Refrigerator Paper Holder

Materials

Clothespins, one for each child
Paintbrushes
Craft paint
Glitter or sequins and glue
Magnet squares
Hot glue gun (adult only)

What to do

1. Give each child a clothespin.
2. Encourage the children to paint their clothespins.
3. The children can sprinkle glitter onto the wet paint and let it dry. Or, they can let the paint dry, then glue on sequins.
4. When the clothespins are dry, use a hot glue gun to attach magnets to the back (adult only).
5. Use them as refrigerator paper holders.

◆Lisa Chichester, Parkersburg, WV

Sandpaper Starfish

Materials

Scissors
Sandpaper
Pictures of sea life
Crayons
9" x 12" (22 cm x 30 cm) construction paper in light colors
Newspaper
Iron (adult only)
Markers

What to do

1. Ahead of time, cut out starfish shapes from the sandpaper, approximately 7″ (17 cm) across.
2. Show the children pictures of ocean life. Discuss the variety of creatures that live under the water.
3. Give each child a sandpaper starfish and a piece of construction paper.
4. Encourage them to color their starfish heavy and dark on the rough side, covering the entire shape. When they are done, ask them to turn their starfish upside down onto the construction paper.
5. Place both sheets onto a thick pad of newspaper and press a warm iron on the sandpaper starfish (adult only). Talk with the children about what heat does to crayons.
6. Encourage the children to add sea life drawings to their pictures with the markers. Or, for a seaside bulletin board, mount the sandpaper starfish onto a beach scene.

More to do

Fine Motor: Provide a variety of other textures for the children to feel and use in their art projects, such as corduroy, wood scraps, aluminum foil, corrugated paper, and cork.

Science: Show the children pictures of a variety of starfish and discuss them. Ask the children to count how many arms the starfish have. (Four, six, or more than the usual five, are not uncommon.)

◆◆Susan Oldham Hill, Lakeland, FL

Leaf Print Pencil Holders

Materials

Scissors
Clean 12-ounce juice cans, one for each child
Construction paper in pastel colors
Felt
Glue
Newspaper
Paint in a variety of bright colors
Shallow containers
Fresh green leaves in various shapes, about 3″ long
Paintbrushes
Clear adhesive paper

What to do

1. Ahead of time, cut the construction paper into rectangles to fit around each can, making sure to leave an overlap for later gluing.
2. Cut out felt circles to fit into the bottom of each can and glue them in.
3. Cover the work surface with newspaper. Pour paint into shallow containers and put brushes into each one.
4. Give each child a leaf and a construction paper rectangle.
5. Show the children how to paint the underside of the leaf gently. Then, demonstrate how to press the paper onto the painted leaf, using the fingertips to smooth the paint onto the paper.

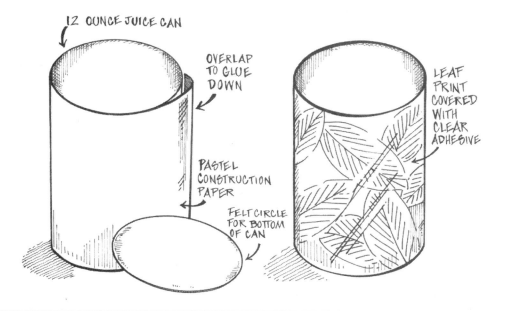

12 OUNCE JUICE CAN

OVERLAP TO GLUE DOWN

PASTEL CONSTRUCTION PAPER

FELT CIRCLE FOR BOTTOM OF CAN

LEAF PRINT COVERED WITH CLEAR ADHESIVE

6. Carefully lift the paper off the leaf and press it down again in a different spot, *without repainting*. This second print will reveal more of the leaf's veins.

7. Encourage the children to make several more prints on the paper, always making two leaf prints from one application of paint. Replace the leaf when it begins to shred.

8. Let the printed paper dry.

9. Help the children cover their leaf printings with clear adhesive and glue them to their cans. This makes a great pencil holder to give as a gift.

More to do

More Art: Make extra leaf prints and cut them out to make bulletin board borders.
Math: Prepare six leaves of graduated sizes for the children to put in order by size.
Outdoors: Take the children for a walk outside and look for leaves of varying shapes.

Related books

Pumpkin Pumpkin by Jeanne Titherington
Red Leaf, Yellow Leaf by Lois Ehlert
School by Emily Arnold McCully
A Tree Is Nice by Janice May Udry
Why Do Leaves Change Color? by Betsy Maestro

◆◆Susan Oldham Hill, Lakeland, FL

Vinegar Hearts

Materials

White vinegar
Small bowls
White construction paper
Paintbrushes
Red tissue paper
Scissors
Markers, optional

What to do

1. Pour white vinegar into small bowls.
2. Give each child a piece of white construction paper. Encourage the children to use paintbrushes to brush vinegar all over their paper.
3. Cut out hearts from red tissue paper.
4. Ask the children to cover their paper with tissue paper hearts. As the vinegar dries, the tissue paper will fall off, leaving red heart prints.
5. If desired, the children can highlight the prints by drawing around them with markers.

◆◆Jean Potter, Charleston, WV

Deer Skin Placemats

Materials

Brown paper grocery bags
Scissors
Cotton swabs
Shallow dishes
Paint in fall colors, such as orange, yellow, brown, green, and red
Clear contact paper or laminate, optional

What to do

1. Cut out flat, rectangular shapes from brown paper grocery bags.
2. Give each child a shape. Encourage the children to crumple and twist the shapes over and over again. Then flatten the paper out again.
3. Pour paint in a variety of fall colors into shallow dishes.
4. Encourage the children to use cotton swabs to paint designs on their placemats.
5. When the placemats are dry, laminate them or cover them with clear contact paper for durability, if desired.

More to do

Instead of making placemats, tear the grocery bags into animal shapes and make "hides." Encourage the children to write or draw pictures on them with black markers to look like cave drawings.

◆◆Jean Potter, Charleston, WV

Hand Cards

Materials

Construction paper, one piece for each child

Pencils

Scissors

Crayons

Glue or glue stick

Decorating materials, such as stickers, sequins, or other sparkly items

What to do

1. Fold each sheet of construction paper crosswise and give one to each child.

2. Ask the children to place their hands on the paper, with their little finger against the folded edge.

3. Use a pencil to trace each child's hand onto his paper. (If desired, as you are tracing each child's hand, encourage the children to sing "Where Is Thumbkin?")

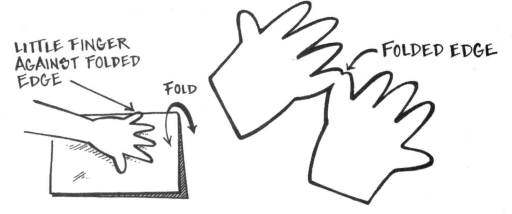

4. Help the children cut out their paper hand, making sure to cut through both pieces of paper. You now have a hand card.

5. Write a verse inside the cards relating to the holiday or special occasion. For example, write, "I hand my heart to you" for Valentine's Day or "Here are my helping hands" for Mother's Day or Father's Day. Or simply write, "I love you" and help the children sign their names.

6. Encourage the children to decorate their cards using crayons, glue sticks, stickers, sequins, or whatever other decorations you have available.

7. You may want to trace the hands one day (making sure to write each child's name on his paper hand) and then cut out the tracings later during naptime. Then ask the children to decorate their cards the next day.

More to do

While doing this activity, discuss with the children how people grow as they get older and how next year, their hands will be bigger than today.

Math: With the children, count the fingers on the card and identify the name of each finger (thumb, index, middle, ring, and pinky).

◆◆Melissa O. Markham, Huddleston, VA

T-Shirt Prints

Materials

Newspaper
Paint smocks
Two small trays
Permanent fabric paint
Printing objects, such as sponges cut into simple shapes, dish mops and scrubbers, thread spools, toy parts, toy cars, plastic ABCs, plastic cups, whisk, and potato mashers
T-shirts
Clothes dryer, optional

What to do

1. Printing with everyday objects makes the most surprising designs!
2. Fabric paint spots are permanent so make sure the children wear paint smocks. Also cover the work area (including the carpet or floor) with newspaper.
3. Pour a puddle of fabric paint onto a small paint tray.
4. Arrange a second tray with printing objects.
5. Give each child a T-shirt. Show the children how to place their T-shirt flat on the work surface with a few layers of newspaper inside so the paint doesn't soak through to the back of the shirt.
6. Demonstrate how to press the flat part of a selected printing object into the paint, and then press it onto the T-shirt.
7. Encourage the children to make prints on their shirts until they are satisfied with the design.
8. Allow the shirts to dry completely overnight. If desired, put each shirt into a clothes dryer by itself for four minutes to set the color, or follow the instructions on the fabric paint box.

Hints and Tips: The biggest challenge with printing T-shirts is for adults to let go of the idea that these shirts must be perfect! Let the children experiment on plain paper with washable paint to get the idea of "printing" before using permanent fabric paint. Place a small sponge or folded paper towel in the paint tray for easier prints. Young artists will invent and explore many methods of printing—this is to be expected and enjoyed.

More to do

Encourage the children to draw with fabric crayons on a piece of paper. Then place the drawing on a T-shirt and iron (adult only). This will transfer the drawing onto the shirt.

Instead of dipping the print item into paint, encourage the children to paint with a brush directly on the item.

Make prints on other items, such as aprons, pillowcases, sheets, quilt pieces, a tablecloth, a table runner, or fabric napkins.

❖❖MaryAnn F. Kohl, Bellingham, WA

Bookworm Bookmarks

Materials

Cardboard
Scissors
Craft paint and brushes
Hot glue gun (adult only)
Green pompoms
Tiny moveable eyes

What to do

1. Beforehand, cut out bookmarks from cardboard.
2. Give the children their bookmarks and encourage them to paint them a bright color.
3. Allow the bookmarks to dry.
4. Help the children glue green pompoms onto their bookmarks to make a caterpillar.
5. Glue eyes onto the caterpillar bookmarks.

❖❖Lisa Chichester, Parkersburg, WV

Bottle Cap Wind Chime

Materials

String
Buttons
Glue
Bottle caps, about 15 per child
Craft paint and brushes
Coffee can lids

What to do

1. Show the children how to push string through buttons and then glue them to bottle cap, as shown.
2. Next, encourage the children to paint the bottle caps with craft paint.
3. Help the children tie all the strings to a coffee can lid as shown. If desired, the children can paint the lid, too, or use stickers to decorate it.
4. Hang the "wind chime" where the wind blows.

◆◆Lisa Chichester, Parkersburg, WV

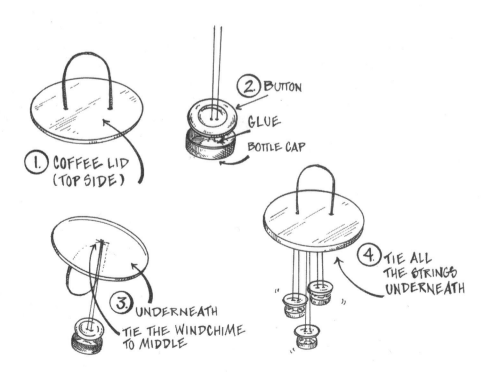

Slipper Socks

Materials

Cardboard pieces
Pencils
Scissors
Inexpensive white socks, one pair for each child
Puffy paints (found in the craft section of any store)
Glue
Scrap materials, such as mini-pompoms

What to do

1. Give each child a piece of cardboard and trace his feet onto it.
2. Help the children cut out their feet shapes.
3. Give each child a pair of socks. Ask them to place the cardboard inside the socks so that the bottom of the sock is flat.
4. Encourage the children to use the puffy paints to make various designs on the bottom of the socks. This forms the non-skid part of the slipper.
5. The children can also glue scrap materials on the tops of the socks.

❖Lisa Chichester, Parkersburg, WV

Fun Magnifiers

Materials

Pipe cleaners
Wax paper
Roll of masking tape
Pencil
Scissors
Glue

What to do

1. Give each child a pipe cleaner and a piece of wax paper.
2. Using the inside of a roll of masking tape as a stencil, help the children trace a circle on a piece of wax paper.

3. Ask the children to cut out the circle. Offer help if needed.
4. Show the children how to form the pipe cleaner into a magnifying glass shape and glue the wax paper circle to it.
5. Let them dry. You now have a pretend magnifying glass!
6. Encourage the children to use the magnifiers throughout the room. Although they don't really magnify anything, it's fun for the children to pretend they are closely inspecting familiar toys and items.

More to do

Games: Hide a small toy in the room and challenge the children to use their magnifiers to find it.

Outdoors: Encourage the children to take the magnifiers outside and use them to search through the grass for bugs.

Related book

The 13th Clue by Ann Jonas

◆◆Virginia Jean Herrod, Columbia, SC

Cool Caps

Materials

Painter's caps or plastic visors, one for each child
Fabric paints (if using painter's caps) or acrylic paints (if using plastic visors)
Small paintbrushes

What to do

1. Give each child a cap or visor.
2. Put the paints in the middle of the work area. Encourage the children to use the paints to decorate their caps or visors as desired.
3. Let the caps or visors dry before wearing them.

More to do

Field Trip: Make field trip caps by decorating the cap or visor as described above. Create a stencil that has a significant design (such as a schoolhouse, bus, or school emblem) and stencil it on the brim of the cap or visor. Ask the children to wear the caps on field trips. **Note:** Do not display any personal information, such as the child's name, on the cap.

Holidays: For Father's Day, make matching father/child caps. Purchase one adult and one child-sized cap or visor for each child. Ask the children to decorate the caps as desired. Create a stencil that says "#1 DAD" and help the children use the stencil on the brim of the adult caps after the other paints have dried. For an added touch, create a stencil that says "#1 Son/Daughter" for the child's cap.

Related books

The 500 Hats of Bartholomew Cubbins by Dr. Seuss
The Cat in the Hat by Dr. Seuss
Felix's Hat by Catherine Bamcroft and Hannah Coale
The Hat by Jan Brett
A Hat for Minerva Louise by Janet Morgan Stoeke
Jennie's Hat by Ezra Jack Keats
Martin's Hats by Joan W. Blos

◆◆Virginia Jean Herrod, Columbia, SC

Pussy Willows

Materials

Pussy willows
Paper
Plastic straws, one for each child
Brown paint
Water-soluble packing curls
Plate
Hot water

What to do

1. Show the children real pussy willows and explain that they will be making their own pussy willows.
2. Give each child a straw and a piece of paper.
3. Pour a small amount of brown paint at the bottom of each piece of paper. Demonstrate how to blow through the straw gently to spread the paint to look like a stem. To help spread the paint further (if needed), hold the paper upside down and at angles to let the paint run.
4. Break the packing curls in half and give a few to each child.

5. Pour a small amount of hot water onto plates. Show the children how to dip one end of a packing curl into the hot water and place it along the paint stem.

6. Encourage the children to place their packing curls along their paint stems until they are satisfied with the pussy willows.

More to do

Instead of using packing curls, put a little gray paint onto the children's pointer fingers and encourage them to make pussy willow fingerprints.

Related poem

The Pussy Willow Poem

I know a little pussy,
Its coat is silver-gray.
It lives down in the meadow
Not very far away.
It will always be a pussy,
It will never be a cat.
For it's a pussy willow
Now what do you think of that?
Meow, meow, meow, meow, meow,
Meow, meow, meow, meow,
Scat!

◆◆Sandra Nagel, White Lake, MI

Telescope Tubes

Materials

Glitter paint
Trays or paint containers
Empty toilet tissue tubes
Easel paintbrushes
Permanent marker

What to do

1. Pour glitter paint into trays or paint containers.
2. Give each child a large paintbrush and a toilet paper tube.
3. Encourage the children to paint the outside of their tubes as desired, using as many paint colors as desired.
4. Use a permanent marker to write each child's name inside his tube.
5. Place the tubes upright on a tray or other drying surface. Make sure it is not a papered surface because the tube will stick to it in the drying process.

More to do

Science: Hang paper stars on the walls and ceiling of the room. Encourage the children to use their tubes to locate the stars.
More Science: Place glow-in-the-dark cosmic shapes under a tabletop and put a dark colored blanket or sheet over the table. Then encourage the child to take his tube under the table to spot the glowing stars and shapes. If the shapes stop glowing, use a bright flashlight to start the glowing again!

❖Tina R. Durham-Woehler, Lebanon, TN

Making an Octupus

Materials

Green, blue, and white construction paper, one sheet of each for each child
Pencil
Scissors
Crayons
Large plastic eggs, divided in half
Glue

What to do

1. Draw eight wavy legs on each sheet of green construction paper or give the children a pattern to trace. Ask the children to cut them out.
2. Draw oval eyeballs on the white paper for the children to cut out. Encourage them to use crayons to color the eyes.
3. Demonstrate how to glue eight legs onto a piece of large blue paper with the tips spreading out to the ends of the paper.
4. Give each child one half of a plastic egg. Encourage the children to glue eyes onto their eggs.
5. Show the children how to glue their eggs onto the center of the blue paper over the legs, so that the legs appear to come out of the eggs.

More to do

Math: Ask the children to count how many legs an octopus has.
Movement: Cut out large paper legs and tape them to the children's sides. Encourage them to crawl and move around the floor as if they were an octopus.

Related book

Herman the Helper by Robert Kraus

◆◆ Sandra Suffeletto Ryan, NY

Making Tracks

Materials

Sand
Sandbox or large container
Water
Heavy paper
Plaster of Paris
Paint and brushes, optional

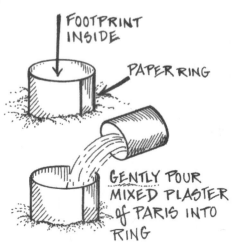

What to do

1. Wet the sand in a sandbox or container.
2. Help each child push his foot into the sand about 1" (2 cm) deep.
3. After the child removes his foot, place a ring of heavy paper around the child's footprint.
4. Mix Plaster of Paris with water and gently pour it into the ring until it completely fills the print.
5. Allow the print to dry for three hours or until it is hard.
6. Carefully remove the print from the sand and brush off any loose sand.
7. If desired, the children may paint their footprints.

FOOTPRINT INSIDE

PAPER RING

GENTLY POUR MIXED PLASTER of PARIS INTO RING

More to do

Make handprints instead of footprints.
Outdoors: Leave the wet sand outside near a bird feeder to try and get a bird print.
Science: With the children, go outside and try to find other animal prints of which to make plaster prints.

DRIED FOOT PRINT

◆◆Tammy Byington, Columbia, MO

Branching Out

Materials

Bucket
Sand or instant concrete
Large tree branch, with or without bark
Paint, optional
Construction paper and markers
Scissors
Hole punch
Pieces of yarn

What to do

1. Pour sand or instant concrete into a bucket.
2. Place a tree branch into the bucket. If the tree branch doesn't have bark, paint it, if desired.
3. Help the children trace their hands onto construction paper and cut them out. Help them write their names on the hand.
4. Punch a hole into the hand and insert a piece of yarn.
5. Invite the children to help tie their hand onto a tree branch.
6. Showcase the classroom "family tree" at an Open House or parent conference.

More to do

Use the branch to hang a variety of drawings with a similar theme, such as favorite foods, weather symbols, or seasonal decorations.

◆◆Margery A. Kranyik, Hyde Park, MA

Hello Jack Frost!

Materials

Large pieces of clear plastic (fabric shops sell it by the yard)
Scissors
Newspaper
Tape
Aluminum pans
White glue
Water
Clear crystal glitter

What to do

1. Cut clear plastic into pieces to fit windowpanes.
2. Tape the pieces to a newspaper-covered table.
3. Pour glue into aluminum pans and dilute it with water.
4. Encourage the children to put their hands into the glue mixture and smear it all over the plastic surfaces.
5. Help the children wash their hands. Then, encourage them to shake clear glitter onto the wet glue, make squiggle designs (or letters if the child is writing).
6. Allow the pieces to dry.
7. Tape the "frosted" panes into the windows.

More to do

Outdoors: On a cold morning, take the children outside for a "frost walk" to see, touch, and hear frost crunch as they step on the grass. Return later in the day. Ask them what happened to the frost.

Science: Make a "Jack Frost Trap." With the children, secure two pieces of clear plastic to a picnic table when frost is predicted that night. Early the next morning, go outside and observe the frosty plastic. Ask the children what will happen if they take one inside and what will happen if they leave one outside. Then, take one in and leave one outside. Observe and discuss the changes.

Related poem

"Jack Frost" (Anonymous)

Jack Frost rapped on the windowpane
And knocked on the door with his icicle cane.
"Excuse me," I said,
"The door is shut tight.
I'd rather you not come in tonight."
So he wrote his name all over the glass,
And the baby sneezed when she heard him pass.
A-choo-o-o!

❖❖Nina Smith, Cameron, SC

Making Cat or Dog Ears

Materials

Plastic headbands
Pipe cleaners
Scissors
White paper
Black marker
Crayons
Tape

What to do

1. Purchase inexpensive plastic headbands. You can find them in the hair care section of department stores or drugstores.
2. For each headband, first cut a pipe cleaner in half. Then, wrap 1 ½" (4 cm) of the wire piece securely around the headband, leaving 3½" (9 cm) sticking up. Repeat with the other half of the pipe cleaner to simulate ear placement.
3. Enlarge ear designs onto white paper using thick black lines.
4. Give each child a set of ears and encourage them to color them as desired. Encourage them to be creative—try spots, stripes, or just bright scribbles!
5. Help the children cut out the ears.
6. Attach the ears to the headbands by lacing the pipe cleaners in and out through the middle of each paper design, fastening them in the back with tape.
7. Encourage the children to act like pets as they wear their dog or cat headbands!

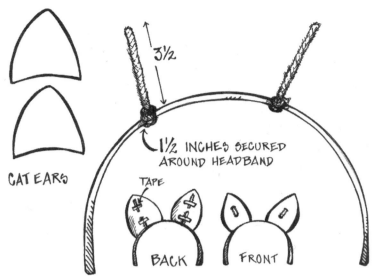

CAT EARS

3½

1½ INCHES SECURED AROUND HEADBAND

TAPE

BACK   FRONT

More to do

More Art: Make cat faces using paper shapes. Cut out an oval head with circle eyes and triangle ears. Use pipe cleaners for the whiskers.

Circle Time: Talk to the children about how to take care of pets. Also discuss how to meet new dogs safely.

Dramatic Play: Set up an adoption center for pets, a veterinarian clinic, or a pet-supply store.

Language: Have a Show and Tell presentation and ask the children to talk about their family pets. If a child doesn't have a pet, he can talk about a friend's pet or about a pet he wants.

◆◆◆Teri A. Schmidt, Silverton, OR

Food Collages

Materials

Food pyramid poster, optional

Large easel and paper or white board

Pens or markers

Magazines or old cookbooks

Scissors

Glue sticks or squeezable tubes of clear glue

White paper plates

What to do

1. Discuss the food pyramid with the children and, if desired, show them a picture of it.
2. Ask the children what foods they like to eat. Write their responses on a piece of easel paper or a white board. Draw a picture of the foods, if desired.
3. When finished, reread the list back to the children. Then explain to them that they will be making food collages of their favorite foods.
4. Give the children magazines or old cookbooks and encourage them to cut out pictures of different foods.
5. Give each child a paper plate. Encourage the children to glue their pictures onto their paper plates to make a collage.
6. Allow time for each child to share their pictures with the rest of the children.

More to do

Dramatic Play: Put empty food boxes in the Dramatic Play Center so the children can play "grocery store."

Literacy: Ask the children to "write" about their collages. They can also dictate stories about their favorite foods and an adult can write them down.

Science: Read *The Carrot Seed* by Ruth Krauss to the children. Give each child a real carrot seed to plant in either a clear plastic cup or in an outdoor garden.

More Science: Fill a clear jar half full with buttermilk. Encourage the children to take turns shaking the jar until butter is formed.

Related books

Bread and Jam for Frances by Russell Hoban
The Carrot Seed by Ruth Krauss
Gregory the Terrible Eater by Michael Sharmat

❖❖Barbara Saul, Eureka, CA

Theme Murals

Materials

Bulletin board paper or old blueprint paper (from a local architect)
Markers

What to do

1. Murals can fit into many themes and you can make them many times throughout the year. As a group, work on a mural that you can hang in the room. Some themes for murals include the ocean, the universe or space, a zoo, a farm, dinosaurs, transportation, a rodeo, and a garden. The possibilities are endless—just use your imagination and your curriculum as a guide.

2. Start by showing the children books and talking about your theme.

3. Then encourage the children to start drawing! Make sure to suggest that they draw scenery on their mural.

4. Play music while the children are working. This can be a creativity booster for the children as they tap their toes and work. (For example, "Octopus' Garden" is a good song to play for an ocean mural.)

5. Ask each child to describe his part of the mural. For example, after reading a book on ocean animals and drawing the animals on a group mural, see if the children know the names of the animals they have created or encourage them to make up names.

6. Hang the mural with pride! This is a great cooperative effort as the children learn to work together.

◆◆Gail D. Morris, Kemah, TX

Season Posters

Materials

Markers
Four pieces of poster board, each a different color
Seasonal stickers, confetti, and party goods
Art materials, such as sand, glitter, pipe cleaners, and cotton balls
Glue sticks
Magazine pictures of different seasonal things, such as clothes, weather, holidays, and so on

What to do

1. Label the top of each poster with the name of the season. For summer, paint the word "summer" with glue and sprinkle over it with sand. For fall, write the word by gluing brown, red, and orange pipe cleaners to it. Write the word "winter" using glue and cotton balls, and write "spring" using glue and glitter in pastel colors.

2. Discuss the different seasons with the children. Talk about the different weather, clothes, activities, and holidays in each season.
3. Give the children a variety of seasonal items, such as stickers, confetti, party goods, and magazine pictures.
4. Encourage them to glue each item onto the correct poster. This works well with small groups. Divide the children into four groups and ask each group to work on one season.
5. Look at the posters during Circle Time and encourage the children to talk about each one.
6. Hang the posters all year for a wonderful display and refer back to the posters as the seasons change during the year.

◆◆Gail D. Morris, Kemah, TX

Stick Puppet Handles Galore!

Materials

Craft sticks, tongue depressors, straws, and chopsticks
Contact cement or hot glue gun (adult only)

What to do

1. Make handles for stick puppets from a variety of materials, such as craft sticks, tongue depressors, straws, and chopsticks.
2. Attach the handles using a hot glue gun or contact cement (adult only).

◆◆Jackie Wright, Enid, OK

Color Days

Materials

Art materials for each color, such as paper, paint, and colored playdough
Variety of colored items to add to other centers

What to do

1. Each week, choose a color to focus on for the week.
2. Do a variety of art projects focusing on the particular color. Encourage the children to use that color paper, paint, and so on.
3. On the last day of the week, ask the children to dress in the specific color and serve a snack that is the color of the week.
4. When you finish all of the colors, have a rainbow week!

Related books

The Color Kittens by Margaret Wise Brown
Little Blue and Little Yellow by Leo Lionni
My Many Colored Days by Dr. Suess
White Rabbit's Color Book by Alan Baker

❖❖Sandy L. Scott, Vancouver, WA

Open-Ended Art Center

Materials

Various scraps, such as fabric scraps, lace scraps, paper scraps, and cork
Miscellaneous items, such as old buttons, glitter, yarn, string, ribbons, rubberbands, and so on
Art paper
Glue or glue sticks
Scissors

What to do

1. Keep a variety of scraps and miscellaneous materials in the Art Center. You can assign specific art projects, or have open-ended art projects. Encourage the children to cut and glue to their heart's content and let their creativity soar!
2. It's a good idea to come up with a list of rules beforehand. Explain the rules to the children before they use the Art Center.
3. Tell them that scissors may be used for cutting scraps only—not hair, each other, and so on!

More to do

Literacy: Encourage the children to create a picture to go along with a book you are reading to them, or help them make their own special art book.

◆◆Sheryl Smith, Jonesborough, TN

Art on the Go

Materials

Several clipboards
Adhesive paper in a variety of colors
Crayons or colored pencils

What to do

1. Cover several clipboards with colorful pieces of adhesive paper. Designate the clipboards as "Art on the Go" boards. Explain to the children that they can carry the clipboards around the room and use them as a hard surface upon which to draw.
2. Encourage the children to take colored pencils or crayons from the art area to other areas in order to draw pictures. Markers (whether washable or not) are not a good option because it is much too tempting to use markers on the walls rather than on the clipboard.
3. Encourage the children to use these portable art boards in other centers. They can make drawings of their block structures, illustrate stories in the reading area, or pretend to help the baby dolls draw in the dramatic living area.

More to do

Field Trip: Bring the "Art on the Go" boards with you on field trips. The children can make on-the-spot drawings of interesting animals at the zoo or the sights at the local museum.
Outdoors: Take the "Art on the Go" boards outside. Encourage the children to draw flowers, trees, bugs, and birds.

Related books

Art Lesson (La Clase de Dibujo) by Tomie dePaola
Draw Me a Star by Eric Carle
The Incredible Painting of Felix Closseau by Jon Agee
The Painter by Peter Catalanotto

◆◆Virginia Jean Herrod, Columbia, SC

Sand Bucket Storage

Materials

Inexpensive sand buckets, one for each child
Stencils
Permanent markers

What to do

1. Give each child a sand bucket.
2. Write each child's name on his bucket using stencils. Then encourage the children to add designs to their buckets.
3. The children can use their buckets to store their outdoor items, such as sunglasses, hats, sunscreen, and so on.

◆◆Lisa Chichester, Parkersburg, WV

Picture Blocks

Materials

Clear contact paper
Scissors
Wooden blocks
A photo of each child

What to do

1. Pre-cut contact paper to fit one side of a wooden block, leaving ½" (1 cm) extra on each side.
2. Attach each photo to a block and cover with contact paper to protect it.
3. Use these blocks to encourage dramatic play within the Block Center.

❖ Charlene Woodham Peace, Semmes, AL

Large Blocks

Materials

Large cereal boxes
Newspaper
Masking tape or duct tape
Colored contact paper or
    paint and brushes

NEWSPAPER

STICKERS

PAINTED BOX WITH DESIGN

LARGE cereal box

What to do

1. Stuff large cereal boxes with newspaper to help retain their shape.
2. Tape the boxes closed.
3. Cover the boxes with colored contact paper or ask the children to paint and decorate them.
4. Add them to the Block Area.

More to do

Outdoors: These blocks also work great outdoors.

◆◆ Sandy L. Scott, Vancouver, WA

Box Blocks

Materials

Boxes in a variety of shapes and sizes
Wide tape
Newspaper
Paint and brushes

What to do

1. Tape a variety of boxes closed.
2. Cover a table with newspaper and put the paints and brushes on the table.
3. Ask each child to choose a box and paint it.
4. When the boxes are dry, add them to the Block Center.

More to do

Dramatic Play: Introduce the children to stories and rhymes they can act out using the box blocks. Add props to support each rhyme. For example, the children can recite "Humpty Dumpty" and build a wall. Or tell them the story of "The Three Little Pigs" and ask them to build the three houses. Supply a wolf mask and three pig masks so they can act it out.

◆◆ Ann Gudowski, Johnstown, PA

Budget Blocks

Materials

Empty, wax-coated milk cartons in assorted sizes
Scissors
Shredded paper or newspaper
Blocks
Contact paper (bright colors, childlike patterns)

What to do

1. Rinse milk cartons thoroughly after use. Cut off the triangular tops along the fold lines to form rectangles. Sort the cartons into pairs of the same size. (You will need two cartons of the same size for each block.)
2. Stuff one carton of each pair with shredded paper or crumpled newspaper. Fill it adequately, but not so much that the sides bulge. Pinch the sides of the stuffed carton so that the upper edges will fit inside its empty mate (turned upside down).

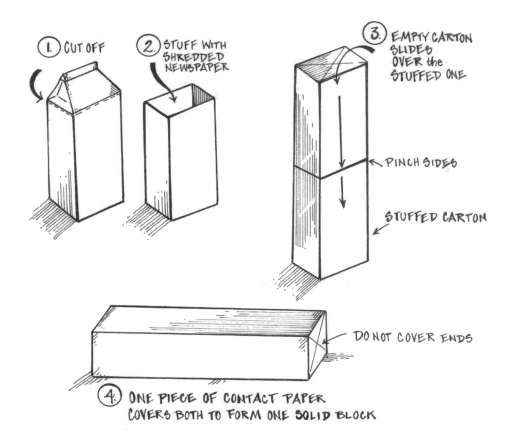

1. CUT OFF
2. STUFF WITH SHREDDED NEWSPAPER
3. EMPTY CARTON SLIDES OVER the STUFFED ONE

PINCH SIDES
STUFFED CARTON

DO NOT COVER ENDS

4. ONE PIECE OF CONTACT PAPER COVERS BOTH TO FORM ONE SOLID BLOCK

3. Carefully slide the empty carton completely over the other. The waxy surfaces allow this to happen as long as you let trapped air escape as you push the two pieces together. As a result, you should have a perfectly formed solid rectangle.

4. Decorate each block with one piece of contact paper, covering the four printed sides and leaving the white ends plain (this leaves less paper edges that might come loose).

5. Add the new blocks to the Block Center. They are lightweight, and virtually accident-proof, enabling children to build head-high structures without endangering their safety.

More to do

Math: Use solid colored self-adhesive paper in basic colors to enable children to sort and stack the blocks by color.

More Math: Cover the blocks in one solid color, and then cut out basic shapes from a contrasting color. Apply the shapes to the sides of the blocks for shape-related activities.

◆◆ Susan A. Sharkey, La Mesa, CA

Triangle Blocks

Materials

Triangle pizza centers from pizza boxes

What to do

1. Collect the triangle centers used in the centers of pizza boxes. You can get them from your local pizza parlors. (Some may come in circles.) Collect about 300 triangles.

2. Encourage the children to construct various shapes and designs using the triangles. They can also make towers or buildings.

3. Challenge them to see how high they can stack them. Have a contest, if desired.

Related books

Albert's Alphabet by Leslie Tryon
Road Builders by B. G. Hennessey

◆◆ Cookie Zingarelli, Columbus, OH

Plastic Blocks

Materials

Variety of plastic containers with lids

What to do

1. Put a variety of plastic containers in the Block Center and watch the children's imaginations soar.
2. Children love exploring how to balance a variety of sizes and shapes.
3. You can also add animals and strawberry containers to create a zoo.

❖ Sandy L. Scott, Vancouver, WA

Blocks and Props

Materials

Old shower curtain or plastic tablecloth
Permanent marker

What to do

1. Draw a village or town on an old shower curtain.
2. Create roads, forests, rivers, and so on.
3. Keep it in the Block Center and encourage the children to build structures on top of it.

More to do

Outdoors: Go outside with the children and collect items such as twigs, rocks, grass, and flowers. Bring them inside and use for the block town.

❖ Sandy L. Scott, Vancouver, WA

"Look What We Built" Photo Album

Materials

Camera
Photo album

What to do

1. Keep a camera loaded with film near your Block Center.
2. When a child or a group of children creates something especially wonderful, take a picture of the structure and the builders, too!
3. Get the photos developed (or printed, if using a digital camera).
4. Place a copy of each picture in a photo album with a caption beneath naming the structure and the "architects." You also may want to include quotes from the children concerning the project.
5. Keep the album in the Block Center. It will be a class favorite!

More to do

Language: This can be incorporated into an enriching language experience if you encourage the children to dictate stories about the process of building their "house" or who might work in their "skyscraper."

❖ Charlene Woodham Peace, Semmes, AL

Dramatic Play for the Block Area

Materials

Safety vests, hard hats (real or toy), and carpenter aprons (child size are available at Lowe's or Home Depot)
Poster board and markers, photos of construction sites
Tape

What to do

1. Put safety vests, hard hats, and aprons in the block area to extend the reality of the play.
2. Make construction signs, such as "Hard Hat Area" or "Construction Underway."
3. Hang the signs and photos of construction sites in the block area.

More to do

Field Trip: To extend the activity, take a field trip to watch construction underway, or ask employees from a hardware store to come in and demonstrate how to use some tools.

Author note: Some employees from our local hardware store visited and helped the children build a planter, and they gave everyone aprons. The children will never forget it. You can also ask parents to come in and help the children build something.

Related books

Construction Critter by Mercer Mayer
The Three Little Pigs

Related song

"Johnny Pounds with One Hammer"

❖❖ Tracie O'Hara, Charlotte, NC

Building an Igloo

Materials

Pictures of different types of homes, including igloos
Styrofoam pieces
Masking tape

What to do

1. Ask the children to bring in pictures of their homes. Discuss what their houses are made of.
2. Show the children pictures of different types of homes that people live in around the world. Compare the houses in hot and cold places. Show the children a picture of an igloo and ask them if they know how to make one.

3. Ahead of time, collect large Styrofoam packing pieces used for shipping and cut them into sections to resemble large blocks of ice.

4. Give the Styrofoam pieces to the children to arrange into the shape of an igloo. Encourage the children to think about how they will get into and out of the igloo once it is built so they will realize the need to leave a doorway. Ask them to make the igloo large enough to be able to crawl inside and sit.

5. Use masking tape to keep the Styrofoam pieces together.

More to do

Dramatic Play: Use the igloo to provide the basis for dramatic play. What will they use for food? How will they sleep? What kind of clothing would they need?

Science: Snow feels cold. How can something cold keep you warm? Go outside and explore how plants live through the winter protected by a cover of snow.

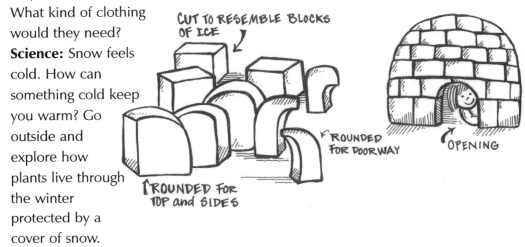

Related books

Building an Igloo by Ulli Steltzer
The Igloo by Charlotte and David Yue

❖❖ Bea Chawla, Vincetown, NJ

Horizontal Blocks

Materials

Variety of blocks and building materials

What to do

1. Three-year-olds love to build with blocks, but usually their focus is on one thing: HIGHER! They love to build towers, but towers can only go so high

before they fall over. The point of this activity is for children to explore using blocks horizontally instead of always "going vertical!"

2. Gather block materials for circle time. Ask the children, "How far do you think these blocks can reach?" Chances are they will want to stack them up.

3. Encourage them to think of what will happen if instead of stacking them, they place them end to end along the floor. How far will they reach?

4. Ask the children to build a "road" from the circle area to the other side of the room. If possible, build a road out into a hallway or into another room.

5. Encourage the children to think of other things they can make with blocks in this way. Some ideas are mazes (either for people or play cars), a paddock for play farm animals, and so on.

More to do

Outdoors: On a non-muddy day, take the blocks outside. Try lining the sidewalks or lines on a black top with blocks placed end to end.

❖❖ Suzanne Pearson, Stephens City, VA

Bear Walk

Materials

It's About Time, Jesse Bear by Nancy White Carlstrom
Short square blocks
Long rectangular blocks

What to do

1. Read It's About Time, Jesse Bear by Nancy White Carlstrom to the children.

2. Put a variety of blocks on the floor. Start lining up the blocks in a line in no particular order.

3. When a child comes to play, ask her if she can hand you all of the short blocks (hold up a short block).

4. Then ask her if she can hand you a long block (hold up a long block).

5. Say, "When the little bear went for a walk, he used the short road. I'm going to use these blocks to make a road for him. Let's build a road with all the short blocks first."

6. Then, let the child make the road. When she is finished, ask her to build another road using only the long blocks.

7. "Look! You have built two roads—one with short blocks and one with long blocks. Now the little bear can take a walk just like in the story. Let's help tear up the roads so he can get back home!" Then start putting the blocks back into the bin.
8. When finished, say:
   This little bear went to the market.
   This little bear went to (area).
   You may go now, too.

More to do

Use different-shaped or colored blocks.
Math: Ask the children to arrange the blocks from shortest to longest.
Outdoors: This is a good sandbox activity.

◆❖ A. Gail Whitney, Dameron, MD

Map It Out!

Materials

Road maps
Rulers, pencils or markers, drawing paper, and masking tape or colored tape

What to do

1. Show the children a road map. Point out various features on the map, such as rivers, mountains, forests, and so on.
2. Place rulers, pencils, paper, and tape in the Block Center and encourage the children to make their own maps. The children will be mapping out new territory in no time at all!

◆❖ Jodi Sykes, Lake Worth, FL

Path Building with Blocks

Materials

Rosie's Walk by Pat Hutchins
Large blocks
Plastic toy chicken or rooster

What to do

1. Read Rosie's Walk by Pat Hutchins to the children.
2. Show the children the pictures of Rosie's path through the barnyard. Discuss the story, paying special attention to directional words, such as over and under.
3. Encourage the children to use blocks to build the path that Rosie took.
4. After they build the path, the children can use a small toy chicken or rooster to recreate Rosie's walk.

❖❖ Cindy Hewitt, Houston, TX

Colored Blocks and Concepts

Materials

Cardboard blocks in various colors
Construction paper (the same color as the blocks)
Scissors
Thick black marker
Clear contact paper

What to do

1. Cut out one construction paper "block" for each color of cardboard blocks on the shelf.
2. Use a marker to write "red block," "blue block," and so on on each cardboard block.
3. Use clear contact paper to attach each paper block to its own shelf (or section of a shelf).
4. At clean-up time, help the children as they put away the blocks by matching them to the colored paper blocks already on the shelf.

5. If desired, assign each child a color to pick up. For example, Sandy is in the blue group so she picks up the blue blocks. Other days, ask the children to pick up their favorite color and put away all the blocks of that color.

More to do

Math: When the children are putting away blocks, talk about big, little, and medium blocks and discuss rectangles and squares. Also, separate block play items into categories. For example, have a bin for people, one for cars, and one for animals. This gives the children lots of practice with sorting and classifying!

Related song

"Rainbow of Colors" on Greg and Steve's *We all Live Together—Vol. 5*

❖❖ Linda N. Ford, Sacramento, CA

Block Blueprints

Materials

Assorted blocks
Tagboard or thick paper
Markers
Clear contact paper or laminate
Empty cereal box

What to do

1. Build a block structure on top of a piece of tagboard or thick paper.
2. Trace the structure, piece by piece, using markers. If using colored blocks, add the colors to the tracing.
3. Laminate the blueprint mat or cover it with clear contact paper.
4. Make as many blueprint mats as desired and store them in an empty cereal box.
5. Keep the blueprint maps in the Block Center and encourage the children to use them as desired.
6. If desired, encourage the children to make their own blueprints and let their classmates build with them.

More to do

Math: Make mats for a variety of math-related activities.

❖❖ Nicole Sparks, Miami, FL

Books Belong Everywhere

Materials

Baskets
Special topic books

What to do

1. So often we tend to limit the books to the library area, but books belong everywhere! Put a basket of books into each center in your classroom to let the children know the importance of reading.
2. The following are some ideas of what kinds of books to put into each center:

Dramatic Play Center: books about dressing up, babies, and jobs; cookbooks
Block Center: books about construction, block play, and cars
Art Center: books about painting, museums, artwork, and child-made art books
Science Center: books about insects, animals, the five senses, and seasons
Music Center: songbooks, books about instruments or playing in a band, books with the words to songs as text
Math and Manipulatives Center: books on counting and books such as the Cheerios or M&M counting books

❖ Tracie O'Hara, Charlotte, NC

Literature-Extension Organizer

Materials

8" x 12" (gallon size) resealable plastic bags
Photocopy of literature-extension activity
Children's book
Cassette tape to accompany children's book, if available
Self-sticking labels or paper and tape

What to do

1. Purchase 8" x 12" resealable plastic bags in quantities of 100 from your local

wholesale food distributor. Plan to use a separate bag for each book.

2. Each time you find an appropriate activity for extending one of your books, put a photocopy of the activity inside the plastic bag along with a copy of the book.

3. If you have a cassette recording of the book, place it in the plastic bag too. All three fit quite nicely and are kept together until needed.

4. Make a label for the bag, including the book title and length (playing time) of the cassette tape.

5. Attach the label to the front of the plastic bag. Now you will always have activities for your favorite stories ready to go!

More to do

If you have flannel board cutouts for the book, add them to the bag, too. Put them into smaller resealable bags first.

◆◆ Jackie Wright, Enid, OK

Book Hunt

Materials

Variety of age-appropriate books
Name tags

What to do

1. Most teachers change the books available to the children with each new theme. However, sometimes the children don't even notice there are new books available. Here is a game I invented to help the children become aware of the new books.

2. The first day of a new theme, instead of putting all the books in the center, write each child's name on a nametag and put one on each book. Then hide the books in various places in the room.

3. When the children arrive, their first "job" is to look around the room and find a book with their name on it. (Remind them not to give away where the other books are hidden.)

4. Tell them that when they find their book, they should take it to the book corner and "read" it. Encourage the children to take at least 3-5 minutes to look through the book, then place it on the shelf or wherever books are kept in the book center (keep the name tag on for now).

5. Later, at circle time, have a "show and tell" with the books. Each child stands up and shows his book to the group. Ask the children to say one thing about something they saw in the book. For example, "This book has lions in it" or "The girl jumps in the water."

6. Throughout the rest of the theme, whenever you read a book to the group, ask the child whose name is on it to stand and hold the book while you read it or help you turn the pages.

More to do

You can also use this game when you introduce new materials in other centers, such as manipulative or art supplies. If the child's name is on the material, he gets to be the first to try it and demonstrate it to the group. Ask the child to talk about the right and the wrong way to use that material.

More Books: Ask the children to bring in books from home to hide for their friends to find and then read.

❖ Suzanne Pearson, Stephens City, VA

Story Read-Alongs

Materials

Any book that has predictable, repetitive phrases, such as:

Brown Bear, Brown Bear, What Do You See? by Bill Martin, Jr. and Eric Carle
Chicken Soup with Rice by Maurice Sendak
The Gingerbread Man
The Little Engine That Could by Watty Piper
Mrs. Wishy Washy by Joy Cowley
Three Billy Goats Gruff

What to do

1. Choose a story with repetitive phrases (see above list) and read it to the children several times over the course of the week.

2. As the children become familiar with the text, invite them to help you read by supplying the repetitive phrases with your support and/or support from the illustrations. For example: "I think I can, I think I can" (from *The Little Engine That Could*), or "Run, run as fast as you can. You can't catch me, I'm the gingerbread man!"

3. As the story becomes even more familiar, ask the children to anticipate what comes next.

More to do

Art: Make stuffed gingerbread dolls using large, brown paper bags. Draw a large outline of a gingerbread man and cut it out, keeping both sides of the bag together. Staple the two sides together, but leave an opening on one side. Encourage the child to decorate his bag as desired. Stuff the bag with crumpled newspaper and staple it closed.

Dramatic Play: Encourage the children to act out the stories.

Literacy: Place the books in the housekeeping corner and invite the children to "read" the stories to the dolls.

◆◆ Iris Rothstein, New Hyde, NY

Tell Me a Story

Materials

Variety of storybooks
3" x 5" (7 cm x 12 cm) cards
Pen
Bag

What to do

1. Read a story to the children. Then discuss different things that happened in the story.
2. Choose one part of the story and write about it on a card. Put the card into the bag.
3. Do this activity every day with different books.
4. After a few days, explain to the children that they are going to play a trivia game.
5. Ask a child to pick one card from the bag.
6. Read the thought and ask the children if they remember which story it came from.

Original rhyme

Tell Me a Story

Tell me a story, tell me a story, tell me a story,
Remember what you said,
Tell me about the birds and the bees,
And why do chickens have knees,
Tell me a story and then I'll have my lunch.

◆◆ Liz Thomas, Hobart, IN

Bags and Books and Tapes

Materials

Cassette tapes and tape recorder
Favorite books
Paper
Stickers
Craft sticks and glue
Gift bags
Markers

What to do

1. Record your favorite books on tape with sound effects (enlist the help of others in your family, if needed).
2. Make paper stick puppets to go with the books.
3. Put each book and tape into their own gift bag. Decorate the outside of the bag with scenes from the story.

◆◆ Lisa Chichester, Parkersburg, WV

Fun Box

Materials

Cardboard box
Paint, markers, construction paper, and so on
Book
Puppet and objects relating to book
Stickers, treats, and so on

What to do

1. Use paint, markers, and so on to decorate a box.
2. Put objects into the "fun box" to use before or after you read a book.
3. Before reading the book, take a character puppet (or any other object that goes along with the book) out of the box and use it to introduce the story.

4. When you finish the book, give the good listeners a treat from the box, such as stickers, edible treats, or a little something that might reinforce the book's message.

❖❖ Tracie O'Hara, Charlotte, NC

Book Basket

Materials

Collection of children's books
Large wicker basket
Seasonal bow, optional

What to do

1. Each time you share a book with the children, place it into a large wicker basket on the floor in your reading area.
2. This allows the children the opportunity to handle the books that were just read aloud to them and to look through them on their own.
3. Keep the basket on the floor so that children have easy access.
4. If desired, add a bow to the basket that reflects the season or your current classroom theme.
5. Rotate the books weekly to correlate with current classroom activities.

❖❖ Jackie Wright, Enid, OK

Book Box

Materials

Empty, sturdy box approximately 6 ½" wide x 11" high x 11" deep
Scissors
Laminated wrapping paper or contact paper
Large label

What to do

1. To make a box similar to a magazine file that can hold a collection of individually bound books, cut the box diagonally along the sides to approximately 5" from the bottom of the box.
2. Discard the top portion of the box.
3. Cover the remaining portion with laminated wrapping paper or contact paper.
4. Label appropriately, for example, "Nursery Rhyme Collection."

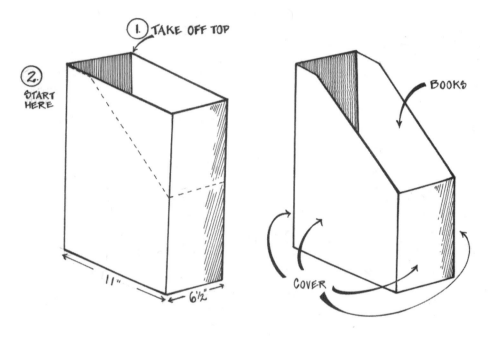

❖❖ Jackie Wright, Enid, OK

Big Birthday Book

Materials

White oaktag or tagboard
Markers, crayons, and colored pencils
Hole punch
Yarn

What to do

1. Give each child a sheet of white oaktag. Ask them to draw a picture of themselves on it using markers, crayons, and colored pencils.

2. Ask the children if they know their birth dates. Record their answers and check your records to make sure each one is right.
3. Print each child's name and birth date on the drawings they made.
4. Punch three holes into the side of each drawing.
5. Arrange the pages in order by month.
6. Help the children create a front and back cover. Punch holes in it.
7. Use yarn to bind the cover and pages into a book.
8. Display the book on each child's birthday.

More to do

Add blank pages for months with no birthdays in them. Have an "unbirthday" party!

Literacy: As the children celebrate their birthdays, ask them to add a page to the book. They can draw a picture of their birthday parties and dictate a short story.

Special Days: If your school follows the public school schedule, celebrate the half birthday of the children whose birthdays fall in the summer months.

Related books

Arthur's Birthday by Marc Brown
Happy Birthday by Gail Gibbons
Happy Birthday Moon by Frank Asch
I Love You, Mary Jane by Lorna Balian
Secret Birthday Message by Eric Carle
Will It Ever Be My Birthday? by Dorothy Corey
You Were Born on Your Very First Birthday by Linda Walvoord Girard

❖ Virginia Jean Herrod, Columbia, SC

Photo Flip Book

Materials

Camera and film
Copier, if needed
Glue
9" x 12" (22 cm x 30 cm) oaktag or tagboard
Paper cutter
Hole punch
Yarn or jump rings

What to do

1. Take a full-length photo of each child. Turn the camera sideways so the child fills the viewfinder. Make sure the child's head is at the very top of the photo (nothing showing above) and his feet are at the very bottom (nothing showing below).

2. Get the photos developed in the largest size you can. If you use a digital camera, print the photos on a full sheet (8" x 10") if possible. If you can't print large photos, then get them developed in the regular size and enlarge them to 8" x 10" on a copier.

3. Glue each photo on a 9" x 12" piece of oaktag, leaving a margin on the left to bind the book later.

4. Let dry.

5. Bend each page at the left margin to create a crease.

6. Stack the photos together, making sure they are all right side up.

7. Use a paper cutter to cut the photos into three equal parts. Cut from the right hand side toward the left. DO NOT CUT ALL THE WAY THROUGH. Leave the margin on the left uncut. The top cut should include the head and shoulders, the middle cut should include the trunk to the mid thighs, and the bottom cut should include the mid thigh to the feet.

8. Create a cover for the book and use a blank page as the back cover.

9. Bind the left-hand edge of the book using jump rings or yarn.

10. Show the children how to mix and match the body sections to create "new" people from the photos. They will have fun creating a child with Susie's head, Tommy's body, and Doug's legs!

More to do

Art: Make several copies of each child's photo. Cut them into pieces by body parts (such as head, trunk, arms, and legs). Put them into the Art Center and encourage the children to glue them together to create a whole new person.

Language: Ask the children to make up names and stories for the "new" people they have created by flipping the pages of the book. Ask leading questions such as: What does the person like to do? What does that person like to eat? Who would be friends with that person?

Related books

Black like Kyra, White like Me by Judith Vigna
A Friend Is Someone Who Likes You by Joan Walsh Anglund
Saturday at the New You by Barbara E. Barber

❖❖ Virginia Jean Herrod, Columbia, SC

Family Collage Book

Materials

Several photos of each member of the child's family
Copier
Scissors
Small containers
Construction paper
Glue
4" x 5" (10 cm x 12 cm) white paper
Pen or marker
Hole punch and yarn or heavy string, or stapler

What to do

1. One week before doing this activity, ask each set of parents to send in several family photos. Make sure that each member of the family is represented (including pets!). Reassure the parents that the photos will be returned unharmed.

2. Copy each photo six times on a copier. Don't worry about making color copies—black and white images are fine for this activity. Return the original photos to the parents.

3. Give the copies of the photos to the children and ask them to cut them apart in any manner they choose. Encourage them to cut around, not through, the faces.

4. The children can put their photo pieces into containers.

5. Give the children a piece of construction paper and some glue. Encourage them to create a collage on the paper using their cut-up photos.

6. While the collages are drying, interview the children about their family members. Ask them questions such as:
   What does your mom/dad like to do?
   What is one thing your mom always says?
   What is one thing your dad always says?
   What is your (sibling's) name?
   What does your (sibling) like to do?
   What is one thing your (sibling) always says?
   What do you like to do?
   What is one thing you always say?
   What is your pet's name?
   What does your pet like to do?

7. Print the answers to the questions in story form on a 4" x 5" piece of paper. Help the children glue this paper to the middle of their collages. Let dry.

8. Create a cover by making a collage that includes at least one photo of each child in the class. Let dry.

9. Print "Our Families" on a piece of paper and glue it to the middle of the cover page. Let dry.

10. Stack the pages together to form a book. Use a blank piece of paper for the back cover.

11. Use the copier to make one copy of the book for each child in the class.

12. Punch holes along the left edge of the book pages and bind them with yarn or heavy string. Or, you can staple along the left edge to bind the books.

13. Send the books home with a note to parents asking them to read the book aloud to their child.

More to do

Invite parents to visit for story time or a special activity. Some parents have talents in areas such as art or drama and would love to share their skills with the children.

Related books

Christina Katerina and the Time She Quit the Family by Patricia Lee Gauch
The Fabulous Firework Family by James Flora
I Got a Family by Melrose Cooper
Poinsettia and Her Family by Felicia Bond
Queenie, One of the Family by Bob Graham
The Surprise Family by Lynn Reiser

❖❖ Virginia Jean Herrod, Columbia, SC

Cereal Book

Materials

Cereal boxes (all the same size)
Scissors
Hole punch
Yarn or heavy string

What to do

1. Collect as many cereal box covers as you would like. Ask parents to bring in cereal boxes, too.
2. Cut out the front cover of each cereal box.
3. Punch three holes on the left side of each cover and bind them together with yarn to make a book.
4. Show the book at circle time. Ask for volunteers to "read" the pages aloud. Chances are, at least one of the children will know the name of the cereal just by being familiar with these products. Environmental print is a great way to start children on their pre-reading skills.
5. Put the book in the Book Center. The children will enjoy a book that they can read all by themselves! They will beam with pride and confidence.

◆◆ Gail D. Morris, Kemah, TX

ABC Construction Picture Book

Materials

Magazines and ads from papers
Scissors
Glue
Construction paper
Hole Punch
Yarn

What to do

1. Cut out pictures from magazines of construction items.
2. Glue them onto paper and bind them together to make an ABC Construction Picture Book.
3. The following are some ideas you can use for each letter:
   A: Alan wrench
   B: Bolts, blueprints
   C: Crow bar, cement truck
   D: Drill, dump truck

E: Enter/Exit signs
F: Foreman
G: Goggles
H: Hard hat, hammer
I: ID badge
J: Jackhammer
K: Knife
L: Ladder, level
M: Measuring tape
N: Nails, nuts
O: Overalls
P: Paint
Q: Quitting time
R: Ruler
S: Saw, screws
T: Truck, tool belt
U: Uniform
V: Vise
W: Wood
X: Excavate
Y: Yardstick
Z: Zoning map

More to do

Sensory Development: Cut out letters from sandpaper and glue them onto poster board so that the children can feel the shape of the letters. This is a good exercise in textures and sensory development. You can glue nuts, washers, bolts, and so on at the top of the letters to provide even more sensory experiences.

Related books

Albert's Alphabet by Leslie Tryon
Chicka Chicka Boom Boom by Bill Martin, Jr. and John Archambault
It's the ABC Book by Joyce Harada

Related song

"The Alphabet Song"

◆◆ Cookie Zingarelli, Columbus, Ohio

What Can You Do?

Materials

Camera and film
9" x 12" (22 cm x 30 cm) oaktag or tagboard
Glue
Marker
Clear contact paper or laminate
Hole punch
Yarn or jump rings

What to do

1. Take photos of the children as they perform daily duties, such as setting up mats for nap or cleaning up after meals or playtime, and as they work in various centers, such as building structures in the block area or working with clay or painting in the art area. Also take photos of them as they achieve certain milestones, such as going across the monkey bars or pedaling a tricycle.

2. After the film is developed, choose one photo of each child that clearly shows him involved in an activity, such as those listed above.

3. Show each child his own photo and ask, "What are you doing in the photo?" Record what the child says on a separate piece of paper.

4. Mount each photo on a piece of oaktag.

5. Create a title page, such as "Children, Children What Can You Do?" (It's a nice touch to include a small photo of each child in the book on the cover.)

6. Put a blank page after the title page and on the back, print "Children, children what can you do?"

7. On the pages with the photos, print a simple text that describes the child's actions. Paraphrase what the child told you. For example, if the photo shows a child putting sheets on her mat for nap, then write "Kathryn can put her own sheets on her mat. Can you?"

8. On the back of each photo page, print "Children, children what can you do?" again. This page should face the next photo page.

9. Continue doing this on every page. Remember to keep the text simple and repetitive and always include the "Can you?" part.

10. On the last page, write "Children, children what can you do? We can do anything! Can you?"

11. Laminate the pages for durability. Punch holes along the left edge and bind them using yarn or jump rings.

More to do

Children often state that they can't do something that seems hard to them. Encourage them to say, "I can try" instead of "I can't."

General Tips: If you have a classroom Camcorder, make short movies of the children involved in activities similar to ones in the book. Show the movies during pick-up time. The parents will enjoy seeing what their children do during the day.

Original song

Try Try Try (Tune: "Row, Row, Row Your Boat")

Try, try, try your best
No matter what you do.
Always keeping on trying hard
It's the best thing for you!

Related books

Howie Helps Himself by Joan Fassler
I Can! Can You? by Carol Adorjan
Now I'm Big by Margaret Miller
Number Nine Duckling by Susan Akass

❖❖ Virginia Jean Herrod, Columbia, SC

Our Class Feelings Book

Materials

Camera and film
Colored paper
Glue
Laminate or clear contact paper
Hole punch
Yarn

What to do

1. Take pictures of each child showing a different emotion, such as sad, happy, and angry.
2. Get the photos developed.

3. Glue each photo onto a piece of colored paper.

4. Write the emotion underneath each photo.

5. Laminate the pages or cover them with clear contact paper for durability.

6. Punch three holes into each page and bind them together.

More to do

Literacy: Ask the children to dictate stories about each emotion. Write down what they say underneath their photo.

❖❖ Nicole Sparks, Miami, FL

My Book About Me

Materials

Paper, six sheets for each child
Marker or pen
Crayons or markers
Hole punch
Yarn or heavy string

What to do

1. Punch holes into six sheets of paper and bind them together with string. Do this for each child in the class.

2. Write the title "My Book About Me" on the front page.

3. On each page of the book, write sentences such as:
   Page 1: *I live with:*
   Page 2: *My favorite book is:*
   Page 3: *On the weekend I like to:*
   Page 4: *My favorite food is:*
   Page 5: *My favorite part of school is:*

4. Give each child a book to bring home to complete. Write a letter to the parents explaining that they should work on it together. The parent can do the writing and the child can illustrate it.

5. When the children bring their books back to class, ask them to share their books one at a time during story time.

Related books

A Book About Me by Gallaudet College Press
Good Books, Good Times selected by Lee Bennett Hopkins
My Book by Me by Dana Rau

❖❖ Liz Thomas, Hobart, IN

My Journal

Materials

Construction paper
Crayons or markers
Laminate or clear contact paper, optional
Blank paper
Hole punch
Yarn or string

What to do

1. Explain to the children what a journal is and that they will be writing in one throughout the year.
2. Ask the children to make a cover for their journal. (A self-portrait makes a great cover.) If desired, laminate the cover or cover it with clear contact paper.
3. About every other week, think of a topic for a journal page, such as a theme or a letter on which you are working. Write a caption at the top of the page in each child's journal. Some examples are:

    If I were a shape, I would be a ____
    If I were an animal, I would be a ____
    When I grow up, I want to be a ____
    If I were going to an island, I would take a ____
    My favorite season is ____
    My favorite nursery rhyme is ____
    If I were president, I would ____
    I can protect our earth by ____
    When the weather is ____ outside, I like to ____

4. Ask the children for their response to the caption and write it for them in the space provided. Then encourage them to draw a picture of their idea.

5. Make sure to date each journal entry and keep them until the end of the year. This is a great way to show parents a child's growth and progress.

More to do

Circle Time: If the journal is too much for the children, depending on your group, you could ask these kinds of questions during Circle Time and then record their responses. Hang the responses for parents to enjoy or put them in your monthly newsletter.

◆◆ Gail Morris, Kemah, TX

A Photo Album of Our Own

Materials

Film and camera
Inexpensive photo album

What to do

1. Take a lot of pictures of the children on field trips, in centers, group time, and so on.
2. Get the photos developed as soon as you finish a roll of film.
3. Put the pictures into a photo album and keep it in the Library Area and continue adding photos throughout the year. Children love to look at pictures of themselves and remember things that they have done throughout the year.
4. At the end of the year, distribute the pictures to the parents in a journal or in an end-of-the-year assessment or conference. Pictures tell a great story and parents will love to have them as a keepsake. (Before giving them to parents, go through them and keep a few for yourself as a reminder of the year!)

◆◆ Gail Morris, Kemah, TX

"Here Are My Hands"

Materials

Here Are My Hands by Bill Martin, Jr. and John Archambault
Chart paper
Markers
Camera and film
White paper
Glue
Construction paper
Stapler

What to do

1. Read *Here Are My Hands* to the children. Talk with them about other things their hands can do.

2. Write each child's name on a piece of chart paper. Ask each child to tell the group one thing his hands can do and write his response next to his name on the chart.

3. Take pictures of each child doing the activity he said his hands can do.

4. After you get the pictures developed, glue each one to a separate sheet of paper. Underneath each photo, write what the child said he could do with his hands.

5. Staple all of the pages together with a sheet of construction paper in front. Write "Here Are My Hands" on the cover.

6. Read the book with the children, and then place it in the class library so they can read it when they desire.

More to do

Make similar books about feet, legs, arms, and so on.

❖❖ Barbara Backer, Charleston, SC

What Color Are You Wearing?

Materials

Mary Wore Her Red Dress and Henry Wore His Green Sneakers by Merle Peek
Camera and film
Glue
Marker
White construction paper
Hole punch
String or ribbon

What to do

1. Read *Mary Wore Her Red Dress and Henry Wore His Green Sneakers* to the children.

2. Take a picture of each child. After you get the photos developed, give each child his own photo.

3. Give each child a sheet of white paper. Help them glue their photos onto the paper.

4. Ask the children to choose something they are wearing in their photos to sing about. Print "(child's name) is wearing (*color word item of clothing*) all day long" underneath his photo.

5. Punch holes into each page and bind them together with string or ribbon. Write "Our Class is Wearing…" on the cover.

6. Sing the song as the group reads the pages during circle and story times.

7. *Mary Wore Her Red Dress and Henry Wore His Green Sneakers* is also available in books with tape packs.

◆◆ Sandra Nagel, White Lake, MI

"It Looked Like Spilt Milk" Class Book

Materials

It Looked Like Spilt Milk by Charles G. Shaw
Paint smocks
Blue construction paper
Tempera paint, white
Black marker
Stapler

What to do

1. Read *It Looked Like Spilt Milk* to the children. Talk about all of the different illustrations in the book. Explain to the children that they will be making their own version of the book.
2. After the children put on paint smocks, give each child a piece of blue construction paper.
3. Demonstrate how to fold the paper in half to make a crease down the middle. Then unfold the paper.
4. Encourage the children to dribble or spoon a blob of white paint in the middle of the paper. Help the children re-fold it on the crease.
5. Ask the children to press on the outside of the fold, causing the paint to spread inside. When they are done, open the paper and let it dry.
6. Ask the children to dictate what they think their "blob" looks like as you write the words underneath.
7. Staple the pages together and add a cover.

More to do

Outdoors: Go outside on a nice day, lie on blankets, and gaze at the clouds. Talk about what the children "see."

◆◆ Vicki L. Schneider, Oshkosh, WI

The Purple Crayon

Materials

Harold and the Purple Crayon by Crockett Johnson
Purple crayons, one for each child
White construction paper
Hole punch
Yarn or string

What to do

1. Read Harold and the Purple Crayon to the children. Talk about the things Harold was able to do with his purple crayon. Ask the children what they would draw if they had a purple crayon.
2. Give each child a purple crayon and a piece of white construction paper. Encourage them to draw something with the purple crayon.
3. Ask the children to dictate something about their drawings and write it on their paper.
4. Put all of the sheets together to make a book. Add text as needed to make it look like the original story.
5. Make up a title and create a cover for the book. Punch holes in the sides of the drawings and bind them together using yarn or string.

More to do

Go on a purple walk around your school. Make a list of things you find that are purple. Create a poster describing what the children saw on their walk.
Art: Create a purple collage using magazine or newspaper pictures.
More Art: Make purple playdough. Create some purple creatures or make some beads and string a purple necklace.
Special Days: Have a purple day. Wear purple clothes, play with purple toys, and eat a purple snack.

Related books

Lilly's Purple Plastic Purse by Kevin Henkes
Purple, Green and Yellow by Robert Munsch

❖❖ Virginia Jean Herrod, Columbia, SC

Classroom Cookbooks

Materials

Recipe from each child in class
Copy machine
Paper
Hole punch
String or ribbon

What to do

1. Send a note home asking parents to bring in a copy of a recipe for your class cookbook.
2. Once all recipes are in, type them on your computer and print them out. Make enough copies for each child in the class.
3. Punch holes into the pages and bind them together with string or ribbon. Each child will have his or her own cookbook.

❖ Lisa Chichester, Parkersburg, VA

Easy, Durable Class Books

Materials

Three-ring binder
Top-loading plastic page protectors
Paper

What to do

1. The next time you want to create a book written by your class, try this easy method. After each page is completed, slip it inside a page protector.
2. Arrange the pages in the three-ring binder, and tape a cover to the front (or use a binder with the plastic pocket on the front).
3. Now it can be on the classroom bookshelf for the children to enjoy and read over and over again without tearing or coming apart.
4. Another advantage of this method is the ability to dismantle the book and send the pages home with their authors to share with family.

❖ Vicki Schneider, Oshkosh, WI

What If...

Materials

If by Sarah Perry
Paper
Markers or crayons

What to do

1. Read the book *If* to the children. During group time, ask the children to think of their own "What if…"
2. After you brainstorm in the group, give the children paper and markers to draw their ideas.
3. Ask the children to tell you something about their drawings and write their responses on their paper.
4. Display the artwork on a bulletin board entitled "What If…" or make a class book.
5. Read the ideas to all the children. They will find them very funny.

❖❖ Gail Morris, Kemah, TX

Making Shadows

Materials

My Shadow by Susan Winter
Large rolled black (butcher type) paper
White crayons or chalk
Scissors
Tape

What to do

1. After reading *My Shadow* to the children, experiment making shadows inside and outside. Encourage the children to find places where they can and cannot make shadows. Discuss.
2. Ask each child to lie down on a long sheet of black paper.
3. Trace around the child and cut out the silhouette.
4. Tape the silhouettes to a long wall space.

Related song

"Just Me and My Shadow"

◆◆ Sandra Nagel, White Lake, MI

Talking About Fears

Materials

Brave Martha by Margot Apple
Props from the story, such as an umbrella, a fur hat, a stuffed animal with horns,
a stuffed animal cat, and a blanket

What to do

1. Read *Brave Martha* to the children. In this book, Martha's cat Sophie checks all of the spooky places in the bedroom each night before Martha goes to sleep. One night Sophie is missing, and Martha imagines that all sorts of creepy things are in her room. She confronts and conquers these fears, and in the end, Sophie returns and they both go to sleep.
2. Discuss the story with the children. Who was making all of the noises that Martha heard? Where was Sophie?
3. Encourage the children to talk about their fears and relate stories of times that they were afraid.
4. Place props in the Dramatic Play Area so the children can act out the story.

◆◆ Barbara Backer, Charleston, SC

Reading Signs and Symbols

Materials

I Read Symbols by Tana Hoban

What to do

1. When walking in the city, or when riding in cars and on the bus, children see many road signs and other informational signs. This book has photographs of many of these signs as well as an information guide to the symbols.

2. Show this wordless book to the children.
3. Ask them to identify several of the most familiar signs, such as symbols for restrooms, "walk," or a school zone.
4. Ask the children if they can tell you some symbols they see when they are not in school. Help them find the symbols in the book.
5. Each time you show them the book, teach them the identity of another symbol.
6. Leave the book where children can enjoy it during reading time and choice time.

More to do

Blocks: Scan or photocopy the signs at the back of the book and cut them out. Glue each sign to a craft stick. Put the signs and a roll of masking tape in the Block Area. Children can tape them to the sides of blocks as they play.

Original song

I Can Read a Sign (Tune: "Farmer in the Dell")

I can read a sign.
I can read a sign.
"Stop" and "Go" and "Please Go Slow"
I can read a sign.

I can read a sign.
I can read a sign.
"Women," "Men," and "No Smoking"
I can read a sign.

◆◆ Barbara Backer, Charleston, SC

Sounds Are All Around Us

Materials

Sounds All Around by Wendy Pfeffer
Objects that make sounds

What to do

1. Read *Sounds All Around* to the children. Discuss how we hear with our ears and talk about different sounds we make.
2. Imitate sounds that animals make. Then sing "Old MacDonald Had a Farm."
3. Ask each child to bring in an object from home that makes a sound, or provide an assortment of objects from around the room.
4. After each child shows and tells about what he brought, put all the objects in another part of the room.
5. Ask one child at a time to go to that part of the room and make a sound with one of the objects. The other children guess what object made the sound.

More to do

There are many activities in the back of the book for you to try.
Music: Ask the children to choose rhythm instruments. One at a time, each child plays his instrument. Talk about the sound. Is it loud? Soft? And so on. Encourage the children to march to music and play their instruments.
Outdoors: Take a walk outside and listen to all the sounds. Back in the room, discuss the sounds heard on the walk. Encourage the children to imitate the sounds they heard as other children guess what they are.

Related book

The Listening Walk by Paul Showers and Thomas Crowell

❖❖ Wendy Pfeffer, Pennington, NJ

Creeping Caterpillars

Materials

The Very Hungry Caterpillar by Eric Carle
Construction paper, one each of several colors

What to do

1. Beforehand, hang the construction paper around the room where children will be able to see it when creeping and crawling on the floor.
2. Read *The Very Hungry Caterpillar* to the children. Talk about caterpillars.
3. Encourage the children to pretend to be caterpillars crawling through a garden and looking at the colorful flowers.
4. Sing the following song as the children creep around the room. Ask the children to point to the matching color construction paper as you sing each verse.

   (Tune: "Jimmy Crack Corn")
   Creeping caterpillar's in the garden.
   Creeping caterpillar's in the garden.
   Creeping caterpillar's in the garden.
   What does he see?

   Caterpillar sees a yellow flower.
   Caterpillar sees a yellow flower.
   Caterpillar sees a yellow flower.
   What else does he see?

5. Continue singing about the other colors in additional verses. The last line of the final verse is "That's what he sees."

More to do

Art: Cut colored tissue paper into 2" (5 cm) circles. Show the children how to place a tissue paper circle on a piece of manila paper and hold it in place with the finger of one hand. Then dip a brush into diluted glue, wiping off excess glue by stroking the brush's side against the shallow dish. Brush the glue mixture on TOP of the circle, brushing from the center to the outside. Place another circle slightly overlapping the first and brush glue on top of it. Continue in this manner forming a tissue-paper caterpillar. Encourage the children to use small scraps of tissue for the caterpillar's facial features.

❖❖ Barbara Backer, Charleston, SC

"The Very Hungry Caterpillar" Puppet Show

Materials

The Very Hungry Caterpillar by Eric Carle
Poster board in the colors of the fruits in the book
Scissors
White poster board
Caterpillar puppet or sock puppet
Butterfly puppet or picture of butterfly
Brown paper bag

What to do

1. Using poster board, cut out large shapes of fruits (apples, oranges, pears, and strawberries) from the book. Cut out a hole in each fruit shape big enough for an arm to fit through. (Enlarge patterns as needed.)

2. On large white poster board, draw the other foods that the caterpillar ate through (cupcake, pickle, sausage). Cut out the shapes and add a large hole in the middle of each.

3. As you read the story to the children, make the puppet eat right through the food shapes.

4. When it is time for the caterpillar to build a cocoon, make the puppet crawl into the paper bag.

APPLE

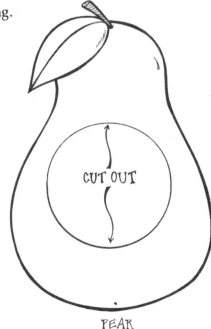

PEAR

STRAWBERRY

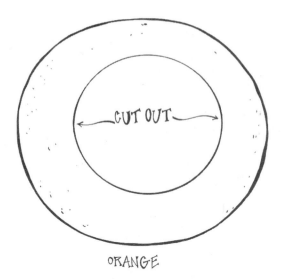

ORANGE

5. Have a butterfly come out of the bag!

More to do

Art: Make "blob" paintings. Spoon colors of paint onto paper, fold and rub, open the paper and cut into butterfly shapes.
More Art: Make egg carton caterpillars.
Music and Movement: Dance to music using scarves (like wings).
Science and Nature: Get a butterfly kit and hatch real butterflies, and then let them fly free.

◆◆ Audrey F. Kanoff, Allentown, PA

My Hungry Caterpillar

Materials

The Very Hungry Caterpillar by Eric Carle
Dark and light green construction paper
Hole punch
Red construction paper
Glue
Black washable markers
Scissors

What to do

1. Read *The Very Hungry Caterpillar* to the children.
2. Cut out leaves about 8" to 12" (20 cm x 30 cm) long from dark green construction paper, one for each child, resembling the leaf in the book.
3. Punch holes into the middle of each leaf until they look like they've been eaten through to resemble the leaf at the end of the story.
4. Cut out circles from red construction paper. These will be the caterpillar heads. Give one red circle to each child.
5. Cut out circles from light green and dark green paper of the same size. Give two of each color to each child. These will be for the caterpillar's body.
6. Encourage the children to glue their circles onto their leaf to form a caterpillar's body.
7. Give the children black markers and encourage them to draw eyes, antennae, and feet on the caterpillar while looking at a picture from the book.
8. Display them on a precut tree or anywhere in the room.

More to do

Science and Nature: Bring in caterpillars for the children to examine. When collecting caterpillars, notice where they are and what they might have been eating, so that you can provide an appropriate habitat for them. Put a small amount of water inside a large jar with a hole-punched lid. Encourage the children to watch the caterpillars eat, move, rest, and so on, using magnifying glasses. Only keep the caterpillars as long as they are healthy and eating or until they have hatched from cocoons. (The caterpillars don't always make a cocoon, but sometimes it happens.)

❖❖ Tina R. Durham-Woehler, Lebanon, TN

What's Big and What's Small?

Materials

Let's Find Out What's Big and What's Small by Martha and Charles Shapp
Tape measure
Chart paper and marker
Objects in the room to measure

What to do

1. Read the book to the children. Discuss which family members are bigger or smaller than the children. Which animals are bigger or smaller than they are?
2. Ask the children which objects in the room are bigger than they are (for example, a piano, window, door, and so on) and which items are smaller (for example, chalk, book, paper, and so on).
3. Measure all of the children and record their heights on a piece of chart paper.
4. Measure all of the items in the room that they talked about and compare these to the children's heights.

More to do

Art: Trace each child's body on a piece of large paper. Encourage the children to color in their shapes. Tape them on a wall and compare heights.

Math: Ask the children to guess how many blocks high they are. Pile a tower of blocks beside each child. Count as you add each block to the stack. Record the appropriate number of blocks for each child. Ask the children, "Who uses the most blocks and is tallest? Who uses the least amount of blocks?"

Related song

"You're Growing" from *Mr. Rogers Songbook* by Fred Rogers

❖❖ Wendy Pfeffer, Pennington, NJ

Individual Spider Webs

Materials

The Very Busy Spider by Eric Carle
Pictures of spider webs
Scissors
Clear adhesive paper
Tape
Colored or white string
Small plastic spiders or bugs

What to do

1. Read *The Very Busy Spider* by Eric Carle to the children. Closely examine the spider web on each page as the spider in the story builds it.

2. Show the children some pictures of spider webs and try to find some real spider webs to observe.

3. Talk about how spider webs all have the same basic form. Point out the concentric circles and connecting lines. Ask the children if they would like to make a spider web of their own.

4. Cut out a 12" x 12" (30 cm x 30 cm) piece of clear adhesive paper for each child.

5. Peel the covers from each paper and tape them to the table in front of each child.

6. Give the children some string. Encourage them to arrange the string on the paper in "spider web" fashion.

7. Provide some small plastic spiders, flies, and other bugs for the children to place on their webs. Or, make your own bugs from paper.

8. Hang the spider webs throughout the room for everyone to enjoy.

More to do

Games: Play "Spider Web Toss" by tossing cotton balls at the sticky spider webs hung around the room.

Movement: When observing spider webs, point out how the spiders move. During movement activities, ask the children to move their bodies like spiders.

Related books

The Itsy Bitsy Spider by Iza Trapani

The Lady and the Spider by Faith McNulty

Miss Spider's Tea Party by David Kirk

The Spider Who Created the World by Amy MacDonald

Related song

"The Itsy Bitsy Spider"

◆◆ Virginia Jean Herrod, Columbia, SC

Class Spider Web

Materials

The Very Busy Spider by Eric Carle
Fence
Large ball of white string or yarn
Scissors
Key ring
Black construction paper, optional

What to do

1. Read *The Very Busy Spider* by Eric Carle to the children. Encourage the children to examine and describe the spider web on each page.
2. Go outdoors and choose a spot on the fence to design your own class spider web.
3. Tie four pieces of string or yarn to a key ring, which will serve as the center of the spider web.
4. Tie the opposite ends of the four pieces of string or yarn that are connected to the key ring to four spots on the fence. This creates the four corners of the spider web.
5. Give the children lengths of yarn or string. Encourage them to weave the string in and out of the four strings on the fence, and the fence itself, to create a web.
6. Continue until the children have created a huge spider web.
7. If desired, cut out paper spiders and add them to the web.

More to do

More books: Get some books about spiders and spider webs. Bring them outdoors and sit next to the spider web while you read them to the children.
Art: Make spiders out of Styrofoam balls and pipe cleaners and add them to the web.

Related books

The Itsy Bitsy Spider by Iza Trapani

❖❖ Virginia Jean Herrod, Columbia, SC

Clothesline Walk

Materials

Mrs. McNosh Hangs Up Her Wash by Sarah Weeks
16' (5 m) of rope

What to do

1. Read Mrs. McNosh Hangs Up Her Wash to the children.
2. Later that day, or on another day when you are outside, ask a few children to help you uncoil the rope and stretch it across the playground.
3. Say, "We're going to take a walk, but we are going to be hooked together just like the clothes, furniture, and dog bone on Mrs. McNosh's clothesline. Let's try to walk together holding onto this rope." Ask each child to hold onto the rope.
4. Then, walk around the playground, holding onto the rope. "Don't pull too hard. We don't want anyone to fall down. If anyone falls, we might fall too! And remember, don't let go!"
5. Walk back to where you started. Sing "Twinkle, Twinkle, Little Star" as you walk back into the center. Ask each child to bring you his part of the rope as he lets go.

❖ Gail Whitney, Dameron, MD

Walking Together

Materials

Three Ducks Went Walking by Ron Roy

What to do

1. Read the book to the children.
2. Later that day, or on another day, get the children's attention by walking around singing "Five Little Ducks."
3. Say, "We're going to play a game. We're going to act like the three little ducks in the story. Everyone will follow me and do what I do. Are you ready? Here we go!"

4. Start leading them around the area by marching, then flapping your arms, then shaking your head.
5. Then, ask a few of the children to lead. After you have had a few leaders, drop out of line and let the children play.
6. When appropriate, jump back into the line and lead the children to the large group circle. Praise each child's activity. For example, say, "I really liked how you waved your arms (child's name)! And (child's name), you really lifted your feet high! Just like the little ducks did in the story.
7. Sing "Five Little Ducks" as you lead them to the next activity.

More to do

Pretend to be bears, wild animals, barn animals, cats, or dogs. Or encourage the children to make up their own animals.

❖❖ Gail Whitney, Dameron, MD

"The Three Billy Goats Gruff" Playlet

Materials

"The Three Billy Goats Gruff" story book or hand puppets, optional
3 or 4 child-sized wooden chairs or stools
Masks of three billy goats and a troll on craft sticks, optional

What to do

1. Read or tell the story of "The Three Billy Goats Gruff." If desired, use any good picture book version of the story or hand puppets. Be sure to use the repetitive phrases and sound effects, such as "trip, trap, trip, trap" and "WHO'S THAT TROMPING ON MY BRIDGE?"
2. Children love to act out a simplified version of this story. When you finish telling the story, line up 3 or 4 chairs or stools to make a "bridge." Ask for volunteers to be the troll and the three billy goats. Give them the hand-held masks to use, if desired.
3. Stand behind the "bridge" to direct the playlet. Ask the "troll" to crouch behind the bridge. One by one, the "billy goats" cross the bridge in order by size. The troll pops up each time and says his or her line (with a little

prompting, if needed). Billy goats one and two respond with, "Wait for my brother—he's bigger and tastier," after the troll says, "I'm going to gobble you up."

4. When the biggest billy goat steps onto the bridge and is challenged by the troll, he or she says, "Come on, then, and try." With coaxing from the director to be gentle, he or she gives the troll a little push off the bridge into the "river."

5. Finish the story by saying, "The biggest billy goat crossed the bridge, and he and his brothers lived happily ever after."

6. Choose more volunteers and repeat as many times as needed for everyone to have a turn. Keep in mind that the fun is in the action: climbing onto the bridge, tricking the mean troll, and "knocking" him or her into the river.

7. This story lends itself to the simple concept of size (small, medium, and big) as well as simple counting. You can reinforce these concepts easily as you remind the children of the importance of the size sequence as each child steps onto the bridge.

8. You can use this same kind of dramatic play with other stories, but they must be very simple tales with easy repetition that young children can follow and remember easily.

More to do

Art: Encourage the children to make paper bag goat puppets. You can find a great goat paper bag puppet reproducible in the book *Farm Animals* by Judy Instructo.

◆◆ Lesley S. Potts, Franklin, TN

Butterfly, Butterfly, What Do You See?

(This activity is adapted from *Brown Bear, Brown Bear, What Do You See?* by Eric Carle.)

Materials

Construction paper in a variety of colors
Scissors
Glue
Large blue mural paper, about 8' (2.5 m) long
Tape

Brown Bear, Brown Bear, What Do You See? by Bill Martin, Jr. and Eric Carle
Pictures of a variety of weather scenes
Chart paper
Paint and brushes
Newspaper
Markers

What to do

1. Ahead of time, cut out white clouds, dark clouds, 25-35 medium-sized raindrops, a sun, and a rainbow. Glue them to the mural paper from left to right in the following order:
   - white cloud
   - dark cloud
   - a group of about five raindrops
   - about 15-20 raindrops
   - another grouping of about five raindrops
   - the sun
   - the rainbow

2. Tape the mural to the wall.

3. Read *Brown Bear, Brown Bear, What Do You See?* over the period of several days until the children are very familiar with the story. Also put out copies of the book for the children to read to each other.

4. Show the children weather pictures and discuss the types of weather shown, the kind of weather in their own climate, and so on. Talk about clouds and rainfall.

5. Write the following adapted story on a large sheet of chart paper.

Butterfly, Butterfly, What Do You See?
White cloud, white cloud,
What do you see?
I see a dark cloud looking at me.

Dark cloud, dark cloud,
What do you see?
I see a raindrop looking at me.

Raindrop, raindrop,
What do you see?
I see a bright sun looking at me.

Bright sun, bright sun,
What do you see?
I see a rainbow looking at me.

Rainbow, rainbow,
What do you see?
I see a butterfly looking at me.

6. Read the adapted story to the children and point to the mural cutouts in order as you read.
7. Demonstrate how to make handprint butterflies. Paint both of a volunteer's palms and ask him to press one palm onto paper with his fingers spread, and then press the other painted hand on the paper so that the wrist areas of the two prints are touching.
8. Spread newspaper on the floor underneath the mural.
9. Working with one child at a time, paint both hands with the child's favorite color of paint. Then, gently holding one hand at a time, carefully guide the child to make a handprint on the mural. Repeat with the other hand, placing the second print on the mural so that the prints are joined at the wrist area.
10. When the child has finished his butterfly print, remind him to clasp his hands together and walk to the sink without touching anything.
11. Repeat until everyone has had a turn, spacing the prints all along the mural under the cutouts.
12. When the mural is dry, encourage the children to use markers to add details to the butterflies or to the weather scene.

More to do

Art: Make individual butterfly handprints on construction paper.
Science: Make a weather chart and track the weather for a week.
More Science: Examine the life cycle of a butterfly.

Related books

Johnny's Lion's Rubber Boots by Edith Thatcher Hurd
Polar Bear, Polar Bear, What Do You Hear? by Bill Martin, Jr. and Eric Carle
Rain Drop Splash by Alvin Tresselt

❖❖ Susan Oldham Hill, Lakeland, FL

Jimmy's Boa

Materials

The Day Jimmy's Boa Ate the Wash by Trinka Hakes Nobel
Newspaper or computer paper
A few pairs of pantyhose
Scissors
Scraps of ribbon or felt
Small pompoms or squiggle eyes
Glue

What to do

1. Read *The Day Jimmy's Boa Ate the Wash* to the children.
2. Explain to the children that they are going to make their own snakes. Show the children how to crumple a pile of newspaper or copy paper. Talk about how "fat" their snake is going to grow.
3. Beforehand, cut off the leg sections of a few pairs of pantyhose. Show the children how to stuff the crumpled paper into the leg section of the pantyhose.
4. When the children finish stuffing their pantyhose, tie the ends for them.
5. Show the children how to glue ribbon or felt scraps on the snake to make a tongue and small pompoms or squiggle eyes to make eyes.
6. Allow the glue to dry.
7. Be sure to make your own snake to add to your props when reading the story.

◆◆ Linda Starling, Rustberg, VA

Measuring Inch by Inch

Materials

Inch by Inch by Leo Lionni
Construction paper in various colors
Scissors
Ruler
Markers

What to do

1. Read the story *Inch by Inch* to the children.
2. Discuss with the children how the inchworm could measure everything he did.
3. Beforehand, cut construction paper into 1" x 12" (2 cm x 30 cm) pieces.
4. Measure each child's hand from his wrist to his middle fingertip. Cut a length of paper to that measurement and write the child's name and date on the strip of paper. Do this for each child.

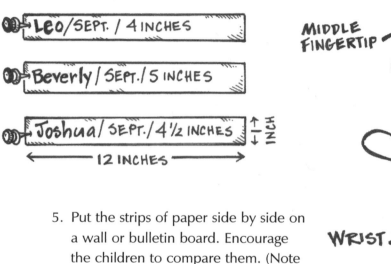

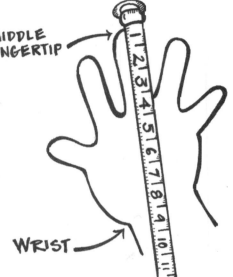

5. Put the strips of paper side by side on a wall or bulletin board. Encourage the children to compare them. (Note that all the hands will be almost the same length.)

◆◆ Diane Weiss, Fairfax, VA

Crazy Mixed-Up Animals

Materials

Pictures of baby animals
Scissors
Tagboard
Glue stick
Laminate or clear contact paper
Felt
Rubber cement
Flannel board
Moo Moo, Brown Cow by Jakki Wood

What to do

1. Beforehand, make a matching game by cutting pictures of baby animals in half across the middle to create tops and bottoms.
2. Glue each piece onto piece of tagboard.
3. Laminate or cover them with clear contact paper for durability
4. Back the pictures with felt using rubber cement.
5. Read *Moo Moo, Brown Cow* to the children. Discuss the special names for the various baby animals: calves, lambs, kids, ducklings, goslings, chicks, piglets, froglets, pups, small fry, and kittens.
6. Encourage the children to match the tops and bottoms of each animal on the flannel board.

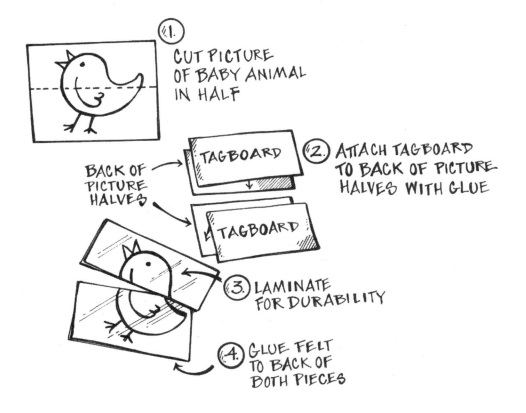

Related book

Baby Farm Animals by Garth Williams

◆◆ Jackie Wright, Enid, OK

The Colors of Cats

Materials

Large cat pattern
White construction paper
White drawing paper
Pen or marker
Scissors
Stapler
Cat Colors by Jane Cabrera
Crayons or magazines and glue

What to do

1. In advance, make a cat booklet for each child. Trace a cat pattern onto one sheet of white construction paper per child and on two sheets of white drawing paper for each child. Cut them out.
2. Staple the white construction paper on top of the two white sheets of drawing paper.
3. Read the story *Cat Colors* to the children.
4. After reading the story, give each child a booklet.
5. Ask the children to choose their favorite color. Then, ask them to color the cat on the front sheet using that color crayon.
6. Then, on the next cat page, ask them to dictate why that color is their favorite while you write down the words.
7. On the last page, help them find things in a magazine or draw things that are their favorite color.

❖❖ Quazonia J. Quarles Newark, DE

"The Itsy Bitsy Spider" Web

Materials

The Itsy Bitsy Spider by Iza Trapani
Dark colored bulletin board paper
White tempera paint
Disposable pie plate
Yarn

What to do

1. Read this book again and again, and talk about the many places the spider goes in his journey. Where else might the itsy bitsy spider go? Where might he go in your classroom?
2. Use the book as a songbook and sing the words in the text. Encourage the children to pantomime the spider's actions.
3. With the children, make a huge spider web and fill it with spiders. Prepare by placing the bulletin board paper on a table and pouring white tempera paint into a pie plate.
4. In turn, ask each child to hold one end of a 12" (30 cm) length of yarn and dip the remaining yarn into the paint. Help the child squeeze some of the excess paint from the yarn by running it between the thumb and index finger of his other hand.
5. Now encourage the child to drag the yarn in random directions across the paper. Repeat this with each child until every child has had a turn and the paper looks like a giant spider web.
6. When the web is dry, the children can draw spiders on it. Demonstrate how to draw a spider by scribbling a circle for the body and drawing eight straight lines going outward from the circle for the legs.
7. Encourage them to use different colors for their spiders.
8. Label the bulletin board "Spider Web."

More to do

Math: Encourage the children to count each color of spiders on the bulletin board spider web (see above).
More Math: Provide plastic spiders for the children to count and classify.
Sensory Table: Hide plastic spiders in the sand of the sensory table.
Snack and Cooking: Make spider snacks with the children. Provide round crackers, cheese spread (or peanut butter), and pretzel sticks. Ask the children to put cheese spread on their cracker. Then ask them to break four pretzel sticks in half and stick them into the cheese for spider legs. Add two raisins for eyes.

❖❖ Barbara Backer, Charleston, SC

"When the Elephant Walks"

Materials

When the Elephant Walks by Keiko Kasza

What to do

1. Read *When the Elephant Walks* to the children. It is a "circular" tale where, in turn, one animal inadvertently frightens another.
2. Encourage the children to act out the story, with every child playing the part of every animal.
3. Talk about fears. What are the children afraid of? What do they do that frightens others? Share your experiences and childhood fears with the children.

More to do

Art: Ask the children to draw a picture of something they are afraid of. With their permission, write their dictated words on their pictures.

Snack and Cooking: The bear in the story was gathering honey. For snack, serve squares of whole wheat bread and 2-ounce cups with a tablespoon of honey inside. Encourage the children to dip the bread squares in honey before eating them.

◆◆ Barbara Backer, Charleston, SC

A Puppy Tale

Materials

The Last Puppy by Frank Asch
Modeling dough

What to do

1. Read *The Last Puppy* to the children.
2. Encourage the children to act out the story. If they desire, they can all play many parts and more than one child can act out each character.
3. Encourage the children to make puppies using modeling dough. Don't be concerned with the final products; for three-year-olds, a lump of clay represents a dog.

4. Count out ten of the clay puppies and put them in front of the children at story time. Designate the largest dough creation as the mother dog. Read the book and ask a child to remove one dog each time a puppy is taken from the litter.

More to do

Blocks: Encourage the children to build a doghouse using blocks.
Dramatic Play: Place the book and a clean, new dog food bowl in the Dramatic Play Area to encourage additional dramatization of the story.

Original song

Children will enjoy acting out the following song.
(Tune: "Ten Little Indians")

One little, two little, three little puppies.
Four little, five little, six little puppies.
Seven little, eight little, nine little puppies,
Born to Mother dog.

❖❖ Barbara Backer, Charleston, SC

Laying Eggs

Materials

Chickens Aren't the Only Ones by Ruth Heller

What to Do

1. Get the children's attention by "clucking" and scratching the ground like a chicken. Pretend to lay an egg.
2. As the children start to gather around, move in a circle and point to each place where you want a child to sit, keeping in the "chicken" character. Keep walking around in a circle (don't forget to cluck!), pointing out spaces for the children to sit until all of the children are seated.
3. Then, plop down where you want to sit and say, "Whew! That's really hard being a chicken! I laid a BIG egg!" Hopefully, the children will laugh and when they have settled, ask a couple of children to name an animal that lays eggs.
4. Read the book to the children. The book is a poem so read it slowly.

5. When you finish, ask the children if they can name other animals that lay eggs besides chickens. Prompt them with hints such as, "What lives in the water?" or "What hops from a lily pad into the water?" or "Are there other kinds of birds that lay eggs?" If no one remembers, open the book to different pages and show them the pictures of the animals. Prompt the children again.

6. Point out some of the beautiful pictures throughout the book. Prompt children's observation skills by asking, "What kind of eyes do you see on that peacock?" or "What color eggs do you think this turtle would lay?"

More to do

Science: Show the children real (blown) eggs from different kinds of animals. Or use life-size cutouts of different eggs to place in the science area.

Transitions: Transition to the next activity by singing the following song to the tune of "I Wish I Had an Apple."

I wish I had a chicken, as big as I could hold.
I'd ask it to lay a really big egg
As big as (child's name) could hold.

Get along home, (child's name), (child's name). Get along home.
Get along home, (child's name), (child's name).
Please go wash your hands now! (or get your coat, and so on)

Repeat the song but change the word "chicken" to "frog," "lizard," "duck," or any other animal that lays eggs until you have dismissed all the children from the group. You may also need to say two children's names if there is a large group.

❖❖ Gail Whitney, Dameron, MD

Let's Put the Hen Back Together Again

Materials

Paper, or colored foam board sheets
Markers or crayons
Scissors
Magnetic strips
Glue
Metal cookie sheet
Draw Right Now by Marie Hablitzel and Kim Stitzer
Chart paper and marker or pen

What to Do

1. Ahead of time, draw a hen and eggs as shown in the book (or use your own) and cut them out.

2. Glue a strip of magnet to the back of each cutout so it will stick to the metal cookie sheet or pan (a metal flannel board!).

3. Get the children's attention by clucking and gather your "chicks" into the large group area. Cluck and scratch the ground as you sit down.

4. Put the cutouts behind your back and read the story to the children. As you read, remove each cutout of the hen's body as you need it and reassemble the hen on the cookie sheet. The children will see parts making a whole, which is also math.

5. Ask the children prompting questions, such as, "Have you ever seen an egg?" or "What would you do if you found an egg?"

6. Have a discussion and write down what the children say. Post the paper where they can see it for a few days.

More to do

Use the "metal flannel board" for all kinds stories, or other activities.
Use refrigerator magnets to make up your own ideas!

❖❖ Gail Whitney, Dameron, MD

"Swimmy"

Materials

Swimmy by Leo Lionni
Large white or blue sheet of butcher paper
Marker
Two small sponges
Scissors
2 shallow dishes
Red and black paint

What to do

1. Read *Swimmy* to the children. Talk about how the fish in the story worked together. Brainstorm ways the children can work together.
2. Draw a large fish shape on the butcher paper.
3. Cut two small sponges into fish shapes. Pour red paint into one dish and black paint into the other dish. Put a sponge next to each dish.
4. Encourage the children to make red and black fish prints on the inside of the fish outline.
5. When the fish shape is filled, ask a child to use the black sponge to make a fish eye. You may need to point out where to put it since the fish is rather abstract.

More to do

Social Development: This is a good activity to practice teamwork.
More Social Development: Make a chart that lists the ways the children work together and mark each time they do.

❖❖ Sandra Nagel, White Lake, MI

Lullabies

Materials

Barnyard Lullaby by Frank Asch

What to do

1. Read Barnyard Lullaby to the children. The animals in the barnyard are singing lullabies to their babies, but to the farmer it sounds like noise.
2. Encourage the children to make the animal noises at the proper places in the story. Just before the farmer yells at the animals, ask different children to make different animal noises so the entire group sounds like a chorus of noises. Let all of the children act out the farmer's part at the end. This will bring the game to a quiet end when the farmer goes to sleep.

More to do

Blocks: Add farm animals to the Block Area.

Rest or Nap Time: When children are on their mats ready for rest, sing the lullaby that the farmer's wife sang to her baby. The music is in the back of the book. If you cannot read music, make up a soft and gentle tune or chant the words quietly. Substitute the word "naptime" for "nighttime." Remind the children that this part of the lullaby quieted the farmer and the baby and put them to sleep.

❖❖ Barbara Backer, Charleston, SC

Nest Dissecting

Materials

Baby Bird's First Nest by Frank Asch
Several abandoned nests
Tweezers
Magnifying glasses
Large sheet of paper
Glue

What to do

1. This activity works well with three to six children.
2. Read *Baby Bird's First Nest* to the children.
3. Give each child or pair of children a nest, tweezers, and a magnifier.
4. Encourage the children to explore and dissect their nests as you ask open-ended questions.
5. Write "What We Found in a Nest" on a large sheet of paper. Ask the children to glue pieces of what they found in their nests on the paper. Write the child's name next to his item.

Related books

Bird Nests by Helen Frost
Nests, Nests, Nests, by Susan Canizares and Mary Reid

❖ Ann Gudowski, Johnstown, PA

"I Went Walking"

Materials

I Went Walking by Sue Williams
Copy machine
Scissors
Glue stick
Oaktag
Felt in various colors, such as pink, red, yellow, green, red, brown, and black
Markers
Flannel board

What to do

1. Before reading the book to the children, photocopy all the animals in the book.
2. Cut out the copies of the animals and glue them onto oaktag to make patterns.
3. Use the patterns to trace the animal outlines on the appropriate colors of felt.
4. Cut out the animals. Draw details on the animals using markers.
5. Now enjoy the book using the animals on a flannel board to retell the story.

❖ Jackie Wright, Enid, OK

Have a "Happy Day!"

Materials

The Happy Day by Ruth Krauss
Copy machine or paper and markers

What to do

1. Beforehand, make copies of each animal in the story and enlarge them. Or draw your own.
2. Read *The Happy Day* to the children.
3. Divide the class into five equal groups. Each group will represent one of the animals in the story. Place one large picture in front of each group, or if your class is small, give a picture to each child to hold.
4. Ask the children to practice each action in the story, as if they are the animals they represent.

> *Sleeping—lie curled up on the floor*
> *Open eyes—sit up and open eyes*
> *Sniff—make sniffing noises with their noses*
> *Run—tap their feet on the floor, quickly.*
> *Laugh—laugh out loud*
> *Dance—stand up and dance around*

5. Read the story again slowly, allowing time for each group of children to act out their part as you read.

More to do

Art: Make flower pictures to celebrate the end of winter and the beginning of spring.
Science and Nature: Talk about animals hibernating.
Sensory Table: Put snow in the water table for play. Point out how it melts over the course of the day.

❖❖ Sandra Suffoletto Ryan, Buffalo, NY

"The Three Bears"

Materials

The Three Bears, any version
Instant oatmeal
Hot water
Plastic bowls
Spoons

What to do

1. Read The Three Bears to the children.
2. Make porridge with the children using instant oatmeal. Pour about one-third of the package into each child's bowl and add a little hot water.
3. Encourage the children to stir it and add milk.
4. This is a great breakfast activity that will also make the story more meaningful.

❖❖ Phyllis Esch, Export, PA

Boats and More Boats

Materials

Ship Ahoy! by Peter Sis
Blue carpet sample
Various pillows
Long cardboard rolls from wrapping paper
Cardboard cartons taped shut
Pictures of boats and ships

What to do

1. Show Ship Ahoy! to the children. Talk about each picture in this wordless book. In this book, a small child on a sofa imagines that the sofa turns into a succession of sailing vessels. At the book's end, the boy imagines he encounters a sea monster. Ask the children what the boy really sees and talk about pretend play.

2. Put the blue carpet sample, pillows, cardboard rolls, and cartons in the Block Center and encourage the children to use them in imaginative building.
3. Hang pictures of boats and ships in the Block Area.

More to do

Home-School Connection: Take photos of the children's creations and make them into a book. Make several copies and let the children have turns taking it home to share with their families.

❖❖ Barbara Backer, Charleston, SC

Patchwork Quilts

Materials

The Patchwork Quilt by Valerie Flournoy, *Sam Johnson and the Blue Ribbon Quilt* by Lisa Campbell Ernst, or *Quilt* by Tomie dePaola
Colored construction paper
Wallpaper samples
Scissors
Glue sticks

What to do

1. Read the children one of the quilt books.
2. Beforehand, cut colored construction paper into 9" x 9" (22 cm x 22 cm) squares and wallpaper samples into 3" x 3" (7 cm x 7 cm) squares.
3. Give each child a construction paper square. Encourage them to choose small wallpaper squares and glue them onto the construction paper, creating a small patchwork quilt.
4. Put the children's quilts together on a bulletin board to form one large quilt.

More to do

Invite parents or members of a local quilt guild to bring in quilts to show to the children and demonstrate how they are made.
Field Trip: Take a field trip to a local museum or fabric store to look at quilts.
Special Days: Have a "quilt day." Invite the children to bring in their favorite blankets or quilts to share.

❖❖ Barbara Saul, Eureka, CA

"Caps for Sale"

Materials

Different colors of felt or paper (gray, brown, blue, and red)
Scissors
Caps for Sale by Esphyr Slobodkina

What to do

1. Cut out oval shapes from different colors of felt or paper so that they resemble caps.
2. From the brown felt or paper, cut out long tails. Cut one for each child.
3. Select one child to be the peddler.
4. Pin a tail on the rest of the children.
5. Encourage the children to act out the story as you read it to them.

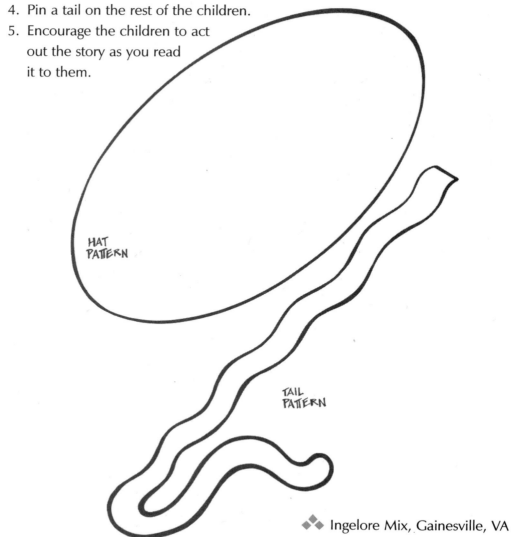

HAT PATTERN

TAIL PATTERN

❖ Ingelore Mix, Gainesville, VA

Hats

Materials

The 500 Hats of Bartholomew Cubbins by Dr. Suess
3 different hats, such as a straw hat, knitted ski hat, and baseball hat

What to do

1. Get the children's attention by walking around with all three hats on your head. Say, "Hats! Hats! Hats for sale!" When you have their attention, ask them which hat they like best.
2. Read *The 500 Hats of Bartholomew Cubbins* to the children.
3. Ask them to whom they think each hat would belong. Ask them to recall how, in the book, the boy carried all the hats. Do they think they can carry hats that way?
4. Put the hats and the book into the Housekeeping Center.
5. Encourage the children (no more than three at a time) to play with the hats. Observe how they play with them. Do they try to stack them on their heads, on each other's head? Do they refer to the book? Do they try to put the hats on each other? (Likely, the children will experience collaborative and pretend play.)
6. After center time is over, read the book again. Be sure to wear the hats while you read.
7. After you finish reading, put the hats on three children. Chant, "One hat, two hats, three hats—go wash your hands (or give other directions)!"
8. Take the hats off the children's heads so they may transition to another area.

More to do

Use coats, sweaters, or shirts instead of hats.

❖❖ Gail Whitney, Dameron, MD

How Many Hats?

Materials

Caps for Sale by Esphyr Slobodkina
A selection of hats

What to do

1. Read *Caps for Sale* by Esphyr Slobodkina.
2. Ask the children how many hats they think they can wear on their heads. Then, encourage them to try on the hats.
3. Show each hat and ask questions about it. For example, ask, "Who might wear this hat? Why might the person wear this hat? What color is this hat? What is this hat made from?"

Related book

Old Hat, New Hat by Stan and Jan Berenstain

◆◆ Wanda Pelton, Lafayette, IN

Where Did the "Runaway Latke" Go?

Materials

The Runaway Latkes by Leslie Kimmelman
Brown paper
Markers
Scissors
Glue
White paper
Hole punch
String

What to do

1. Read *The Runaway Latkes* to the children.
2. Draw a large circle onto each sheet of brown paper (brown paper bags work well) and give one to each child.
3. Help the children cut out their circles (latkes) and glue them onto a sheet of white paper.
4. Ask each child where he thinks the runaway latke would go. Write his words underneath his latke.
5. Punch holes in the sides of the papers and use string to bind them together into your own "Runaway Latkes" book.

More to do

More Books: Also read *The Gingerbread Man* and make comparisons.
Snack: Make latkes using the directions in the back of the book. The ingredients are: three large potatoes, peeled and grated; ½ onion, grated; 1½ cup flour; ½ teaspoon baking powder; 1 egg; salt, pepper, and cinnamon; and olive oil. You can also purchase potato pancake mix at the grocery store.

Related book

A Taste for Noah by Susan Remick Topek

❖❖ Sandra Nagel, White Lake, MI

"The Spooky Old Tree"

Materials

The Spooky Old Tree by Stan and Jan Berenstain
A slide

What to do

1. The book, *The Spooky Old Tree* by Stan and Jan Berenstain, is always a popular story. It has a catchy rhyme at the end that the children quickly memorize. It has great words such as "through," "down," and "out," as well as rhyming words. Read the book several times.
2. Take the children outside to a slide and help them act out the rhyme while they say, "Up a ladder, through the floor, down a slide, and out the door!" They can move their arms like a door as they reach the bottom.

3. Copy the page in the book so the children can bring it home to "read" to their parents. Suggest they act it out at home if they have a slide.

More to do

More Books: Read *Bears in the Night* by the same authors. This book has similar words such as "down," "over," "under," "around," and "between." There is a page in this book that illustrates these words.

Dramatic Play: Turn a large box into a spooky old tree with pretend spider webs. The children could decorate it with bats. Put in a flashlight, a rope, and a (safe) stick.

Language: Put little counting bears in a toy house or in the block area. Encourage the children to manipulate them using words such as "through," "over," "under," and so on.

Music: Sing the rhyme to the tune of "Twinkle Twinkle Little Star."

Related book

There's a Wocket in My Pocket by Dr. Suess

❖ Laura Durbrow, Lake Oswego, OR

Friendship Soup

Materials

Growing Vegetable Soup by Lois Ehlert
Vegetables: fresh green beans, pea pods, one zucchini or squash, one or two carrots, one or two tomatoes, two or three small potatoes, two or three broccoli stalks, one onion, one green pepper, and one small head of cabbage
Small plastic serrated knife
Four vegetable bouillon cubes
Crock-pot
Large serving spoon or ladle
Small bowls and spoons (one for each child)

What to do

1. Read *Growing Vegetable Soup* by Lois Ehlert. Talk about the different ingredients that go into vegetable soup.
2. Explain to the children that everybody will bring in a different vegetable and they will make vegetable soup together.

3. Assign a soup ingredient to each child in the class. Send a note home to parents asking them to send in the ingredient with the child on a designated day.

4. On the day of the activity, help each child rinse the vegetable he brought in.

5. Help the children cut up the various vegetables. The children should be able to cut most of the vegetables with a small plastic serrated knife. Closely supervise the children during this stage of the activity. (Make sure you observe health rules by having everyone wash their hands thoroughly).

6. When all of the ingredients have been cut, begin to put the soup together in the crock-pot. You can follow the recipe provided in the book or use one of your own. Ask each child to add his ingredient.

7. Add the remaining ingredients according to your recipe.

8. Let the children take turns stirring the soup. At this point the soup is not hot, so it is safe for them to stir.

9. Put the crock-pot in a safe area and turn it on high. Let the children know that it will take several hours for the soup to cook. Do not leave the crock-pot unattended and remember to stir it occasionally throughout the day.

10. Several times during the day, ask the children to sniff the air and see if they can smell the soup.

11. After the soup is done, sit down and enjoy it together.

12. As you are eating, make sure you talk about how everyone contributed something to make the soup. Mention the children by name and let them tell what they brought in.

More to do

Invite parents in for a Friendship Soup Lunch or Snack. This is a good way for them to get to know each other.

Share the soup with another class in your school. Deliver the soup to them or invite them to your room for snack.

More Books: Take lots of photos as the children work together to make soup. Use the photos to make a book entitled "How to Make Friendship Soup". Let the children take turns taking the book home to share with their parents.

Social Development: A few days before this activity, take photos of the children in small groups of two or three friends. Try to catch them as they are working or playing cooperatively together. Hang these photos on the wall underneath the heading "Good Friends Work Together."

Original song

Soup Song (Tune: "If You're Happy and You Know It")

We are friends working together to make some soup (make some soup).
We are friends working together to make some soup (make some soup).
We cut up all the veggies
Peas, carrots, and cabbage too,
We are friends working together to make some soup (make some soup).

Related books

Chicken Soup, Boots by Maira Kalman
Dumpling Soup by Jama Kim Rattigan
Growing Vegetable Soup by Lois Ehlert
Mean Soup by Betsy Everitt
Monkey Soup by Louis Sachar
Mouse Soup by Arnold Lobel
Stone Soup by Tony Ross

❖❖ Virginia Jean Herrod, Columbia, SC

Picnic

Materials

Picnic basket (with lid or cloth covering)
Assortment of common picnic items, such as plates, cups, plastic food, salt
shakers, serving spoons, beach balls, and so on
The Teddy Bear's Picnic by Jimmy Kennedy
Tablecloth

What to do

1. Beforehand, place the picnic items into a picnic basket.
2. Seat the children in a circle. Read *The Teddy Bear's Picnic* to the children. If desired, also play the theme song if you have it.
3. Invite the children to join you for an imaginary picnic. Spread out the tablecloth and name each object as you bring it out of the picnic basket and place it on the tablecloth. Pretend to serve and enjoy a delicious meal and play some games together.

4. Then say, "Our tummies are so full, and our heads are so sleepy, we'll need to take a little nap now. Everybody close your eyes, cover them up, and wait for me to choose a little teddy bear to come out of the woods. Listen while I call your name to hide something in our picnic basket."

5. Give each child a turn to remove something from the tablecloth and conceal it in the basket. Invite others to open their eyes and guess what's missing.

More to do

Children can use teddy bear counters for sorting activities, enjoy gummy bears as a treat, draw teddy bears on brown construction paper, or have a teddy bear tea party in the Dramatic Play area.
(For many more ideas, see Chapter 11, "Teddy Bears and Other Bears" in *Story S-t-r-e-t-c-h-e-r-s* and *More Story S-t-r-e-t-c-h-e-r-s* by Shirley C. Raines and Robert J. Canady.)

Related recording

"Teddy Bear's Picnic"

❖❖ Susan A. Sharkey, La Mesa, CA

"Rain Drop Splash"

Materials

Rain Drop Splash by Alvin Tresselt
Construction paper
Crayons
Glue
Shallow containers
Paintbrushes
Silver icicles

What to do

1. Read *Rain Drop Splash* several times, inviting the children to join in on the parts repeating "drip drop splash."
2. Discuss the book with the children. Ask them to identify all the things on which the rain fell and make a group list. Then, ask them to name some things that the rain falls on at their homes and in their yards.
3. Give each child a sheet of construction paper. Encourage the children to draw a picture of their house or yard without adding any rain at this point.
4. Pour glue into shallow containers. Demonstrate how to brush glue on their drawings and add icicles to represent rain falling.

More to do

Dramatic Play: Provide raincoats, rain hats, and galoshes in the housekeeping area.
Music: Simulate a thunderstorm by having the children gradually increase the volume of the following sounds: snapping fingers, patting laps, and stomping feet. Then, reverse the order and gradually soften and stop.
Science: Keep a weather chart and mark the rainy days.
More Science: Go outside with the children and observe the different shapes and kinds of clouds.

Related books

Big Sarah's Little Boots by Paulette Bourgeois
Johnny Lion's Rubber Boots by Edith Thacher Hurd
Rain by Peter Spier

❖❖ Susan Oldham Hill, Lakeland, FL

Sand Treasure Sorting

Materials

Sand table filled with sand (or substitute a tub of sand)
Various blue and yellow small, plastic toys and manipulatives, such as counting bears, buttons, pattern blocks, and jar lids
Little Blue and Little Yellow by Leo Lionni
Sieves, optional
Blue and yellow construction paper

What to do

1. Prior to reading the book, hide the blue and yellow treasures under the sand in the sand table. Also, cut out 6" (15 cm) squares of blue and yellow construction paper.
2. Read *Little Blue and Little Yellow* to the children.
3. During free choice, encourage the children to scoop into the sand with their hands or sieves to discover "a little blue and a little yellow."
4. Encourage the children to name and sort the treasures by color and put them onto the squares of paper.

More to do

Language: Use this activity with other units to encourage vocabulary development. For example, hide shells for an ocean unit; acorns, leaves, nuts for a fall unit; and so on. Changing the treasures on a weekly basis keeps interest in the activity at a high level.

❖❖ Ann Wenger, Harrisonburg, VA

Getting Into the Garden

Materials

Come Into My Garden by Cynthia Rothman
2 or 3 medium-size cardboard boxes
Shredded brown paper
Plastic vegetables
Small plastic rakes and shovels
Aprons, straw hats, gardening gloves, and overalls
Wicker baskets or paper grocery bags (Do not use plastic grocery bags, which are a safety hazard.)

What to do

1. Read *Come Into My Garden* to the children. Encourage the children to examine the illustrations closely as you point out the various things in the garden.
2. Make a pretend garden with the children. Fill two or three cardboard boxes with shredded brown paper. This represents the dirt.

3. Ask the children to "plant" plastic vegetables by digging in the shredded paper with plastic rakes or shovels.

4. Remember to point out that certain vegetables grow above the ground (such as lettuce, beans, spinach, squash, and zucchini) and certain ones grow under the ground (such as potatoes and carrots). Encourage the children to plant their plastic vegetables accordingly.

5. Later, ask the children to use the shovels and rakes to dig up the garden. They can harvest the vegetables and place them into a wicker basket or paper bag.

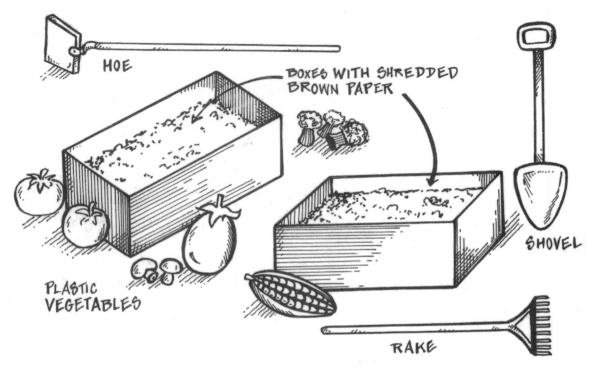

HOE

BOXES WITH SHREDDED BROWN PAPER

SHOVEL

PLASTIC VEGETABLES

RAKE

More to do

Art: With the children, make a huge mural of a garden scene and put it on the wall in the Dramatic Play Center. This can serve as a backdrop for your garden.

Dramatic Play: Set up a Farmer's Market in another area of the room. The children who dig up the vegetables can take them to the market for sale. The children who buy them can have the fun of planting them again.

More Dramatic Play: Create a fruit area in your Dramatic Play Center by adding a fake tree. Tape string to plastic pieces of fruit and hang them from the tree. To save space, you can put all the fruit on one tree and label it "The Fruit Salad Tree." Also string plastic ivy along a shelf unit and add plastic grapes. Use your imagination to create a fun and fanciful garden!

Math: When the children are digging up the vegetables, ask them to sort them into two bags: above-ground vegetables and below-ground vegetables. Talk about the differences in plants that grow above and below the ground.

Original song

(Tune: "The Farmer in the Dell")

(Show an example of each food as you sing about it)

Carrots grow under the ground,
Carrots grow under the ground,
Hi-ho the derry-o
Carrots grow under the ground.

Grapes grow on a vine,
Grapes grow on a vine,
Hi-ho the derry-o
Grapes grow on a vine.

Lettuce grows above the ground,
Lettuce grows above the ground,
Hi-ho the derry-o
Lettuce grows above the ground.

Related books

Come Into My Garden by Cynthia Rothman
The Garden of Happiness by Erika Tamar
The Lady and the Spider by Faith McNulty
Miss Penny and Mr. Grubbs by Lisa Campbell Ernst
The Surprise Garden by Zoe Hall
This Year's Garden by Cynthia Rylant

❖❖ Virginia Jean Herrod, Columbia, SC

Flower Identification Book

Materials

Camera and film
Flower garden near the playground
Tape
Oaktag or tagboard
Markers
Hole punch
Yarn or heavy string

What to do

1. Take photos of the flowers in your playground garden. Take one photo of each type of flower.
2. Tape each photo to a piece of oaktag, leaving some space below the picture for text.
3. Underneath each flower photo, print the flower's common name.
4. Continue in this manner until you have created a page for each flower photo.
5. Create a cover with a title such as, "Our Flowers."
6. Punch three holes in the left edge of the cover and each page.
7. Thread yarn or heavy string through the holes to bind the book together.
8. Take your flower identification book outside. The children can use it to aid them as they identify familiar flowers on the playground.

More to do

Art: Encourage the children to draw flowers on construction paper. Also make a copy of each flower photograph. Glue or tape the photos and pictures on the wall to create a garden scene.

Literacy: Ask the children what they think about each flower. Choose a few statements about each flower and print them underneath that flower in the book. Make sure to reference the children whose quote you use, such as "Jason thinks paper whites are as white as paper."

Related books

Almira's Violets by Claudia Fregosi
Dancers in the Garden by Joanne Ryder
Flower Garden by Eve Bunting
The King's Flower by Mitsumasa
Planting a Rainbow by Lois Ehlert
The Rose in My Garden by Arnold Lobel

❖❖ Virginia Jean Herrod, Columbia, SC

Theme-Based Reading Lists

Materials

Children's books

What to do

1. There are many ways to use children's books effectively in your curriculum. The most obvious way is to incorporate story time into your daily schedule.

2. After reading a book, do extension activities to reinforce concepts as well as just have fun with the book's ideas. A good place to start is to use the small group activities suggested in this activity guide. After trying several, it will become easier to identify age-appropriate activities for any of the books in your collection.

3. Another way to use books and stories is to encourage children to create their own books based on the story read to them. A variety of prompts can encourage them to contribute their own ideas to their books. For example, ask them, "What part of the story did you like the most? Can you make a picture of it?" or "Have you ever had anything happen to you like what happened in the story?"

4. Then, write down the children's verbal responses. Ask the children to illustrate their ideas.

5. When the children are finished, assemble all the pages to make a classroom version of the book that was shared.

6. There are many different ideas you can use for child-created books. For example, if you read a book about apples, give the children apple-shaped papers on which to draw. Or, invite children to complete a line from the story using their own words, such as:

   Brown bear, brown bear, what do you see?
   I see a _____ looking at me!

The following is a list of books arranged by themes. These are broad themes, and some books may overlap with more than one. Many of the small group activities can be used in connection with these book selections.

All About Me

Amazing Grace by Mary Hoffman
Arthur's Tooth by Marc Brown
Beady Bear by Don Freeman

Bear Shadow by Frank Asch

Big Dog Little Dog by P. D. Eastman

A Color of His Own by Leo Lionni

The Ear Book by Al Perkins

Fox Eyes by Margaret Wise Brown

From Head to Toe by Eric Carle

Good Night, Owl by Pat Hutchins

Hand, Hand, Fingers, Thumb by Al Perkins

Happy and Sad, Grouchy and Glad by Constance Allen

Happy Birthday Moon by Frank Asch

I Can Do It Myself by Emily Perl Kingsley

In a People House by Theo LeSeig

It Wasn't My Fault by Helen Lester

It's My Birthday by Helen Oxenbury

Leo the Late Bloomer by Robert Kraus

Madeline by Ludwig Bemelmans

Milton the Early Riser by Robert Kraus

Mop Top by Don Freeman

The Napping House by Audrey Wood

The Nose Book by Al Perkins

Pigby Pig Grows Up by David McPhail

Places I Like to Be by Evelyn M. Andre

Quick as a Cricket by Audrey Wood

The Runaway Bunny by Margaret Wise Brown

Running Away from Home by Nigel Gray

Teddy's Ear by Niki Daly

Thank You Henrietta by Niki Daly

Things I Like to Do by Beth Clure

Titch by Pat Hutchins

When Bunny Grows Up by Patsy Scarry

The Wobbly Tooth by Nancy Evans Cooney

The Wonderful Tree House by Irene Schultz

Alphabet

The Accidental Zucchini: An Unexpected Alphabet by Max Grover

The Alphabet Tree by Leo Lionni

A My Name Is Alice by Jane Bayer

A My Name Is Annabel by Michaela Muntean

Alphabears by Kathleen Hague

Animalia by Graeme Base

Bird Alphabet by Teresa McKemen
Chicka Chicka Boom Boom by John Archambault
Clifford's ABC by Norman Bridwell
D Is for Dinosaur by Ken and Mally Ham
Dr. Seuss's ABC by Dr. Seuss
Eating the Alphabet: Fruit & Vegetables from A to Z by Lois Ehlert
Have You Ever Seen...? An ABC Book by Beau Gardner
Letters from Calico Cat by Donald Charles
Potluck by Anne Shelby
Shaggy Dog's Animal Alphabet by Donald Charles
The Z Was Zapped by Chris Van Allsburg

Back to School

Cleversticks by Bernard Ashley
The Day the Teacher Went Bananas by James Howe
Franklin Goes to School by Paulette Bourgeois
Going to School by Anne Civardi
Miss Nelson Is Missing by Harry Allard
Morris Goes to School by B. Wiseman
See You Tomorrow, Charles by Miriam Hoban
Tough Eddie by Elizaeth Winthrop
Twenty One Children by Virginia Ormsby
We Laughed a Lot, My First Day of School by Sylvia Root Tester

Christmas

Alabaster's Song by Max Lucado
The Animals Christmas Eve by Gale Wiersum
Baby's Christmas by Esther Wilkins
A Child's Story of Jesus by Barbara Kanaar
Christmas in the Big Woods by Laura Ingalls Wilder
The Christmas Miracle of Jonathan Toomey by Susan Wojciechowski
The Christmas Star by Marcus Pfister
The Christmas Story by Jane Werner
The Christmas Story by Ruth J. Moorehead's Holly Babes
The Christmas Tree That Grew by Phyllis Krasilovsky
The Crippled Lamb by Max Lucado
Danny and the Kings by Susan Cooper
The Fir Tree by Hans Christian Andersen
Frosty the Snowman by Annie North Bedford
Heaven's Little Helpers by Michael Newton

I Can't Wait Until Christmas by Linda Lee Maifair

The Night Before Christmas by Clement C. Moore

One Tiny Baby by Mark A. Taylor

One Wintry Night by Ruth Bell Graham

The Pine Tree Parable by Liz Curtis Higgs

A Silent Night by Mary Manz Simon

The Story of the Nutcracker Ballet by Deborah Hautzig

The Wild Christmas Reindeer by Jan Brett

Community Helpers

Arthur's Tooth by Marc Brown

Clifford Gets a Job by Norman Bridwell

Curious George Gets a Job by H. A. Rey

Curious George Goes to the Hospital by H. A. Rey

Curious George Visits the Police Station by Margaret Rey

Dear Garbage Man by Gene Zion

Dr. DeSoto by William Steig

The Fire Engine Book by Jesse Younger

He Bear, She Bear by Stan and Jan Berenstain

Madeline by Ludwig Bemelmans

Mr. Grigg's Work by Cynthia Rylant

My Apron by Eric Carle

People in Your Neighborhood by Jeffrey Moss

The Sailor Dog by Margaret Wise Brown

There's a Canary in the Library by Don Freeman

Timothy Tiger's Terrible Toothache by Jan Wahl

The Tool Box by Anne Rockwell

Walter the Baker by Eric Carle

Dinosaurs

Dinosaur Roar! by Paul and Henrietta Strickland

The Dinosaurs Are Back and It's All Your Fault Edward by Wendy Hartmann

If the Dinosaurs Came Back by Bernard Most

It Zwibble by Werenko Ross

Little Danny Dinosaur by Janet Craig

My Dinosaur by Mark Weatherby

Saturday Night at the Dinosaur Stomp by Carol Shields

Ten Terrible Dinosaurs by Paul Strickland

A Trio of Triceratops by Bernard Most

Fall/Apples/Pumpkins

The Apple Pie Tree by Zoe Hall

Autumn Days by Ann Schweninger

The Bear Detectives: The Case of the Missing Pumpkin by Stan and Jan Berenstain

The Biggest Pumpkin Ever by Steven Kroll

Big Honey Hunt by Stan and Jan Berenstain

A Busy Year by Leo Lionni

It's Pumpkin Time! by Zoe Hall

My Favorite Time of Year by Susan Pearson

Nuts to You! by Lois Ehlert

The Parable Series: The Pumpkin Patch Parable by Liz Curtis Higgs

Pumpkin! Pumpkin! by Jeanne Titherington

Red Leaf, Yellow Leaf by Lois Ehlert

The Seasons of Arnold's Apple Tree by Gail Gibbons

Six Crows by Leo Lionni

Ten Apples Up on Top! by Dr. Seuss

Where Are You Going Emma? by Jeanne Titherington

Why Do Leaves Change Color (Let's Read And Find Out Science Book and Cassette) by Betsy Maestro

Farms

Baby Animals on the Farm by Liza Alexander

Baby Calf by P. Mignon Hinds

Big Red Barn by Margaret Wise Brown

The Cow that Went Oink by Bernard Most

Farm Babies by Ann Rice

Friska: The Sheep that Was too Small by Rob Lewis

Good Morning, Chick by Mirra Ginsburg

Henny Penny by Paul Galdone

Julius by Angela Johnson

Liam's Day Out by Kati Teague

The Littlest Pig by Erica Frost

The Milk Makers by Gail Gibbons

Moses the Kitten by James Herriot

Mr. Brown Can Moo! Can You? by Dr. Seuss

My First Counting Book by Lillian Moore

Noggin and Bobbin in the Garden by Oliver Dunrea

Only One Woof by James Herriot

Robert the Rose Horse by Joan Heilbroner

Rock-A-Bye Farm by Diane Johnston Hamm

Rosie's Walk by Pat Hutchins

Small Pig by Arnold Lobel
The Surprise Party by Pat Hutchins
Three Little Pigs by Margaret Hillert
The Ugly Duckling by Hans Christian Andersen

Food

The Biggest Cookie in the World by Linda Hayward
Bread and Jam for Frances by Russell Hoban
The Cheerios Counting Book by Barbara McGrath
Cloudy with a Chance of Meatballs by Judi Barrett
Don't Forget the Oatmeal by B.G. Ford
Eating the Alphabet: Fruits and Vegetables from A to Z by Lois Ehlert
The Giant Jam Sandwich by John Vernon Lloyd
Green Eggs and Ham by Dr. Seuss
Growing Vegetable Soup by Lois Ehlert
Hundred and Hundreds of Pancakes by Audrey Chalmers
It Looked Like Spilt Milk by Charles G. Shaw
The M&M's Chocolate Candies Counting Book by Barbara McGrath
One Potato: A Counting Book of Potato Prints by Diana Pomeroy
Pancakes! Pancakes! by Eric Carle
Pizza for Everyone by Josh McDowell
Popcorn: A Frank Asch Bear Story by Frank Asch
The Popcorn Book by Tomie dePaola
Stone Soup by Ann McGovern
Vegetable Soup by Judy Freudberg
Wednesday Is Spaghetti Day by Maryann Coccaby Leffler

Friends/Family

Are You My Mother? by P. D. Eastman
A Baby Sister for Frances by Russell Hoban
A Baby Sister for Herry by Emily Perle Kingsley
A Bargain for Frances by Russell Hoban
Bear Shadow by Frank Asch
Best Friends for Frances by Russell Hoban
Best Nest by P. D. Eastman
Big Dog... Little Dog by P. D. Eastman
Blueberries for Sal by Robert McCloskey
Come Again, Pelican by Don Freeman
Frog and Toad Together by Arnold Lobel
Goggles by Ezra Jack Keats

Grover, Grover Come on Over by Katherine Ross

Grover's Mommy by Liza Alexander

Guess How Much I Love You? by Sam McBratney

Hands by Lois Ehlert

Happy Birthday Mama by Bonnie Pryor

Home for a Bunny by Margaret Wise Brown

Hop on Pop by Dr. Seuss

How Joe the Bear and Sam the Mouse Got Together by Beatrice DeRegniers

I'm Glad I'm Your Brother by Bill and Kathy Horlacher

I'm Glad I'm Your Dad by Bill and Kathy Horlacher

I'm Glad I'm Your Grandma by Bill and Kathy Horlacher

I'm Glad I'm Your Grandpa by Bill and Kathy Horlacher

I'm Glad I'm Your Mother by Bill and Kathy Horlacher

I'm Glad I'm Your Sister by Bill and Kathy Horlacher

I'm Moving by Martha Whitmore Hickman

Ira Sleeps Over by Bernard Waber

Is Your Mama a Llama? by Deborah Guarino

Jumanji by Chris Van Allsburg

Little Blue and Little Yellow by Leo Lionni

Little Fur Family by Margaret Wise Brown

The Little House by Virginia Lee Burton

Love You Forever by Robert Munsch

Make Way for Ducklings by Robert McCloskey

Mama Zooms by Jane Cowen Fletcher

Mr. McMouse by Leo Lionni

My Friend William Moved Away by Martha Whitmore Hickman

Natasha's Daddy by Constance Allen

Nathan and Nicholas Alexander by Lulu Delacre

Nathan's Fishing Trip by Lulu Delacre

Owl Babies by Martin Waddell

Papa Please Get the Moon for Me by Eric Carle

Peter's Chair by Ezra Jack Keats

Robert the Rose Horse by Neil Heilbroner

The Runaway Teddy Bear by Ginnie Hofmann

Stellaluna by Janell Cannon

The Story About Ping by Marjorie Flack

A Terrible Thing Happened at Our House by Marge Blaine

Ton and Pon, Big and Little by Kazuo Iwamara

Ton and Pon, Two Good Friends by Kazuo Iwamara

Town Mouse, Country Mouse by Jan Brett

Traveling Again Dad by Michael Lorelli

Grandparents

Blue Barry Bear Counts from 1 to 20 by Marilyn Sadler
A Gift for Grandpa by Angela Elwell Hunt
Grandfather and I by Helen E. Buckley
Grandfather's Journey by Allen Say
Grandma and Grandpa Smith by Edith Kundhart
Grandpa and Me Together by Susan Goldman
Grandpa Had a Windmill, Grandma Had a Churn by Louise A. Jackson
The Great Town and Country Bicycle Balloon Chase by Barbara Douglass
Happy Birthday Grandpa by Harriet Zieffert
Miss Rumphius by Barbara Cooney
My Great Aunt Arizona by Gloria Houston
Now One Foot Now the Other by Tomie dePaola
Strega Nona by Tomie dePaola
We're Very Good Friends, My Grandmother and I by P.K. Hallinan
When I Was Young and in the Mountains by Cynthia Rylant
Where Are You Going Emma? by Jeane Titherington
With Love, From Grandma by Harriet Zieffert

Pets

Always Arthur by Amanda Graham
And I Mean It, Stanley by Crosby Bonsall
Angus and the Ducks by Marjorie Flack
But No Elephants by Jerry Smath
Clifford, the Big Red Dog by Norman Bridwell
Clifford, the Small Red Puppy by Norman Bridwell
Clifford's Kitten by Norman Bridwell
Clifford's Puppy Days by Norman Bridwell
The Curious Little Kitten Around the House by Linda Hayward
Educating Arthur by Amanda Graham
A Fish Out of Water by Helen Palmer
Harry and the Lady Next Door! by Gene Zion
Have You Seen My Cat? by Eric Carle
Hi! Cat by Ezra Jack Keats
I'll Teach My Dogs 100 Words by Michael Frith
Just Like Archie by Niki Daly
Little Black, a Pony by Walter Farley
Millions of Cats by Wanda Gag
Mister Dog by Margaret Wise Brown

Moses the Kitten by James Herriot
Never Give a Fish an Umbrella by Mike Thaler
No Roses for Harry by Gene Zion
Only One Woof by James Herriot
The Poky Little Puppy by Janette Sebring Lowrey
Puppy Love by Madeline Sunshine
The Shy Little Kitten by Cathleen Schurr
Three Little Kittens by various authors
We Love Them by Marin Waddell
Whistle for Willie by Ezra Jack Keats
Who Wants Arthur? by Amanda Graham

Spring/Easter/Bugs

All Falling Down by Gene Zion
Baby Lamb by Beth Spanjian
Bambi, Friends of the Forest by Walt Disney
Come Out, Muskrats by Jim Arnosky
The Golden Egg Book by Margaret Wise Brown
Golly Gump Swallowed a Fly by Joanna Cole
The Grouchy Lady Bug by Eric Carle
Home for a Bunny by Margaret Wise Brown
Hurry, Hurry! by Mary Manz Simon
Jelly Beans for Sale by Bruce McMillan
The Lamb and the Butterfly by Arnold Sundgaard
Little Cloud by Eric Carle
The Little Lamb by Judy Dunn
Max and Maggie in Spring by Janet Craig
Mr. Mead and His Garden by John Vernon Lord
The Parable of the Lily by Liz Curtis Higgs
Planting a Rainbow by Lois Ehlert
Really Spring by Gene Zion
Runaway Bunny by Margaret Wise Brown
The Story of Miss Moppet by Beatrix Potter
The Tale of Peter Rabbit by Beatrix Potter
The Tale of Squirrel Nutkin by Beatrix Potter
The Tiny Seed by Eric Carle
The Velveteen Rabbit by Margery Willliams
The Very Busy Spider by Eric Carle
The Very Clumsy Click Beetle by Eric Carle
The Very Hungry Caterpillar by Eric Carle
The Very Lonely Firefly by Eric Carle

The Very Quiet Cricket by Eric Carle
Wait Till the Moon Is Full by Margaret Wise Brown
The Whispering Rabbit by Margaret Wise Brown

Thanksgiving/Harvest

Best Thanksgiving Book by Pat Whitehead
Cranberry Autumn by Wendi Devlin
Cranberry Thanksgiving by Wendi Devlin
The Deer in the Wood by Laura Ingalls Wilder
Dinosaur Thanksgiving by Liza Donnelly
Giving Thanks by Rita Walsh
The Legend of the Blue Bonnet by Tomie dePaola
Sometimes It's Turkey, Sometime's It's Feathers by Lorna Balian
Thank You God, for All My Friends by Kath Mellentin
A Turkey for Thanksgiving by Eve Bunting
Winnie the Pooh's Thanksgiving by Bruce Talkington

Transportation

Away Go the Boats by Margaret Hillert
Boats by Byron Barton
Freight Train by Donald Crews
Go, Dog, Go! by P.D. Eastman
Harbor by Donald Crews
Harriet and the Roller Coaster by Nancy Carlson
Hey! Get Off My Train by John Burmingham
Hold the Bus by Arlene Alda
Hot Air Henry by Mary Calhoun
The Little Engine that Could by Watty Piper
The Little Red Caboose by M. Potter
Little Toot by Hardie Gramatky
Mike Mulligan and His Steam Shovel by Virginia Lee Burton
Richard Scarry's Best Balloon Ride Ever by Richard Scarry
Road Builders by B.G. Hennessy
Sam Goes Trucking by Henry Horenstein
School Bus by Donald Crews
Scuffy the Tugboat by Gertrude Crampton
Trains by Gail Gibbons
The Truck Book by Bill Gere

Winter

The Big Snow by Berta and Elmer Hader
The Cat and the Hat Comes Back by Dr. Seuss
Curious George Goes Sledding by Margaret Rey
Dance at Grandpa's by Laura Ingalls Wilder
First Snow by Kim Lewis
Ice Cream Is Falling by Shigeo Watanabe
January Brings the Snow by Sara Coleridge
Katie and the Big Snow by Virginia Lee Burton
The Mitten by Jan Brett
The Mystery of the Missing Red Mitten by Steven Kellogg
Sadie and the Snowman by Allen Morgan
The Shiny Red Sled by Barbara Davoll
Snowballs by Lois Ehlert
Snow Lion by David McPhail
Snow on Bear's Nose by Jennifer Bartoli
The Snowy Day by Ezra Jack Keatts
White Snow, Bright Snow by Alvin Tresselt
Winter Days in the Big Woods by Laura Ingalls Wilder

Zoo/Animals

1,2,3, to the Zoo by Eric Carle
Bearymoore by Don Freeman
Brown Bear, Brown Bear, What Do You See? by Bill Martin, Jr. and Eric Carle
Caps for Sale by Esphyr Slobodkina
Cuckoo by Lois Ehlert
Elephants Aloft by Kathi Appelt
Fish Eyes by Lois Ehlert
The Foolish Tortoise by Richard Buckley and Eric Carle
The Greedy Python by Richard Buckley and Eric Carle
The Happy Hippopotami by Bill Martin, Jr.
Hello, Red Fox by Eric Carle
A House for Hermit Crab by Eric Carle
If You Give a Moose a Muffin by Laura Numeroff
If You Give Mouse a Cookie by Laura Numeroff
Jamberry by Bruce Degen
The Lion's Paw by Jane Werner Watson
Mole's Hill by Lois Ehlert
Mouse Count by Ellen Stoll Wash
Mouse Paint by Ellen Stoll Wash

Mr. Grumpy's Outing by John Burmingham

Polar Bear, Polar Bear, What Do You Hear? by Bill Martin, Jr. and Eric Carle

The Right Number of Elephants by Jeff Shepherd

The Saggy Baggy Elephant by Kathryn Jackson

Stand Back Said the Elephant, I'm Going to Sneeze by Patty Thomas

Ten Things I Know About Elephants by Wendy Way

There Are Rocks in My Socks by Patricia Thomas

Tiger, Tiger Growing Up by Joan Hewett

Top Cat by Lois Ehlert

Watch Where You Go! by Sally Noll

Why Can't I Fly by Rita Golden Gelman

❖❖ Susan E. May, Madison Hts., VA

Fun Bags

Materials

Bags

Books

Puppets and stuffed animals

What to do

1. This activity is very popular with busy parents, who can't always get to the library.

2. Put a children's book Into a sturdy bag. Add a list of songs, activities, and recipes that can be done easily at home. Add a stuffed animal or puppet that looks like the main character. The items don't have to be expensive—yard sales, dollar stores, consignment stores, and donations keep it inexpensive.

3. Make these bags available for parents to sign out the same as they would a library book. You may want to include an evaluation sheet to rate the bag for effectiveness.

4. A good way to get started with putting the bags together is to have a workshop after school for teachers, or use a workday. Parent volunteers can also help.

Author note: I was initially worried about losing a lot of the materials that we put together, but the families loved it so much, they were very careful. Keeping the stuff "cheap" made it easier, too. This is a great way to get families reading together!

❖ Tracie O'Hara, Charlotte, NC

Placemat Seating

Materials

Inexpensive plastic-coated or vinyl placemats

What to do

1. Purchase a variety of inexpensive plastic-coated or vinyl placemats.
2. Ask the children to choose a mat to sit on during circle time. These are helpful in designating a child's personal space.

More to do

Use the mats for musical chairs and other circle time games.

◆❖ Charlene Woodham Peace, Semmes, AL

Meet Penelope Panda!

Materials

Large box (the boxes that reams of paper come in with lids are good)
Construction paper
Markers or crayons
Glue
Scissors
Stuffed panda bear (or any animal character)

What to do

1. Beforehand, decorate a large box to make a "home" for the stuffed panda. Cover the box with construction paper and draw windows, a door, flowers, and so on to make a house.
2. Introduce Penelope Panda as the classroom "friend" or mascot. Explain to the children that Penelope can only come out during circle time if they are very quiet and are being good listeners.
3. Bring out Penelope and speak for her. (The children will know it's you talking, but will also think it's Penelope!) Say hello to the children and let Penelope "tell" the children what the plans are for the day. Sometimes Penelope sings and sometimes she might tell them a funny story!

4. If you have a theme for the week, dress Penelope for the part. For example, at Halloween, put a piece of white cloth over her with the eyes cut out. This is her Halloween ghost costume. For Christmas, dangle ornaments from her ears. For Teddy Bear Day, give her a teddy bear and for Pet Week, give her a stuffed puppy. The possibilities are endless!

5. Collect miniature things for Penelope to use. For example, collect small sunglasses, Frisbees, a small beach ball, baby items, and so on. Another good idea is to collect miniature toys from fast-food restaurants.

6. You will be amazed at how the children are so surprised by what Penelope keeps hidden in her "house." Only she can get into it and bring things out (with your help, of course).

7. Penelope can come out any time and sometimes the children like to play with her at non-circle times. This is okay as long as they know she is special and circle time is her special time.

8. This special classroom friend is VERY REAL to three-year-olds. Sometimes when a child is sad, Penelope can come out and sit with her. Penelope loves to be hugged!

More to do

As mentioned in #4, you can use Penelope to introduce any theme. Be creative!
Literacy: Penelope can begin a story, and the children can finish it. Write down the children's story and encourage them to illustrate it.

❖❖ Sheryl Smith, Jonesborough, TN

Numbers

Materials

None needed

What to do

1. Each day, assign a different child to be in charge of the "number of the day."
2. The child gets to choose the motion that everyone will do for the chosen number. For example, if the number is six, the child may choose six jumps, six toe touches, six arm circles, and so on.
3. This is a concrete way for the children to understand what the number represents.

❖❖ Sandy L. Scott, Vancouver, WA

I Am...

Materials

Tagboard
Scissors
Marker

What to do

1. Cut out rectangle strips from tagboard. Write each child's name on a strip.
2. During circle time, read each name to the children so they are familiar with it.
3. Hold up a nametag and ask questions such as, "Is this person here today? Whose name is this? What letter does this name begin with?"

Related books

Fibblestax by Devin Scillian
From Anne to Zach by Mary Jane Martin

❖ Liz Thomas, Hobart, IN

Name Game

Materials

Small toy or other object

What to do

1. Ask the children to sit in a circle. Teach them to say:
   Round is the circle,
   Round is the game,
   When I come to you
   Please say your name.
2. As the children say the verse, pass around a small toy or other object. When the verse ends, the child with the object responds, "My name is (child's name)."
3. For variation, change the last line to favorite sport, color, animal, food, and so on.

4. Children love to play this game! It helps promote self-esteem, language skills, and socialization skills. It's great to play at the beginning of the year.

◆❖ Noreen Berrington, Camarillo, CA

I Like School

Materials

White, yellow, and green construction paper
Black and green marker
Glue
Scissors

What to do

1. Cut yellow and green construction paper into 3" (8 cm) diameter circles, two of each color for each child. Draw a happy face on each circle.
2. Give each child a piece of white construction paper. At the top of each sheet, write "I Like School" using a green marker.
3. Give each child four happy face circles and ask them to glue them on the paper so the happy face shows.
4. During circle time, talk with children about what they like best about school. If desired, record their answers and post the list in the room.

◆❖ Diane Weiss, Fairfax, VA

Guess What?

Materials

None needed

What to do

1. This is a fun guessing game to play during circle time, or whenever you have a few extra minutes. Give the children clues about an animal (or something else) and encourage them to guess what it is.

2. Without telling the children, choose an animal to describe. For example, if you choose a turtle, say, "I'm thinking of an animal. It's green, has a hard shell, and moves very slowly." When a child thinks she knows the answer, she can raise her hand.

3. As the children get better at the game, give more obscure clues. You can also increase their knowledge by throwing in clues that they probably don't know about the animal, but that they can learn from other clues. For example, "This animal is gray and has a long trunk. Some live in India and some live in Africa."

4. Vary the game by having the children guess people in the class ("This person has a new baby sister and his birthday was last week") or common objects ("This is something we use to get our teeth clean and it comes in a tube").

5. Once the children get the hang of the game, they can take turns giving the clues. You will hear a lot of repetition but that's okay—this is a great language developer.

More to do

Art: Give clues and ask the children to draw their answer.

Gross Motor: Give clues and encourage the children to act out the animal they think you are describing. Or, play the game like charades. Instead of giving verbal clues, one child acts like the animal and the other children try to guess what it is.

❖❖ Suzanne Pearson, Stephens City, VA

Body Alphabets

Materials

A group of children

What to do

1. Talk about the alphabet with the children and ask them to think about ways that they can form the letters of the alphabet with their bodies.

2. Then divide the children into small groups, or if they know the alphabet really well, they can do this individually.

3. Pick a group or an individual and call out a letter for them to make with their bodies. They can stand or lie down depending on the letter. Some letters may require more than one person. This is really fun, and the children can be so creative.

4. You also can call out a letter and ask the children to make the letter together. You're sure to hear, "Look at me," and "Try it this way!"

◆◆ Gail Morris, Kemah, TX

Shape Bear

Materials

Cardboard
Scissors
Bright paint and brushes
Glue gun
Velcro
Small teddy bear

What to do

1. Ahead of time, cut out different shapes from cardboard and paint them bright colors.
2. Use a glue gun to attach Velcro to the back of each shape. Also attach a piece of Velcro to the teddy bear's hand.
3. As you talk about different shapes during circle time, attach them to the bear's hand using the Velcro.

◆◆ Lisa Chichester, Parkersburg, WV

Color Boxes

Materials

Cardboard boxes or gift bags in various colors
Various child-safe items in the same color as the bag or box
Labels or index cards and tape
Magnifiers

What to do

1. Purchase boxes or bags in different colors. If colored boxes or bags aren't available, wrap, color, or paint them various colors.

2. Place items that match the color box or bag inside each one.

3. Write the color of the bag or box on a label or index card and tape it to the front.

4. During circle time, give each child a bag and ask her to pull an item from the bag while guessing what it may be.

5. Place the bags on a table with the magnifiers for further exploration.

◆◆ Tina R. Durham-Woehler, Lebanon, TN

Colors of My World

Materials

Large paper plates

Large pictures of flowers in different colors, such as red roses and carnations, yellow daffodils, purple pansies, and so on (seed catalogs are good sources for pictures)

Glue

Mirror

What to do

1. Beforehand, glue a different flower picture onto each paper plate.

2. Ask the children to close their eyes and ask, "What do you see?" They may say, "Black" or "Nothing." Now say, "Open your eyes. What colors do you see?" Talk about the colors around the room or out the window.

3. Give each child a paper plate with a flower on it. One at a time, each child will hold it in front of her face and ask the other children what colors they see on the plate.

4. Give one child at a time a mirror and ask her to look into it. Encourage the other children to stand around her and describe the colors they see (for example, blue eyes, red hair, brown freckles, brown skin, and so on). Encourage them to look closely and see the different variations of colors such as the eyes.

5. Explain that we all are different colors, and like the flowers, we are all beautiful.

More to do

Art: Encourage the children to draw flowers, birds, butterflies, or animals using different colors.

Housekeeping: Put dolls of different ethnicities as well as with different hair, eyes, and so on in the Housekeeping Center.

Science: Show the children a collection of bugs or butterflies of different colors.

Related poem

Colors and Me

If you look around you will see
Flowers, trees, the sky, and me.
Browns, yellow, pinks, and greens
Colors everywhere it seems.
Dogs, cats, birds, and me too
Black, white, purple, and blue
Different colors we will see.
When I look at you and you look at me.

❖❖ Helene De Witt, Cochise, AZ

Rainless Rainbows

Materials

Solid color 24" streamers or ribbons, one for each child

What to do

1. Ask the children to join hands and form a circle, singing the "Rainbow Song."
2. At the end of the song, ask each child, "What rainbow color would you like?" Give the child the color streamer she chooses.
3. When everyone has a streamer, sing the song again as the children twirl and swirl the streamers all around.

More to do

Science: Make sprinkler rainbows. On a sunny day, turn on a water sprinkler and ask the children to stand with their backs to the sun. Show them the rainbow. Turn off the sprinkler off. What happens to the rainbow?

More Science: Hang a crystal in a sunny window. Ask the children to find the rainbow that is cast on the wall or floor. Discuss what happens when the sun no longer shines through the window.

Snack: Make Rainbow Ice. Fill ice cube trays with water and squeeze a few drops of food coloring into each compartment. Freeze them. Put the colored ice cubes into clear plastic cups with water or other clear beverages.

Original song

Rainbow Song (Tune: "Bringing Home a Baby Bumblebee")

I wish I had a big rainbow.
I'd take it with me everywhere I'd go.
And if you smile and ask me to
I would give a piece to YOU!

Related books

Planting a Rainbow by Lois Ehlert
A Rainbow of My Own by Don Freeman
The Storm by Charlotte Zolotow

❖ Nina Smith, Cameron, SC

My Favorite Color

Materials

White construction paper
Construction paper or tissue paper in various colors
Scissors
Glue
Markers
3" by 5" index cards
Chart paper

What to do

1. Pick a date for "Favorite Color Day" and send home a note to parents asking that their children wear their favorite color that day.
2. On the designated day, cut out large hearts from white construction paper and give one to each child. Cut a variety of colors of construction or tissue paper into 1" squares.
3. Show the children how to make collages using glue and paper squares in their favorite color.

4. Ask each child why she chose her color and write her response on a 3" by 5" card. Glue the card to the back of the heart shaped paper.

5. During circle time, write all the colors on the left side of a piece of chart paper. Next to each color, make a mark for each child who is wearing that color.

6. Total up marks to see how many children like each color. Compare which color is liked the most and which color is liked the least.

More to do

Say the following rhyme as the children act out the motions.

If your favorite color is red,
Put both hands on your head.
If your favorite color is blue,
Put your fingertips on your shoes.
If your favorite color is yellow,
Give a smile like a happy fellow.
If your favorite color is green,
Wave your hands so they can be seen.
If your favorite color is white,
Clap your hands with all your might.
If your favorite color is black,
Hide your hands behind your back.
If your favorite color is pink,
Nod your head and give a wink.
If your favorite color is brown,
Stand up and turn yourself around.
If your favorite color is purple,
Spin your hands in a circle.
(Add color words and rhymes as necessary.)

Related books

Cat's Colors by Jane Cabrera
Color Dance by Ann Jonas

❖❖ Diane Weiss, Fairfax, VA

Occupation Days

Materials

Chart paper

Markers

What to do

1. Do a unit on occupations. Each day during circle time, talk about different jobs.
2. One day, talk about parents' jobs. Another day, talk about community helpers and what they do.
3. Spend time discussing what the children want to do when they grow up. Chart their responses and hang it up.
4. If desired, ask parents or other people to come in and talk about their jobs.

❖❖ Lynn Reihl, Lynchburg, VA

Learning Responsible Pet Care

Materials

Cardboard pet carrier (available at your local Humane Society)

Stuffed dog and cat

Cat and dog collars and nametags

Blanket

Food dish and water bowl

Pet brush

Leash

Toy vet items, such as a toy syringe, medicine dropper bottle, and stethoscope

Pet toys, such as yarn, a furry cat toy, and a ball

Dog bone

What to do

1. Beforehand, put collars and nametags onto a stuffed dog and cat and place them in a cardboard pet carrier.
2. Gather the children and introduce the pet carrier.
3. Ask the children what kind of pet could fit into the carrier. Discuss the different types of pets. Then gently lift the dog and cat from the carrier using two hands.
4. Engage the children in a discussion about responsible pet care as you show them the things that pets need (see materials list).
5. Demonstrate each job through dramatic play. For example, children can take turns:
   - Spreading the blanket to make a pet's bed.
   - Giving the pets food and water.
   - Brushing the pets to groom them.
   - Exercising the dog with his leash on.
   - Playing with the cat using toys and yarn.
   - Taking both pets to the veterinarian for a check-up, shots, and medicine.
6. While children are still in a circle, roll the ball to each child and encourage him or her to roll it back to the dog for play and training. They can reward the dog by giving him a dog bone.
7. Tell the children, "Don't forget—give them lots of love!"

More to do

Dramatic Play: Set up an adoption center for pets, a veterinarian clinic, or a pet supply store.

Language: Encourage the children to talk about their family pets during show and tell.

❖❖ Terri A. Schmidt, Silverton, OR

Hats, Hats, Hats

Materials

Hats or pictures of hats
Construction paper
Scissors
Markers or crayons
Glue, staples, and so on

What to do

1. Talk about hats. Why do we wear hats? What kinds of hats are there?
2. Show the children a variety of hats, or pictures of them, such as rain hats, cold weather caps, firemen's hats, baseball caps, football helmets, "Cat in the Hat" hats, military caps, fancy Easter hats, and so on.
3. Send a note home asking parents to let their children bring in various hats. During circle time, ask the children to put on their hats and talk about them.
4. Help the children make hats from paper. They can be as simple as just cutting out two circles of paper and stapling them together, or as complicated as origami samurai hats.

More to do

Language: Compare the hats using opposite words. For example, large/small, big/little, tall/short, and so on.
Math: Count the hats.
Science: Explore with the children which kinds of hats keep out the cold (paper? cloth? football helmet?) and/or rain.

Original song

(Tune: "Three Blind Mice")

This is my hat.
This is my hat.
See how I look.
See how I look.
I smile and wave and show my hat.
So what do you really think of that?
This is my hat.
This is my hat.

Related books

The 500 Hats of Bartholomew Cubbins by Dr. Seuss
Caps for Sale by Esphyr Slobodkina
The Cat in the Hat by Dr. Seuss

❖❖ Lucy Fuchs, Brandon, FL

Chef's Hats

Materials

Pictures of chefs, optional
Small white plastic bags (13" garbage bags)
White sentence strips or long strips of card stock cut 3" wide
Stapler
Scissors

What to do

1. During circle time, discuss the job of a chef. If possible, show the children pictures of a chef.
2. Using a sentence strip or card stock, measure around each child's head.
3. Staple it in place. (**Tip:** Staple from the inside out so the sharp ends won't poke the children.)

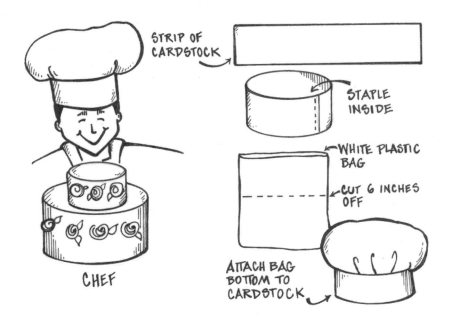

STRIP OF CARDSTOCK

STAPLE INSIDE

WHITE PLASTIC BAG

CUT 6 INCHES OFF

CHEF

ATTACH BAG BOTTOM TO CARDSTOCK

4. Cut about 6" off the top of each plastic bag and staple a bag to each headband, gathering and stapling the bag to fit.
5. Write each child's name on her headband.

More to do

Invite a chef to come in and discuss his or her job.

Art: Give the children modeling clay and encourage the children to make clay "food."

Dramatic Play: Set up a restaurant in the Dramatic Play Center.

Field Trip: Go to a restaurant and ask for a tour of the kitchen.

Snack and Cooking: Using pre-made bread dough (or help the children make their own dough), give each child a handful of dough. Show them how to knead it into a small ball. Bake the bread and eat it for snack.

Related books

How My Parents Learned to Eat by Ina Friedman
If You Give a Mouse a Cookie by Laura Joffe Numeroff

❖❖ Barbara Saul, Eureka, CA

My Feet and Me

Materials

Paper
Pencil and marker
Scissors
Variety of footwear, such as boots, shoes, slippers, and so on (or pictures of them)

What to do

1. During circle time, ask the children to look at their feet. Talk about feet and ask questions. What do we have on our feet? What do we do with our feet? What would it be like if we had no feet?
2. Ask the children to take off their shoes and socks and stand on a piece of paper. Trace their feet and cut out their footprints. Talk about the different prints and compare the sizes. Explain how we each have a right and a left foot.

3. Write each child's initials on her footprints and place them around the room. Play games with the footprints. (Who is sneaking into the cupboard? Who is at the chalk board? Who is in the sand?)

4. Talk about footwear as you show the children different types of footwear (or pictures of them). Teach the children words such as *shoes, slippers, sandals, boots, baby booties, mules,* and so on.

5. Point out to the children how important their feet are as they engage in running, skipping, jumping, and other activities.

6. If possible, encourage the children to go barefoot some days so that they can feel the sand and the grass and learn how to avoid rocks. They will also learn how cold or wet or hot the sidewalk can be.

More to do

Art: Encourage the children to draw different kinds of shoes, real or imaginary.
Language: Ask the children to talk about their shoes. Who bought them for them? Do they like them? Are they comfortable?
Math: Count how many people are in the room, and then count the shoes. Children will learn, in an elementary way, that the number of shoes is twice that of the people.

Original song

(Tune: "Three Blind Mice")
These are my feet.
These are my feet.
I have two.
I have two.
I can walk and jump and run.
I can dance and skip and have lots of fun.
These are my feet.

Related book

Grandma Summer by Harley Jessup

❖❖ Lucy Fuchs, Brandon, FL

All About Hands

Materials

Construction paper
Pencils
Scissors
Pictures of people and animals

What to do

1. Ask the children to form a circle and hold their hands in front of them. Ask them to put their palms out and move them around.

2. Talk about hands as they examine them. Ask them questions, such as:
   What do your hands look like?
   How many fingers? How many thumbs?
   Which is your longest finger?
   What do you call the little finger?
   Look at your fingernails. What are they good for?
   What can we do with our hands?
   What couldn't we do if we didn't have hands?

3. Make a circle and ask everyone to hold hands.

4. Ask the children to compare their hands with a partner. Encourage them to compare their hands at home with their parents and siblings.

5. Ask the children to trace their partner's hand onto a piece of paper. Cut them out and paste them around the room.

6. Show the children pictures of people and animals, pointing out their hands (and paws). Talk about what animals do with their paws. Compare animal paws with human hands.

More to do

Art: Draw pictures of hands.
Dramatic Play: Encourage the children to paste faces on the palms of their hands and tell little stories with them.
Games: Using the cut-out handprints, encourage the children to guess to whom they belong.
Sand and Water: Encourage the children to feel the difference between hot and cold water, sand and stones, and so on.

Original song

(Tune: "Three Blind Mice")

These are my hands.
These are my hands.
I can wiggle them.
I can wiggle them.
I like to do things with my hands.
I work and play and move my hands.
These are my hands.

Other verses:
I can open them.
I can close them.
I can clap them.
I can hide them.

Related book

My Hands, My World by Catherine Brighton

❖❖ Lucy Fuchs, Brandon, FL

I Am Special Because I Am Me

Materials

This Thumbprint by Ruth Krauss
Old catalogs
Scissors
Paper
Paste

What to do

1. During circle time, encourage the children to look carefully at their hands, especially at the fingerprints on each finger. Explain that each child's fingerprints are different from everyone else's fingerprints.

2. Talk about other ways each child is special.
3. Read *This Thumbprint* to the children.
4. Give the children old catalogs and encourage them to cut out pictures of things they like, such as hamburgers, books, bicycles, and so on.
5. Encourage the children to paste their pictures onto a piece of paper. Explain that they are making a picture story of one special person—themselves!
6. When they are finished, encourage the children to share their pictures with the rest of the children.

More to do

Art: Pour tempera paint into saucers. Put a folded paper towel into each saucer and soak it with paint. Help the children make thumbprints by pressing their thumbs onto the paper towels soaked in paint and then onto a piece of manila paper with their own thumbprint designs. If desired, write the child's name, and then encourage her to make thumbprints all over it.

Movement: Make "Me Shadows." Hang a white sheet in a doorway and shine a light behind it. Divide the group into two teams. Ask one person to stand behind the screen and move around, but not talk. The other team guesses who is behind the screen.

Related song

"You Are Special" from Mr. Rogers Songbook

◆◆ Wendy Pfeffer, Pennington, NJ

I Can Be Happy

Materials

Snow White and the Seven Dwarfs book, optional
A Child's Garden of Verses by Robert Louis Stevenson, optional

What to do

1. During circle time, tell the children the story (or read the book) of *Snow White and the Seven Dwarfs*.
2. Talk about the dwarfs' personalities, such as Happy, Grumpy, Bashful, and so on. Discuss what makes each of us feel different emotions, such as happy, sad, and so on.

3. Ask the children to look at each other and make faces, such as happy, joyful, sad, and so on.

4. If desired, read the poem "Happy Thought" by Robert Louis Stevenson.

More to do

Art: Make "happy-sad thermometers." On pieces of 9" x 12" cardboard (one for each child), cut a 1" horizontal slit 2" from the top and another one 2" from the bottom, each cut centered on the page. Give each child a piece of pre-cut cardboard, a piece of ?" x 17" ribbon, and crayons. Help the children thread the ribbon through the two slits and staple the ends together in the back. Ask the children to draw what makes them the happiest at the top of their thermometer, something that makes them happy in the middle, and something that makes them sad at the bottom. Ask the children questions such as, "You fell and scraped your knee." Or, "Grandma just brought you a new toy." Encourage the children to move the ribbon on their thermometer to "very happy," "happy," or "sad."

Related books

Feelings by Aliki
Grandma Gets Grumpy by Anna Grossnickle Hines
If You're Happy and You Know It by Nicki Wiess

Related song

"If You're Happy and You Know It"

◆◆ Wendy Pfeffer, Pennington, NJ

Blue Whale, Blue Whale, What Do You See?

(This activity is adapted from *Brown Bear, Brown Bear, What Do You See?* by Bill Martin, Jr. and Eric Carle.)

Materials

Pieces of felt in blue, red, pink, orange, yellow, white, gray, black, purple, and green
Scissors
Flannel board

What to do

1. Cut the following shapes from felt: a blue whale, red crab, pink shrimp, yellow starfish, white shark, gray dolphin, black eel, purple jellyfish, and a person wearing a green swimsuit (beachcomber).
2. At circle time, introduce the shapes as you hand one to each child.
3. Explain that you will tell them a story and when they hear their shape named, they can bring it up and put it on the flannel board.
4. Tell the following story:

   Blue whale, blue whale, what do you see?
   I see a white shark looking at me.
   White shark, white shark, what do you see?
   I see a gray dolphin looking at me.
   Grey dolphin, gray dolphin, what do you see?
   I see a black eel looking at me.
   Black eel, black eel, what do you see?
   I see a red crab looking at me.
   Red crab, red crab, what do you see?
   I see a pink shrimp looking at me.
   Pink shrimp, pink shrimp, what do you see?
   I see a yellow starfish looking at me.
   Yellow starfish, yellow starfish, what do you see?
   I see a purple jellyfish looking at me.
   Purple jellyfish, purple jellyfish, what do you see?
   I see a green beachcomber looking at me.
   Green beachcomber, green beachcomber, what do you see?
   I see a lively ocean looking back at me.

Related books

Across the Big Blue Sea: An Ocean Wildlife Book by Jakki Wood
In the Ocean by Neecy Twinem
Water by Frank Asch
Who Lives in the Ocean? by Peggy Tagel

❖❖ Ann Gudowski, Johnstown, PA

Felt Board Tree

Materials

Brown felt
Scissors
Black marker
Green felt
Flannel board

What to do

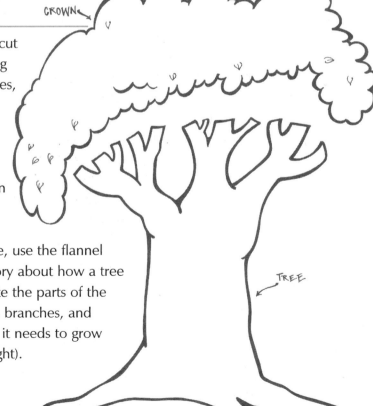

1. Using brown felt cut out a tree showing the trunk, branches, and roots.
2. Draw the roots using a black marker.
3. Cut out the crown of the tree using green felt.
4. During circle time, use the flannel board to tell a story about how a tree grows. Incorporate the parts of the tree (roots, trunk, branches, and crown) and what it needs to grow (soil, water, sunlight).

5. After circle time, leave the felt pieces and the flannel board out so the children can reconstruct the tree and retell the story on their own.

More to do

Outdoors: Plant a tree on the playground. Encourage the children to share in the planting and care of the tree.

Related songs

"The Little Nut Tree"
"The Green Grass Grows All Around" (*Wee Sing Silly Songs* cassette, Price Stern Sloan)

❖❖ Jackie Wright, Enid, OK

The Daily Weather Report

Materials

Felt
Scissors
Markers
Flannel board

What to do

1. Cut out a boy and girl, clothing for different seasons, and weather-related items (such as sun, rain, clouds, snowflakes, and so on) from felt.
2. Each day, choose a child to be the weather person.
3. Using the flannel board and felt pieces, the child can dress the girl or boy in clothing that would be appropriate for that day's weather.
4. Encourage the child to show and discuss her completed flannel board during circle time.

More to do

Science and Nature: With the children, make a weekly graph of the weather.

❖❖ Sandy L. Scott, Vancouver, WA

Weather Graph

Materials

Felt
Scissors
Markers
Flannel board

What to do

1. Cut out several of each of the following weather symbols from felt: sun, clouds, raindrops, and snowflakes.
2. Make columns on the flannel board for the following: sun, clouds, rain, and snow.
3. Choose a "weather child" each day. Encourage the child to describe the day's weather to the rest of the children.
4. The child will then pick one of the symbols and put it in the correct column on the flannel board.
5. At the end of the month, tally the symbols in each column.

More to do

Art: Encourage the children to draw a variety of weather pictures.
Dramatic Play: Add appropriate clothing that represents different types of weather to the Dramatic Play area.
Sand and Water Table: Add items to the sensory table that remind the children of the weather.

❖❖ Sandy L. Scott, Vancouver, WA

Seasonal Sorting

Materials

Suitcase
Clothing from winter and summer seasons, such as a boot, shorts, mittens, sandals, ear muffs, and sunglasses

What to do

1. Beforehand, put a variety of winter and summer clothing into a suitcase.
2. At group time, present the suitcase. Tell the children that you'd like their help sorting the clothes that are inside. Explain that there are some winter things and summer things all mixed up.
3. Show each item, one at a time, and ask the children to name the season in which they would need that item. Ask them to explain their answer.
4. If desired, sort them into piles.

More to do

Ask the children which clothes would be appropriate for the current weather outside, or what they should wear to go sledding, water skiing, and so on.

❖❖ Vicki Schneider, Oshkosh, WI

Old MacDonald's Vegetable Farm

Materials

Raw vegetables
Knife
Tray

What to do

1. Cut up raw vegetables and place them on a tray.
2. Sing "Old MacDonald Had a Farm" with the children.
3. Discuss with the children what else they might find on a farm besides animals. Prompt them, if necessary, to say vegetables or food.
4. Ask each child to name a vegetable and say one thing about it.
5. Incorporate this information into a new version of the song. For example:
   Old MacDonald had a farm, E-I-E-I-O,
   And on that farm he had some carrots, E-I-E-I-O,
   With an orange carrot here, and an orange carrot there,
   Here a carrot, there a carrot, everywhere an orange carrot, E-I-E-I-O.

6. Continue making up new verses, using "crunchy carrot," "leafy lettuce," "juicy tomato," "smelly onion," and so on.

More to do

Math: Encourage the children to count each of the vegetable pieces on the tray.

❖❖ Angela Williamson La Fon, Lynchburg, VA

Grandmas

Materials

Paper
Pencils and crayons
Objects from home that grandma made or gave to the children
Grandmothers

What to do

1. Talk about grandmothers. Ask the children to talk about at least one of their grandmothers. What does grandma look like? Is she big or small? Does she wear glasses? When do you see your grandmother?
2. Encourage the children to draw pictures of their grandmothers.
3. Send a note home to parents asking them to let their child bring in an object they received from their grandmothers. These can be anything, including cookies or candy. Encourage the children to discuss these objects during circle time.
4. Invite the grandmothers to come in for "Grandmother Day." The children can sing to them and serve them cookies and juice.

Note: Children who do not have a grandmother may substitute another significant adult, such as a parent, babysitter, aunt, and so on.

More to do

Math: Ask the children to count how many people are in their families (mom, dad, brothers, sisters, grandparents, and so on)
Snack and Cooking: If a grandmother sends cookies (or another food) to school, ask her to supply the recipe. Make the cookies with the children and call them "Sally's grandmother's cookies," and so on.

Social Development: When the grandmothers come in, teach the children how to make simple introductions.

Original song

(Tune: "Happy Birthday")

I love my grandma very much.
I love my grandma very much.
She likes to see me,
And I like to see her!

My grandma bakes cookies.
My grandma bakes cookies.
They are so good to eat,
I love her for them.

My grandma tells stories.
My grandma tells stories.
They are funny and sad,
I love her stories.

Related books

Abuela's Weave by Omar Castenada
Grandma Summer by Harley Jessup
Grandmama's Joy by Eloise Greenfield
Grandmother's Dreamcatcher by Becky Ray McCain
My Gran by Debbie Boon
My Grandmother's Journey by John Cech
Quinnie Blue by Dinah Johnson
Willy's Silly Grandma by Cynthia DeFelice

❖❖ Lucy Fuchs, Brandon, FL

Circle Day

Materials

Round parachute
Kiddie pools
Circular toys, such as bubbles, hula hoops, Frisbees, and assorted balls

What to do

1. Send a note home to parents explaining that their children will be learning about circles. Ask the parents to let their children bring in balls, hula hoops, and other toys that are circles, making sure their names are on them. It would be helpful to have parents volunteer to help with some of these activities. Someone should be supervising the water play at all times.

2. Following are some ideas you can try:
   - Play parachute games.
   - Blow bubbles.
   - Have water play or sand play in kiddie pools.
   - Play "Ring Around the Rosie," Duck Duck Goose," and "Here We Go 'Round the Mulberry Bush."
   - Teach the children how to throw Frisbees.

More to do

Art: Make potato prints with tempera paint.
More Art: Put a little tempera paint in with the bubbles and encourage the children to blow bubbles and let them pop onto a light-colored piece of construction paper.
Snack: Serve round sandwiches, cookies, crackers and cheese, and other snacks that have been cut with a cookie cutter.

Related books

Pancakes, Pancakes by Eric Carle
Round and Round and Round by Tana Hoban

Related song

"The Wheels on the Bus"

❖❖ Vicki Whitehead, Citronelle, AL

Dramatic Play Art

Materials

Any size boxes
Paint and brushes

What to do

1. Paint a variety of boxes and allow them to dry.
2. Put the boxes in the Dramatic Play area and outdoors. Encourage the children to use their imaginations and turn the boxes into anything they desire!
3. Larger boxes can become cars, caves, and so on. Children can also use tissue boxes and paper towel holders for a variety of things.

Note: Explain to the children that if a child is inside a box on its side, they should wait their turn and not lie down on top of the box.

❖❖ Ann Chandler, Felton, CA

Dramatizing Nursery Rhymes

Materials

Simple props related to nursery rhymes, such as a cylinder block for a candle ("Jack Be Nimble"), a cushion ("Little Miss Muffet"), and a horn ("Little Boy Blue")

What to do

1. This activity helps young children begin to identify with the characters in structured make-believe, and is a first step to role playing or simple drama as opposed to dramatic play.
2. Say the nursery rhyme out loud, inviting the children to recite it with you.
3. Then encourage the children to take turns acting out the rhyme as the others recite it. Use the props as desired.
4. After the children become at ease acting out familiar rhymes, read a simple story and encourage the children to act out scenes as you read.

More to do

Make up role plays using situations that are meaningful for the children. Encourage them to make up their own parts. For example: "Today is Mike's first day at school. What can Ben do to make Mike feel better?" (If Ben does not know what to do, ask the other children to make suggestions. If they do not think of something, suggest that he tell Mike his name and invite him to play). "I am Ben. Would you like to help me build a house?" You may need to model and give them the words several times, but soon this will be a favorite activity. Be sure not to use the children's real names so they will understand they are role playing.

❖❖ Mary Jo Shannon, Roanoke, VA

Purposeful Productions

Materials

None

What to do

1. Creative dramatics is pretending you are something that you're not. All children dramatize to various degrees. Following are some tips for encouraging creative dramatics.

   Plan classroom dramatizations. This allows children to "try out" various roles, increases their oral language development, and provides opportunities for them to work together to meet common goals. Begin by playing "Let's pretend to be…" or acting out familiar fingerplays and/or songs.

   Re-enact a favorite story. Familiarize children with the story through several readings, then select and prepare characters. Be sure to repeat (over several days/weeks) the dramatization until all the children have a turn to be the part of their choice. Begin the dramatization by telling the story to yourself. Pause to give children the chance to join in at the appropriate times, and stop when children pick up their lines and your narration is no longer necessary.

2. Keep the following things in mind when planning classroom dramatics: Dialogue doesn't have to be word-for-word to be beneficial and meaningful. Productions can be spontaneous. Props and costumes are wonderful, but not necessary for children to gain the benefits offered from creative dramatics.

3. As with all creative endeavors, the *process* is more important than the *product!*

❖❖ Rebecca McMahen Giles, Mobile, AL

Paper Plate Mask

Materials

Paper plates
Scissors
Glue
Popsicle sticks
Craft paint and paintbrushes
Sequins, glitter, star stickers

What to do

1. Give each child a paper plate. Help them cut their plates in half and cut out eyes.
2. Show the children how to glue a Popsicle stick to the paper plates.
3. Encourage the children to paint their masks and decorate them with glitter, stickers, sequins, feathers, and so on.
4. The children can use their masks in the Dramatic Play area.

❖ Lisa Chichester, Parkersburg, WV

"Stick It to Me" Stick Puppets

Materials

Stickers
Tagboard or poster board
Scissors
Laminate or clear contact paper
Craft stick
Glue or contact cement

What to do

1. Save stickers from sticker books. Carefully remove the stickers by pressing them out.

2. Lick the backs (or use self-adhesive stickers) of each sticker and attach them to tagboard.

3. Cover them with clear contact paper or laminate them. Trim the excess laminate.

4. Glue a craft stick to each puppet using contact cement.

5. When you're not using these to add sparkle to your songs, stories, and units, place them in the Dramatic Play area for the children to manipulate.

❖❖ Jackie Wright, Enid, OK

Greeting Card Puppets

Materials

Greeting cards
Scissors
Craft sticks
Contact cement

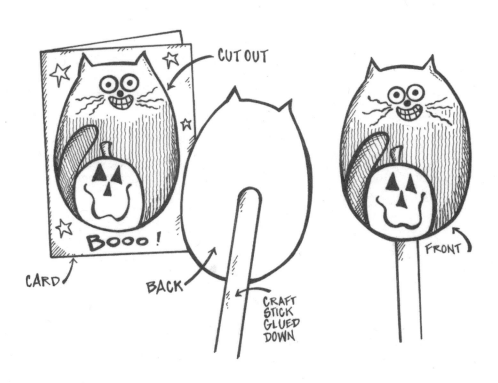

What to do

1. Save cute greeting cards in the shapes of fish, ducks, teddy bears, cats, and so on. Party invitations and Christmas cards are good to use.
2. Cut the card apart and discard all but the part you want to use.
3. Glue a craft stick to the back of each one using glue or contact cement.
4. When you're not using these to add sparkle to your songs, stories, and units, place them in the Dramatic Play area for children to manipulate.

◆◆ Jackie Wright, Enid, Oklahoma

"Wrap It Up" Stick Puppets

Materials

Wrapping paper with appropriate pictures
Scissors
Tagboard
Glue stick
Laminate or clear contact paper
Craft sticks
Glue or contact cement

What to do

1. Throughout the year, save wrapping paper with pictures you can cut out to use for craft projects or stick puppets.
2. Cut out pictures from wrapping paper and glue them to tagboard or poster board using a glue stick.
3. Laminate the pictures or cover them with clear contact paper for durability.
4. Trim away excess poster board and contact paper.
5. Glue a craft stick to each puppet using glue or contact cement.
6. Place them in the Dramatic Play area for the children to manipulate.

◆◆ Jackie Wright, Enid, OK

Online Picture Puppets

Materials

Pictures from the Internet
Color printer
Scissors
Tagboard or poster board
Laminate or clear contact paper
Craft sticks
Glue or contact cement

What to do

1. The Internet is a wonderful source for adorable pictures to use for stick puppets.
2. Print out the pictures using a color printer directly onto tagboard.
3. Cut out the pictures.
4. Laminate or cover them with clear contact paper.
5. Glue a craft stick to the back of each one using glue or contact cement.
6. Place them in the Dramatic Play area for children to manipulate.

❖ Jackie Wright, Enid, OK

"Stop and Go" Stick Puppets

Materials

Pictures of safety signs
Scissors
Tagboard
Glue stick
Laminate or clear contact paper
Craft stick
Glue or contact cement

What to do

1. Locate pictures of safety signs or make your own using construction paper. Some good ones to use are a yield sign, stop sign, school-crossing sign, railroad-crossing sign, and so on.
2. Cut out the pictures and attach them to tagboard using a glue stick.
3. Laminate or cover them with clear contact paper. Trim away the excess contact paper.
4. Glue a craft stick to each puppet using glue or contact cement.
5. Place them in the Dramatic Play area for the children to manipulate.

Related book

Bumper to Bumper: A Traffic Jam by Jakki Wood

❖❖ Jackie Wright, Enid, OK

Seasonal Fun

Materials

Dress-up clothes and accessories for all seasons
Newspaper
White paper
Clear packing tape
Camping gear (real or play)
Summer gear, such as beach towels; pool toys; empty, clean sunscreen bottles; and so on
Plastic rakes
Plastic, silk, or die-cut fall leaves

What to do

1. Choose a day or week to set up each season in the Dramatic Play center.
2. Set up the seasonal play as follows:

Winter: Put out boots, snow suits, gloves, mittens, hats, scarves, and coats. Make snowballs by scrunching up newspaper into different size balls and covering them with white paper and clear packing tape. Encourage the children to stack them, roll them, or toss them while dressed for cold weather.

Spring: Set up a camping center with backpacks, canteens, pots and pans, cans of beans, binoculars, rope flashlights, and a tent. If you do not have a real or play tent, make one from a sheet.

Summer: Encourage the children to pretend they are going to the beach or the pool. Give the children towels, empty sunscreen bottles, pool toys, goggles, diving sticks, and beach chairs. You could even play some "Beach Boys" music for a fun touch.

Fall: Rake, rake, rake the leaves! Put a bunch of pretend leaves and plastic rakes into the Dramatic Play center and the children will have a great time raking and dumping the leaves.

❖❖ Gail Morris, Kemah, TX

Prop Boxes

Materials

Empty boxes with lids
Marker
Variety of dress-up clothes (see below)

What to do

1. Collect the following items, place them into boxes, and label them. Keep in mind the age of the children and do not add anything that is sharp or small enough to swallow.

Theme Ideas		

FIREFIGHTER:
Fire hats
Vacuum cleaner hose
Black boots
Toolbox with tools
Steering wheel
Posters of fire engines
	HOSPITAL:
	Doctor/nurse scrubs
	Small toy plastic doctor
	  tools
	Medical kit bag
	Clipboard
	Paper and pencils
	Posters of doctors and
	  nurses
		VET:
		Small stuffed animals
		Medical kit
		Doctor tools
		Bandages
		Cotton swabs
		Pet carriers
		Small bowls
		Clipboard
		Paper and pencils

OFFICE: Paper Clipboards Telephones Calculators Typewriter Computer Envelopes Stickers Inkpads Rubber stamps	GROCERY STORE: Cash register Play money Grocery carts Aprons Empty food containers Grocery bags	

2. For more information on enhancing your Dramatic Play area through the use of prop boxes, see *Young Children* (NAEYC), July 1993.

More to do

Books: Read stories about firefighters, the hospital, the vet, and so on.
Field Trip: Visit a grocery store, hospital, vet office, and so on.

❖❖ Sue M. Myhre, Bremerton, WA

Thematic Dramatics

Materials

See below

What to do

1. There are many opportunities to develop rich dramatic play in the pre-school classroom. Consider going beyond the customary Housekeeping area, Block Center, and so on and think about realistic themes to enhance language development, social interaction, and creativity.
2. Following are some ideas for themes and props.
   Theme: A Restaurant
   Props can include menus, order pads, placemats, dishes, real or play food, pots and pans, aprons, and a telephone. Roles include host, cook, wait staff, and customers.
   Theme: The Doctor's Office
   Props can include a sign-in sheet, prescription pads, doctor tools, play money, checkbooks, tickets, a telephone, and so on. Roles include patients, parents, nurse, doctor, and receptionist.
   Theme: A Travel Agency
   Props can include office furniture, a computer, brochures, travel posters, play money, checkbooks, tickets, and a telephone. Roles: customers and agents. Other possible themes could be a post office, grocery store, bank, library, bakery, and so on.
3. Invite the children to suggest themes, props, costumes, and characters.

More to do

Literacy: Record some aspects of the play, using a simple chart or encourage the children to dictate a story. Tape Polaroid photos during the course of the dramatic play to illustrate the chart or story. Make sure to include children's names. For example, "This is Mary. She is the nurse."

❖❖ Iris Rothstein, New Hyde Park, NY

Table Tent

Materials

About five yards of lightweight fabric
Scissors
Fabric paint, optional
Sewing machine
Standard card table

What to do

1. Cut out a 30" x 30" square of fabric (large enough to cover the top of a card table).
2. Cut out eight 16" x 27" panels of fabric.
3. If desired, encourage the children to decorate the fabric using fabric paint. (If this is the case, use plain fabric.)

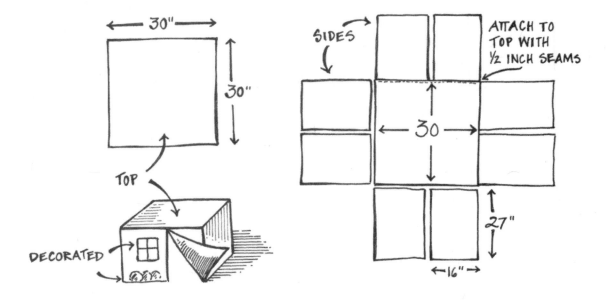

4. Sew two panels to each side of the fabric square, leaving ½" seams.

5. Hem the raw edges.

6. Drape the finished product over the card table—now you have a tent! The children can also use it as a cave, house, garage, or anything else they desire. It also can be used as part of an obstacle course, or a place to read books.

❖❖ Sharon Dempsey, Mays Landing, NJ

Teepee

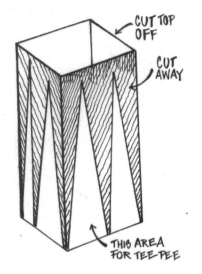

Materials

Large box, such as a refrigerator box
Utility knife (adult only)
Duct tape
Tempera paint
1" to 2" paintbrushes
Shallow dishes or plates
Liquid soap
Play items, such as a drum, fire pit, and so on

What to do

1. Cut off the top of a large box, and then cut out triangle strips along the sides of the box (see illustration). Remove the V shapes and corner pieces, leaving the rest.

2. At the top of the box, pull together all the points of the pieces that are left to form a teepee shape. Put tape around them to hold them together. Put tape midway down and at the base.

3. Cut an opening for the door.

4. Ask the children to paint it brown.

5. After the brown paint dries, pour different colors of tempera paint into plates and mix in a little liquid soap. Encourage the children to make handprints on the sides of the "teepee" for decoration.

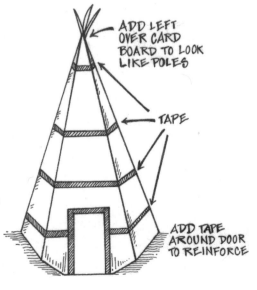

6. When the teepee is dry, place play items such as a plastic fire pit, fake furs, a drum, pretend food that Native Americans may have eaten, bowls, a large pot, and so on in the area.

More to do

Books: Have books available about Native Americans.
Circle Time: Read stories about Native Americans. Talk about the types of dwellings they had.
Music: Play Native American music.

❖❖ Sandra Nagel, White Lake, MI

Rocket Ship

Materials

Large box, such as a refrigerator box
Matte knife (adult only)
Two empty wastepaper baskets
Silver duct tape
Small chairs
Tempera paint and brushes

What to do

1. Make the rocket ship before the children arrive. Start by turning the refrigerator box on one side, with both ends closed.
2. Cut a door into the side of the box.

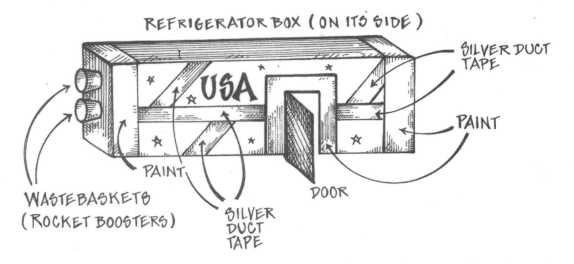

REFRIGERATOR BOX (ON ITS SIDE)

SILVER DUCT TAPE

USA

PAINT

WASTEBASKETS (ROCKET BOOSTERS)

PAINT

SILVER DUCT TAPE

DOOR

3. Turn two wastepaper baskets on their sides and tape them to one end of the box. These are the "rocket boosters."

4. Put two chairs inside the box for the astronauts to sit on.

5. Use tempera paint to decorate the outside and inside of the spaceship, creating dials and gauges. If desired, ask the children to help you with this step.

6. Put the rocket ship into the Dramatic Play area and encourage the children to take turns playing "spaceship."

More to do

Science: Put peel-off stickers of the planets on the window of the room and discuss them. Brainstorm what they think they would find on another planet. Ask them what they would take with them if they traveled in a spaceship.

Related book

Little Bear Goes to the Moon by Frank Ashe

❖❖ Barbara Saul, Eureka, CA

"I've Been Working on the Railroad"

Materials

Large refrigerator box
Matte knife (adult only)
Four sheets of black railroad board
Hot glue gun (adult only)
One sheet of white railroad board
Small chairs
Tempera paint and brushes
Railroad play items, such as a conductor's hat, whistle, and so on

What to do

1. Make a train using a large box before the children arrive. Turn the refrigerator box on one side, with one end open and the other closed. The closed end will be the front of the train.

2. Cut out a square approximately 12" x 12" to be the window of the train engine.

3. Cut out a large circle, about 36" diameter, from each of the four pieces of black railroad board. Use the hot gun to attach these to the large box for the wheels.

4. Cut two lengths of white railroad board about 6" wide. Glue each end of a piece to connect the two wheels onto each side of the train.

5. Put two chairs inside the train for the engineer and helper.

6. Use the tempera paint to decorate the outside of the train. If desired, ask the children to help you with this step.

7. Put the train engine in the Dramatic Play area. You can also place small chairs behind the engine for the passengers to sit on.

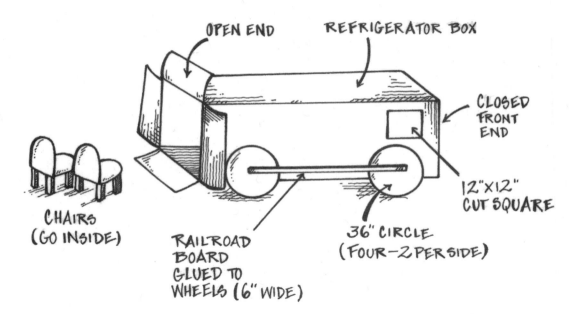

More to do

Invite parents to set up a model train in the room.
Field Trip: Take a field trip to a local train station or museum.

Related song

"I've Been Working on the Railroad"

Related books

The Little Engine that Could by Watty Piper
Thomas the Train book series

❖❖ Barbara Saul, Eureka, CA

The Wet and Dry Laundromat

Materials

4 large boxes
Duct tape
Matte knife (adult only)
Poster board
Markers
Laundry baskets, variety of clothes, plastic hangers, magazines,
    change sorter (for pretend change machine),
    empty soapboxes, fabric softener containers, and so on
Table and chairs

What to do

1. Tape the four boxes closed.
2. Cut out a large circle on any untaped side of each box.
3. Put a piece of poster board over each circle and cut it to fit that side of the box. Tape one edge to the box, so that it can be lifted much like you would lift the lid of a washing machine.
4. Label two of the boxes "washer." Label the other two boxes "dryer."
5. Place the four boxes in the Dramatic Play area, so that the washers have the circle on top and the dryers have the circle facing front.

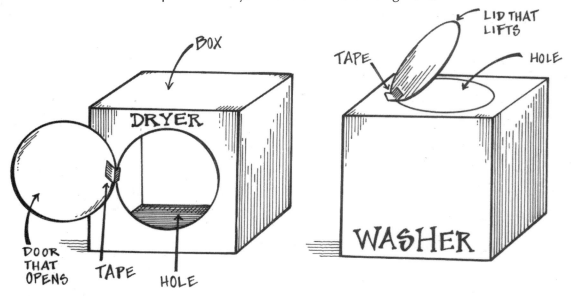

6. Put a small table at one end of the boxes. Put the change machine, empty soap boxes, and softener containers on it.
7. Put baskets, hangers, and clothes at the other end of the washers and dryers.
8. Line up a few chairs against the wall and place magazines nearby. The other furniture in the area can be used as a clothes-folding area.
9. Label the entrance to this area "The Wash and Dry." Encourage the children to play in the laundromat!

More to do

Math: Encourage the children to sort the clothes by color and match socks.

❖❖ Ann Gudowski, Johnstown, PA

Ice Cream Shop

Materials

Cardboard
Scissors
White, pink, and brown yarn
Lightweight tagboard
Tape
Shoebox
Empty, clean ice cream bucket
Ice cream scoop
Pretend cash register and play money, optional

What to do

1. Cut out a 5" (12 cm) piece of cardboard.
2. Make white, pink, and brown pompons by wrapping yarn around the piece of cardboard. When you have wrapped the desired amount, slide the yarn off the cardboard and tie it in the middle with a matching piece of yarn. Cut the end loops and fluff. These are the balls of "ice cream."
3. Cut out cones from tagboard using a pattern similar to the one in the illustration.
4. Roll the tagboard into a cone shape and tape the edges together.
5. Cut six circles in the top of a shoebox just big enough to hold the cones.
6. Put the pompoms into an empty ice cream bucket and the cones into the cone holder. Use an ice cream scoop to serve up ice cream cones!

7. Help the children make signs for an ice cream shop. If desired, add a cash register and a place to sit.

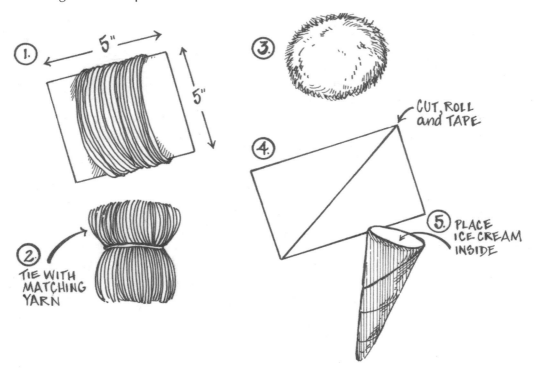

❖❖ Catherine Shogren, Eagan, MN

Hair Salon

Materials

Items typically found in a beauty shop, such as empty shampoo bottles, empty hair color boxes, combs, brushes, curlers, toy blow dryers and curling irons, mirrors, and kitchen play furniture

Old magazines

Scissors

What to do

1. Set up play furniture to look like a beauty shop. Use the refrigerator as a cabinet to hold beauty supplies. Place a chair in front of the sink to make a hair washing area. Tape construction paper over the top of the stove to hide the burners and tape a small mirror on the back of it. Place a small chair in front of the stove. This is where the "customer" will sit.

2. Place a few other chairs in the area to make a waiting area for customers. Put some books on a small table next to the chairs.
3. Cut out large pictures depicting a variety of hairstyles from magazines. Tape the pictures on a wall in the area.
4. The children can take turns being hairstylists or customers.

More to do

Art: Encourage the children to draw pictures of their own heads on paper or paper plates. They can use different kinds of yarn to make hair.
More Art: Show the children how to paint pictures using old combs and brushes to create different textures and lines on the paper.
Books: Read the children stories about different occupations.

Related book

Uncle Jed's Barbershop by Margaret King Mitchell

❖❖ Sandra Suffoletto Ryan, Buffalo, NY

Pet Store

Materials

Stuffed animals
Play money and play cash register
Toy comb and brushes
Old dog leashes
Collars
Empty dog biscuit boxes
Labels and markers

What to do

1. Put a play cash register with play money on a table in the Dramatic Play area. Put the stuffed animals, combs, leashes, collars, and so on in the area too.
2. Encourage the children to play pet store. Some of the children can be the animal caretakers, some can work as cashiers, and some can be the customers.
3. The children can make price tags using labels and markers, brush the pets and feed them, and purchase the pets.

❖❖ Lisa Chichester, Parkersburg, WV

Post Office

Materials

Cardboard box
Markers
Table
Post Office sign
Stickers
Large bag
Newspaper, postcards, letters, magazines, small boxes

What to do

1. Beforehand, make a "mail box" using a large cardboard box and markers. If desired, make letters for the children and write each child's name on an envelope.
2. Place materials on a table in the Dramatic Play area. The children can use stickers for stamps and a big bag as a mail carrier bag.
3. Encourage the children to "sort" the mail and pretend to be mail carriers delivering mail to their friends.

❖❖ Barbara Lindsay, Mason City, IA

Outdoor Hospital

Materials

Dr. Shawn by Petronella Breinburg, optional
Large outdoor area
Large wood blocks
Old washable blankets and quilts
Doctor props such as stethoscopes, thermometers, blood pressure cuffs, medicine bottles with the caps removed, ice bags, and so on
Tricycles ("taxi trike" type, which have an extra seat in the back) or wagons
Baby dolls
Clipboards, marker, yarn, and paper, optional

What to do

1. If desired, read *Dr. Shawn* to the children. Ask the children if they would like to play hospital outside.
2. Use large wooden blocks to outline a hospital area in the playground.
3. Set up a "treatment" area using old quilts, blankets, and other doctor materials.
4. Encourage the children to act out getting hurt or becoming sick on the playground. One child can use a taxi trike or wagon to transport the sick child to the hospital area, and the "doctors" can treat the child.
5. The children can also bring hurt or sick baby dolls to the hospital for treatment.
6. If desired, make "patient charts." Attach a chunky crayon or washable marker to a few clipboards with a length of string or yarn. Demonstrate how doctors, nurses, or hospital personnel use the clipboard to hold papers that track each patient's progress, medications, and treatments.

More to do

Make patient ID bands. Give each child a 3" x 6" piece of oaktag or tagboard. Encourage the children to use markers and small stickers to decorate the oaktag in any manner they wish. Print each child's name on his oaktag, put the band on his wrist, and secure with tape. Explain that every patient in a hospital must wear a patient identification band to assure they get the right medications and treatments.

Related books

Curious George Goes to the Hospital by Margaret Rey
Island Baby by Holly Keller
When Mommy Is Sick by Ferne Sherkin-Langer

❖❖ Virginia Jean Herrod, Columbia, SC

Class Restaurant

Materials

Playhouse items, such as a play stove, refrigerator, sink, table, and so on
Plastic "food" or pictures of food
Clipboard with paper and pencil
Plastic knives, forks, and spoons
Paper plates
Pieces of white drawing paper for "menus"
Aprons
Chef's hats
Play cash register and plastic coins, optional

What to do

1. During circle time, ask the children to share experiences they have had eating in a restaurant.
2. Discuss the roles of cook, wait persons, and customers.
3. Set up the Dramatic Play center like a restaurant.
4. Encourage the children to take turns being the waiters, cooks, and customers.

More to do

Use real food in the "restaurant." This can be the children's snack.

Related books

Bread and Jam for Francis by Russell Hoban
Green Eggs and Ham by Dr. Seuss
Gregory the Terrible Eater by Mitchell Sharmat

❖❖ Barbara Saul, Eureka, CA

"Check It Out" Library

Materials

Books
Index cards
Marker or pen
Old keyboard or computer
Pillows and tables

What to do

1. Talk to the children about their visits to the library. Ask them what kinds of things they see and what librarians do. Talk about what "borrowing" means.
2. Make a "library card" for each child by writing his name on an index card.
3. Encourage the children to play "library" in the book area or Dramatic Play area. One child can be the librarian, another child can reshelve the books, and someone else can be the storybook person.
4. The other children can use their library cards to check out books. The librarian can use an old keyboard to "check out" the books. (You may want to tell them how many books they can check out at a time.)
5. Make sure you put pillows and tables in the "library" so they can read there.
6. Let each child check out one book from the room to take home for the night.

More to do

Send a letter home to parents telling them about your class library and invite them to take their child to the library to get a card and check out books.
Field Trip: Take the children on a field trip to a library.

❖❖ Holly Dzierzanowski, Brenham, TX

Beautiful Jewelry

Materials

Jewelry box
Necklace holders
Ring boxes
Mirror
Assortment of inexpensive costume jewelry

What to do

1. Put the jewelry box, ring boxes, necklace holders, and a mirror in the Dramatic Play area. Add inexpensive clip-on earrings, bracelets, old watches, rings, necklaces, and so on. Don't forget to include jewelry for boys!
2. Ask parents to donate to this collection, and look for inexpensive costume jewelry at yard sales.
3. Encourage the children to be creative with the jewelry in their dramatic play. Ask them if there are other ways they could use the jewelry, such as in a jewelry store or as part of a fashion show.

More to do

Art: Cut drinking straws into ½" lengths. Cut out circles ½" in diameter from construction paper and punch holes into each circle. Cut 20" lengths of yarn and wrap one end of each length with a small amount of masking tape to stiffen the end. Encourage the children to make necklaces and bracelets to add to the jewelry boxes. After they string items on the yarn, help them tie the ends together.

Math: Encourage the children to cut out pictures of jewelry from magazines. Collect the pictures and show the children how to sort the pictures into separate groups, such as rings, bracelets, pins, and necklaces.

◆◆ Barbara Backer, Charleston, SC

Felt Board Snowman

Materials

White felt
Scissors
Pictures of hats, gloves, shoes, and so on
Glue stick
Tagboard
Rubber cement
Flannel board

What to do

1. Cut out three different sizes of balls for the snowman's body from the felt.
2. Cut out an assortment of pictures to add to the snowman: pipe, hat, gloves, sticks (for arms), scarf, and so on.
3. Glue the pictures to tagboard using a glue stick. Cut them out.
4. Attach felt to the backs of the pictures using rubber cement.
5. Put out the snowmen items with the flannel board for the children to manipulate during playtime. They can decorate him as desired.

More to do

Art: Make snowmen for a craft project using white tempera paint and crayons to add details.

◆❖ Jackie Wright, Enid, OK

Sandy Printing

Materials

Large trays with low sides, such as a cafeteria tray
Clean sterilized sand
Popsicle sticks or dull pencils, optional

What to do

1. Pour a couple of cups of sand into each tray, enough to cover the tray's surface to about a ½" depth.
2. Put the trays on a low table within the children's reach.
3. Demonstrate how to use a finger, Popsicle stick, or dull pencil to print and draw in the sand on the tray.
4. To erase the design, simply smooth the sand with your hand.
5. Encourage the children to practice their fine motor skills by using the sand trays.

More to do

Make colored sand. Put a couple of cups of sand in a zipper closure plastic bag and add food coloring and a drop or two of alcohol. Close the bag and shake it vigorously. Spread the colored sand on newspaper to dry.

Art: Create plaster cast impressions of interesting sand drawings by filling the depression on the sand with plaster of Paris. After the plaster has cured, lift it from the sand. Brush the sand off to reveal the plaster impression. Paint, if desired.

Sand and Water Table: If the trays are impractical or impossible for your group, then put a shallow amount of sand into the sensory table and let the children experiment there.

◆❖ Virginia Jean Herrod, Columbia, SC

Homemade Etch-a-Sketch

Materials

Hair gel
Large zipper-closure plastic bag
Tempera paint
Glitter
Duct tape
Lid from a plastic storage container or Tupperware box

What to do

1. Fill a zipper closure plastic bag half full with hair gel.
2. Add a little tempera paint and glitter. Zip the bag closed.
3. Tape the edges of the bag onto the edges of the square lid.
4. Encourage the children to move their fingers through the bag of gel. It acts like an etch-a-sketch.

More to do

Put a few small objects into the bag, such as buttons, for the children to feel.

◆◆ Jean Potter, Charleston, WV

Dinosaur Eggs

Materials

Dough
Small dinosaur figures
Plastic bag

What to do

1. Before the children arrive, cover each dinosaur figure with dough to resemble an egg shape.
2. Give each child a "dough egg" in a plastic bag.
3. Ask the child to carefully break apart his egg to see the treasure inside.

More to do

Blocks: Put dinosaurs in the Block Area to add a new dimension.

Related books

Bones, Bones, Dinosaur Bones by Byron Barton
Danny and the Dinosaurs by Syd Hoff
Digging Up Dinosaurs by Aliki
How I Captured a Dinosaur by Henry Schwartz

◆◆ Sandy L. Scott, Vancouver, WA

Polishing Silver

Materials

A tarnished silver teaspoon
Small sponge
Small piece of soft cloth
Toothpaste
Other silver items, optional

What to do

1. Put a little toothpaste on a damp sponge.
2. Rub a small area of a tarnished spoon in a circular motion. Point out the tarnish on the sponge.
3. Rub the polished area with the dry cloth, pointing out the shine.
4. Encourage the children to take turns polishing the spoon.
5. If desired, polish other silver items.
6. This activity seems almost like magic, as the children watch blackened metal turn shiny and bright. Using toothpaste instead of silver polish makes this perfectly safe.

More to do

Language: Vocabulary development—silver, tarnish, polish, metal.
Science: Explain that the silver reacts to oxygen in the air and makes tarnish.

◆◆ Mary Jo Shannon, Roanoke, VA

Cut and Stop

Materials

Construction paper
Thick black marker
Safety scissors

What to do

1. On a few sheets of construction paper, draw a single line extending from one edge of the paper to midpoint.
2. Give each child a piece of the marked paper and a pair of safety scissors.
3. Explain to the children that the line on the paper marks a place for them to cut. Hold up a paper and demonstrate where to place the scissors to start.
4. Open your scissors wide and say, "Open them." Close the scissors to make the first cut and say, "Close them."
5. Encourage the children to mimic your actions and words. Chant "Open them, close them" as you cut on the black line to the end.
6. Remember to cut slowly so that the children can keep up with you.
7. At the end of your line, stop cutting and say, "Stop."
8. Praise the children for their efforts and encourage them to keep practicing.

Note: Always supervise young children when they use scissors. The child who cannot cut paper will find it amazingly easy to cut a friend's hair.

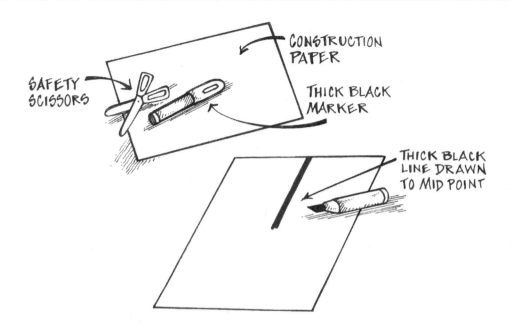

SAFETY SCISSORS

CONSTRUCTION PAPER

THICK BLACK MARKER

THICK BLACK LINE DRAWN TO MID POINT

More to do

Encourage the children to cut out pictures from old magazines. Offer help as needed but don't control the children's cutting. They will learn by doing. If desired, draw a thick black line around the picture to help the child cut it out.

Music and Movement: Practice starting and stopping in other ways. Play "freeze dance" by having the children dance to music and freeze when the music stops.

More Music and Movement: Use the chant below to lead the children in other start and stop activities. Simply change the chant to suit your needs. For example:

> *We're going to hop, hop, hop*
> *Hop, hop, hop*
> *Hop, hop, hop*
> *And stop!*

Original chant

Cut and Stop Chant

> *We're going to cut, cut, cut*
> *Cut, cut, cut*
> *Cut, cut, cut*
> *And stop!*

❖ Virginia Jean Herrod, Columbia, SC

It's Hammer Time!

Materials

Log, approximately 18" (45 cm) x 12" (30 cm)
12" (30 cm) square of cardboard
Bag of roofing nails
Hammers
Safety goggles

What to do

1. Place the log on top of the cardboard square.
2. Hammer a few nails far enough into the log so the children won't smash their fingers when they try to do it.

3. Ask the children to put on safety goggles. Encourage them to drive the nails all the way into the log. Supervise closely!

4. Limit two children at a time unless the length of the log is longer.

5. Once the children have filled up one side of the log, just flip it over and use the other side.

More to do

Math: Count the number of times it takes for each child to hit the nails all the way into the log.

Related books

Building a House by Byron Barton
Construction Zone by Tana Hoban
Mike Mulligan and His Steam Shovel by Virginia Burton

Related song

"If I Had a Hammer"

◆◆ Vicki Whitehead, Citronelle, AL

Hammer Fun

Materials

Several sturdy toy hammers
Several sturdy pieces of Styrofoam in a variety of shapes and sizes
Golf tees (wood or plastic)

What to do

1. Give each child a hammer and pieces of foam.

2. Encourage the children to hammer tees into the Styrofoam. They can attach smaller pieces to larger ones so they can build buildings, or whatever they wish.

3. Show the children how to use the "claw" on the hammer to remove the "nails" and use them again to build something different.

More to do

Math: Provide rulers or tape measures and ask the children to measure what they are working on. Incorporate counting skills by giving them some instructions such as, "Use 10 nails on this building."

Related books

A Carpenter by Douglas Florian
Tools by Venice Shone

Related song

"Johnny Hammers with One Hammer"

❖❖ Maxine Della Fave, Raleigh, NC

Wind Me Up

Materials

Assortment of bolts, nuts, and wing nuts
Metal washers in a variety of sizes
Small bowls

What to do

1. This activity must be supervised at all times. Put all of the nuts, bolts, and washers into a small pile.
2. Give the children small bowls and ask them to sort the materials.
3. When they are done, demonstrate how to screw the nuts and washers onto the bolts. Encourage them to practice doing this.

More to do

Put construction toys nearby. If small dump trucks are available, include small objects suck as Popsicle sticks or small blocks for the children to haul and dump.

❖❖ Barbara Saul, Eureka, CA

Feel and Tell

Materials

3-pound coffee can
Metal file
Colored self-adhesive plastic
Ribbed sweater sleeve
Plastic, colored duct tape
Objects to put inside the can:
    Shapes: circles, triangles, and so on cut from cardboard, plastic, or wood
    Textures: a cotton ball, rock, piece of fur, modeling clay, and so on
    Common objects: a pencil, coin, plastic spoon, and so on

What to do

Directions for Making the Feely Can

1. Remove both ends of the coffee can. Use a metal file to smooth any rough edges.
2. Cover the can with self-adhesive plastic. Place the plastic lid on one end of the can.
3. Stretch the cut end of the sweater sleeve to fit over the other end of the can and attach it with duct tape.
4. Remove the lid and add objects to the can. Change categories occasionally to keep the activity interesting.

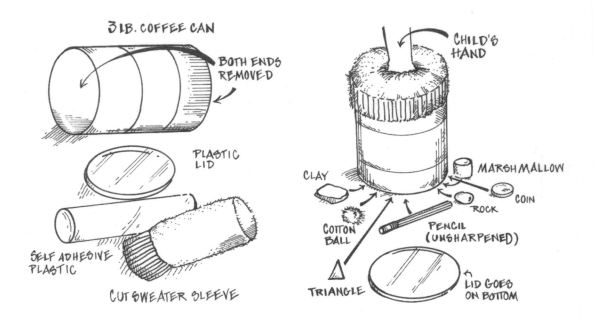

3 LB. COFFEE CAN   BOTH ENDS REMOVED   PLASTIC LID   SELF ADHESIVE PLASTIC   CUT SWEATER SLEEVE

CHILD'S HAND   CLAY   MARSHMALLOW   COIN   ROCK   COTTON BALL   PENCIL (UNSHARPENED)   TRIANGLE   LID GOES ON BOTTOM

Procedure:

1. Encourage the child to reach through the sleeve to feel an object.
2. Before removing her hand, ask the child to identify the object.
3. The child removes the object through the sleeve, to see if she was correct.
4. Repeat with the other children.

More to do

Language: Encourage the children to describe the textures of the objects, such as hard, soft, round, sharp, pointed, cold, rough, and smooth.

Math: When all objects have been identified, ask the child to remove the plastic lid and count them as she drops them into the can.

◆❖ Mary Jo Shannon, Roanoke, VA

Shape to Shape

Materials

Marker
Scissors
Two colors of heavy stock poster board
Glue or paste

What to do

1. Draw shapes, such as circles, squares, and triangles about 4" in diameter on one color of poster board. Cut out the shapes, without cutting the area of board around them (like a template).
2. Glue the template to the other color of poster board to form a shape puzzle.
3. Invite the child to choose cutouts and match them to the shapes on the board.

More to do

Math: If desired, use white poster board and color code individual shapes to the shapes on template. Ask the children to identify both the shape and color.

◆❖ Margery A. Kranyik, Hyde Park, MA

Matching Shapes

Materials

Tagboard or heavy paper
Scissors
Laminate or clear contact paper
Clothespins in different colors (or plain clothespins and markers)
Markers

What to do

1. Cut the heavy paper into shapes such as circles, squares, and triangles.
2. Laminate them or cover them with clear contact paper for durability.
3. Purchase colored clothespin at a dollar stores or hardware store. If you cannot find clothespins in different colors, purchase wooden ones and color the pincher part with a marker.
4. Color the paper shapes to match the color of the clothespins. The object is to match the color of the clothespins to the same colored shape.
5. Encourage the children to match the colors by squeezing the clothespin and attaching it to the shape. This is a great way to strengthen fingers for pre-writing skills.

More to do

Math: This is a great activity that includes colors and shapes. Once the children have mastered this activity, add numbers to the shapes. Ask the children to add that number of pins.

❖❖ Laurie Nied, Charlotte, NC

Key Match

Materials

Variety of keys, such as house keys, car keys, mail keys, small lock keys, and so on
Copy machine
Paper
Marker
Laminate or clear contact paper
Small tray

What to do

1. Collect a variety of old keys. Parents, friends, and relatives are good sources.
2. Place keys on the copier very gently so you don't scratch the glass. Then make a copy of the keys. When placing the keys on the copier, try to make sure that any distinguishing markings are facing down on the copier.
3. On the back of the copy, write how many keys there are. Then laminate it or cover it with clear contact paper.
4. Place the keys on a small tray.
5. Encourage the children to match the keys on the tray with the keys on the laminated copy. This is a very quick matching activity to make, and the children love to handle keys.
6. It is a good idea to count the keys before putting this activity away. Remind the children to keep the keys in the tray and not in their little pockets.

COPY OLD KEYS
ON TO 8½ × 11
SHEET OF PAPER
and LAMINATE

More to do

This is a good activity to use during a transportation unit.

◆◆ Debbie Barbuch, Sheboygan, WI

Match the Tops

Materials

Several small jars and bottles with screw-on tops
Tray

What to do

1. Collect several jars and bottles with different diameters. Cosmetic jars are good to use, especially those that are plastic or heavy glass that will not break easily if dropped.
2. Place the jars on a tray to define the workspace.
3. Remove the tops from the jars, emphasizing the turn of your hand to the left.
4. Mix up the tops. Then, match the tops to the jars.
5. Screw the tops onto the jars, emphasizing the turn of your hand to the right.
6. Now invite the child to repeat the procedure.
7. This activity develops coordination, left/right discrimination, and visual discrimination.

More to do

Vary the jars and bottles. Nuts and bolts may be used when children have mastered handling the larger objects.

❖ Mary Jo Shannon, Roanoke, VA

Clipping Clothespins

Materials

A plastic bowl (large, empty margarine containers work well)
Colored plastic clothespins

What to do

1. Place a few clothespins into the bowl. (Increase the number as skill develops.)
2. Demonstrate grasping the clothespin with the thumb and two fingers, squeezing to open the clothespin.
3. Place the clothespin on the rim of the bow, demonstrating the releasing your grasp to close the clothespin.

4. Repeat step 2, removing the clothespin and placing it in the bowl.

5. Invite the child to clip the clothespins to the bowl, then remove them.

6. This activity is excellent for developing small muscles of the fingers, fine motor control, and the three-finger-grasp necessary for writing.

More to do

Games: Play a relay game with clothespins. Divide the children into two teams and give each child a clothespin. The children grasp a paper cup with the clothespin, race to the goal line, return and transfer the cup to the next child in line.

Language and Color Recognition: Ask the children to sort and name the colors.

Math: Count the clothespins. Group them by color, leaving space between the colors. How many are there of each color? Which color has the most? The least?

❖❖ Mary Jo Shannon, Roanoke, VA

Clipping Colors

Materials

Clothespins
Markers
Construction paper
Scissors
Plastic bowl or box
Glue

What to do

1. Beforehand, use a marker to color each clothespin a different color.

2. Cut construction paper into squares. You should have one square for each color of clothespin.

3. Glue each square to the outside of the container. Put the clothespins into the container.

4. Show the children how to open and close the clothespin. Next ask where they think you should put the blue pin. It doesn't take long before the children realize that the blue pin goes on the blue paper, and so on

5. Encourage the children to practice this activity. Even if they don't get the colors right at first, they're using their small muscles.

Related books

Color, Shapes, and Sizes by Michelle Warrence
The Colors by Monique Felix

❖❖ Sandra Hutchins Lucas, Cox's Creek, KY

Tweezer Pick Up

Materials

Masking tape
Small bowls or plates in a variety of colors, two of each color
Variety of items to pick up that match the tong sizes, such as wooden cubes,
    cotton balls, sunflower seeds, grapes, and so on
Different size tongs, such as tongs to pick up ice cubes and tongs to pick up corn
    (Montessori catalogs are a good source for unique tongs)
Tweezers

What to do

1. Mark boundaries on a table in front of each chair using masking tape. This is
   where the children are to keep the items that they are working with. It will
   provide a visual cue and help keep the materials on the table.
2. Place two bowls or plates of the same color inside each of the marked
   boundaries.
3. Fill one of each color bowl or plate with the items to pick up.
4. Place the matching size tongs or tweezers with the items.
5. Show the children how to pick up the items and transfer them from one plate
   or bowl to another using the tongs or tweezers.

More to do

Math: Using paper plates, write one number in the center of each plate (1, 2, 3,
4, 5, and so on, as high as appropriate for your children). Ask the children to
count out the appropriate number of items using the tongs or tweezers and place
them on the plates.

❖❖ Ann Gudowski, Johnstown, PA

Lacing Cards

Materials

Picture of item relating to theme
Construction paper
Marker
Scissors
Laminate or clear contact paper
Single hole punch
Shoestring with coated ends

What to do

1. Find a simple picture of an object that relates to your theme or unit. For example, if you are studying farms, copy a large outline of a barn, pig, cow, tractor, and so on.
2. Enlarge and copy the picture onto construction paper.
3. Cut out the picture of the object so that there is no extra paper around the outline.
4. Laminate it or cover it with contact paper.
5. Punch holes around the outside edge of the object. Leave about 1 cm between the hole and the outside edge, and space the holes about ?" apart.
6. Finally, tie a shoestring to one of the holes. Then, show the children how to lace the card. They do this by weaving the string under and over the card until all the holes have been passed through.

1. ENLARGED COPY
2. CUT OUT
3. LAMINATED

SHOE STRING

More to do

This activity is easily transferred into any area of the curriculum. You can create lacing cards to fit any subject, such as a microscope or a moon shape for science; a ship or picture or a historical character for social studies; an apple or tooth for health and nutrition; a guitar or music note for music; and so on.

❖ Kacie Farmer, Dale, IN

Sewing Card

Materials

Pencil
3" x 5" index cards
Hole punch
Scissors
Yarn
Transparent tape

What to do

1. Using a pencil, draw each child's first initial on an index card.
2. Punch holes along the outline of the initial, leaving about ½" in between each hole.
3. Cut the yarn into large strips, and wrap one end of each strip with tape to prevent fraying. Make a knot at the other end.
4. Give each child a strip of yarn and her index card. Help the children sew around their initial.

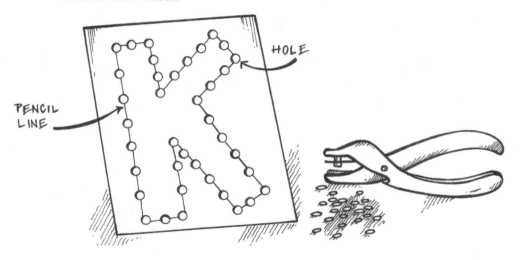

More to do

Fold 3" x 5" index cards in half, and punch holes along the open edges. Encourage the children to sew the cards closed with the yarn.

❖❖ Dotti Enderle, Richmond, TX

Texture Books

Materials

Construction paper
Hole punch
Variety of textured items, such as sandpaper, fabric (corduroy, satin, flannel, velour, terrycloth), wallpaper, buttons, old towels, and burlap sack pieces
Glue
Yarn

What to do

1. Fold construction paper in half widthwise (five pieces per child). Punch two holes into one side of each piece of paper.
2. Give each child five pieces of folded paper.
3. Ask the children to choose five textured items, one for each page. Be creative. The goal is to provide the children with different textures to experience.
4. Encourage the children to glue the items on the pages.
5. Give each child a piece of yarn and help her thread the yarn through the two holes on each page and tie the yarn into a bow. Her book is complete.

More to do

Put a sample of each of the different textures into a bag. Ask the children to take turns reaching in (without looking) and describing how the item feels (smooth, rough, soft, hard, and so on).

❖❖ Melissa O. Markham, Huddleston, VA

Cornstarch Beads

Materials

¾ cup (90 g) flour
½ cup (125 g) salt
½ cup (60 g) cornstarch
Warm water
Mixing bowl
Toothpicks
Paint and brushes
String

What to do

1. Pour flour, salt, and cornstarch into a mixing bowl and add warm water until the mixture can be kneaded into a stiff dough.
2. Lightly dust the children's hands with flour.
3. Encourage the children to shape the dough into beads.
4. Poke a toothpick through each bead and allow them to dry.
5. Encourage the children to paint the beads.
6. Show the children how to string the beads onto string to make bracelets.

More to do

Make little people out of the dough.

❖ Sandy L. Scott, Vancouver, WA

Rhyme Die

Materials

Cube-shaped box (at least 1′ x 1′ x 1′)
Construction paper
Glue
Permanent marker
Clear contact paper

What to do

1. Cover the box with construction paper and glue it in place.
2. Write the title of a nursery rhyme on one side and draw (or use clip art) a picture to represent that rhyme. For example, Humpty Dumpty sitting on a wall.
3. Cover each side with a different rhyme and picture that represents that rhyme.
4. Cover the box with clear contact paper.
5. Use the "rhyme die" at circle time. Pick a child to roll the cube, and together recite or sing the rhyme that is on top.

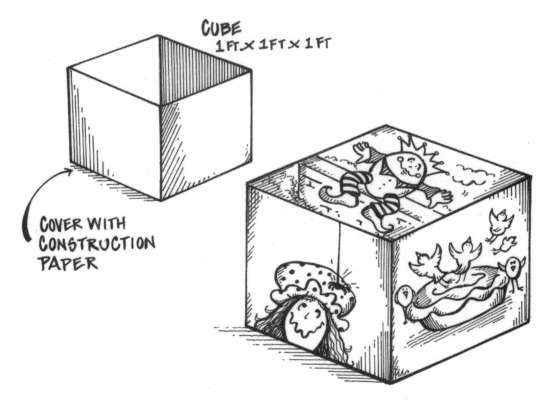

CUBE
1 FT x 1 FT x 1 FT

COVER WITH CONSTRUCTION PAPER

More to do

After the children are familiar with the rhymes, begin asking questions about the rhyme that is selected. For example, how did the king's horses and king's men put Humpty Dumpty back together again?

❖ Ann Gudowski, Johnstown, PA

Let's Sing Song Cards

Materials

Poster board
Pictures
Glue
Markers
Laminate or clear contact paper

What to do

1. For each song and fingerplay you use in your class, make a song card for it. Draw or glue appropriate pictures on poster board. For example, for "Old McDonald," use a picture of a farmer, a barn, and animals.
2. Write the words in large print underneath the photos.
3. Laminate the cards or cover them with clear contact paper.
4. The children can use the cards to learn the words to a song, to choose a song during music time, or to sing during free time.

❖ Brenda Miller, Olean, NY

Silly Songs

Materials

None

What to do

1. Sing the following song to the tune of "Frère Jacques."

    Where is Frankenstein? Where is Frankenstein?
    On a slab, in the lab.
    Getting brand new fingers, getting brand new toes,
    And there he goes, there he goes.

    Using new feet, using new feet
    To trick or treat, trick or treat.
    Showing up in knickers,
    Go and hide the Snickers!
    Give him Cream of Wheat, give him Cream of Wheat!

2. Sing the following song with the children.

Old Dan Tucker

Old Dan Tucker was a mountain man,
Washed his face in a frying pan.
Combed his hair with a wagon wheel,
Died with a toothache in his heel.
Get out the way for old Dan Tucker,
Get out the way for old Dan Tucker,
Get out the way for old Dan Tucker,
Came too late to eat his supper.

Old Dan Tucker saw a ghost,
Sitting in his kitchen eating his roast.
Old Dan Tucker got such a scare—
He ran out the door in his underwear!
Get out the way for old Dan Tucker,
Get out the way for old Dan Tucker,
Get out the way for old Dan Tucker,
Came too late to eat his supper.

(Additional verses by Penni Smith):
Old Dan Tucker rode his horse,
To town to find a new golf course.
Got into a fight with a cook named Ross
Went home wearing spaghetti sauce!

Old Dan Tucker went to town
To buy himself a suit of brown.
He got lost in Chinatown,
Slid on rice and he fell down!

Repeat chorus of:
Get out the way for old Dan Tucker,
Get out the way for old Dan Tucker,
Get out the way for old Dan Tucker,
Came too late to eat his supper.

3. Sing the following song to the tune of "Five Little Ducks."

Five little elves went out to play
Over the hills and far away.
When Santa Claus called, "Ho, ho, ho, ho!"
Only four little elves went home real slow.

Four little elves went out to play
Over the hills and far away.
When Santa Claus called, "Ho, ho, ho, ho!"
Three little elves decided to go.

Three little elves went out to play
Over the hills and far away.
When Santa Claus yelled, "Ho, ho, ho, ho!"
Only two little elves decided to go.

Two little elves went out to play
Over the hills and far away.
When Santa Claus yelled, "Ho, ho, ho, ho!"
Only one little elf went home real slow.

One little elf went out to play
Over the hills and far away.
When Santa Claus called, "Ho!"
And the last little elf went home real slow.

❖❖ Penni L. Smith, Riverside, CA

Songs throughout the Day

Materials

None

What to do

1. Sing the following songs throughout the day.

Find Your Cubby (by Deborah R. Gallagher)
Find your cubby
Put your things in.
Have a seat
And we'll begin.

Find Your Mat (by Deborah R. Gallagher)
(Tune: "London Bridge")
Find your mat and have a seat,
Have a seat, have a seat.
Find a mat and have a seat
It is storytime/songtime.

The Sun (adapted by Deborah R. Gallagher)
(Tune: "The Farmer in the Dell")
In the morning the sun comes up
And marches all the day.
At noon it stands right overhead;
At night it goes away.

2. Sing the following songs about animals.

All Around My Backyard (adapted by Deborah R. Gallagher)
(Tune: "I'm a Little Teapot")

All around my back yard
My dog runs.
He runs around in circles
He runs back and forth.
When I call to him
He comes right then.
He jumps up and down
Then runs around again.

Bark, Bark Little Doggie (adapted by Deborah R. Gallagher)
(Tune: "Ten Little Indians")

Bark, bark little doggie.
Bark, bark little doggie.
Bark, bark little doggie
All around the yard.

In the Pond (adapted by Deborah R. Gallagher)
(Tune: "The Farmer in the Dell")

The frog lives in the pond,
His tongue is oh, so long.
It reaches high to catch a fly,
A yummy treat for him.

Ladybugs (adapted by Deborah R. Gallagher)
(Tune: "She'll Be Coming 'Round the Mountain")

Oh, I love the little spotted ladybugs.
Oh, I love the little spotted ladybugs.
Oh, they are so very tiny
And their spotted shells are shiny.
Oh, I love the little spotted ladybugs.

Meow, Meow Little Kitty (by Deborah R. Gallagher)
(Tune: "Ten Little Indians")

Meow, meow little kitty.
Meow, meow little kitty.
Meow, meow little kitty
All around the house.

3. The following songs are circus songs.

I'm a Little Circus Clown (by Deborah R. Gallagher)
(Tune: "I'm a Little Teapot")
I'm a little circus clown short and fat.
Here is my funny face and here is my hat.
I have a great big smile and a big red nose
And great big silly shoes covering my toes.

When you come to the circus
You'll have lots of fun
There's lions and bears
And elephants that weigh a ton.
Just come to the big top
And sit yourself right down
There'll be lots of laughter,
The best in the town.

We're Going to the Circus (by Deborah R. Gallagher)
(Tune: "Did You Ever see a Lassie?")
We're going to the circus,
The circus, the circus.
We're going to the circus, we'll have so much fun.
There are lions, and bears,
And clowns with bright hair.
We're going to the circus, we'll have so much fun.

We're going to the circus,
The circus, the circus.
We're going to the circus, we'll have so much fun.
There are horses and elephants
And clowns wearing funny pants
We're going to the circus, we'll have so much fun.

4. The following songs are food songs.

Popcorn (by Deborah R. Gallagher)
(Tune: "Frère Jacques")
Pop, pop, popping.
Pop, pop, popping.
Our popcorn, our popcorn.

Popping, popping, popcorn.
Popping, popping, popcorn.
Pop, pop, pop. Pop, pop, pop.

Vegetable Soup (adapted by Deborah R. Gallagher)
(Tune: "Farmer in the Dell")
We're going to make some soup,
We're going to make some soup.
Stir slow, around we go.
We're going to make some soup.

First we add the broth...
Now we add some carrots...
Next we add some celery...
(add any additional vegetables)

We're Gonna Make Some Pizza (by Deborah R. Gallagher)
(Tune: "Heigh-ho the Derry-O")
We're gonna make some pizza.
We're gonna make some pizza.
Heigh-ho the derry-o
We're gonna make some pizza.

First you take the bread,
Then you add the sauce,
Sprinkle on the cheese,
Put it in the oven.
Pizza is so yummy.
Pizza is so yummy.
Hi-ho the derry-o
Pizza tastes so good.

5. The following songs are "me, my friends, and my family" songs.

Friends Are Here (by Deborah R. Gallagher)
(Tune: "Jingle Bells")
Friends are here, friends are there,
Friends are everywhere.
Lots of laughter, songs, and play
All throughout the day.

Friends have fun in the sun
And even in the rain.
Friends love to play and share.

I Look in the Mirror (adapted by Deborah R. Gallagher)
(Tune: "I'm a Little Teapot")

I look in the mirror
And who is that I see?
A very special person
Who looks a lot like me.
Eyes so bright and shiny,
A smile that's pearly white.
It's great to be me,
What a lovely sight!

I Love My Family (by Deborah R. Gallagher)
(Tune: "I Love the Flowers")

I love my daddy.
I love my mommy, too.
I love my family,
My brother and my sister too.
We love to have some fun,
In the house and in the sun.
Boom-de-ah-dah, Boom-de-ah-dah,
Boom-de-ah-dah, Boom!
Boom-de-ah-dah, Boom-de-ah-dah,
Boom-de-ah-dah, Boom!
To show how much they care.

Manners Song (by Deborah R. Gallagher)
(Tune: "If You're Happy and You Know It")

If you want something, what do you say? Please!
If you want something, what do you say? Please!
If you want something given to you;
If you want something, what do you say? Please!

When you get something, what do you say? Thank you!
When you get something, what do you say? Thank you!
When you get something you asked someone for;
When you get something, what do you say? Thank you!

If someone's in your way, what do you say? Excuse me!
If someone's in your way, what do you say? Excuse me!
If someone's in your way and you need to get around;
If someone's in your way, what do you say? Excuse me!

6. The following songs are about safety.

Matches (by Deborah R. Gallagher)
(Tune: "Did You Ever See a Lassie?")

Have you ever played with matches?
With matches, with matches?
Have you ever played with matches?
I hope that you don't.
When you light a match
A fire could catch.
Have you ever played with matches?
I hope that you don't.

Have you ever played with matches?
With matches, with matches?
Have you ever played with matches?
I hope that you don't.
Playing with matches
Can turn things to ashes.
Have you ever played with matches?
I hope that you don't.

Safe Shopping (by Deborah R. Gallagher)
(Tune: "Skip to My Lou")

No one knows me at the store.
No one knows my address or name.
I only see strangers all around,
At the mall it's just the same.

So when shopping I follow this rule:
I stay close to my Mom and Dad.
I don't want to wander off
Staying safe makes me so glad!

Scissor Cutting (by Deborah R. Gallagher)
(Tune: "Open, Shut Them")

Open, shut them, open, shut them
Give a little snip.
Open, shut them, open, shut them
Make another clip.

Cut along the dotted lines
To cut out your design.
Use the scissors carefully,
And you'll do just fine.

Open, shut them, open, shut them
Give a little snip.
Open, shut them, open, shut them
Make another clip.

Walking Feet (by Deborah R. Gallagher)
(Tune: "Rock Around the Clock")

Walking feet, walking feet.
We must use our walking feet.
We got to walk, walk, walk, down the hall.
We got to walk, walk, walk, down the hall.
Walking feet, down the hall we go.

7. The following songs are about the seasons.

Fall Is Here (by Deborah R. Gallagher)
(Tune: "Row, Row, Row Your Boat")

Fall, fall, fall is here.
Let's all have some fun.
Leaves are falling everywhere,
Bright colors, every one.

Fall, fall, fall is here.
Rake the leaves up high.
Gather leaves both far and near,
Let's all give it a try.

I'm Dressed Warmly (by Deborah R. Gallagher)
(Tune: "Twinkle, Twinkle, Little Star")
When the winter's cold has come,
Dress up warmly everyone.
Put on your coat and zip it up,
Scarf and mittens, hat on top.
Winter's cold won't bother me,
I'm dressed warmly as can be!

Leaves Are Falling (by Deborah R. Gallagher)
(Tune: "Frère Jacques")
Leaves are falling, leaves are falling,
On the ground, all around.
Yellow, red and orange,
Many different colors,
To be found, to be found.

❖❖ Deborah R. Gallagher, Bridgeport, CT

Count in Spanish Song

Materials

None

What to do

1. Sing the following song to the tune of "Row, Row, Row Your Boat."

   Uno, dos, tres,
   Quatro, cinco, seis,
   Siete, ocho, nueve, diez
   Los nombres español.

❖❖ Lisa Chichester, Parkersburg, WV

Spanish Days of the Week

Materials

None

What to do

1. Sing the following song to the tune of "Bingo."

   Lunes, martes, miercoles,
   Jueves, viernes,
   Sabado, domingo,
   Que dia es hoy?
   Hoy es _____.

   (English translation)
   Monday, Tuesday, Wednesday
   Thursday, Friday
   Saturday, Sunday
   What day is today?
   Today is _____.

   ◆◆ Lisa Chichester, Parkersburg, WV

Senses Song

Materials

None

What to do

1. Sing the following song to the tune of "The Farmer In the Dell."

   I see with my eyes,
   I see with my eyes,
   Heigh ho the derry-o,
   I see with my eyes.

I hear with my ears, …
I feel with my hands, …
I taste with my tongue, …
I smell with my nose, …

❖❖ Phyllis Esch, Export, PA

Swinging

Materials

None

What to do

1. Sing the following song when the children are playing on the swings. It always puts smiles on their faces.

Swinging

Swinging, swinging, high in the sky.
Swinging, swinging, watch me fly.
Up so high
Like a bird in the sky.

Swinging, swinging, high in the sky.
Swinging, swinging, watch Susie fly.
Up so high
Like a bird in the sky.

2. Repeat using the other children's names.

❖❖ Diann Spalding, Santa Rosa, CA

Sitting in the Park

Materials

None

What to do

1. With the children, sit in a circle and sing the following song to the tune of "The Farmer in the Dell."

   We are sitting in the park.
   We are sitting in the park.
   Oh, tralala, oh, tralala
   We are sitting in the park.

   A butterfly flies by. (stand up and walk around while flapping your arms)
   A butterfly flies by.
   Oh, tralala, oh, tralala
   A butterfly flies by.

   A worm is crawling by. (get down on the ground and crawl around)
   A worm is crawling by.
   Oh, tralala, oh, tralala
   A worm is crawling by.

2. Encourage the children to think of other creatures and things in the park, such as a grasshopper hopping, leaves falling, ducks swimming, and so on.

❖❖ Ingelore Mix, Gainesville, VA

"Bugs on the Move"

Materials

None

What to do

1. Ask the children, "What kind of bug would you like to be?"
2. Tell them, "Put on your antennas and your wings. It's time to turn yourself into a BUG!"
3. Sing the following song and do the actions mentioned, including marching in the first verse, crawling in the second verse, and flying in the last verse.

Bugs on the Move

The bugs come marching in our room, hurrah, hurrah!
The bugs come marching in our room, hurrah, hurrah!
They wiggle their hands and they wiggle their feet, (wiggle hands and feet)
They think they're oh so very neat, (one hand on head, one hand on hip)
When the bugs come marching, marching in our room.

The bugs come crawling in our room, hurrah, hurrah!
The bugs come crawling in our room, hurrah, hurrah!
They wiggle their hands and they wiggle their feet, (wiggle hands and feet)
They think they're oh so very neat, (one hand on head, one hand on hip)
When the bug's come crawling, crawling in our room.

The bugs come flying in our room, hurrah, hurrah!
The bugs come flying in our room, hurrah, hurrah!
They wiggle their hands and they wiggle their feet, (wiggle hands and feet)
They think they're oh so very neat, (one hand on head, one hand on hip)
When the bugs come flying, flying in our room.

4. Finish by saying, "Let's fly back to our seats, little bugs!"

Related books

Have You Seen Bugs? by Joanne Oppenheim
Icky Bug Alphabet Book by Jerry Pallota

❖❖ Diann Spalding, Santa Rosa, CA

Mrs. Hubbard Had a Garden

Materials

Large pictures of flowers (flower catalogs are great to use—enlarge flowers on a copy machine)

What to do

1. Give each child a picture of a flower.
2. Sing the following words to the tune of "Old MacDonald." As you sing the song, the child with the picture of the flower you are singing about holds it up.

   Mrs. Hubbard had a garden, e, i, e, i, o.
   In this garden she had some roses, e, i, e, i, o.
   With a rose here and a rose there,
   Here a rose, there a rose, everywhere a rose.
   Mrs. Hubbard had a garden, e, i, e, i, o.

3. Continue adding different flowers to the song. End it with "Mrs. Hubbard took good care of her garden, e, i, e, i, o."

   ❖ Darleen A. Schaible, Stroudsburg, PA

Red Light, Green Light

Materials

None

What to do

1. When learning about transportation or personal safety, use the following simple song to emphasize the proper response to traffic signals. Sing it to any simple tune you know.

   Red light, green light,
   Stop and go.
   Red light, green light,
   Stop and go.
   Red light, green light,
   Don't you know?
   Red light means "stop,"
   And green light means "go."

   Yellow light in the middle,
   Go very slow.
   Yellow light in the middle,

Go very slow.
Yellow light in the middle,
Don't you know?
Yellow light in the middle
Means "go slow."

More to do

Games: When the children are out on the playground riding trikes and scooters, play a simple traffic game. Stand in one spot as the children wheel around. As they approach you, call out "red light," "green light," or yellow light." The children should respond appropriately by stopping, continuing, or slowing. If desired, give tickets to those who run red lights. The children love this!

Outdoors: Provide props for outdoor traffic play, if possible. Make a traffic signal using a refrigerator box, have police hats and badges available, and provide notepads for writing tickets.

Related books

The Little Auto by Lois Lenski
Night Driving by John Coy
On the Go by Ann Morris

❖ Virginia Jean Herrod, Columbia, SC

Name Your Animal Song

Materials

Stuffed animals, animal puppets, or play animals from farm sets

What to do

1. Give each child a stuffed animal, animal puppet, or play animal.
2. Sing "Mary Had a Little Lamb" with the children.

   Mary had a little lamb,
   Little lamb,
   Little lamb,
   Mary had a little lamb
   Whose fleece was white as snow.

3. In turn, ask each to child say his name, his animal's name, and one thing about the animal.

4. Incorporate the child's name, animal, and fact about the animal into a personal song. For example, "Joey had a little dog," or "Taylor had a little cat."

5. Sing the personalized songs. For example:

Joey had a little dog,
Little dog,
Little dog.
Joey had a little dog
Whose ears were black and brown.

❖❖ Angela Williamson LaFon, Lynchburg, VA

Stick Puppet Frogs

Materials

Copy machine
Crayons or markers
Craft sticks
Stapler or tape

What to do

1. Make copies of the frog head (see illustration on the following page) and songs (see below).

2. Give each child a copy of the frog head to color. If desired, the children can add a tongue to the puppet and a bug on the end of the tongue.

3. Attach a craft stick to the base of each child's frog head using tape or a stapler.

4. Sing "Grump Went the Little Green Frog" and encourage the children to hold their frog puppets and jump as they sing. The children can stoop down in a frog position, with their hands on the floor and elbows between their knees. Then, leap forward each time they sing the word "gr-ump."

Grump Went the Little Green Frog
Gr-ump went the little green frog one day,
Gr-ump went the little green frog.
Gr-ump went the little green frog one day,
And the frog went gr-ump, gr-ump, gr-ump.

5. Encourage the children to act out "Five Little Speckled Frogs." Choose five children at a time to stand in front of the group. As the group sings the song, one "frog" pretends to leap into a pool until there is none left. Rotate the groups of children so that everyone gets a turn.

Five Little Speckled Frogs

Five little speckled frogs,
Sat on a great big log,
Eating some most delicious bugs
YUM! YUM!

One jumped into the pool,
Where it was nice and cool,
Now there are four green speckled frogs,
GLUMP! GLUMP!

(Start the song over with four frogs, then three, and so on.)

❖ Sandra Nagel, White Lake, MI

Zickity Zockity Zackity Zoo

Materials

None

What to do

1. When calling the children for a specific activity, use the following fun rhyme. (Notice how the second and third words rhyme with the child's name by simply substituting a W or B for the initial sound in the child's name.)

   Andrew Wandrew Bandrew Boo
   Zickity Zockity Zackity Zoo
   Andrew Wandrew Bandrew Bop
   Zickity Zockity Zackity Zock

2. Try to time the cadence of the rhyme so that the last word, "Zock," coincides with the child's arrival at the designated place.
3. Be enthusiastic! Children love nonsense rhymes.
4. Find other ways to add fun to your day by using rhymes. For example, when announcing that you are about to serve snack, instead of saying, "It's snack time," say, "I'd like to announce to this pack, it's about time for your snack." At lunchtime you might say, "Hey, you bunch, it's time for lunch."

More to do

Encourage the children to make up silly nonsense rhymes. Don't expect them to create whole rhymes, but they can make up silly rhymes such as, "I found my shoe, boo be doo boo."

Books: Make a simple rhyming book using magazine pictures. Glue pictures of things that represent rhyming words to sheets of paper and bind them into a book. For example, place a picture of a dress next to a picture of a nest, or a picture of rose next to a picture of someone's toes, and so on.

Related books

Bug in a Rug by Joanna Cole and Stephanie Calmenson
"Quack!" Said the Billy-Goat by Charles Causky

◆◆ Virginia Jean Herrod, Columbia, SC

"Apples, Apples, Applesauce"

Materials

None

What to do

1. Say the following poem with the children and act it out.

Apples, Apples, Applesauce

Apples, apples, applesauce, (clap...clap...clap, clap, clap)
Pick the apples from the tree. (reach up, picking pretend apples)
Apples, apples, applesauce, (clap...clap...clap, clap, clap)
Peel the apples carefully. (circle one hand around the other, pretending to peel)
Apples, apples, applesauce, (clap...clap...clap, clap, clap)
Now you cut the apples up. (hold one hand flat, making chopping motions
    with other hand)
Apples, apples, applesauce, (clap...clap...clap, clap, clap)
Add some sugar from a cup. (raise one hand and "pour" into other hand)
Apples, apples, applesauce, (clap...clap...clap, clap, clap)
Put it all into a pot. (scooping motions with one hand into the other hand)
Apples, apples, applesauce, (clap...clap...clap, clap, clap)
Stir it up and make it hot. (both hands together, using an imaginary spoon)
Apples, apples, applesauce, (clap...clap...clap, clap, clap)
Let it cool and then we'll eat. (wave one hand over the other, while blowing
    on cupped hand)
Apples, apples, applesauce, (clap...clap...clap, clap, clap)
What a fresh and tasty treat! (rub tummy and lick lips)

More to do

Art: Make apple magnets. Give each child a 3″ red construction paper circle and a 1 ½″ green leaf shape. Demonstrate how to glue the leaf on the circle (apple). Give each child a 1″ piece of self-adhesive magnetic tape to put on the back of the apple.

Related books

Apples, Apples, Apples by Nancy Elizabeth Wallace
Applesauce by Shirley Kurtz
Picking Apples and Pumpkins by Amy Hutchins

❖❖ Christina R. Chilcote, New Freedom, PA

"Five Little Pumpkins"

Materials

None

What to do

1. Say the following rhyme with the children and act it out.

Five Little Pumpkins

Five little pumpkins sitting on a gate.
The first one said, "Oh my, it's getting late."
The second one said, "It's cool this air." (hug, like you're trying to keep warm)
The third one said, "But we don't care." (shrug shoulders)
The fourth one said, "Let's run and run and run." (run in place)
The fifth one said, "It's only Halloween fun."
Then "Whooooooo" went the wind, and out went the lights, (clap hands
  loudly on "out went the lights")
And the five little pumpkins rolled out of sight. (roll arms together)

❖❖ Sandra Nagel, White Lake, MI

"Autumn Leaves"

Materials

None

What to do

1. Say the following poem with the children and act it out.

Falling, Falling Autumn Leaves

Falling, falling autumn leaves, (move hands above your head, tap your toes,
*   and wiggle your fingers)*
Autumn leaves, autumn leaves,
Falling, falling autumn leaves,
Falling to the ground.

Whirling, whirling, autumn leaves, (turn around in a circle)
Autumn leaves, autumn leaves,
Whirling, whirling, autumn leaves
Whirling all around. (fall to the ground)

Related book

Red Leaf, Yellow Leaf by Lois Ehlert

❖❖ Sandra Nagel, White Lake, MI

Snowflakes

Materials

None

What to do

1. Point to the different parts of your body as you recite the following poem with the children.

Did snowflakes ever…
Land in your hand?
Freeze on your knees?
Meet in your feet?

Have snowflakes ever…
Spread on your head?
Slid on your eyelid?
Clung to your tongue?

They have? Fun! Fun! Fun!

More to do

Science and Nature: Discuss snowflakes and how they are each unique. Ask the children to name other things that are different from each other (such as faces, fingerprints, and so on).

❖❖ Dotti Enderle, Richmond, TX

Let's All Make a Snowman

Materials

None

What to do

1. This winter fingerplay is fun to do after the children have had experience making a real snowman outside.
2. Say the following rhyme with the children and act it out.

   Let's all make a snowman. (stand in a circle)
   Help me roll the ball. (make rolling motion with hands as if rolling ball away
        from you)
   First he is so little; (kneel down with hands out and palms down near floor)
   Then he starts getting tall. (gradually stand up as you say words and raise hands)
   Put on the bottom, (make motion of placing a ball on the ground)
   Then the middle, (place imaginary ball on top of first "ball")
   Lastly goes the top. (place third ball on top)
   Give him two eyes, (point twice)

A nose, a mouth, (point for nose and make a curved line in the air for mouth)
Three buttons (point three times, going down in a row)
Then we'll stop! (clap on the word "stop")

More to do

Art: Use clay or playdough to make three-dimensional snowmen. As the children make their snowmen, repeat the fingerplay as they roll and mold clay. This is also great for teaching concepts such as little/tall, bottom/middle/top, and counting to three.

Related book

The Snowman by Raymond Briggs

❖❖ Bea Chawla, Vincentown, NJ

Five Fat Snowmen

Materials

None

What to do

1. Say the following rhyme with the children.

Five fat snowmen standing in a row,
Out comes the sun—Oh no!

Four fat snowmen standing in a row,
The temperature is rising—Oh no!

Three fat snowmen standing in a row,
The day gets warmer—Oh no!

Two fat snowmen standing in a row,
Icicles dripping—Oh no!

One thin snowman sinking very low,
Now he's a puddle—Oh no!

❖❖ Dotti Enderle, Richmond TX

A Box of Crayons

Materials

None

What to do

1. Say the following poem with the children and act it out.

This is Andy Rayon's box of crayons.
When I open the top (put hands together palm to palm)
Out they pop. (lift up top hand and wiggle fingers)
They are the best colors
I have ever seen.

One is red. (wiggle thumb while naming the color)
One is green. (wiggle index finger while naming the color)
One is yellow. (wiggle middle finger while naming the color)
One is blue. (wiggle ring finger while naming the color)
This one is purple, (wiggle little finger while naming the color)
Like Peter's turtle.
Now I close the top
And stop. (put hands together with a loud clap)

❖❖ Ingelore Mix, Gainesville, VA

My Toy Box

Materials

None

What to do

1. Say the poem on the following page with the children.

I have a box
Stuffed with toys.
Some are quiet,
Some make noise.
I have a ball,
Puzzles and blocks,
A teddy bear
With green socks.
I have crayons,
Watercolors and playdough,
And a puppet called
SPAGHETTIO.

2. Ask the children what they have in their toy box. If desired, ask them to bring in a quiet toy for "Show and Tell."

❖❖ Ingelore Mix, Gainesville, VA

"Oliver Twist"

Materials

Playground or space in which to move around

What to do

1. Recite the following poem with the children and act it out.

   Oliver Twist, Twist, Twist,
   Can do this, this, this
   Touch your hair, hair, hair
   Touch your nose, nose, nose
   Touch your knees, knees, knees
   Touch your toes, toes, toes.

2. If desired, say it faster and faster and encourage the children to keep up.
3. Begin loud and get softer with each recitation, until you are just moving your lips.

❖❖ Barbara Saul, Eureka, CA

"Ten in a Bed"

Materials

Area rug

What to do

1. Ask ten children to lay on a rug, side by side, all turned in the same direction.
2. When you begin the following rhyme, the children roll over in the same direction. The child on the end in the direction the line rolled "falls" out. On the next verse, the children will roll in the opposite direction. The child on the end falls out. Continue until there is one child left.

Ten in a Bed

There were ten in a bed and the little one said, "Roll over, roll over."
So they rolled over and one fell out.
There were nine in the bed and the little one said, "Roll over, roll over."
So they all rolled over and one fell out.
(Continue with 8,7,6,5,4,3,2)
There was one in the bed and the little one said, "Good night."

More to do

Substitute "one fell out" with a child's name. For example, "Michael fell out."

❖❖ Nicole Sparks, Miami, FL

Spider Legs

Materials

None

What to do

1. Say the following poem with the children and act it out.

A spider has eight legs. (show 8 fingers)
One for creeping, (one finger creeps up child's leg)
One for crawling, (two fingers crawl up child's other leg)
One for spinning, (one finger on left hand spins around two fingers on right hand)

One to stop falling. (left hand catches four falling fingers on right hand)
One for walking, (five fingers walk across child's tummy)
One to help it run, (six fingers run up child's head)
One for tickling, (seven fingers tickle child under the chin)
One for sitting in the sun. (eight fingers rest on child's lap)

Related books

Little Miss Spider by David Kirk
The Very Busy Spider by Eric Carle

❖❖ Christina Chilcote, New Freedom, PA

I Spy

Materials

None

What to do

1. Use the following silly rhyme to learn about parts of the body.

   I spy, here is my eye.
   Ear, ear, I hear with my ear.
   Nose, nose, it blows and blows.
   Here's my chin, now give me a grin.
   Hair, hair, it goes everywhere.
   Hand, hand, let's play in the band.

2. Point to each part of the body as it is named.
3. Follow the rhyme with a pretend band and march around the room playing pretend instruments.

More to do

Circle Time: Teach a circle time activity about musical instruments.

Related books

The Foot Book by Dr. Seuss
Hand, Hand, Finger, Thumb by Al Perkins
The Tooth Book by Theo LeSieg

❖❖ Wanda Pelton, Lafayette, IN

Five Senses Fingerplay

Materials

None

What to do

1. Begin with the following fingerplay.

   I have eyes so I can see (curl fingers of both hands around eyes like
   *   binoculars)*
   The smallest leaf (point fingers close together)
   On the tallest tree. (hands go high overhead)
   My ears can hear the cars go by. (cup hands behind ears)
   My lips can taste some apple pie. (lick your lips)
   My nose can smell a rose so sweet, (touch your nose)
   And tell me when it's time to eat. (rub your tummy)
   My hands can pet a kitten's fur, (make stroking motion)
   And touch its chest to feel it purr.
   My five senses help me very well,
   To see, hear, taste, touch and smell. (touch related body part with each word)

2. Now ask the children answer each of the following questions by pointing to a
   body part (or parts) and naming the sense.

   How can you tell…

   There's a cake in the oven? (nose/smell)
   The radio is on? (ears/hearing)
   The lemonade is too sour? (mouth/taste)
   Your friend is wearing a red shirt? (eye/sight)
   An ice cube is cold? (fingers/touch)
   It's dark outside? (eyes/sight)
   The telephone is ringing? (ears/hearing)
   The candy is sweet? (mouth/taste)
   A bunny's tail is soft? (fingers/touch)
   Your mom is wearing perfume? (nose/smell)

More to do

Set up five "Sensation Stations" around the room.

Sight: Make and decorate telescopes or binoculars from paper towel or toilet paper tubes for outdoor visual discoveries.

Hearing: Put a tape recorder or tape player in the Dramatic Play area.

Taste: Serve pieces of fresh fruit (five or more different kinds) to eat with toothpicks for snack. Compare and enjoy the distinct flavor of each fruit.

Smell: Put scented markers and paper on the art table.

Touch: Place a "feely box" (or bag) in the Science area. Put objects with different textures inside the box for the children to feel and identify.

❖❖ Susan A. Sharkey, La Mesa, CA

Wishy Washy

Materials

None

What to do

1. Use the following fun rhyme when discussing personal hygiene.

   Wishy washy
   Splishy splashy
   I have fun in the tubby wubby.
   Wishy washy
   Splishy splashy
   I make sure I wash my armsies warmsies.
   Wash wash wash
   Wash wash wash.

2. As you say the body part in the rhyme, pretend to wash it.
3. Repeat the rhyme using other body parts, such as:
   Toesies woesies
   Earsies wearsies
   Feetie weetie
   Necky wecky
   Tummy wummy
   Legsies wegsies

More to do

Art: Make personalized washcloths. Give each child a white washcloth. Encourage the children to decorate them using permanent paint pens. Put each child's initial in the center of his cloth.

Housekeeping: Encourage the children to wash baby dolls. Provide a small tub of water or set up the sensory table as a baby washtub. Provide small soaps and washcloths and towels for drying. This activity will also help those with younger siblings as you emphasize the importance of handling a baby gently.

Related books

Harry Takes a Bath by Harriet Ziefert
Harry the Dirty Dog by Gene Zion
King Bidgood's in the Bathtub by Audrey Wood

❖❖ Virginia Jean Herrod, Columbia, SC

"Imagination Zoo"

Materials

None needed

What to do

1. Say the following poem with the children and act it out.

Imagination Zoo

If I were a monkey, I'd swing from trees. (scratch and pretend to swing around)
If I were a bear, I'd steal honey from bees. (stretch your "claws" up high and growl)
If I were a horse, I would prance and run. (prance and run in place)
If I were a bird, I'd fly for fun. (spread your arms and pretend to fly)
But I am a child, as you can see. (child points to self)
Won't you come and play with me? (child points to another person and then to self)

More to do

Cut out the appropriate animal and child shapes from felt for a flannel board presentation.

Art: Cut out animal and child shapes from construction paper. Attach the shapes to a hanger with different lengths and colors of yarn to make a mobile.

Related books

Ape in a Cape: An Alphabet of Odd Animals by Fritz Eichenberg
Pretend You're a Cat by Jean Marzollo

❖❖ Christina R. Chilcote, New Freedom, PA

"Big Brown Dog"

Materials

None

What to do

1. Say the following poem with the children and act it out.

Big Brown Dog

A little blue bird sits on a tree, (move hand like a bird, land on other arm)
But big brown dog is sitting here with me. (point to yourself)
A lazy gray cat watches a busy honeybee, (pretend to be a cat washing his face)
But big brown dog is sitting here with me. (point to yourself)
A fuzzy yellow duck paddles down to the sea, (make a paddling motion with
*   two hands)*
But big brown dog is sitting here with me. (point to yourself)
A bright green grasshopper jumps on my knee, (have one finger bounce on knee)
But big brown dog is sitting here with me. (point to yourself)
Come little bird, all downy and blue. (move hand like a flying bird)
Fluffy gray cat, we want you, too. (wash face like a cat)
Here, little duck, with orange webbed feet. (make a paddling motion with
*   two hands)*
Stay, tiny grasshopper, in the summer heat. (bounce one finger on a knee)
But go away busy, buzzy honeybee, (wave hand in front of face)
Or big brown dog won't sit with me! (shake head side to side and point to
*   yourself)*

More to do

Cut out the appropriate animal and child shapes from felt for a flannel board story.

Related books

Clifford, the Big Red Dog by Norman Bridwell
Go, Dog, Go by P.D Eastman

❖ Christina R. Chilcote, New Freedom, PA

Little Ducks

Materials

None

What to do

1. Say the following poem with the children and act it out. It is a good transition activity between the playground and the next indoor activity.

Quack, quack, quack
Ducks are talking. (children imitate ducks quacking)

Waddle, waddle, waddle
Ducks are walking. (children imitate ducks walking)

Splash, splash, splash
Ducks are flapping. (children flap their arms)

Shhh, shhh, shhh
Ducks are napping. (children rest their heads in the folds of their arms while sitting at the table)

❖ Ingelore Mix, Gainesville, VA

Three Little Owls

Materials

Brown, yellow, and black construction paper
Marker or pencil
Scissors
Two-sided tape
Flannel board or bulletin board

What to do

1. Draw three owls (about 3" tall) on brown construction paper. Cut them out.
2. Draw a moon on the yellow construction paper and a tree on the black construction paper and cut them out.
3. On the back of each cutout, stick a piece of double-sided tape.
4. Place the moon and tree on the bulletin or flannel board.
5. As you begin the verse, place the three owls somewhere on the tree. As you continue with the verse, take away one owl at a time while the children name the number of owls left. (To help with number recognition, you may want to put numbers on the owls.)

Three little owls stay awake all night,
Sitting in the tree in the moon's bright
light.
One flies away whooo,
whoo, whoo
Left are…two.

Two little owls stay
awake all night,
Sitting in the tree in the
moon's bright light.
Another flies away and hoots,
"This is great fun!"
Left is …one.

One little owl stays awake all night,
Sitting in the tree in the moon's bright light.
It flies away and cries, "I'm the last one."
Left are…none.

❖❖ Ingelore Mix, Gainesville, VA

Sea Animal Song

Materials

Poster board
Markers

What to do

1. Draw the sea animals mentioned in the following song on a piece of poster board.
2. Sing the following song to the tune of "The Itsy Bitsy Spider" and point to the animals on the poster.

   D is for dolphin.
   F is for fish.
   W's for whale.
   And S is for swish.

   Swish goes the dolphin.
   Swish goes the fish.
   Swish goes the whale.
   S is for swish!

3. You might want to introduce this song after learning about sea animals.

More to do

Art: Make puppets by cutting out pictures of the animals and gluing them to Popsicle sticks. The children can use them to "swish."

❖ Angela Williamson LaFon, M.Ed., Lynchburg, VA

5 Wiggly Worms and a Bird

Materials

Small paper plates, one per child
Yellow and black paint
Paintbrushes
Black and orange paper
Glue

What to do

1. Paint a paper plate yellow on one side and black on the other. Let dry.
2. Fold the plate in half so that the black is on the inside.
3. Fold orange paper in half and cut out a triangle about 6 ½" by 11." This will be the beak.
4. Glue the beak along the folded line inside the plate.
5. Cut two circles from black paper and fold them in half. Glue them on the lower part of the plate.
6. Make a paper plate "bird" for each child

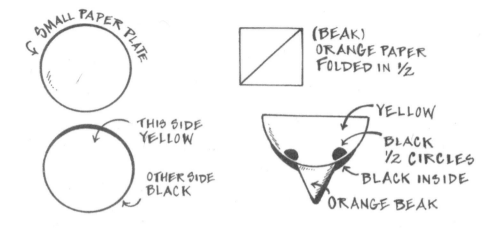

7. As you say the following poem, the children will hold their birds in one hand and use the fingers of their other hands to be the worms.

While little bird sang a song
Five little worms wiggled along. (wiggle fingers)

Little bird smiled with glee
"I'll get me one," said she. (the "bird" eats one—thumb disappears)

While little bird sang a song
Four little worms wiggled along.

Little bird smiled with glee
"I'll get me one," said she. (the "bird eats another one—index finger disappears)

Continue until the five worms (fingers) have disappeared.

❖ Ingelore Mix, Gainsville, VA

Sniff Bottles

Materials

6 plastic film canisters
Cotton balls
Vanilla extract
Cinnamon and peppermint oils

What to do

1. Put vanilla extract on two cotton balls, cinnamon oil on two, and peppermint oil on two more.
2. Place one cotton ball into each film canister or "bottle." (You will have two of each smell.)
3. Invite the children to sniff one of the bottles and find the other that smells just like it.
4. Continue with the other bottles.
5. Cap the containers when not in use.

More to do

Make bottles with other smells, such as coffee (put dry coffee in the bottom, and a cotton ball on top) or pine (crush a twig of pine and a few needles). Be cautious not to use chemicals that could be hazardous.

Language: Teach the children the names of the smells. Ask the children to name something the smell reminds them of, such as ice cream, Christmas, or toothpaste.

❖ Mary Jo Shannon, Roanoke, VA

Fruit Game

Materials

Actual fruit (bananas, pears, apples, oranges)
Oak tag
Scissors
Paper lunch bags
Crayons
Stapler

What to do

1. Discuss the names, colors, tastes, and shapes of the actual fruit. Talk about the differences between the fruit.
2. Choose a child and ask her to put her hands behind her back. Then place one of the fruits into her hand and see if she can identify it by touch.
3. If desired, do the same activity with taste. Ask the child to close her eyes and then put a small piece of fruit into her mouth. Can she identify it by the taste?
4. Make fruit puppets with the children. Beforehand, cut out pear, orange, apple, and banana shapes from oak tag.
5. Ask each child to pick either a pear, orange, or apple shape for the head and four banana shapes for the arms and legs.
6. Give each child a paper bag. This will be the body of the hand puppet.
7. Encourage them to decorate the bag and color the shapes with crayons.
8. Staple the head onto the closed end of the bag, and attach two bananas for the arms and two for the legs.
9. The children's hands will fit comfortably inside the opening of the bag.

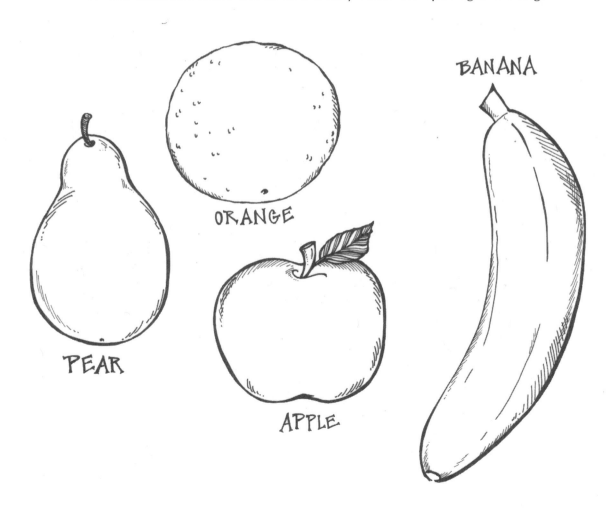

BANANA

ORANGE

PEAR

APPLE

More to do

You can also make vegetable puppets using a potato or green pepper shape for the head and carrots for the limbs. The children can choose between a fruit or vegetable puppet. This will allow for some classification experience.

Original fingerplay:

Way up in the apple tree, (child pretends to be a tree)
Two little apples looked at me. (hold up two fingers, then make eyeglasses
    with your thumb and forefinger)
I shook that tree as hard as I could, (child wiggles up and down)
Down fell the apples (fingers flutter down)
Mmmmmmm—were they good! (rub tummy)

Related book

The Very Hungry Caterpillar by Eric Carle

❖❖ Iris Rothstein, New Hyde Park, NY

Sock Sense: A Touching Game

Materials

Variety of small items, such as a rock, coin, marble, wooden cube, and a bottle top
Dark-colored child's sock

What to do

1. Show the assorted objects to the children, naming and describing them together.
2. Without the children seeing, put one item into the sock. Encourage one child to feel the item through the sock and try to identify it without peeking inside. If the child has difficulty naming the object, suggest asking a friend to help.
3. When the child has identified the item, remove it and discuss its identifying features, such as round edges, smooth surfaces, or sharp corners.
4. Repeat the game with other objects.

More to do

Literacy: Make a class book of drawings of the children's favorite things to touch, accompanied with the completed sentence: "I like to feel _____ because…"
Science: Repeat the game using items with similar shapes or features, such as all round items or all wooden objects.
More Science: Play other guessing games using the sense of taste, the sense of smell, and so on.

❖❖ Susan Oldham Hill, Lakeland, FL

Hide the Hippopotamus

Materials

A small stuffed hippo or toy hippo figure

What to do

1. Choose a child to be "It." Ask "It" to either leave the room or hide her eyes.
2. Choose another child to hide the hippo. Explain that the toy must stick out a little from the hiding place, but not be in plain view.
3. "It" starts looking for the toy by walking around the room.
4. The rest of the children clap softly when "It" is far away from the toy, and they clap louder as she gets closer, and VERY loudly when she is right next to it. The child will soon realize that she must listen carefully to judge whether the clapping is getting louder. She will also learn not to look carefully when she is near a place where the clapping is soft, but to look thoroughly when the clapping is loudest.
5. Of course the game is over when the child finds the toy. If she cannot find the toy and becomes frustrated, the child who hid it can show where the toy is.
6. You can use any stuffed animal for this game—just remember to change the name. For example "Find the Fox," "Discover the Dinosaur," "Locate the Lion," "See the Seal," and so on.

More to do

Substitute other actions, such as stamping feet, tapping fingers, and so on.
Language: Discuss how the words in the title of the game have the same beginning sounds, such as Hide/Hippo, Find/Fox, and so on.

Original chant

Clap, clap, clap your hands
Softly as can be.
Clap, clap, clap your hands,
Do it now with me.
Clap, clap, clap your hands
Loudly as can be.
Clap clap, clap your hands,
Do it now with me.

❖❖ Iris Rothstein, New Hyde Park, NY

Find the Sound

Materials

Beans
Small plastic container with a lid (small enough to be concealed in a child's hand)

What to do

1. Ask the child to sit in a circle.
2. Choose one child to be "It." Ask "It" to leave the circle and stand so that she cannot see you or the other children.
3. Put a couple of beans into the container and put the lid back on. Give the container to a child to conceal in her hand.
4. Ask all the children to hold their hands balled up in fists in front of them.
5. The children shake their hands, while the child who is "It" tries to locate the hand making the sound.

❖❖ Mary Jo Shannon, Roanoke, VA

Who's Making that Noise?

Materials

Toy that produces a sound
Box or bag
Paper
Markers or crayons

What to do

1. Place the sound-producing toy inside a box or bag and place it on a table. Make sure that the toy is making a sound.
2. Ask the children open-ended questions about what could be inside the box.
3. Write down their predictions.
4. Ask them to draw pictures of what they think is inside the box.
5. After all the children have taken a turn guessing, open the box to reveal what is making the noise. Compare the predictions of the children with the item in the box.

More to do

Literacy: Begin reading a new story to the children and ask them to predict what will happen on the next page.
More Literacy: Make a class book about the children's predictions.

❖❖ Linda S. Andrews, Sonora, CA

Do You Hear What I Hear?

Materials

Objects that make sounds, such as scissors, rhythm sticks, a bell, a drum, an alarm clock, tambourines, silverware, and maracas
Bag
Curtain or sheet

What to do

1. Put all of the objects that make sounds into a bag.

2. Choose one child at a time to come up and pick out an item from the bag and show it to the class.
3. Encourage the children to guess what kind of sound it will make, such as "crash," "boom," so on.
4. Ask the child to demonstrate the sound it makes.
5. After all the objects have been shown, place them back into the bag. Hang up a sheet or curtain and put the bag behind it.
6. Now play a guessing game. Ask one child at a time to go behind the curtain and pick an item from the bag. The child makes the noise while the class decides which object they just heard.

More to do

Discuss *loud* and *soft* and ask the children to classify the objects into those categories.

Related books

Little Frog Learns to Sing by Lucille LeBlanc
My Five Senses by Aliki
Polar Bear, Polar Bear, What Do You Hear? by Bill Martin, Jr. and Eric Carle

❖❖ Vicki Whitehead, Citronelle, AL

Find the Alarm Clock

Materials

Alarm clock

What to do

1. Without the children seeing, hide an alarm clock somewhere in the room. Set it to go off about five minutes after you hide it.
2. Gather the children together and explain that they are to use their senses to find the clock.
3. When the alarm sounds, encourage the children to search for the clock.
4. When the clock is found, ask the children to explain how they found it and which senses they used.
5. For children who have a hearing impairment, hide a flashlight with or instead of the clock.

More to do

Hide a small radio or a music box instead of a clock.

Ask the children to cover their eyes and use only their sense of hearing to find an object.

❖❖ Tammy Byington, Columbia, MO

Construction Time!

Materials

Pictures of tools, construction worker clothing, and things one could build
Glue
File folders
Scissors

What to do

1. Cut out or draw pictures of tools, trucks, clothing a construction worker wears, or things one can build.
2. Glue each picture inside a file folder.
3. Cut three or four openings into the front cover of each folder to make peep holes. Only cut around three sides to keep the flap in place so the children can't see the whole picture.
4. Hold up a closed file folder and give hints about the picture. Open one flap so the children get a glimpse of what the picture is inside the folder. Continue giving hints and opening more flaps until they can guess what the picture is. If the children are unable to guess, then show them the picture.

More to do

Ask a parent to bring in various types of tools and tell the children how they are used. Have a supply of wood handy so the children can use the tools to build small structures.

Art: Collect old nuts, bolts, screws, and washers. Encourage the children to glue them onto cardboard to make structures and designs. This is a great activity because the children can write their names, stack or build something, or just make a design.

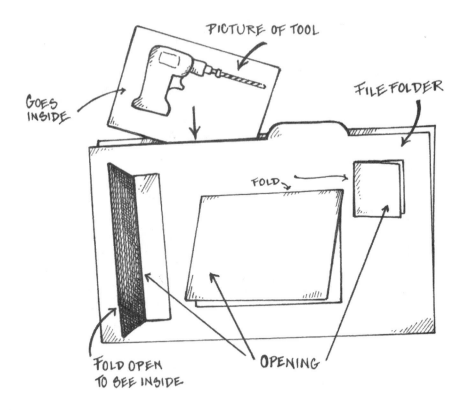

PICTURE OF TOOL

GOES INSIDE

FILE FOLDER

FOLD

FOLD OPEN TO SEE INSIDE

OPENING

Original songs

Peter Works with One Hammer

Peter works with one hammer, one hammer, one hammer.
Peter works with one hammer all day long.

Peter works with two hammers, two hammers, two hammers.
Peter works with two hammers all day long.

Continue until you get to five hammers.

If desired, sing the song and substitute the following Hebrew words: hammer (patysh), one (achad), two (shteim), three (shalosh), four (arbab), and five (chamesh).

The Happy Worker
(Tune: "The Happy Wanderer")

I love to go a-wandering along the construction site.
And as I go I love to sing,
My hard hat on my head.

Chorus:
Valaree, a valarah, a valaree, valarahahahahaha
Valaree, valarah, my hard hat on my head.
I love to climb the steel frames and drill all day long.

So joyously they call to me, "Come join my big tall frames."
High overhead the birds sing, they never rest at home.
But just like me, they love to sing as I wear my hard hat.

❖❖ Cookie Zingarelli, Columbus, Ohio

What Could Be in the Box?

Materials

A common object, such as a doll, cup, or block
Box with a top (any size will do, just gear your questions accordingly)
Gift wrap and ribbon, optional

What to do

1. Without the children seeing, put the object into a box and put the lid on.
2. If desired, wrap the box like a gift and tie a ribbon around it.
3. Sit in a circle on the floor with the box in the center.
4. Ask the children questions about what could be in the box. For example, "Could it be a dog? Why not?" (Too big. Accept other reasons: dog would need air, dog would bark, and so on.)
5. Continue asking if it could be other objects, some small enough, some too large.
6. Finally, give clues to let the children guess the identity of the object. For example, "It's something you play with," "It looks like a real baby," "You build with it," or "It's made of wood."
7. Open the box and encourage the children to examine the object.

More to do

Vary the size of the box and its contents.
Science and Nature: Relate the object to science by using a seashell, leaf, pinecone, rock, or other natural object.

❖❖ Mary Jo Shannon, Roanoke, VA

Bugs for Lunch!

Materials

Small pictures of bugs or paper and markers
Scissors
Tape
Tray or table
Party blowers with roll-out tongues (preferably the silent kind)

What to do

1. Cut out small photos of bugs, or draw pictures of bugs on small pieces of paper.
2. Put a piece of looped tape on the front of each bug picture.
3. Put the photos on a tray or table, with the tape facing up.
4. Give the children party blowers and encourage them to blow out their "tongues" and catch the bugs.

More to do

Science and Nature: Study frogs and their eating habits. Show the children video clips of amphibians or reptiles that eat bugs in this manner.

Related song

"I Know an Old Lady Who Swallowed a Fly"

◆◆ Shirley R. Salach, Northwood, NH

Flyswatter Zap

Materials

New, clean flyswatters
2 identical sets of flashcards for whatever skill you're trying to reinforce (You can buy these or make them with 3" x 5" index cards.)

What to do

1. Seat two children facing you, and give them each a flyswatter.

2. Spread one set of the flashcards face up in front of them, making sure that the children aren't seeing them upside down.

3. Display the other set of flashcards one at a time to the children. The first child to zap the matching card with her flyswatter gets the card.

4. See if the children can zap all of the cards, or who can zap the most.

More to do

This game can be adapted to reinforce all kinds of skills, depending on what type of flashcards you use: letters, numbers, shapes, colors, and so on.

❖❖ Vicki L. Schneider, Oshkosh, WI

Can You Find Me?

Materials

Variety of small classroom items
Copy machine

What to do

1. Make paper copies, one each, of a variety of small classroom items such as scissors, a crayon, a puppet, a magnet, a BINGO card, a doll dress, a block, and so on.

2. Before the children arrive, hide the classroom items that you made copies of.

3. Give each child a paper copy and challenge the children to find their items in the classroom. Classmates can help guide the child by giving verbal cues.

More to do

Math: Use the copies to make a matching game. In a box or basket, place the copies and their matching items. Encourage the children to spread the pictures on the floor and place the real items on top of their matching pictures.

❖❖ Barbara Backer, Charleston, SC

Seed Matching

Materials

Old science books or workbooks
Scissors
Index cards
Glue stick
Marker, optional

What to do

1. Use old science textbooks or workbooks as a source of pictures to use for making simple matching activities. For example, cut out pictures of fruit dissected to expose the seeds.
2. Glue each picture to a separate index card using a glue stick.
3. Now cut out pictures showing the whole fruit.
4. Glue each of these to separate index cards. If desired, label them with the name of the fruit.
5. Ask the children to match the seeds to the correct fruit.

❖❖ Jackie Wright, Enid, OK

Open and Closed

Materials

Old books or workbooks
Scissors
Glue stick
Index cards
Felt and flannel board, optional

What to do

1. Cut out pictures depicting the opposite concepts of "open" and "closed" in old books or workbooks. Glue each one to a separate index card.
2. Encourage the children to play a sorting game by placing the pictures that depict "open" on one side and the pictures that depict "closed" on the other.
3. If desired, back them with felt and use them as a flannel board activity.

❖❖ Jackie Wright, Enid, OK

Looking for the Color

Materials

Construction paper in a various colors or white paper and markers
Scissors
Old magazines
Paper
Glue sticks
Stapler

What to do

1. Cut out rectangles from different colored construction paper. Or use white paper and color the rectangles with markers.
2. Give each child a different color rectangle. Ask the children to identify the color they have.
3. Then ask the children to look through old magazines to find something that is the same color as their rectangle. When they find something that is their color, help them cut it out.

4. Encourage them to glue the magazine picture and their rectangle on a piece of paper.

5. Make a color book with the children. Staple all of the papers together and make a cover for the book. Keep it in the Library area.

Related books

The Colors by Monique Felix
Colors Around Us by Shelly Rotner and Anne Woodhull
Colors Everywhere by Tana Hoban

❖❖ Sandra Hutchins Lucas, Cox's Creek, KY

Classification Game

Materials

Old magazines or catalogs
Scissors
Construction paper
Glue
Container
Books with pictures of toys, animals, things that go, and things to wear
Chairs
Music

What to do

1. Beforehand, prepare classification cards. Cut out large pictures of the following classification objects: toys, animals, things that go, and things to wear. Glue each picture to a piece of construction paper.

2. Put the cards into a container.

3. Read books to the children that give examples of the classification items.

4. Ask the children to sit in chairs in a circle. Then, ask each child to choose a card from container.

5. Go around the circle, and ask each child to identify the picture and give the correct classification of that object.

6. Next ask the children to stand up and place their card on their chair. Play some music as the children march around the circle. When the music stops, the child takes the card on whatever chair is in front of her and sits down.

TOY (CLOWN)

TRICYCLE (THINGS THAT GO)

ANIMAL (CAT)

THINGS TO WEAR (SLIPPER)

Related books

Things That Go by Anne Rockwell
Whose Socks Are Those? by Jez Alborough

❖❖ Liz Thomas, Hobart, IN

Big Corner Games

Materials

Pictures of objects that relate to the current theme (shapes, colors, action pictures)
Scissors
Glue
Construction paper
Laminate or clear contact paper

What to do

1. Cut out pictures of objects that relate to your theme.
2. Glue each picture onto a piece of construction paper (8" x 10" is good, but any size will do). It's a good idea to use larger paper for younger children.

3. Laminate the cards or cover them with clear contact paper to preserve them.
4. Clear a big space on the floor.
5. Place four cards face down, one in each corner of the space (see illustration).
6. Ask a child to select a card, turn it over, and say what is on the other side of the card.
7. Take that card away.
8. Continue with other children, until all the cards are gone.
9. Put down another set of cards and start over again.

LAMINATED PICTURES AT EACH CORNER

More to do

Extend this activity by adding more cards to the formation.

Gross Motor: Draw different motions on the cards and have the children duplicate the motion.

Literacy: Make a story out of the cards. Put down cards that need to go in sequence to tell a story, and when all the cards are off the floor, ask the children to put them in the correct sequence.

◆◆ Jane Hibbard, Stryker, OH

What's My Line?

Materials

Old magazines

Scissors

Glue

5" x 8" (12 cm x 20 cm) unruled index cards

Laminate or clear contact paper

Basket

Clothesline rope, about 10' long

Clip clothespins

What to do

Prepare:

1. Cut out magazine pictures of 10 or more different articles of clothing (such as shirts, pants, dress, hats, socks, nightgown, and so on).
2. Cut out an equal number of items one couldn't possibly wear (such as a dog, truck, teakettle, computer, and so on).
3. Glue one picture onto each index card. Laminate or protect them with clear contact paper.
4. Shuffle the cards and place them face down in a basket.
5. Set up for the game in front of your circle time area. Tie the clothesline between two chairs or any two objects that allow the line to spread within a child's reach. Attach the clothespins.

Play the Game:

1. Settle the children into a semi-circle facing the clothesline. Place the basket of cards in the middle.
2. Say, "It's laundry day—such a CHORE! I'm so glad you're all here to help me out. Oh no, my clothes dryer is broken! I'll have to hang everything outside on the clothesline to dry in the sunshine. Let's take turns picking cards from the basket. If the card shows something to wear, please hang it on the clothesline for me. If not, place the card beside the basket, because it belongs somewhere else."
3. Guide the children to make the proper choices. Encourage a good giggle about the idea of wearing a bicycle, a television set, a refrigerator, or whatever.

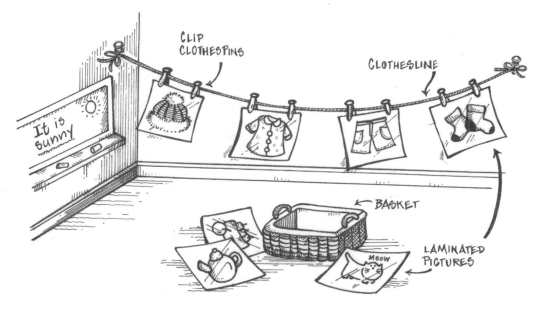

More to do

Instead of a laundry theme, make sets of cards for classifying other groups of objects or themes (such as animals, fruits, things that fly, dinosaurs, and so on). **Fine Motor:** Play "Clothespin Pick-up." Give each child a clip-type clothespin and an assortment of small objects (such as crayons, wooden beads, cotton balls, and so on) on a tray. Challenge the children to pick up these objects using the clothespin. (Make sure the clothespins are good quality so that the hinges don't fall out.)

Related books

Animals Should Definitely Not Wear Clothing by Judi Barrett
The Day Jimmy's Boa Ate the Wash by Trinka Hakes Noble
The Three Little Kittens by Paul Galdone

❖ Susan A. Sharkey, La Mesa, CA

Tricky Tools of the Trade

Materials

Assorted small household objects (see activity for examples)
Gallon-size zipper closure bags
Plastic bin
Placemat

What to do

1. Collect a variety of small household objects.
2. Make sets of four objects—three of the objects should belong to the same category, and one item should not belong in the group. For example:
   - Tools: hammer, screwdriver, pliers, book
   - Art supplies: pencil, crayon, marker, necklace
   - Cooking utensils: slotted spoon, meat fork, soup ladle, toy car
   - Clothing: sock, mitten, ball cap, water bottle
   - Toys: dolls, ball, truck, bowl
   - Grooming items: brush, comb, fingernail clippers, battery
   - Hygiene items: soap, tube of toothpaste, bottle of shampoo, soup can
   - Stuffed animals: bear, bunny, dog, sunglasses
3. Put each set of objects into a zipper closure bag. Then put all of the bags into a plastic bin.
4. Ask the children to sit on the carpet or at a table. Conceal the bin so that each bag can be revealed separately.
5. Put the placemat in the center of the area or table, bring out the first group of objects, and place them in a row on the placemat.
6. Say, "Three of these things belong together. One of them does not. Can you guess which thing does not belong with the others?"
7. Discuss the use of the three matching objects and what they have in common.
8. Repeat the procedure for each bag of objects.

More to do

Use this activity for themes such as "Careers" and "Community Helpers." Select three "tools" used for each occupation and one that does not.

You can also play this game with colors. For example, show three red objects and one yellow and ask, "Which color is different?"

❖❖ Susan A. Sharkey, La Mesa, CA

Puzzle Scramble

Materials

6-8 simple puzzles

What to do

1. To renew the children's interest in puzzles, try this fun game. Ask the children to sit in a circle and show them a puzzle.
2. Then dump the pieces of the puzzle into a pile in the center of the circle. Mix up all the pieces.
3. Now it's time to scramble! Explain to the children that at the count of "1, 2, 3, GO!", they will scramble to get the puzzle back together again.
4. Once the children get the hang of this, put the pieces of two different puzzles into the circle and mix them all up. Again, at your count, they will scramble to put together TWO puzzles.
5. As the children get better at this game, you can add more puzzles to the mix.
6. For a challenge, play an upbeat song and encourage the children to try to get the puzzle(s) together before the song ends. You can even do a "freeze" type game by turning off the music and asking the children to freeze until you start the music again.

More to do

You can play a similar game to practice sorting. Put a variety of objects, such as crayons, markers, and glue sticks, into a big pile. Encourage the children to see how fast they can get them all into the correct bins. Play this game in any center where the children are having trouble putting things into the right place at clean-up time.

Art: Put old, mismatched puzzle pieces in the Art Center for children to paint.

◆◆ Suzanne Pearson, Stephens City, VA

Any Theme Musical Chairs

Materials

One chair for each child

Theme-related pictures, one for each chair (for example, food, fruits, vegetables, winter or beach items, pets, zoo animals, items used by a firefighter, colors, shapes, and so on)

What to do

1. Set up chairs in typical "Musical Chairs" fashion, either in a long row with chairs facing forward and backward, or in a circle with chairs facing outward.

2. Place pictures on the floor, face down, underneath the chairs, or tape them to the bottom of the chairs.

3. Begin playing musical chairs as usual—the children walk around the chairs until the music stops, and then quickly sit down in a chair.

4. Once all the children are sitting, each child picks up the picture under her chair and identifies the picture when called upon.

5. After each child has identified her picture, continue playing. You may choose to put new pictures under the chairs, or if the pictures were taped, switch the chairs around so that children do not know which picture will be under her chair next. With some groups, you may be able to encourage the children to choose a new chair each time.

6. Instead of putting whole pictures under the chairs, put two halves of a picture underneath two different chairs. After the children find their pictures, they have to match it to a half that someone else is holding. (For example, zoo animals can be cut in half, so one child finds the head and another child finds the tail.)

More to do

The same pictures can be used throughout the day or week, during different activities. For example, ask the children to find a picture at group time and identify it, tape the pictures to the backs of chairs at snack time, and so on.

❖❖ Sandra Suffoletto Ryan, Buffalo, NY

Over, Under, Up, and Down

Materials

Small chairs, one for each child

What to do

1. This exercise is one that can be repeated frequently to reinforce the concepts of *over, under, in, on,* and *beside.*
2. Ask the children to sit IN their chair. Explain that they are going to play a game. When you give a command, they are to go to that place on their chair.
3. Give the following commands:
   Get UNDER your chair.
   Stand OVER (on top of) your chair.
   Stand BESIDE your chair.
   Stand IN BACK OF your chair.
4. End the series by saying, "Sit IN your chair."
5. If desired, let the children take turns giving the commands.

More to do

Use beanbags to place "over your head," "under your arm," and so on.
The children can use stuffed animals to place in the positions around the chair.

Related book

Rosie's Walk by Pat Hutchins

❖❖ Barbara Saul, Eureka, CA

Circle Action Games

Materials

Garden hose (50' will make about a dozen circles)
Scissors
Wooden dowel, the same diameter as the hose (½" to ¾") For 12 circles, you will need about 2'.

What to do

1. Remove the metal connections from the hose.
2. Cut the hose into 3' (1 m) segments.
3. Cut the dowel into 2" (5 cm) segments.
4. Force half of a dowel piece into one end of a hose piece. It should fit tightly.
5. Force the other end of the dowel into the opposite end of the hose, forming a circle.
6. To teach spatial concepts, ask the children to step *inside* the circle, walk *around* it, step *over* it, stand *beside* it, hold the circle in one hand and put their other hand through it, put their free hand under the circle and over it.
7. To teach body parts, place the circles on the floor and instruct the children to put their hands, then feet, knees, elbows, fingers, toes, heels, chins, and noses (be prepared for laughter!) inside the circle.

More to do

Music and Movement: Put on a record and practice hopping into and out of the circles in time to the music.

❖❖ Mary Jo Shannon, Roanoke, VA

Stand Up Game

Materials

A place where children can sit and stand easily and safely

What to do

1. Ask the children to sit in a circle. Explain the rules of the game to the children.
2. Tell them that you will give clues about a child and when the child thinks the clue describes her, she should stand up.
3. For example, stand up if…

   You have on a red shirt.

   You have brown hair.

   Your name is Emily.

   You have two feet.
4. Include clues that will allow one, several, and all the children to stand.

More to do

Math: Count the number of children standing after each clue.

❖❖ Angela Williamson La Fon, M. Ed., Lynchburg, VA

Nighttime Animals

Materials

Large space

What to do

1. This game is played just like "Goodnight Mr. Fox," but with some changes.
2. Ask all the children to line up at one end of the room. Choose one child to stand at the other end of the room.
3. The child by herself chooses an animal to imitate, for example, a dog.
4. The other children ask, "What time is it, Mr./Mrs. Dog?"
5. The "dog" calls out a number, and the children walk forward that many steps making dog sounds (barking, and so on).
6. When the children get close to the dog, she calls out, "Nighttime." Then they all run back to where they started. The dog tries to tag someone and that child is the next animal.

❖❖ Catherine Shogren, Eagan, MN

Bunny Races in Pillowcases

Materials

2 or more pillowcases
Large carpeted area

What to do

1. Encourage the children to practice hopping on two feet, like bunnies.
2. Ask two or more children at a time to put pillowcases over their feet, and pull them up to their stomachs.

3. Have a pillowcase race! When you say, "Go," the children can race to a designated point and back.

More to do

Encourage the children to try to hop around a circle, or other objects without falling.

Related book

The Great Bunny Race by Kathy Feczko

❖❖ Sandra Suffoletto Ryan, Buffalo, NY

Firefighter Relay Races

Materials

Red and orange paper or white paper and markers
Scissors
Clear contact paper, optional
Outside grassy area
4 bins
Water
Tape
2 cups

What to do

1. Beforehand, cut out paper flames using red and orange paper or white paper and markers. Cover them with clear contact paper, if desired.
2. Talk to the children about fire safety.
3. After your discussion, go outside with the children to have a relay race.
4. Fill two of the bins with water and space them about 3' (1 m) apart.
5. Place the other two bins at a distance appropriate for the children to run to, directly across from the water bins. Tape the paper flames to the front of the empty bins.
6. Ask the children to form two lines, one behind each of the water bins.
7. Ask the first child in each line to fill a cup with water from the bin, run to the empty bin, and pour the water into it (putting the fire out). Then the child runs back to the line and hands the cup to the next child in line.
8. Continue in relay fashion until all the children have had a turn.

More to do

Discuss other ways to put out fires.

Ask the children to think of ways to prevent the water from spilling out of their cups when they run.

Related books

Fire Engines by Anne Rockwell
Fire Fighters by Norma Simon

◆◆ Sandra Suffoletto Ryan, Buffalo, NY

Any Theme Parachute Games

Materials

Construction paper
Scissors
Markers
Parachute

What to do

1. Beforehand, make theme-related cutouts based on the class curriculum. For example, cut out snowflakes for winter, tissue paper ghosts and black paper bats for Halloween, autumn leaves, stars, hearts, shamrocks, and so on.
2. Ask the children to stand or sit around the outside edge of the parachute.
3. Distribute a few cutouts to each child. Ask the children to toss their cutouts into the parachute.
4. Go through a variety of movements with the parachute. For example:
   - Shake it fast and then slow.
   - Lift the parachute up high on the count of three to shoot the cutouts into the air.
   - Hold the parachute in one hand and walk in a circle like a merry-go-round, lifting the parachute up and down gently.
5. After shooting the items up into the air, some may fall on the ground around the parachute. The children can pick up the items that fall near them and throw them back into the parachute.

6. Toss the items under the parachute and call on children one or two at a time to go under and pick up the items while the others hold the parachute up high (e.g., John and Mary will go under the parachute and pick up "just one" star, or find "two" stars, or "pick up as many as they can." If you are using colored leaves, you may ask the children to go under the parachute and find "just a red leaf" or "just the yellow leaves."

7. Some parachutes have a hole in the middle of them. If so, you can have children gently shake the parachute until all the items fall through the hole.

More to do

Use the same items from the parachute games for other activities throughout the day. For example, hide the cutouts around the room for children to find, tape them on the floor for the children to sit on at group time, and so on.

❖❖ Sandra Suffoletto Ryan, Buffalo, NY

Pass It

Materials

Ball (or another safe hand-sized object, such as an apple or bean bag)

What to do

1. Ask the children to form a circle and sit down.
2. Explain that to play this game, they will have to work together and listen carefully to what the words in the poem say to do.
3. Say the following poem a few times as the children clap to the beat.
   Pass, pass, pass the ____,
   As slowly as you can.
   Pass, pass, pass the ____,
   As quickly as you can.
   Pass, pass, pass the ____,
   As high as you can.
4. Before beginning the game, pass the ball (or other object) around the group so that each child has a chance to look at it and feel it.
5. Explain that when they get the ball, they should pass it to the person next to them, going around the circle.

6. As the children pass the object, encourage them to say the poem and listen to you for directions. To make the activity easier, repeat the same direction three or more times.

More to do

If the children appear to be losing interest, pick up the pace by passing more than one object. If the children get really good at passing the object, try passing two objects, one in each direction.

Sensory: Increase the sensory and exploration experience during the game by using a variety of objects.

❖❖ Sandra Nagel, White Lake, MI

Balls and Windmills

Materials

Tennis ball

What to do

1. Ask the children to sit cross-legged on the ground opposite a partner.
2. One child holds a tennis ball, and the other child is the "windmill."
3. The "windmill" closes her eyes while the other child places the tennis ball on the ground within reach of her.
4. With her eyes still closed, the windmill swings her arms around herself, low to the ground.
5. Her partner then has to retrieve the tennis ball without being touched by the windmill.
6. The game is over when the windmill touches the ball, the child picking up the ball is touched, or when the child has picked up the ball successfully.

More to do

Alter the amount of windmills and ball collectors. Try one windmill with three balls, or three windmills sitting with their backs together using six balls and partners.

Music and Movement: Play music during the game and ask the windmills to move in time to the beat.

❖❖ Elizabeth Bezant, Quinns Rocks, Australia

Beanbag Toss

Materials

Beanbags, one each child
A space to throw beanbags, such as a rug area

What to do

1. Throwing and catching beanbags is great for improving hand-eye coordination. There are a variety of beanbag games children can play either individually, in pairs, or in a large group.
2. Individually, children can:
   - throw the beanbag up in the air and catch it with one or both hands
   - toss the beanbag up and try to have it land on their head, shoulder, or back of their hand
   - throw their beanbag and try to clap before they catch it
   - toss the beanbag from their right hand to their left hand
3. In pairs, the children can sit or stand and try to throw and catch the beanbag to each other.
4. In large groups, you can use one beanbag and the children can take turns throwing the bag to each other. If desired, the children can say letters, numbers, shapes, or names when they catch the beanbag.
5. For children not ready for throwing, start out by having the children pass the beanbag around different parts of their body or around a large circle of children. This will help to develop hand-eye coordination for future toss and catch games.

❖❖ Melissa Browning, Milwaukee, WI

Roll the Ball

Materials

Ball

What to do

1. Ask the children to hold hands and make a circle, then sit down.
2. Explain that you will sing the following song, and when the child states her name, you will roll the ball to her. Then she can roll it back to you.
   Roll the ball.
   Play the game.
   When you get the ball,
   You say your name.
3. After singing it a few times, encourage the children to sing along.
4. Continue until everyone has had a turn.
5. This is a great game to play at the beginning of the year because it helps the children learn each other's names.

More to do

After the children are able to say their names and are familiar with each other, change the last sentence of the song to work on other skills. For example, say your last name, …favorite color, …what you like to do, and so on.

❖❖ Sandra Nagel, White Lake, MI

Twister for Threes

Materials

"Twister" board game
Stuffed animals

What to do

1. "Twister" is a fun game for all ages, but little children don't always have the balance and coordination to play the traditional way, so here is a way for three-year-olds to play.

Note: No more than four children can play at once, so you may want to set this game up as one of several stations so children not playing Twister have another activity to go to.

2. Ask a child to stand on each side of the Twister mat. (You can have a fifth child do the spinning if you'd like.) Give each child two stuffed animals. They can hold them or place them on the floor near their feet.

3. On the game board, instead of left foot, right foot, left hand, and right hand, use these four divisions: hand, foot, bear, and dog (or whatever the animals are—if you don't have enough of the same animals, go by color, or tie a colored ribbon around the stuffed animals' necks to designate).

4. Give the spinner a spin! You will come up with choices such as "Hand on red," or "Bear on green." As in the regular game, the object of the game is to try to maintain your position. In other words, if you get "dog on blue" and your foot is on red, keep it there!

More to do

Art: Put blue, red, green, and yellow paint in the art center. Ask the children if they can make a line of four colored circles like the game board.

Dramatic Play: Leave the game board in the dramatic play area for the children to use with the dolls and stuffed animals on their own.

❖❖ Suzanne Pearson, Stephens City, VA

Leap Frog Leap

Materials

2 clean, cardboard ½ gallon milk cartons
Ruler
Marker
Scissors
Construction paper in various colors
Glue
3" (7 cm) wide clear tape
Clear contact paper

What to do

Prepare:

1. Measure 4" (10 cm) up from the bottom of the milk cartons. Mark the 4" point around the entire carton and cut off what remains above the line.
2. Slide the two cartons together, open ends facing each other, until you have formed a cube.
3. Glue a different color piece of construction paper to each side of the cube and cover the entire cube with clear tape.
4. Cut out five lily pad shapes of each color that you put on the cube (30 in all). Make them large enough for a child's feet to fit on.

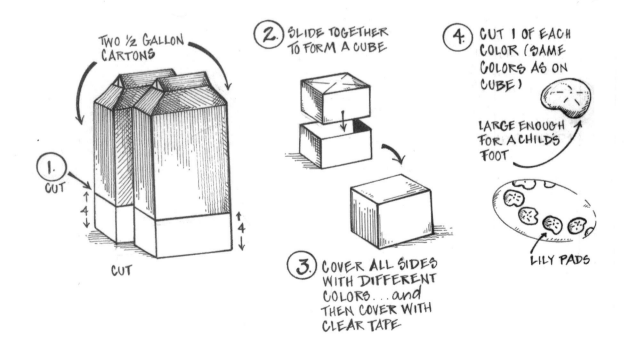

5. Put the lily pads in a line on the floor, varying the colors. Leave approximately 1' (30 cm) between each one and zigzag the line. Put clear contact paper over each lily pad to attach it to the floor.

Play the game:

1. Ask a small group of children to line up at the beginning of the lily pad line.
2. Ask the first child to roll the color cube and leap from lily pad to lily pad until she comes to the color she rolled.
3. The next child rolls the color cube and does the same thing. The first child also leaps to the next pad of the color that was just rolled.
4. Continue until everyone has leaped off the end of the line and start again.

Related books

It's Mine by Leo Lionni
Jump, Frog, Jump! by Robert Kalan
Once There Was a Bull…(Frog) by Rick Walton
Spotted Yellow Frogs: Fold-out Fun with Patterns, Colors, 3-D Shapes, and Animals by Matthew Van Fleet
The Wide-Mouthed Frog: A Pop-Up Book by Keith Faulkner

❖❖ Ann Gudowski, Johnstown, PA

Guidelines for Small Group Times

Materials

None

What to do

1. Small group times are a part of every preschool program. A simple definition for small group time is a time during the day's activities where children are involved with a small group of their peers (eight or less) in a planned, teacher-facilitated activity. The role of the teacher is to encourage and facilitate the learning and exploring process, not dominate and stifle creativity. Following is a list of ideas to guide you in successful small group times.

2. The adult/child ratio should be no more than 1:8. This allows opportunity for adults to become directly involved with all the children in a group.

3. Each child should have a defined space to work that can be designated as his or hers.

4. Children will need certain materials of their own to be available during small group times, including such things as scissors, glue, tape, crayons, and markers. These can be kept in the children's own art boxes or be made available when needed.

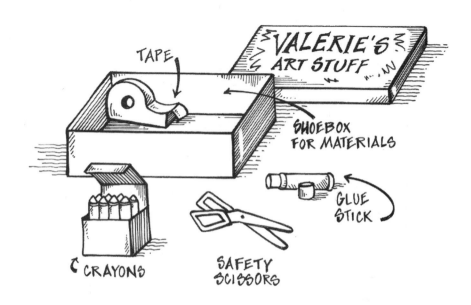

5. Each child should have access to all materials being used in an activity. Put several containers of the same materials in various places throughout the work area. This eliminates anxiety on the part of the child by keeping wait time at a minimum.

6. Adult language during small group times should encourage and facilitate the child's exploration and creativity. Open-ended statements that encourage the child to be involved with conversation are preferable to comments that seek one specific answer or yes/no answers. For example: "Billy, tell me about what you are making" is a better approach than "What is it you are making?"

7. Small group activities do not always have an end product that the child takes with them. Small group times will often include the use of manipulatives from the classroom in different ways.

8. Always have additional materials to add to your original idea in case your plan does not go in a direction you intended. Asking children what else can be used is a good way to add to and extend an activity.

9. Recording a child's conversation during small group times is a wonderful way to add to a child's creation. Writing responses on paper and using them later to discuss the activity is an excellent follow up. These responses can be shared with parents and incorporated into further activities.

10. Use the "Small Group Planning Sheet" (see following page) for future planning. Your changes and recommendations can be noted as well.

11. Small group activities will often lead to new centers. Materials used for the activity can be transferred to the appropriate learning center in the room or a separate center can be established.

❖❖ Susan E. May, Madison Heights, VA

SMALL GROUP PLANNING SHEET

Small Group Idea:

_____
_____
_____
_____
_____
_____

Individual Materials:

_____
_____
_____
_____
_____

Group Materials:

_____
_____
_____
_____
_____

Explanation:

_____
_____
_____
_____
_____

Key Comments:

_____
_____
_____
_____

Extension Materials:

_____
_____
_____
_____

Evaluation/Changes:

_____
_____
_____
_____
_____

Building Quality Teacher-Child Relationships

Materials

None

What to do

The following are some tips for building quality teacher-child relationships.

1. **Respect children.** Treat children as living, loving individuals, and show them respect by listening attentively, communicating on their level, and responding positively.
2. **Be accepting.** Embrace all children regardless of ethnic, religious, physical, linguistic, or socioeconomic diversity. Remember that you can accept a child without necessarily approving of his behavior.
3. **Provide warmth.** Create an open and inviting classroom atmosphere where you are welcoming and approachable.
4. **Treat children as individuals.** Compare children to themselves at an earlier time rather than comparing children to one another.
5. **Provide alternatives.** Give children some control over their environment by allowing them to make choices and contribute to class decisions.
6. **Have high expectations.** Expect the best from your children and provide them with many, varied opportunities to be successful.
7. **Be honest.** Answer children's questions simply but truthfully and offer only sincere praise.
8. **Be a learner.** Know your own strengths and weaknesses and be willing to learn along with, and from, your children.

❖❖ Rebecca McMahen Giles, Mobile, AL

Managing Misbehavior

Materials

None

What to do

Following are some tips for managing misbehavior:

1. **Address the child directly.** Go over to the child and positively state what the child did wrong. Explain why the exhibited behavior is not permissible, and provide appropriate alternatives. For example, "The blocks are for building. Throwing the wooden blocks could hurt someone. If you want to throw something, you may go to the bean bag toss."

2. **Remove the child from the situation.** Calmly remind the child of your previous conversation and state that the result of his choice to act inappropriately is the loss of privilege. For example, "I explained that throwing wooden blocks is dangerous. Because you chose to continue throwing the blocks, you have to leave the Block Center."

3. **Keep the child with you.** Briefly reflect on the child's choice of behavior and discuss the feelings behind his action. Avoid preaching to the child or talking too much.

4. **Let the child decide when to return.** Personally escort the child to the chosen activity whether or not it is the same activity where the problem situation occurred. Make the child's transition comfortable by offering suggestions and reinforcing appropriate behavior.

5. **If the problem persists, remove the child again.** Talk to the child again. Allow the child to return to an activity with teacher assistance when he or she is ready. The child, however, should not return to the problem area for the rest of the day.

◆❖ Rebecca McMahen Giles, Mobile, AL

Constructive Communication

Materials

None

What to do

The following are some tips for constructive communication with the children:

1. **Listen attentively.** The first consideration in being an effective communicator is being a good listener. Eliminate distractions; make eye contact; and pay attention to what the child is saying. If you are unable to listen attentively, let the child know that this is not the best time to talk.

2. **Talk with (not at) children.** Talking "at" someone is a one-sided conversation. Talk to children as you would a friend in order to create an atmosphere that fosters discussion and encourages confidences.

3. **Use conversation starters.** Phrases such as "Tell me about that." And "Really?" invite children to say more about a particular topic while expressing the idea that their thoughts are worthy and appreciated.

4. **Use more "Do's" than "Don'ts."** State directions positively, telling children what you want them to do rather than what not to do.

5. **Make requests simple.** Avoid giving several directions at one time to increase children's chances of understanding.

6. **Make important requests firmly.** Get the child's attention before speaking, and speak as if you mean it. Be sure to state the reason why the child must do this particular thing.

7. **Use considerate language.** Communicate acceptance by using kind, encouraging words and avoiding sarcasm. Common courtesies such as "please" or "thank you" show respect while modeling appropriate manners.

❖❖ Rebecca McMahen Giles, Mobile, AL

Objectives by the Numbers

Materials

List of teaching objectives

What to do

1. Write down your teaching objectives for the month and number each one.
2. As you write your lesson plans for the week, simply jot down the number of the objective instead of writing it out.

❖❖ Jackie Wright, Enid, OK

Portable File Boxes

Materials

9 all-purpose, clear storage boxes with lids
Labels and markers
Outline of themes for the year
Theme-related instructional materials you plan to use during the year

What to do

1. Purchase a clear storage box for each month of the school year. A good size is about 12" high x 19" wide x 15" deep (WhatchamaBoxes or Long-Term File Tote boxes).
2. Label each box with the name of the month.
3. Into each box, put all of the hands-on materials you plan to introduce during that month.
4. Arrange all of your instructional materials such as manipulatives, file-folder games, flannel board stories and activities, and so on by weekly themes you plan to use during the school year.
5. This keeps all of your hands-on materials in one place, which makes locating them each month easy.
6. If desired, you may list the contents of each box to make sure everything is returned and ready for next year.

❖❖ Jackie Wright, Enid, OK

Three-Ring Binder Management System

Materials

Three-ring binder (3" or 4"), one for each month of school
An outline of themes for the year
8 ½" x 11" top-loading, plastic sheet protectors
Master copies of all your activities
Photocopier

What to do

1. Label the months on each spine of the binders, one for each month of the school year.
2. Once you have established your weekly themes for the year, divide each month into weeks. Keep a photocopy of all your planned activities for the week organized in page protectors in the appropriate binder.
3. At the beginning of each month, gather materials and prepare for the following month to ensure all items are cut out and ready for use.
4. At the end of the month, store any unused materials inside the page protector with that activity to be used again next year.
5. Continue in the same manner, rotating through all of the binders each year.

❖ Jackie Wright, Enid, OK

Monthly Room Plan

Materials

Paper and pencil

What to do

1. Make a comprehensive list of all the hands-on materials you plan to use during the year.
2. Then, complete a one- or two-page monthly record listing all the materials you plan to introduce to the children during the month. Include on the list all

of the manipulatives, audiocassette tapes (to use in listening centers), flannel board activities, and learning mat activities that you plan to use and that children may use on their own. Be sure to designate where the materials will be stored and displayed.

3. Use a pencil to make the list because the space in which you work and the availability of materials will sometimes change during the year.
4. Update the plans monthly.
5. Reuse this record from year to year. It's a great way to jog your memory about the resources you have collected and remind you how actively engaged and involved in the activities the children have been. It also makes rotating the materials throughout the year much easier when you have a plan in writing.

❖❖ Jackie Wright, Enid, OK

Portfolios for Three-year-Olds

Materials

Samples of the children's work
Manila folders, one for each child
Portfolio box
Camera, optional

What to do

1. Throughout the year, keep samples of the children's work. For example, keep something from August, January, and May.
2. This is a good tool to use for parent conferences and data collection.
3. At the end of the year, put the items together into a memory book for the child's family.
4. You may also want to use a developmental checklist throughout the year to record what skills the child has learned and when. Include this in the memory book.

More to do

Field Trip: Take photos of the children during field trips to add to the portfolios.

❖ Melissa Browning, Milwaukee, WI

Group Time Preparation Form

Materials

Paper and pen
Copy machine

What to do

1. Make your own form entitled "Things to Do to Prepare for Group Time," "Things to Remember to Do," "From the Teacher's Desk," or whatever title seems appropriate.
2. Divide the paper into five sections, one for each day of the week. Write the names of the days of the week.
3. Under the title at the top, make three columns. Label them: "At Home," "In the Office," and "In the Classroom." In the top margin write, "Week Themes."
4. Make multiple copies of the form so that you will have one to use each week.
5. Use this form to jot down materials you need to locate, items you need to bring from home, things you need to turn in to the office, things you need to turn in for purchase, things you need to pick up from the office, and so on.
6. It's also a good idea to note when it's time to change a bulletin board, make a class quantity of pages for the next week, cut out a craft project, fold and staple little books, mix paints, or anything that will require preparation time before group time begins.

❖ Jackie Wright, Enid, OK

Snack Ease

Materials

None

What to do

1. If you work in a school where the parents bring in the snacks each day, then this timesaving tip will work for you. Depending on the number of children in your class, you may need to adjust this idea to suit your needs.
2. At the beginning of the year when you meet with all of the parents, assign a number to each child. This can be done to correspond with the alphabetical listing of the class.
3. Explain to the parents that whatever number their child is assigned is the day of the month that they will need to bring in the class snack each month. They will have the same date each month, but not the same day of the week.
4. This way parents won't easily forget what day of the month to send in a snack because it will always be the same date. This saves you from sending home constant reminders.

Note: If their date hits on a weekend, then they can bring in a snack at the end of the month.

◆◆ Mike Krestar, White Oak, PA

Pictorial Agenda

Materials

See below and following page

What to do

1. Because three-year-olds find comfort in structure and routine, I developed a pictorial agenda for my classroom that I use daily with the children. Instead of clock time, I use the numbers 1-10. I also use pictures of activities instead of words. This immediately gives the children control of the agenda and begins the process of early language and reading.

2. Following is an example of a pictorial agenda:
   - pictures of little children=welcoming and begin to play
   - picture of a circle=circle time
   - pictures of numbers, markers, ABC's, blocks, and so on=center time
   - picture of a book=language experience: story, music, drama
   - picture of a lunchbox=lunchtime
   - picture of outdoors=outside play
   - picture of an empty sack=surprise activity of the day
   - pictures of blankets and pillows=quiet time
   - picture of snack=snack time
   - picture of coats and backpacks=time to go home

3. As the year progresses, the children rely on the agenda more and more. It will also help them to understand sequence. For example, if a child asks, "When is lunch?" You might respond with, "We are finishing #3 very soon." Children will go to the agenda and use pre-reading skills to answer their own questions.

4. Following numbers instead of a clock allows the teacher greater flexibility. For example, you might cut #7 a little shorter to provide ample time for a #9 birthday celebration.

5. You can also change the agenda for special circumstances. For example, if you are on a half-day schedule, cover up #6-9 on the agenda. If the class is having a special visitor or a field trip, draw the corrected agenda first thing in the morning. If someone is leaving early, sit down individually with that child and plan his day so he knows his schedule.

❖❖ Diane L. Shatto, Kansa City, MO

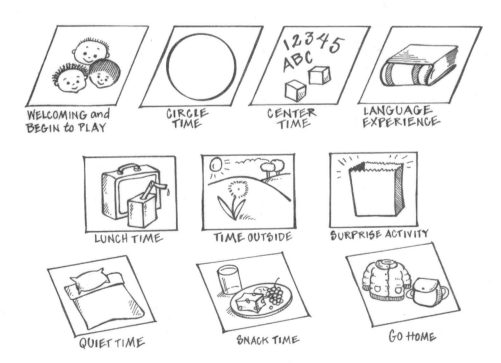

WELCOMING and BEGIN to PLAY CIRCLE TIME CENTER TIME LANGUAGE EXPERIENCE

LUNCH TIME TIME OUTSIDE SURPRISE ACTIVITY

QUIET TIME SNACK TIME GO HOME

Sequencing Our Day

Materials

Camera and film
Card stock
Glue
Marker
Pocket chart

What to do

1. Take pictures of the children doing various activities throughout the day.
2. After the pictures are developed, glue each one on a piece of card stock. Label them. For example, "Hanging Up Our Coats," "Eating Our Snack," and so on.
3. Show the pictures at circle time and ask the children to tell each other what is happening in the photo.
4. Use a pocket chart to put the pictures in the correct order from first to last.
5. Leave the photos at a table and let the children practice putting them in sequential order.

More to do

Give each child a picture. Help the children work together to put them all in sequential order. Ask them to explain what is happening in their picture.

Home Connection: Ask the parents to help the children write and draw pictures of what happens during their day.

Math: Buy two copies of a book—one to read and one to cut up. Ask the children to put the story in sequential order.

Related books

The Gingerbread Man by K. Schmidt
The House that Jack Built by Jeanette Winter

◆❖ Barbara Saul, Eureka, CA

Pick a Pocket!

Materials

Construction paper in a variety of colors
Scissors
Laminate or clear contact paper
Marker
Index cards, one for each child
Library pockets

What to do

1. Make a large color dot for each center in your classroom using a different color of construction paper for each center. A good idea is to trace around a dinner plate on the paper and cut out the circle.
2. Write the name of the center on the dot or on a matching sheet of construction paper.
3. Laminate the dots or cover them with clear contact paper. Hang a different color dot in each center.
4. Write each child's name on an index card and put each index card into a library pocket. Keep them where the children can access them easily, such as the front of your desk. Also put three or four library pockets into each center.

5. Whenever there is free choice for centers, each child brings his name card to the center of his choice and puts it into an empty library folder. If all the pockets in a particular center are filled, the child must choose another center to go to. This helps keep the number of children in each center small, and it also helps the teacher see where each child should be.

6. When center time is over, ask the children to clean up their area. Then each child will return his index card to his own library pocket.

❖❖ Sheryl Smith, Jonesborough, TN

Durable Nametags

Materials

Baseball card sleeve
Paper and pen

What to do

1. Have the children carry around a nametag while rotating through centers.
2. To make the nametags more durable, write each child's name on a piece of paper and slip it into a hard baseball card protector.
3. In my classroom, the cards went through the water table, the children's mouths, and lots of other three-year-old messes and still lasted a long time!

❖❖ Laurie Nied, Charlotte, NC

Morning Attendance and Greeting

Materials

None

What to do

1. When taking attendance each morning, say each child's name.

2. Allow time for the child to say, "Good Morning." Then ask the child a question about his morning or the night before, or comment about an article of clothing he is wearing or other outward appearance.

3. This allows for a personal interaction between the teacher and the child each day.

More to do

Have a "style show" of new items that the child has brought in. For example, a new hat for winter will lend itself to a discussion of the different types and purposes of hats.

❖❖ Melissa Browning, Milwaukee, WI

Lunchbox Tree

Materials

Construction paper, green and brown
Scissors
Tape
Coat rack

What to do

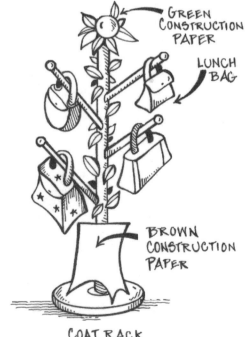

GREEN CONSTRUCTION PAPER

LUNCH BAG

1. Cut out leaves and a tree trunk from brown and green construction paper. Tape the cutouts to a coat rack to create a tree (see illustration).

2. Place the coat rack by the door in your room.

3. Each day as the children arrive, they can hang their lunch bags on the "lunchbox tree."

BROWN CONSTRUCTION PAPER

COAT RACK

❖❖ Lisa Chichester, Parkersburg, WV

Picture Passer

Materials

Clothespin

What to do

1. When sharing photos with the children in your class, simply clip a clothespin to the bottom of each photograph and pass it on. This will help keep the photos in good condition.

◆◆ Jodi Sykes, Lake Worth, FL

Name Find

Materials

3" x 5" note cards
Markers
Variety of large stickers, one for each child

What to do

1. Print each child's name on separate note cards.
2. Ask each child to select a sticker to add to his note card.
3. Use the name card to label the child's coat hook, cubby, or some other location in the classroom where the child places personal items.
4. Since most three-year-olds are unable to identify their names in print, the addition of the sticker to the name card will assist them in identifying which card belongs to them.
5. If space does not allow for the use of a 3" x 5" note card, you can also use this "sticker concept" on other appropriate materials such as file folder labels or construction paper cutouts.

◆◆ Mary Volkman, Ottawa, IL

Stick with Me

Materials

Packs of animal stickers

What to do

1. Since many three-year-olds can't recognize their written name, this tip will help them not only recognize the letters of their name but also where to hang their coat, put their lunch box, stand in line, and so on.
2. On the first day of class, ask each child to pick a pack of their favorite animal stickers. Make sure that each pack has all the same animal in it.
3. Then, wherever you write that child's name, place his animal sticker beside it. For example, write the name "Mike" on a tag on Mike's desk, and then place his elephant sticker beside his nametag.
4. The children will begin to recognize the letters of their name every time they see their animal sticker. They will also know that if their animal is on a desk, it must be their desk.

◈ Mike Krestar, White Oak, PA

Snack Helper Picture

Materials

Construction paper
Scissors
Snapshot of each child, requested from parents when each child enrolls in school
Markers
Glue

What to do

1. Cut pieces of construction paper in half. When each child enrolls in the school or center, glue a picture of the child onto a half sheet of construction paper and clearly print the child's name under it. The child can participate in this by choosing colors and gluing.
2. Each day, before the children gather in the first circle time of the day, post one child's picture on the wall or bulletin board.

3. This child will be the special person of the day and will be first in everything, such as line leader, first one to start a game, and first to do a special craft or project. This gives each child a day to feel extra-special.

❖❖ Nancy DeSteno, Andover, MN

Pet Parade

Materials

Blue construction paper
Scissors

What to do

1. Cut out blue paper ribbons for each child.
2. On the second or third day of school, when many young children begin to miss being at home, ask them to bring in their favorite stuffed animal.
3. Plan a "Pet Parade" for that particular day. March to the beat of a tambourine through the school, playground, and other classes (if possible). This way the children familiarize themselves with the school surroundings and see other children in different rooms playing and being busy.
4. When you return to your own room, give out blue ribbons for different categories, such as largest, smallest, cutest, whitest, greenest, cuddliest, biggest, tallest, and so on. Make sure that everyone receives a blue ribbon.

❖❖ Ingelore Mix, Gainesville, VA

First Day Pictures

Materials

Camera (a Polaroid is best so you can get instant results)
Contact paper

What to do

1. On the first day of class, take a picture of each child and their parents as they arrive.

2. Use contact paper to adhere the picture to the child's place at the table, cubby, or in a photo album.

3. This allows the child to look at their parents throughout the day, which helps them to get through first day jitters.

❖❖ Melissa Browning, Milwaukee, WI

Clean Up Photos

Materials

Camera
Pictures of all the items in the room
Contact paper

What to do

1. Take photos of all the items in the room and how they are to be put away.

2. Use contact paper to adhere the photos to the shelves so that the children will know where the items are to be placed at clean-up time.

❖❖ Melissa Browning, Milwaukee, WI

Keep It Simple

Materials

Plastic containers
Buckets or tubs

What to do

1. If the children are having difficulty cleaning up at the end of activity time, there may be too many materials available for them to clean up!

2. Start the year with a minimum of materials on the shelves:
   - two easy, four-piece puzzles
   - one bucket of Legos, cardboard blocks, and a bucket of vehicles
   - one doll, one pot, two place settings, and a play pizza

3. As the children grow accustomed to the classroom and learn how to clean up, gradually add more materials. If you notice that cleanup is consistently difficult, remove some materials!

Original song

This is the way we clean our room,
Clean our room, clean our room,
This is the way we clean our room so early in the morning." (or late in the afternoon)
Andy's picking up a block, up a block, up a block,
Adam's cleaning up the blocks so early in the morning.

Related books

Berenstain Bears and the Messy Room by Stan and Jan Berenstain
Tracy's Mess by Elise Peterson

❖❖ Linda N. Ford, Sacramento, CA

Where Do I Belong?

Materials

Basket
Items from around the room that the children will use

What to do

1. At the beginning of the year, put a bunch of items from around the room into a basket.
2. Gather the children into a group and ask each child, one at a time, where one of the items belongs.
3. The other children watch as the child puts the item away.
4. This really helps when it is time to clean up.

❖❖ Melissa Browning, Milwaukee, WI

Felt Theme Boxes

Materials

Felt with adhesive back (found in hardware stores in the area of products
designed to protect wooden floors)
Scissors
Assorted felt pieces
Plastic videotape storage boxes
Marker

What to do

1. Cut felt to fit around the outside of the tape storage box. Remove the
   adhesive backing to adhere it to the plastic case.
2. Cut or purchase felt shapes to match your theme or concept (such as letters,
   numbers, shapes, farm animals, clothing shapes, story characters, and so on).
3. Put the felt cutouts into the box.
4. Label the end of the box with words or pictures for identification.
5. Over a period of time, you can create a variety of theme boxes. These
   provide great activities for children to do during quiet times.

More to do

This also works with pizza boxes, but VCR cases are stronger and last longer.
Language: Supervise and talk with the children about their use of the materials
to encourage language development.

◆◆ Bev Schumacher, Dayton, OH

Puppet Storage

Materials

Gallon size, zipper-closure plastic bags
Hand puppets
Labels and markers

What to do

1. Store each of your hand puppets in separate 8" x 12" (gallon-size) zipper-closure plastic bags.
2. Put a copy of the poem, song, or script that belongs with the puppet inside the bag with it.
3. Label the outside.

❖ Jackie Wright, Enid, Oklahoma

Easy Flannel Board Storage

Materials

Large three-ring binder
Top-loading plastic page protector sheets (same size as binder)

What to do

1. Place page protector sheets into the binder.
2. In each page protector, store a different set of flannel board pieces, along with the accompanying story or poem.
3. Place the binder your bookshelf so your stories are always at your fingertips.

❖❖ Vicki L. Schneider, Oshkosh, WI

Chart Storage Made Easy

Materials

Large, clear plastic sacks
Scissors
Clear mailing tape
Charts, posters, graphing projects, and bulletin boards
Spring-style clothespins
Zipper-closure plastic bags, optional
Clothes rod

What to do

1. Save plastic bags from the cleaners or use large, clear plastic garbage sacks. Cut the bottoms so that they are open and no longer pleated together.
2. Tape the bottoms closed with clear mailing tape, leaving an opening at the top.
3. Store charts, posters, graphing projects, and bulletin boards in separate bags.
4. Clip each bag to a wire clothespin for easy storage.
5. It is not necessary to label the bags. However, if desired, it is a good idea to label the bulletin board titles and put each set of cut-out letters into small zipper-closure bags inside the large bags.
6. Hang them on a clothes rod in the order you plan to use them to keep them neatly organized and easily accessible.

❖❖ Jackie Wright, Enid, OK

Make Your Own File Jackets

Materials

12" x 18" construction paper
Scissors
Transparent tape
Markers
Theme-related pictures
Glue
Laminate or clear contact paper

What to do

1. Cut along one 12" side of the construction paper to form an opening (pocket).
2. Fold along the 12" side slightly short of folding in the middle. This should create a top resembling store-bought jacket folders (9" x 12").
3. Tape the side closed.
4. Label the front to depict the contents.
5. Glue a cute, theme-related picture on the front.
6. Laminate or cover with clear contact paper for durability.
   Author note: I like to laminate mine twice.
7. Trim away the excess laminate and you have a handy container for a flannel board activity, book and book extension, stick puppets and script, and so on.

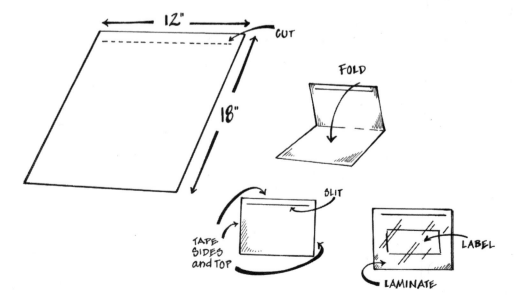

8. Create as many of these as you need for managing your materials. They fit perfectly in filing cabinets or plastic storage boxes.

❖❖ Jackie Wright, Enid, OK

Display Stands

Materials

Cardboard display stand
Flannel board
Big books

What to do

1. Ask the manager of your local grocery store to donate a display stand to your classroom. Put your flannel board on the display stand.
2. This is a unique way to show off your flannel board. It works nicely holding the flannel board at the correct slant so that nothing falls off and it is approximately 16" off the floor, just at children's eye level.
3. This is great for holding big books as you read aloud to the children. It frees up your hands to turn the pages and your arms don't tire out trying to hold the weight of the book.
4. These stands fold flat and can be stored out of sight when not in use.

Author note: In my 18 years of teaching preschool children, I consider this one teaching tool most helpful.

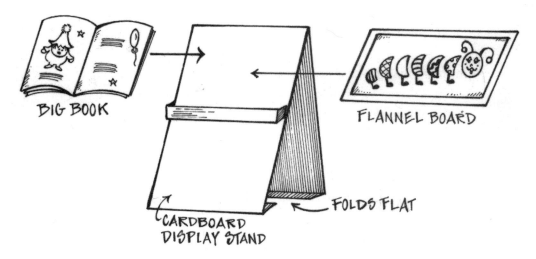

BIG BOOK

FLANNEL BOARD

FOLDS FLAT

CARDBOARD DISPLAY STAND

❖❖ Jackie Wright, Enid, OK

Material Magic

Materials

See below

What to do

1. Following are some ideas of how you can use wallpaper, upholstery samples, coffee cans, candy boxes or shoeboxes, and Styrofoam trays in your classroom.

Wallpaper use in classrooms:

1. Call local paint stores or other places where wallpaper sample books are used. Ask if there are any books about to be discarded and see if they will donate the books to your school.
2. Wallpaper samples make excellent bulletin board borders. There are endless possibilities. For example, animal print wallpaper is great as a bulletin board background when doing a theme such as jungle animals or the zoo.
3. You can use wallpaper for many holiday themes. For example, use green plaid wallpaper to make shamrocks for St. Patrick's Day. Roses and flower patterns are great for cutting out hearts for Valentine's Day. Cut out autumn leaf patterns to make Halloween or Thanksgiving placemats.
4. Another good use for wallpaper samples is to make scrapbook covers with them. Put sheets of colored paper between wallpaper samples, fold in half, and staple to make "Good Listener" sticker books. When you read the children a story, if they have been good listeners, place a special sticker inside their sticker books that have their names on them. The children love collecting stickers this way. And when the book is full, they can take them home and you can begin all over again.

Upholstery samples:

1. These also come in sample books. They are somewhat different from wallpaper samples because they are cloth.
2. Cut upholstery samples out of the books and use a sturdy cloth glue such as Liquid Stitch to make wallets, purses, clothes for dolls, and cut-outs for the felt board. Use the large pieces of upholstery samples to make book bags.
3. You can also use them for background scenes on display boards, parent information boards, and so on.

Coffee cans:

1. Coffee cans can be decorated and used to hold many things.
2. Cover the cans with wallpaper or upholstery samples. Glue faux jewels or beads or buttons on the sides or spray paint them any color.
3. Use them to hold marbles (for marble painting), sequins, glitter, buttons, ribbons, or any number of small craft items that need to be in a container.
4. These cans make great flowerpots. Decorate the outside of the can and add a bit of floral Styrofoam to hold artificial flowers, or make tissue flowers using strong and sturdy straws as the stems. This is a great gift for Mother's Day.

Candy and shoeboxes:

1. Candy boxes and shoeboxes are great for making treasure boxes. Children love the idea of having their own box to store treasures in. Whitman's candy boxes are particularly good for this because the lids are attached to the box.
2. Children can use many things to decorate their box, such as wrapping paper, wallpaper, lacy doily napkins, newspaper comics, magazine pictures, and so on.

Styrofoam trays:

1. Styrofoam trays make excellent picture frames. Glue a picture from a magazine, greeting card, or cereal box in the middle of the tray. Secure a piece of yarn or string to the back to hang the picture. Decorate the sides with ribbon or even puzzle pieces if most of the puzzle has been lost or misplaced.

❖❖ Penni L. Smith, Riverside, CA

Shower Curtain Sanity Savers

Materials

Inexpensive shower curtains or liners (available at "dollar" stores)

What to do

1. Before beginning a messy activity, place shower curtains on the floor where the activity will take place. The curtains catch drips of paint, water, glue, and more.

2. With these on the floor, children can engage in many activities while sitting or sprawling on the floor (their favorite positions).

3. Use shower curtains with sponge painting, printing with gadgets, using huge amounts of modeling dough with several children, playing with bins of rice, painting footprints, and more. (When using modeling dough, use shower curtains on the tables, too.)

4. At the end of the activity, shake loose items into the trash. Wipe down the curtains or wash them using the gentle cycle of your washing machine.

❖ Barbara Backer, Charleston, SC

Tips for Working with Modeling Dough

Materials

12" tile squares used for flooring
Modeling dough

What to do

1. Give each child a tile square to use as a workspace when using modeling dough. This keeps the modeling dough in one place and minimizes dough on the floor, where it can be tracked into carpeted areas.

2. Make sure children wash their hands before and after using modeling dough. Washing first keeps the dough clean and relatively free from germs.

3. Some children will spend days squeezing and mashing the dough, discovering and enjoying its tactile qualities. Don't rush children through this stage. It is an important stage in learning and is also a good experience for strengthening small muscles and coordination.

4. Some children will work with dough by putting small pieces together to make a larger figure; others, by pulling small amounts from a large piece. Respect both ways of creating—both are valuable.

5. For three-year-olds, the pleasure of using modeling dough is in the process of playing with it. Don't rush children to make specific items.

6. To keep children interested in playing with the modeling dough, add other items

7. Alternate adding rolling pins, plastic knives, craft sticks, blunt scissors, or cookie cutters. Avoid adding too many items at once. Too many might distract from the modeling experience.

More to do

Math: Encourage the children to divide their dough into several balls. Ask the group to help each child count the balls he made.

More Math: Encourage the children to divide their dough into four balls of different sizes. Have them arrange their dough balls in order from largest to smallest or from smallest to largest.

❖❖ Barbara Backer, Charleston, SC

Egg Cartons and Glue

Materials

Styrofoam egg cartons
Scissors (for adult use only)

What to do

1. Young children have difficulty squeezing the bottles that dispense glue. Avoid this frustration by giving each child his own glue cup.
2. Cut off and discard the tops of the egg cartons.
3. Cut the bottom of each egg carton bottom into six pieces, so that there are two connected egg cups in each section.
4. Pour a small amount of glue into each cup and give each child a double cup. The child can use his fingers to dip into, apply, and spread the glue.
5. If desired, the children can share the glue cups.

❖❖ Barbara Backer, Charleston, SC

Glue Pots

Materials

Glue
Plastic caps from milk bottles
Jar lids

What to do

1. Three-year-olds have difficulty handling glue bottles with their small hands. For each child, squirt a small amount of glue into a plastic cap from milk bottles or into a small jar lid.
2. Let the children apply the glue with their fingers.

❖❖ Barbara Backer, Charleston, SC

Book Sale

Materials

None

What to do

1. Watch for notices of "Friends of the Library" book sales in your area. Often, these are held on the same weekend of the same month every year. Plan on attending the Early Bird Sale (for Friends of the Library members only), which is usually held on the first evening of the three- or four-day sale.
2. This is an economical way to add to your collection of children's books. Many times, children's books are only 25 cents each or five for a dollar. The membership, which allows you to enter the Early Bird (Preview) sale, is usually about $10.00. There is no admission charge during the remaining days of the sale.
3. Another good source for children's books are garage sales. Even if the books aren't in good condition, consider cutting them up to help you with your teacher-made materials.

❖❖ Jackie Wright, Enid, OK

Arrange your Books by Themes

Materials

Personal collection of children's books
Computer and database program
Outline of themes for the year

What to do

1. Keep track of all of your children's books by putting them in a database on your computer.

2. List them by title, but also include fields for author and thematic unit.

3. Once you have your outline of themes for the coming year, sort your database for all the books in each thematic unit. (I change themes on a weekly basis.)

4. Your books for the week will appear in alphabetical order on the database. Print out a hard copy of your books for each week of the year. (See examples on following page.)

5. Use this list to sort your books. Place each of the children's books in the same order on your bookshelves as they are on the database. Start with the first unit you plan to use and continue throughout the year.

6. As each new week arrives, take the books from home that you will need for the current unit.

7. This not only helps you keep your books organized at home, it is also a ready resource to turn in with your lesson plans each month. (I like to include favorite poetry selections and flannel board stories to make a complete literature list for each unit.)

Sample weekly literature lists are on the following pages.

LITERATURE FOR WEEK 1

Title	Author	Thematic Units
Across the Stream	Mirra Ginsburg	Farm
Ask Mr. Bear	Marjorie Flack	Farm/Birthdays
The Bremen-Town Musicians	Ruth Belov Gross	Farm/Value of Friendship
Cat Goes Fiddle-I-Fee	Paul Galdone	Farm
The Chicken Book	Garth Williams	Farm
Chickens Aren't the Only Ones	Ruth Heller	Farm
Cock-a-Doodle Dudley	Bill Peet	Farm
The Day Jimmy's Boa Ate the Wash	Trinka Hakes Noble	Farm
Farm Alphabet Book	Jane Miller	Farm/ABC
The Farm Book	Jan Pfloog	Farm
Farming	Gail Gibbons	Farm
Good Morning, Chick	Mirra Ginsburg	Farm
Happy Birthday, Dear Duck	Eve Bunting	Farm/Birthdays
Hattie and the Fox	Mem Fox	Farm
The Little Red Hen	Paul Galdone	Farm
Make Mine Ice Cream	Melvin Berger	Food/Farm
Old MacDonald	Pam Adams, illus.	Farm
Old MacDonald Had a Farm	Carol Jones	Farm
Over in the Meadow	Ezra Jack Keats	Farm
Over in the Meadow	Olive A. Wadsworth	Farm
Ox-Cart Man	Donald Hall	Farm
Rosie's Walk	Pat Hutchins	Farm
Too Much Noise	Ann McGovern	Farm/Homes
The Very Busy Spider	Eric Carle	Farm
The Year at Maple Hill Farm	Alice & Martin Provensen	Farm

LITERATURE FOR WEEK 2

Title	Author	Thematic Units
Angus and the Cat	Marjorie Flack	Pets
Angus and the Ducks	Marjorie Flack	Pets/Curiosity
Annie and the Wild Animals	Jan Brett	Pets
Carl Goes Shopping	Alexandra Day	Pets
Clifford, the Small Red Puppy	Norman Bridwell	Pets
Clifford's Good Deeds	Norman Bridwell	Pets
Clifford's Tricks	Norman Bridwell	Pets
Cookie's Week	Cindy Ward	Pets
The Duel	Eugene Field (p. 174)	Pets
Have You Seen My Cat?	Eric Carle	Pets

I Want a Pet	Barbara Gregorich	Pets/Colors
The Kitten Book	Jan Pfloog	Pets
The Last Puppy	Frank Asch	Pets
Millions of Cats	Wanda Gag	Pets
Mysterious Tadpole	Steven Kellogg	Pets
No Roses for Harry	Gene Zion	Pets
The Owl and the Pussy Cat	Edward Lear (p. 175)	Pets
Pinkerton, Behave!	Steven Kellogg	Pets
The Poky Little Puppy	Janette Lowrey	Pets
The Three Little Kittens	Paul Galdone	Pets
What Do You Do with a Kangaroo?	Mercer Mayer	Animal found on bed
Whistle for Willie	Ezra Jack Keats	Pets/Air

LITERATURE FOR WEEK 3

Title	Author	Thematic Units
All Fall Down	Brian Widsmith	Zoo Safari
The Animal Fair	Anonymous (p. 178)	Zoo Safari
The Biggest Bear	Lynd Ward	Zoo Safari
Caps for Sale	Esphyr Slobodkina	Monkeys
The Crocodile's Toothache	Shel Silverstein	Water Animals/ Zoo Safari
Curious George	H. A. Rey	Monkeys
Dear Zoo	Rod Campbell	Zoo Safari/Pets
Edward the Emu	Sheena Knowles	Zoo Safari
Going to the Zoo	Tom Paxton	Zoo Safari
The Happy Day	Ruth Krauss	Zoo Safari/Snow
I Asked My Mother	Anonymous (p. 37)	Zoo Safari
If I Ran the Zoo	Dr. Seuss	Zoo Safari
Is Your Mama a Llama?	Deborah Guarino	Zoo Safari
Leo the Late Bloomer	Robert Krauss	Zoo Safari
Little Gorilla	Ruth Bornstein	Zoo Safari
Miss Mary Mack	Mary Ann Hoberman	Elephants
Norma Jean, Jumping Bean	Joanna Cole	Zoo Safari
Sam Who Never Forgets	Eve Rice	Zoo Safari
Stand Back, Said the Elephant, I'm Going to Sneeze	Patricia Thomas	Zoo Safari
The Trek	Ann Jonas	Zoo Safari
What a Tale	Brian Wildsmith	Zoo Safari
The Zoo Book	Jan Pfloog	Zoo Safari
Zoo for Mister Muster	Arnold Lobel	Zoo Safari

◆◆ Jacki Wright, Enid, OK

Rubber Date Stamp

Materials

Collection of children's books
Library card pockets
Rubber cement
3" x 5" index cards
Marker
Inkpad

What to do

1. Inside the cover of each of your children's books, attach a library card pocket with rubber cement.
2. On a 3" x 5" index card, write the title of the book.
3. Insert the card into the pocket and stamp the month and year with a rubber stamp each time you read the book aloud to the children.
4. Advance the rubber stamp setting with each new month and year, as needed.
5. This lets you know at a glance if you have read a book to the children and when.

◆❖ Jackie Wright, Enid, OK

Parent Book Sharing Day

Materials

Schedule with times on it
Letter to parents
Books

What to do

1. Designate a week or two for parents and grandparents to come in and be guest book readers.
2. Send home a letter explaining that you will have a schedule with times on it that they can sign up for. Ask the parents or grandparents to choose a time that would be good for both them and your class.

3. Ask them to bring in one or two books they like to read to their child or grandchild. Let them know that you will also have some of the children's favorite books available for them to read.

4. When the parent or grandparent comes in, encourage their child to introduce them to the class.

5. At the end of the two weeks, ask the children to make thank-you pictures, copy them, and send them to each parent or grandparent that read to the class.

❖❖ Darleen A. Schaible, Stroudsburg, PA

Library Books Are Special Books

Materials

Large basket
Library books

What to do

1. If you have a library in your school or center, the children probably are allowed to check out books using a library card.

2. Keep these books in a special basket so that the children know these books are different from the classroom books.

3. This helps children learn responsibility for the care of library books.

❖❖ Melissa Browning, Milwaukee, WI

"This 'n That" Helpful Ideas and Hints

Materials

See below

What to do

1. Following is a list of supplies to keep on hand to use during small group times:

1" cubes	Glitter	Scoops
Aluminum foil	Glue	Shaving cream
Assorted papers	Golf tees	Small plastic
Big bowls or tubs	Keys	figures
Cardboard tubes	License plates	Soap pieces
Carpet scraps	Magazines	Sponges
Chalk	Markers	Spoons
Chenille stems	Masking tape	Staplers
Clothespins	Old greeting	Stickers (all kinds)
Coins (real and	cards	Strainers
play)	Paintbrushes	Straws
Colored pencils	Paper clips	Tape
Containers with	Paper plates	Tissues
lids	Paper towels	Wallpaper
Cookie cutters	Party streamers	Watercolors
Cookie sheets	Plastic lids	Wax paper
Craft sticks	Poker chips	Yarn
Crayons	Ribbons and	Zipper-closure
Egg cartons	bows	plastic bags
Eyedroppers	Rolling pins	
File folders	Rubber bands	
Fingerpaints	Salt shakers	
Fly swatters	Sand	
Funnels	Scissors	

2. Each child should have his own art box for small group time. By keeping certain supplies in each child's art box, small group set up can go quickly. Art boxes can contain the following: scissors, crayons, roll of clear tape, pencils, glue, and markers. Ask parents to send these supplies in a plastic container already labeled with their child's name. Children will ask about storing other "treasures" in their boxes. Be flexible with their requests as long as the lid can be closed!

3. To add to your inventory, post a "Needs List" once a month for parents to contribute supplies for your classroom. Ask for things that may be theme-related or are a special need, such as an apple for each child. You will rarely get 100% participation, but any contribution will help both the program's and the teacher's budget. Local craft, wallpaper, and fabric stores will often contribute their leftover merchandise. Simply make a phone call and ask them to save items for you. Don't forget to follow up with a written thank you, either from your class or from yourself. Contributors will be more likely to remember you in the future.

4. How to offset the cost of children's books: Children's books can be expensive but are a worthwhile purchase. Try to obtain hardcover copies when possible. Post a list of books you would like to have and encourage parents to give one to the class instead of buying teacher gifts. Ask for a parent volunteer to check books out for you from the public library. You can supply the parent with specific titles or your monthly theme. Often libraries will extend check out times for teachers. Hosting a book fair or a book shower is another creative way to obtain new books for your classroom library. Don't forget yard sales.

5. As you develop your own small group ideas, you can keep them organized on index cards and filed in a file box. Simply jot down the idea and file it away under the theme or book title you will use it with. You can develop the full idea later using the small group planning sheet. You can also keep your small group ideas in a three-ring notebook, filing them in a way that is most useful to you. Using clear page protectors gives opportunity to keep a sample of the idea or odd shaped supplies such as patterns.

6. Make story baskets. Decorate a story basket or box that children will identify as being used to share an exciting children's book. You can have one for each monthly theme or one that is used all year long. Use it to keep storytelling props in as well as keeping the book a secret until storytelling time.

7. Make theme boxes using children's books. Find props that the children can use to retell stories you have read. You can have some standard props for book series such as *Curious George* (a monkey, yellow hat, toy car, and so on). Add dress-up clothes when appropriate and encourage children to offer their ideas from the story.

More to do

Use your small group activities for party days and special events. You can have bowls and soap for a "Bubble Day," or paint animal cookies at a Noah's Ark Party. Encourage children to act out a favorite book for visiting parents or have them "read" a book with you such as "Brown Bear, Brown Bear, What do You See?" Parents will also love reading child-created books. Make them available during a Parent's Night or check out.

❖ Susan E. May, Madison Heights, VA

Special Days and Themes

Materials

Items related to theme (see below)

What to do

1. At the beginning of the year, plan themes (including holidays and special days) that you would like to do throughout the year.
2. For each theme, plan how you will decorate the room, what snacks you might serve, what kind of cross-curricular activities you could include, and what kind of celebration to have at the end.
3. Following are some ideas of themes and special days.

All About Me: The children can glue photos of their families on poster board and share it with the others. For snack, they can make Pizza Faces and for art, they can draw pictures of themselves on paper plates and decorate them.

Fall: Have Apple Day, Tree Day, or Scarecrow Day. Bring in leaves and the children can sort them and graph the results(math) and use them to make leaf rubbings (art).

Halloween: Have Imagination Day, Pumpkin Day, and tell scary stories. For snack, make "booberry" muffins, ghost cookies, and so on.

Thanksgiving: The children can make books about being thankful, have a feast, dress up in clothes a Native American or pilgrim might have worn on the first Thanksgiving. Ask a Native American to come in and be a guest speaker. Bring in artifacts.

Christmas: Ask the children to bring in favorite toys, stories, traditions, food, and so on. Decorate a tree with decorations made by the children. Make crafts and gifts for parents.

Winter: Have a Winter Picnic, Pajama Day, Mitten Day, Polar Bear Day, Snow Day, and so on. Serve hot chocolate for snack. Hang big snowflakes from the ceiling.

Senses: Do activities for each sense. Do listening activities (sounds of nature, music, and so on) for hearing. Play "I Spy" for sight. Do finger painting with hands for touch, using different mediums. Have a tasting day for taste. Use sour, sweet, salty, bland, and so on.

Valentine's Day: Learn about the heart! The children can make valentines and decorate paper bags to hold their valentines. Talk about the post office and how mail is delivered.

Food Pyramid: Decorate the room with giant food pictures. Have a tasting day for each food group.

Colors: Ask the children to wear one color each day.

Easter: Have an egg hunt, make bunny cookies, and dye Easter eggs. If you can, tell the real story of Easter (if you are in a Christian school).

Spring: Have Umbrella Day, Balloon Day, Bubble Day, and Flower Festival. Plant flowers for mom for Mother's Day.

Community Helpers: Visit a fire station or police station. Invite a doctor, dentist, banker, and so on to come in and talk to the children.

Animals: Visit a farm if possible. Have Pet Visitation Day. (Parents can bring in a pet each day and stay for about ten minutes.)

Summer: Have a Beach theme. Have a Luau, Water Day, and Beach Day. Ask the children to wear sunglasses one day. Listen to Caribbean music.

❖ Sheryl Smith, Jonesborough, TN

Field Trip Fun

Materials

None

What to do

1. Exploring the sights in your neighborhood can provide valuable learning experiences and expand your teaching resources while adding realism to any area of study. Every community is full of great places to visit. You can maximize the potential of your locale by not overlooking the simple choices close to home and focusing on the options readily available to you and the children. Remember, the best trips are those that serve as extensions of children's play and interests.

2. Following are a few suggestions to get you started:

Airport
Animal Show
Aquarium
Auction
Aviary
Bakery
Bank
Barber Shop
Beach or Seashore
Beauty Salon
Berry Farm
Blood Bank
Bottling Plant
Building Site
Bus Depot
Campground
Cannery
Car Wash
Car Dealership
Christmas Tree
    Farm
Circus
Dairy Farm
Dentist's Office
Department Store
Diner
Dock or Harbor
Doctor's Office
Dog Kennel
Farm

Fast Food
    Restaurant
Fields (corn,
    peanut, cotton,
    and so on)
Fire Station
Fish Hatchery
Flower Show
Garden
Gas Station
Greenhouse
Grocery Store
Health Club or
    Gym
Health Food Store
Hospital
Landfill
Livestock Show
Lumber Yard
Mill
Movie Theater
Museum
Newspaper
Nursery
Nursing Home
Orchard
Pet Store
Petting Zoo
Photography
    Studio

Pizza Parlor
Planetarium
Police Station
Post Office
Poultry Farm
Produce Stand
Public Library
Pumpkin Patch
Radio Station
Recycling Center
Repair Shop
    (watches, bike,
shoes, and so on)
Restaurant
Sewage Disposal
    Plant
Stable
Stadium
State Park
Subway Terminal
Television Studio
Train Station
Water (dam, lock,
    lake, pond,
    stream, and so
    on)
Zoo

❖ Rebecca McMahen Giles, Mobile, AL

Catchy Titles List

Materials

Various teacher resource books and magazines

What to do

1. As you look through your favorite new teacher resource book or magazine, list any caption or title you think is cute and may be usable in the future.
2. When labeling new teacher-made materials or coming up with a new room theme or bulletin board idea, glance over your list of catchy titles for inspiration.
3. Use the list as a springboard to add to your current thematic units when planning your school year.
4. Following are some examples of catchy titles:

'Tis the Season
A B C Express
A Birthday Blowout
A Job for Me
A Penguin Adventure
A Season of Fun
A Time to Shine
ABCDEFG, School Where We Want to Be
All About Animals
All About Apples
All About Bats
All About Boats
All About Family
All About Whales
Amazing Alphabet
Amazing Animals
An Alphabet of Apples
Animals All Around
Apples Aplenty
April Showers Bring May Flowers
At the Circus
Awesome Owls
Becoming a Butterfly

Birds of a Feather
Blowing in the Wind
Bring on the Bees
Bubble Magic
Bundle Up!
Calling All Community Helpers
Calling All Cows!
Candy Cane Christmas
Circus Sights
Count Me In!
Cowpoke Roundup
Crazy About Colors
Creepy Crawlers
Dolphin Delights
Down on the Farm
Egg 'em On!
Fabulous Friendship
Fabulous Fall
Fall Frolics
Family Ties
Fantastic Fall
Far Out! (Space)
Fine Feathered Friends

Flipped Over Frogs
Flower Power
Flowers and Showers
Flying High (Airplanes)
For the Birds
Forever Fall
Frog Follies
Fun on Wheels
Get Ready for Rabbits
Get Ready for Rainbows
Getting into Shapes!
Gingerbread Time
Give a Cheer for the End of the Year!
Giving Thanks
Grow, Garden, Grows
Halloween Happenings
Halloween Hoopla
Happy Haunting
Hats Off to You!
Hats Off! (Careers)
Have a Ball
Have a Heart
Head to Toe
Heading South (Migration)
Hello, Mr. Sun
Here Comes Spring
Here We Go A-Camping
Holiday Happenings
Home Sweet Home
Hooray for the Seasons
Hot Diggity Dog!
How Does Your Garden Grow?
In a Springtime Garden
In Praise of Pets
It's a Spring Fling!
It's in the Bag!
It's Pumpkin Time
It's Raining
It's Springtime!
It's Turkey Time
Land Ho!

Leapin' Leprechauns!
Let It Snow
Let's Compare
Let's Talk Turkey
Little Critters (Bugs)
Looking Good!
Lots of Colors
Love Is in the Air
Luscious Leaves
Making Spirits Bright
Marvelous Mice
Me and My Shadow
Mice Are Nice!
Mitten Magic
Monkeying Around
Mother Goose Is on the Loose!
Nighttime Skies
Oh Goodness! Ghosts!
On the Right Track
On the Road Again
Opposites All Around
Out of the Blue (Sky)
Over the Rainbow
Peculiar Plants
Penguin Antics
Penguins on Parade
Picnic, Anyone?
Pigs Aplenty!
Pretty Posies
Purposeful Parts (Part of a tree)
Put Your Best Foot Forward
Reach for a Rainbow
Rock around the Clock
Roundup Time
S-S-Simply Snakes
Santa's Coming
Santa's Workshop
Scurrying Critters (Beach Life)
Scurrying Squirrels
See You Later, Alligator
Send in the Clowns

Show Shenanigans
Signs of Spring
Snowflakes Falling
Something to Crow About
Sort It Out!
Soup's On!
Special Delivery
Spread Your Wings
Spring Is in the Air
Spring Is on Its Way
Spring Treasures
Springtime Weather
Start Light, Star Bright
Step Right Up!
Stop! Look! and Listen!
Strike Up the Band
Sunflower Power
Take Me Out to the Ball Game!
Taking Off!
Thanksgiving Fun
The Inside Outs of Opposites
The Land of Nursery Rhymes
The Price Is Right
The Scoop on Ice Cream
The Wonder of Watermelons

Time Flies
Time for Bed
Turtle Time
Under the Big Top
Under the Sea
Under the Weather
We're Proud to Be Americans
We're Talkin' Turtles
Welcome Aboard
Welcome Spring
Welcome Winter
What a Pair (mitten pairs)
What's Bugging You?
What's New at the Zoo
What's the Weather?
Whooo Knows! (Owls)
Winter Weather
Winter Wonderland
Wintry Weather
Wish Upon a Star
World of Waterfowl
You Are My Sunshine
You've Got Mail
Zoo Safari

◆❖ Jackie Wright, Enid, OK

My Beanbag

Materials

Felt
Patterns
Straight pins
Material scissors
Sewing machine or needle and thread
Funnel
Bags of dry split peas
Fabric paints

What to do

1. Ask each child to choose a color of felt and a beanbag pattern.
2. Pin the pattern to the felt and cut it out.
3. Sew the pieces together for the children using a sewing machine or needle and thread. Leave an opening on one side to add the peas.
4. Once the felt is sewn together, turn it right side out.
5. Place the funnel opening in the open space. Help the children fill the felt bag with the split peas.
6. Stitch up the opening for the children.
7. Print the child's name on his beanbag with fabric paint. When the bag is dry, encourage the children to decorate their beanbags with fabric paints.
8. Use the beanbags with activities at circle time and during movement activities. The children love having their own bag.

More to do

Change the shapes of the beanbags to go with specific themes, such as a fish, bunny, or lion head.

❖❖ Sandra Nagel, White Lake, MI

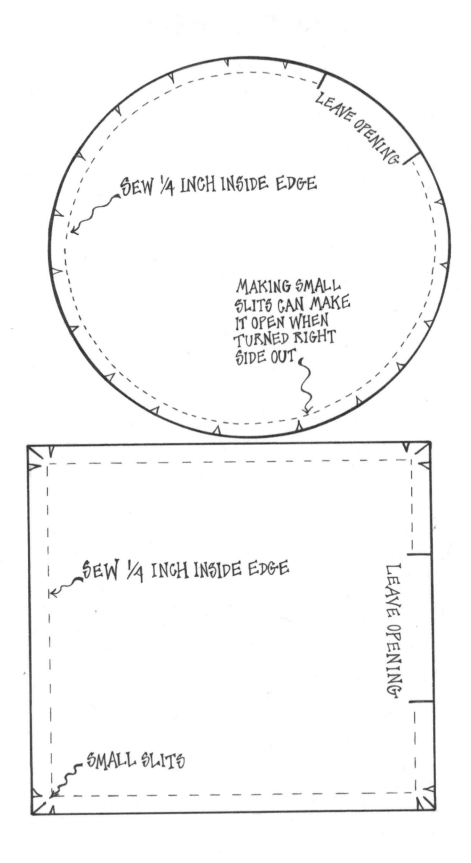

LEAVE OPENING

SEW ¼ INCH INSIDE EDGE

MAKING SMALL
SLITS CAN MAKE
IT OPEN WHEN
TURNED RIGHT
SIDE OUT

SEW ¼ INCH INSIDE EDGE

LEAVE OPENING

SMALL SLITS

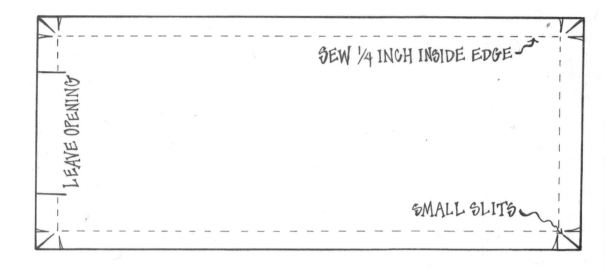

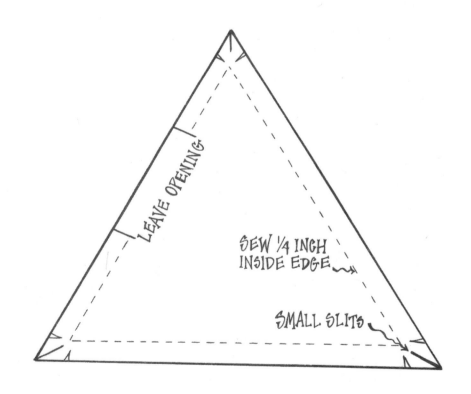

Rainy Day Shoes

Materials

Heavy brown grocery bags or heavyweight brown paper
Pencils
Scissors
Hole punch
Gummed circles (notebook paper hole reinforcers)
Yarn

What to do

1. Ask the children to remove their shoes. Trace their feet onto brown paper and help them cut out their feet shapes.
2. Punch three holes along the left and right side of each "paper shoe."
3. Show the children how to attach gummed hole reinforcers over the holes. Then, help them "lace" each paper shoe with yarn pieces.
4. Print each child's name on his "paper shoes."
5. Whenever it rains and the children have wet shoes, they can remove their shoes and wear their "paper shoes."

❖❖ Joan Stevenson, North Ft. Myers, FL

Cleaning Plant Leaves

Materials

Plotted plants (snake plant, a fichus trees, and peace lilies are good)
Plastic cotton swabs
Small bottle of soapy water

What to do

1. This activity lets the children contribute to the care of the room environment, which helps build self-esteem. Because the child works alone, this activity helps calm an overactive child.
2. Encourage the child to dip a cotton swab into a bottle of soapy water.
3. As the child supports the leaf with his left hand, he carefully wipes the leaf with the wet swab to remove dust. Children are fascinated with the shiny wet leaf with its deepened color.

4. The child can repeat with other leaves until he is satisfied.

5. Empty the bottle and discard the swab.

More to do

Language: Teach the names of the plants.

Science: Explain how the leaves need to be clean to absorb light. The leaves use light, carbon dioxide from the air, and minerals from the earth to make food for the plant grow.

◆◆ Mary Jo Shannon, Roanoke, VA

Move and Play Four Different Ways

Materials

Construction paper and scissors
Hinge

What to do

1. Ask the children if they know ways they can move their bodies. You may need to come up with a few examples to get the discussion started. A few good examples are shaking their arms, stomping their feet, running in place, shrugging their shoulders, and bending their elbows and knees. Once you have covered ways to move their bodies, you are ready for the following activities.
2. These activities do not need to be done in any particular order and are easily adapted. Depending upon the size of your group, you may wish to enlist the help of another enthusiastic adult.

Activity 1: Stars

1. Cut out two stars or other shapes from construction paper. Place one star at each end of the room.
2. Ask the children to form a line near one of the stars.
3. Each child takes a turn showing the other children ways they can move their bodies by going from one star to the other.
4. Some examples they may use are: skipping, jumping, twirling, hopping, slithering, walking very fast or very slow, and any other invented ways to walk. One invented walk is the "crab walk." To do this, sit on the floor and place your hands behind you with the fingers pointed towards your feet. Push up on your hands, so your weight is supported by your hands and feet (your belly should be pointed up). This is a particularly silly way to move the body. It can be done backwards or forward.

Activity 2: The Glass Box

1. Ask the children to stand in place, about an arm's length apart, and draw an imaginary square around their feet. This is the base of their glass box. Let them know that they are inside a glass box and they must move inside it, without stepping out.

2. Pretend to be a little mouse. Ask the children to move like a very little mouse inside their glass box.

3. Then pretend to be a very large elephant. Ask the children how they think a very large elephant would move inside a tiny glass box.

4. Pretend to be a bird inside the glass box. Encourage the children to flap their arms like wings.

5. Pretend to be a fish inside the glass box, or the wind, or trees blowing in the wind. The possibilities are endless.

Activity 3: Sticky Bubble Gum

1. Ask the children to imagine they are sticky pieces of bubble gum.

2. Now tell them to imagine that they are a great big wad of icky, sticky bubble gum and that they are all stuck together. They can stick together by holding onto one another.

3. Encourage the "big wad of bubble gum" to try to move together, a few steps at a time, first in one direction, and then another.

4. Ask the children if they can tell you how it was different to move all together rather than moving by themselves.

Activity 4: Hinges

1. Show the children a hinge. Tell them that their bodies have hinges that move just like the hinge you are holding.

2. Ask them if they know where their hinges are, and how they move. Ankles, wrists, elbows, shoulders, knees, waists, and necks are all good examples of hinges.

3. Show the children ways to move their "hinges." Start with neck rolls. Ask the children to roll their necks one way a few times, and then change to the other direction.

4. Demonstrate how you can roll your wrists in the same way. Point out that when you roll your wrists, your elbows move too.

5. Ask them to rotate their shoulders with you, one at first, and then the other. Do the same exercises with your waist, knees, and ankles.

6. Teach the children how to do jumping jacks. This is a great exercise that incorporates a whole bunch of hinges.

7. Point out to the children that it is a good thing we have hinges so that when we bend, we won't crack in two!

❖ Jayne Morrison, Magna, UT

Move Your Body

Materials

Large area

What to do

1. Ask the children to stand in a large area. Give them commands such as:
   - Make your body as tall as you can.
   - Make your body as flat as you can.
   - Make your body as wide as you can.
   - Make your arm the tallest part of your body.
   - Make your foot the tallest part of your body.
   - Make your tummy the tallest part of your body.
2. Encourage the children to take turns calling the directions.

◆❖ Barbara Saul, Eureka, CA

I Was Just Thinkin'

Materials

None

What to do

1. Encourage the children to either sit quietly in a circle or lie down with their heads forming the inside of a circle.
2. Start by saying, "I was just thinkin' and I think I'd like to be a …" (Choose an animal or moveable item the children are familiar with, such as a stapler.)
3. Invite everyone to move like the animal or object named.
4. Ask everyone to lie or sit still again and ask the next person to say, "I was just thinkin' and I think I'd like to be a …"
5. Repeat the process until everyone has had a chance to say what she has been "thinkin' about."
6. When finished, everyone says, "I was just thinkin' and I'm glad to be me!"

◆❖ Jeannie Gunderson, Casper, WY

On, Over, Around, and Through

Materials

8½″ x 11″ piece of paper
Pen or marker
Scissors
8 strips of tag board

What to do

1. On the piece of paper, write "top" at the top, "bottom" on the bottom, "right" on the right side, and "left" on the left. Cut a round hole in the middle of the paper.

2. Write the following instructions on each strip of tag board:
   - Stand on top of the paper.
   - Stand on the bottom of the paper.
   - Stand on the right side of the paper.
   - Stand on the left side of the paper.
   - Stand over the paper.
   - Stand under the paper. (See if they think to pick up paper and put it over their head.)
   - Walk around the paper.
   - Put your finger through the paper.

3. Put the paper on the floor. Ask each child in turn to choose a card. Read the instruction on the card and ask the child to do what the card says.

More to do

Language: Encourage the children to use the words. For example, "Let's go *through* the door," "Look on *top of* the bookcase," and so on.

❖❖ Helen De Witt, Cochise, AZ

Five Green and Speckled Frogs

Materials

Brown blanket or rug, big enough for five children

Six or more hula hoops (fewer will work, but it won't be as much fun)

What to do

1. Most three-year-olds can jump, but not over objects very well. One way to work on this gross motor skill is by playing green and speckled frogs.

2. Sing the familiar song, "Five Green and Speckled Frogs" (see below) until the children are very familiar with it.

3. Then place a brown rug or blanket on the floor (this will be "log"). Ask the children to stand on the rug.

4. Place the hula hoops on the floor at various distances away from the rug, the closest right up against the rug. Encourage the children to act like frogs and take turns jumping into the ponds (hula hoops). Each child sees how many ponds she can jump into.

More to do

Books: To extend the activity, read *Frog and Toad* by Arnold Lobel or a book about real frogs.

Science and Nature: Go outside and observe how real frogs jump before playing the game.

Related song

Five Green and Speckled Frogs

Five green and speckled frogs sat on a speckled log
Eating a most delicious bug
Glub, glug.

One jumped into the pool where it was nice and cool
Now there are four green and speckled frogs.

(Continue until there are none left.)

❖ Kathleen Wallace, Columbia, MO

Jumping

Materials

None

What to do

1. Encourage the children to practice jumping with their feet together, with their feet apart, forward, backward, and sideways.
2. After a bit of practice, sing the following song with the children and joyfully fall down at the end.

   (Tune: "This Old Man")
   Jumping up, jumping down,
   Jumping, jumping all around.
   Jumping, jumping, jumping all around.
   One more jump and then FALL DOWN!!

3. Children find this is a positive way to use energy, and teachers like to use the activity on rainy days.

More to do

Math: Using the numbers one through five, encourage the children, in turn, to decide how many times the group should jump. With the group, jump slowly, counting each jump until you come to the chosen number. Let each child have a turn to decide how many times to jump.

Related books

Jump, Frog, Jump! by Robert Kalan
Jump Like a Frog by Kate Burns.

◆◆ Barbara Backer, Charleston, SC

Jump Over the River

Materials

Rope or tape

What to do

1. Put a rope or a line of tape on the floor in a straight line. This will be the "river."
2. Demonstrate how to jump over the river. Start with both feet flat on the floor. Bend your knees and jump forward, over the river.
3. Encourage the children to jump, one at a time.
4. If the children have difficulty, let them jump off a stool a few times.

More to do

Use two ropes and make the "river" wider. Raise the rope (tie each end to a chair) and practice crawling under it.

❖❖ Mary Jo Shannon, Roanoke, VA

Skating Bags

Materials

Paper grocery bags
Scissors
Music

What to do

1. Discuss skating with the children. Show them pictures of people ice skating and roller blading and watch short segments of professional figure skating.
2. Cut off the top two-thirds of the grocery bags. Give two bags to each child.
3. Show the children how to place one foot into each bag (with or without shoes on). Encourage them to slide their feet on the floor in a skating movement.
4. Add music and skate around the room!

More to do

More Gross Motor: Do short relays while wearing the skating bags.

Art: Encourage the children to decorate the bags with markers, crayons, or chalk.

❖❖ Sandra Nagle, White Lake, MI

Fun with Cones

Materials

Game cones or any other objects that can be upright such as soda bottles,
bowling pins, paper cups, and so on
Music, optional

What to do

1. Place the objects around the room in an open space.
2. Ask the children to walk around the room, being careful not to knock over the objects. The children could also jump, crawl, or run. If a child knocks over an object, she sets it back up.
3. Play music, if desired, and encourage the children to start and stop according to the music.
4. At the end, the children can knock over the objects while crawling, using their heads and noses!

More to do

Art: Make cones with the children. They can put stickers or tape on soda bottles or decorate construction paper and fold it into a cone shape.

❖❖ Brenda Miller, Olean, NY

Obstacle Course

Materials

Masking tape or board
Pillows
Chairs
Tables
Bookshelves

What to do

1. Push all unnecessary furniture aside. Make an obstacle course for the children.
2. Place either a board or a line of tape on the floor (this is for the children to practice walking a straight line).
3. Pile pillows in such a way as to make steps up, and then down.
4. Arrange the tables so that children can crawl under them.
5. Set up chairs so the children have to zigzag through a maze of them.

More to do

Language: Enhance language understanding by emphasizing *on, over, under, up, down, through, between,* and *around* so the children will get a better understanding of these direction words.

Outdoors: Set up an obstacle course outside using whatever items you may have available on the playground.

❖❖ Melissa O. Markham, Huddleston, VA

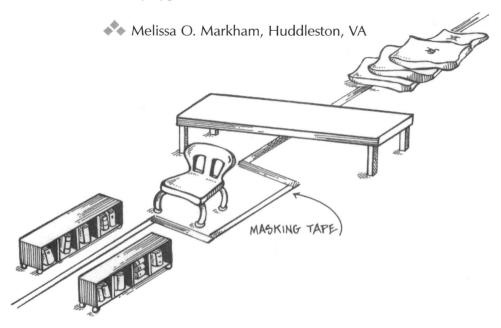

MASKING TAPE

Juice Can Bead Toss Toys

Materials

Yarn or string
Exacto knife, knife, or sharp adult scissors (adult only)
Plastic juice cans
Beads
Wallpaper scraps or tissue paper, optional

What to do

1. Pre-cut pieces of string, approximately 1' (30 cm) in length, one for each child.
2. Use a knife or sharp scissors to pre-score a slit near the top edge of each plastic juice can.
3. Place beads, cans, and yarn on a table and encourage the children to choose one of each.
4. Challenge them to string their bead on their yarn.
5. Tie the bead onto one end of the yarn and push the other end of the string through the juice can slit.
6. Make a knot on the end of the string that is in the juice can. The bead should be out of the juice can, and the plain knot should be in the juice can.

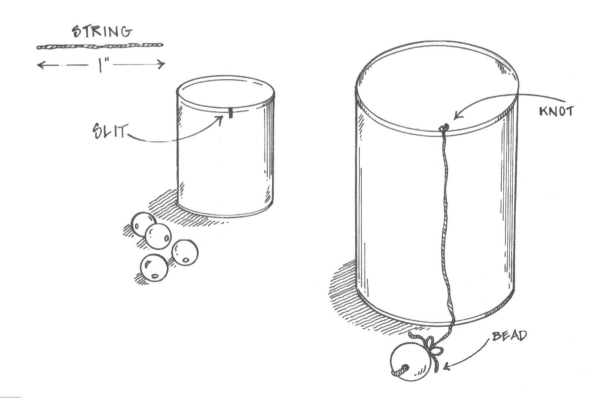

7. Encourage the children to hold their juice cans, toss the bead up, and attempt to catch the bead in their cans.

8. Shorten or lengthen the string for varying difficulty levels.

9. If desired, encourage the children to decorate their juice cans with scraps of wallpaper or tissue paper.

More to do

Compare beads with different textures or sizes and determine which are easiest to catch.

❖❖ Shirley R. Salach, Northwood, NH

Class Tree

Materials

Large branch
Pot
Plaster of Paris
Supplies to make seasonal/holiday decorations, such as construction paper, markers, paint, glue, and scissors

What to do

1. Mount a large branch in a pot using plaster of Paris.
2. Make holiday decorations with the children to hang on the branches.
3. In the fall, cut out paper leaves and sponge paint them; at Christmas, make ornaments; and at Easter, make paper Easter eggs.

More to do

Books: Read stories to correspond with the season.
Circle Time: During circle time, encourage the children to pretend to be animals of the season (for example, bunnies at Easter).

❖❖ Sandy L. Scott, Vancouver, WA

Holiday Napkins for the Flannel Board

Materials

Holiday napkins
Scissors
Felt
Rubber cement
Clear contact paper
Flannel board

What to do

1. Throughout the year, save holiday napkins that feature pumpkins, turkeys, bunnies, and so on.
2. Cut out the holiday shapes (such as a turkey) and glue them to felt using rubber cement.
3. Cover them with clear contact paper.
4. Put the flannel board characters with your flannel board out in the room for the children to manipulate during playtime.

◆◆ Jackie Wright, Enid, OK

Paper Plate Puppets

Materials

Seasonal paper plates
Scissors
Craft sticks
Glue (contact cement)

What to do

1. Throughout the year, save holiday paper plates.
2. Cut out the shape of pumpkins, turkeys, Santas, hearts, leprechauns, bunnies, and so on from the plates.
3. Glue a craft stick to the back of each shape using Contact Cement.
4. These colorful puppets will add sparkle to your songs, stories, and units. When you're not using them, place them in the Dramatic Play area for the children to manipulate.

◆◆ Jackie Wright, Enid, OK

Making Doggie Bones

Materials

1 cup flour
1 cup wet dog food
⅓ cup water
Mixing bowl and spoon
Rolling pin
Dog bone cookie cutter
Cookie sheet
Oven
Ribbon

What to do

1. These doggie bones make great gifts for holidays.
2. Mix all the ingredients in a bowl. Add more flour if it is too sticky to roll out.
3. Refrigerate the dough for one hour.
4. Sprinkle flour on the working surface and encourage the children to roll out the dough and cut it into bone shapes.
5. Bake at 350° for 8-10 minutes (adult only).
6. After they have cooled, help the children tie a ribbon around the middle of each bone. Give them to your favorite pooch!

❖❖ Lisa Chichester, Parkersburg, WV

Teddy Bear Day

Materials

Brown construction paper
Scissors
Stapler
Slice-and-bake sugar cookie rolls (enough to have two slices per child)
Cookie sheets
Oven
Tubes of frosting

What to do

1. Designate a day to be "Bring Your Teddy Bear to School Day." Send a note home to parents notifying them of the date.
2. On Teddy Bear Day, make each child a bear headband to wear all day. Cut out ears and bands from brown construction paper. Staple two ears to each band. Give one to each child and staple it to fit around the child's head.
3. For snack, slice cookie dough and put it on a cookie sheet. Bake as directed.
4. After the cookies cool, give each child two cookies to decorate bear heads using tubes of frosting.
5. Sing songs or use finger rhymes that relate to teddy bears and ask the children to make their bears do the movements.

More to do

Music and Movement: Play Raffi's song *Teddy Bear Hug* and act out the motions with bears.

Related books

My Friend Bear, by Jez Alborough
Where's My Teddy? by Jez Alborough
You and Me Little Bear by Martin Waddell

❖❖ Diane Weiss, Fairfax, VA

"I Have Birthdays"

Materials

Chart paper and marker
Mr. Rogers record, optional
Paper
Crayons
Baking materials, if possible

What to do

1. Write all the children's birthdays on a piece of chart paper and hang it in the room. On each child's birthday, do some of the following activities.
2. At circle time, talk about how old the birthday child is and discuss all the things we can do as we get older. If desired, play "You're Growing" by Mr. Rogers.

3. In the Art Center, give each child a large piece of paper. Encourage them to draw a birthday gift they would like to give to the birthday child.
4. Give each child a piece of paper titled, "Now I Can..." Encourage them to draw something they can do this year that they couldn't do last year.
5. If you have the facilities to bake, do so each time a birthday occurs. Ask the birthday child to choose what to bake (such as muffins, oatmeal cookies, and so on). Let the birthday child serve it at snack time.

More to do

Ask senior citizens to come in and talk about their childhood and their birthdays as they grew up.

Math: Make a pictograph of the birthdays each month, using candles for markers. See which month has the most birthdays and the least birthdays.

Related books

Benny Bakes a Cake by Eve Rice
Birthday by John Steptoe
A Birthday for Francis by Russell Hoban
Happy Birthday, Sam by Pat Hutchins

❖❖ Wendy Pfeffer, Pennington, NJ

Valentine Match Up

Materials

At least 10 pairs of identical children's Valentine's Day cards with different themes
3" x 5" strips of construction paper, all in same color
Glue or rubber cement
Clear contact paper or laminate

What to do

1. Attach each Valentine's Day card to construction paper strips using glue or rubber cement.
2. Laminate the cards or cover them with clear contact paper.
3. Place all 20 cards face up on a table and encourage the children to scan the collection to locate pairs of cards.
4. Use other cards for other holidays, if desired.

More to do

Add more sets of matching Valentine's cards to make the game more challenging.

Games: Shuffle five of the matching pairs and place them face down on the table in two rows of five cards. Play a memory game where each child turns over two cards to try to locate a match.

Language: Ask the children to describe the action on each of the cards. For example, Winnie the Pooh is holding a big heart.

❖❖ Mary Volkman, Ottawa, IL

Valentine Tote Bag

Materials

Red, pink, or purple construction paper, 2 pieces per child
Scissors
Hole punch
White and red yarn, approximately 1 yard per child
Glue
Construction paper in a variety of valentine colors
Black marker

What to do

1. Cut out two matching large hearts for each child.
2. Use a hole punch to punch holes, about one every inch, through both hearts. Leave the top of the heart without holes (to leave an opening for the valentines). See illustration on following page.
3. Give each child about 1 yard of yarn. Help them lace their two hearts together, leaving several inches at the beginning and end to tie a knot when done.
4. After the hearts are laced together and tied at the top, cut out a variety of small hearts from construction paper. Encourage the children to glue the hearts and other materials (if desired) on one side of the large heart. On the other side of the heart, help the children print their name in large letters using the black marker.
5. As the friends pass out valentines, they can do name recognition/matching as they place the valentines into each heart.

Related books

Franklin's Valentine's by Paulette Bourgeois
Froggy's First Kiss by Jonathan London
Roses Are Pink, Your Feet Really Stink by Diane deGroat
Teeny Witch and the Perfect Valentine by Liz Matthews
Valentine Mice! by Bethany Roberts

❖❖ Mindy Britt-Nellis, Evansville, IN

President's Day Hats

Materials

12" x 18" (30 cm x 45 cm) white construction paper, two pieces per child
Stapler
Red and blue crayons, markers, or paint
American flag, optional

What to do

1. Give each child two pieces of white construction paper.
2. Demonstrate how to put the two pieces of paper together and fold them as if making a newspaper hat.
3. When the children have done this (with adult help), help them staple the papers together at both ends to hold the hat together.
4. Encourage the children to decorate their hats using red and blue crayons, markers, or paint. This is a good time to show them the American flag and talk about the colors in the flag. Ask if anyone knows the name of our president.
5. After the children finish their hats, have a parade using rhythm band instruments.

❖❖ Phyllis Esch, Export, PA

Luck o' the Irish

Materials

Map of Ireland
Copy machine
Green construction paper
Glue
St. Patrick's Day stickers
Laminate or clear contact paper
Small copper pot with lid
Rainbow confetti
Play coins and acorns, optional
Gold spray paint, optional

What to do

1. Make photocopies of a map of Ireland. If necessary, draw a map.
2. Give each child a map and a piece of large green construction paper. Encourage the children to glue the map in the center of the green paper to make a placemat.
3. The children can use St. Patrick's Day stickers to decorate the placemat.
4. Laminate the placemats or cover them with clear contact paper. These make great party placemats for the children to eat their party foods on (see More to do).
5. Make "A Bit o' Rainbow Dust." Before the children arrive, put confetti into a small copper pot. If desired, spray paint play coins and acorns using gold paint and add them to the pot.
6. Go outside to the playground and select a spot to put the tiny copper pot, with the lid off. Sprinkle a bit of the confetti around it.
7. At recess, lead the children to the pot of rainbow dust and tell them the following story:

   At dawn on St. Patrick's Day, if the leprechauns find the gold at the end of the rainbow (as they always do), they collect every last coin and nugget and put it into tiny copper pots and carry it to their underground fortress. But leprechauns are greedy. Even when they see that they can't get it all into their hole before it closes up until the next St. Patrick's Day, they still try to squeeze every last copper pot through. But there is never enough time. One small copper pot is always left behind—with gold that comes from the end of the rainbow inside of it—along with a wee bit o' rainbow dust. (Story by Penni Smith)

More to do

Make "Keep from Getting Pinched Pins": Cut out shamrock shapes from green felt. Give one to each child and encourage him or her to glue gold and green sequins onto it. Use gold safety pins to pin the shamrocks onto the child's clothing.

Snack: Make a St. Patrick's Day snack. Bake shamrock-shaped cookies and decorate them with green icing. Mix lime sherbet and ginger ale to make green punch. The children can eat their snack on their Ireland placemats.

Original song

Sing the following song to the tune of "The Farmer in the Dell."

A leprechaun found some gold
A leprechaun found some gold
Heigh-ho the Blarney stone
A leprechaun found some gold.

He found it by the stream
He found it by the stream
Heigh-ho the Blarney stone
He found it by the stream.

It twinkles bright and gold
It twinkles bright and gold
Heigh-ho the Blarney stone
It twinkles bright and gold.

He took it home in bags
He took it home in bags
Heigh-ho the Blarney stone
He took it home in bags.

He danced an Irish jig
He danced an Irish jig
Heigh-ho the Blarney stone
He danced an Irish jig.

Original fingerplay

Five little leprechauns lookin' for a rainbow
The first one said, "It's down the road of gold!"
The second one said, "Ah, no, it's where secrets are told."
The third one said, "It's by the waterfall."
The fourth one said, "You're all wrong. It's by the castle tall."
And the fifth one knew exactly where to look—and he found it
Gold and all!

❖❖ Penni L. Smith, Riverside, CA

Easy Easter Eggs

Materials

Hard-boiled eggs
Colored tissue papers
Bowl of water

What to do

1. Give each child a hard-boiled egg and their choice of tissue paper.
2. Demonstrate how to wrap the paper around the egg. Then dip the egg in water and pat all over. Point out how the color changes to become brighter.
3. Encourage the children to practice on their own.
4. Although the color will fade a bit when dry, the paper will stick nicely and they will have beautiful colored eggs without the mess of paints or dyes.

More to do

Math: Count the eggs and name the colors.

❖❖ Angela Williamson LaFon, M.Ed., Lynchburg, VA

Tissue Paper Mosaic Easter Eggs

Materials

Tagboard
Scissors
Glue sticks or paste
Scraps of colored tissue paper

What to do

1. Cut tagboard into egg shapes and give one to each child.
2. Ask the children to apply glue to an area of the egg. Then demonstrate how to squeeze a piece of tissue to make a ball.
3. Ask them to place the paper ball in the sticky glue surface.
4. Encourage the children to continue to fill in the area until they are satisfied with their design.

More to do

Language: Help develop vocabulary by using the words mosaic, tissue paper, sticky, and design.

❖❖ Mary Jo Shannon, Roanoke, VA

Easter Bonnets

Materials

Paper plates
Hole punch
Colored tissue paper
Glue sticks or paper paste
Ribbons or yarn

What to do

1. Give each child a paper plate.
2. Punch two holes, one on each side, into each paper plate.
3. Show the children how to scrunch pieces of tissue paper to resemble flowers. Encourage them to glue the flowers to the bottom of their plate.
4. Give each child a piece of ribbon or yarn. Run it through one hole, over the tissue flowers, and through the other hole.
5. Tie the ribbons to secure the bonnets on the children's heads.
6. If desired, have an Easter parade when all the hats are complete.

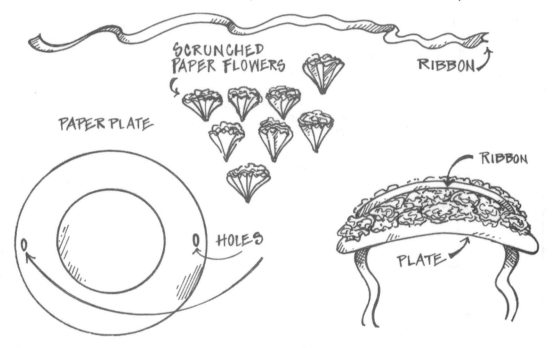

◆◆ Mary Jo Shannon, Roanoke, VA

Cinco de Mayo Village

Materials

Large piece of cardboard and assorted boxes (cereal, crackers)
Scissors, tape and glue
Paint and brushes
Pie tin
Marker piece from old game, small plastic animals, wagons, and so on
Fabric scraps

What to do

1. Use assorted boxes to create a Mexican villa with the children. Start with a large piece of cardboard for the base of the villa. Tape the assorted boxes closed.
2. Paint the boxes with rustic colors such as salmon pink or terra cotta, tan, or brown.
3. Paint a small silver pie tin turquoise blue (to assimilate water) and glue it in the center of the cardboard square. Use a marker piece from an old board game (such as Clue or Pictionary) to put in the center of the pie pan. This will be the village fountain.
4. Paint a variety of boxes to make houses, barns, a general store, and a church, and cut little windows and doors into them. Glue little squares of fabric on cut-out windows for curtains. Glue the boxes to the large cardboard square.
5. Glue small plastic figures around the villa. Add plastic animals, wagons, barrels, wagon wheels, and so on. These items can often be found in cake decorating sections of craft stores.
6. This is a wonderful project for children to create for Cinco de Mayo!

❖❖ Penni L. Smith, Riverside, CA

My Mom Has Curly Hair

Materials

Photos of your mother and pictures of mothers with children
9" x 12" (22 cm x 30 cm) construction paper in skin tones, such as manila, pale pink, tan, and soft browns
Crayons
Scissors
Construction paper in hair colors, such as light and dark brown, yellow, black, white, and red-brown
Jumbo crayons
Glue
Damp paper towels

What to do

1. Show the children pictures of mothers with children. Discuss mothers and the caring things they do for their children every day.

2. Ask the children to think about their mothers' faces. Give each child a 9" x 12" sheet of construction paper in the color closest to his mother's skin tone.

3. Ask the children to draw a large circle or oval shape for the mother's face. Encourage them to add facial features using crayons, but not to draw hair.

4. Help the children cut out their shapes.

5. Cut hair-colored construction paper into strips about 1" x 4" (2 cm x 10 cm).

6. Give the children strips of paper in the color that most closely matches their mother's hair. Show the children how to put a curl into the paper strip by rolling the paper tightly around a jumbo crayon, holding it for a moment, and then slipping the crayon out (keeping the curl intact).

7. Ask the children to put a small dot of glue on the inside edge of the curl. Show them how to slip the glued end under the edge of the face cutout so that the curl winds up and over the edge of the face.

8. The children can repeat this step with other strips, curling and gluing them around the hairline. Encourage them to look in a classroom mirror to see where their own hair grows around their faces.

9. Provide damp paper towels for finger wiping as they alternately curl and glue. Allow the glue to dry before displaying the pictures.

More to do

Bulletin Board: Create a classroom Mother's Day display by hanging the portraits and sentences (see below).

Language: Ask the children to complete this sentence: "I love my mother because…" Write down their dictated thoughts.

More Language: Invite the children to contribute to a classroom list of ways their mothers help them.

Original song

You Are My Mother (Tune: "You Are My Sunshine")

You are my mother,
There is no other;
No one can love me like you do!
I want to show it,
So you will know it:
I have a heart full of love for you!

Related books

A Chair for My Mother by Vera B. Williams
Are You My Mother? By P.D. Eastman
Our Mother's Day Book by Jane Belk Moncure

❖❖ Susan Oldham Hill, Lakeland, FL

July Fourth Fingerpaint Fireworks

Materials

Paint smocks
Fingerpaint paper
Blue and red fingerpaint
Newspaper
White glue
Shallow containers
Swabs
Red and silver glitter

What to do

1. Help the children put on smocks.
2. Give each child a sheet of fingerpaint paper and a dollop of blue paint. Encourage them to use both hands, not just their fingertips, to spread the paint all over the paper to resemble a night sky.
3. When the blue is distributed, give each child a small amount of red paint to create a dark purple color. It is not necessary to blend the two colors completely.
4. Let the paintings dry overnight.
5. The next morning, weight the dry paintings with heavy books for a few hours to flatten the pictures.
6. Cover the work surface with newspaper and pour glue into shallow containers. Return each child's fingerpaintings.
7. Show them how to dip swabs into the glue and swipe the swab onto the "night sky" to represent fireworks. Before the glue dries, sprinkle glitter on the glue lines. Repeat to create additional fireworks.

More to do

Music: Sing "I'm a Yankee Doodle Dandy."

Snack: Serve strawberries, cool whip, and a blue drink for a red, white, and blue snack!

Social Studies: Examine the American flag, discussing the colors and shapes. Compare it to the state flag.

Original song

(Tune: "I've Been Working on the Railroad")

When you ask about my country, I am proud to say
If you ask about my country, I'm from the USA.
U reminds me it's united;
S is for each state;
A is for A-mer-i-ca,
And that's the USA!

◆◆ Susan Oldham Hill, Lakeland, FL

Black and Orange Chain

Materials

Orange and black construction paper
Scissors
Glue

What to do

1. Cut orange and black paper into strips about 3" to 4" (7 cm to 10 cm) long and ½" (1 cm) wide.
2. Grip both ends of one strip and make a circle. Glue the ends together.
3. Take another strip in a different color and loop it through first circle and glue the ends. Continue making the chain as long as desired.

More to do

Decorate the strips with scary creatures before looping them together.

◆◆ Jean Potter, Charleston, WV

Pumpkin Sun Catchers

Materials

Clear contact paper
Tape
Red and yellow tissue paper

What to do

1. Tape contact paper to a table with the sticky side up.
2. Place bits of red tissue paper in a single layer on one side of the sticky paper. Then add bits of yellow tissue paper on the other side of the paper.
3. Fold the sticky paper in half. Put it in a sunny window and watch what happens when the red and yellow tissue overlap.

More to do

After placing bits of tissue on the paper, use a pattern or stencil outline to cut around it. This will make an object with bits of paper showing through. Hang it in a sunny window to get the full effect. Also experiment with mixing different colored tissue paper.

❖❖ Jean Potter, Charleston, WV

Felt Board Jack-o-Lantern

Materials

Orange felt
Scissors
Black felt
Flannel board

What to do

1. Cut out a jack-o-lantern from orange felt.
2. Cut out a variety of shapes from black felt for the eyes, mouth, and nose.
3. Put the pumpkin and the shapes with your flannel board in the room for the children to manipulate during playtime.

More to do

Carve a real pumpkin to make a jack-o-lantern for the classroom.

Related books

Five Little Pumpkins by Iris Rynbach
Pumpkin, Pumpkin by Jeanne Titherington

❖❖ Jackie Wright, Enid, OK

Halloween Wreath

Materials

Paper plate
Scissors
Green tempera paint
Paintbrushes
Markers
Black and orange construction paper
Black and orange ribbon

What to do

1. Cut out the center of a paper plate and discard the middle part.
2. Paint the "wreath" with green tempera paint.
3. On black and orange construction paper, draw Halloween figures such as ghosts, bats, black cats, and so on. Cut them out.
4. Glue the shapes around the circle.
5. Add ribbon to complete the wreath.

More to do

Make paper chains of Halloween creatures. Cut out lots of black cats and "chain" them together.

❖❖ Jean Potter, Charleston, WV

Thanksgiving Cookbook

Materials

Picture of a turkey
Copy machine
Paper
Pen
Watercolors and brushes or crayons
Feathers, sequins, and glue optional

What to do

1. Ask the children what their favorite Thanksgiving foods are.
2. Ask each child to explain how to make his favorite dish. Write down their exact words. (This will make your recipe book more original.)
3. Copy your notes in the center of the paper, no more than two on a page.
4. Place a picture of a turkey on top to make a cover. Make a copy for each child to give to his family as a Thanksgiving present.
5. Before binding the books, encourage the children to paint or color the turkey cover page. If desired, use feathers and sequins for added decoration.

More to do

Art: Make a "Horn of Plenty." Encourage the children to paint or color with crayons or markers on the back of a large paper plate. Then, fold the plate in half to form a cone. Help the children cut out pictures of food found in old grocery ads and glue them inside the wide open end of the paper plate. This can be used as a centerpiece for the table on Thanksgiving Day.

Related books

Clifford's Thanksgiving Visit by Norman Bridwell
My First Thanksgiving by Tomie dePaola
Our Thanksgiving by Kimberly Weinberger
Thanksgiving Day by Gail Gibbons

❖❖ Cookie Zingarelli, Columbus, Ohio

Friendship (Thanksgiving) Soup

Materials

Variety of vegetables
Chopping knife (adult only)
Plastic knives
Large cooking pot
Stove

What to do

1. This is a good soup to make around Thanksgiving and share it with friends and other teachers.
2. Talk about the first Thanksgiving with the children and discuss how the Native Americans and Pilgrims shared food with each other.
3. Explain that they will be making soup to share with their friends.
4. Ask each child to bring in a vegetable. It is a good idea to hang up a list of suggestions outside your room (such as onion, carrots, potatoes, sweet potatoes, frozen corn, frozen peas, celery, large can of stewed tomatoes, and so on).
5. Use a chopping knife to cut all the vegetables into chunks. Ask the children to use plastic knives to cut the vegetable chunks into smaller chunks. Talk about the smell, color, and texture of each vegetable.
6. Put all of the vegetables into a large pot on a stove. Add a little water, salt, and pepper and cook it for about 45 minutes, or until all the vegetables are soft.
7. As the children are eating it, talk about friendship and sharing.

Related books

Growing Vegetable Soup by Lois Ehlert
Rainbow Fish by Marcus Phister

❖❖ Audrey Kanoff, Allentown, PA

Thanksgiving Wreath

Materials

Construction paper in autumn colors
Scissors
Heavy cardboard
Glue
Pinecones
Assortment of nuts
Ribbon, optional
Thin wire

What to do

1. Beforehand, cut out leaves in a variety of sizes and colors from construction paper.
2. Cut out a large circle (about the size of a large salad bowl) from heavy cardboard.
3. Cut out a smaller circle (about the size of a saucer) from the center of the large circle.
4. Encourage the children to glue paper leaves, pinecones, and nuts to the cardboard to make a Thanksgiving wreath.
5. If desired, add ribbon.
6. Make a hook using a thin piece of wire and attach it to the back of the wreath. Hang the wreath on a door or wall.

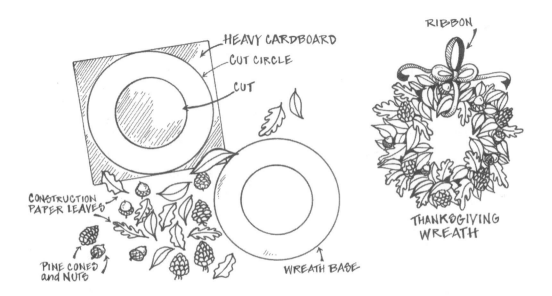

More to do

Art: With the children, make great smelling "pumpkin pies." Give the children small paper plates and ask them to paint them orange. Then encourage them to sprinkle nutmeg and cinnamon onto the wet paint. This will make a nice centerpiece on Thanksgiving Day.

Related books

Albert's Thanksgiving by Leslie Tryon
Thanksgiving by Miriam Nerlove
Thanksgiving Day by Anne Rockwell
'Twas the Night Before Thanksgiving by Dav Pilkey

❖❖ Cookie Zingarelli, Columbus, OH

The Menorah

Materials

Paper plates
Paper
Birthday wrapping paper decorated with candles or plain paper strips
Scissors
Glue

What to do

1. Explain to the children that there are eight candles on a menorah, in addition to the shammas. The shammas has the important job of lighting the other candles on the menorah.
2. Give each child a paper plate folded in half.
3. Cut out 1" x 2" (2 cm x 5 cm) rectangles from a piece of paper and give one to each child. Show them how to glue the rectangle in the middle of the folded part of the plate. The longer side should be vertical (see illustration).
4. Help the children cut out candles from the wrapping paper (or give them paper strips). Ask them to glue one candle on the top of the rectangle in the center. This candle, called the *shammas*, will be higher than the other candles.
5. Ask the children to count out four candles and glue them to the plate beside the tall shammas candle. Then they can count out four more and glue them on the other side of the tall candle.

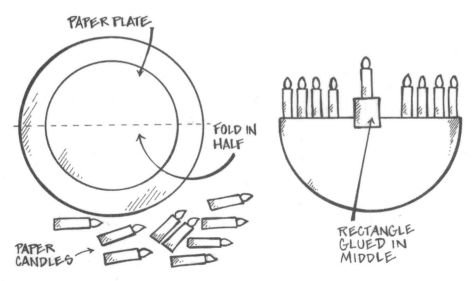

PAPER PLATE

FOLD IN HALF

PAPER CANDLES →

RECTANGLE GLUED IN MIDDLE

More to do

If paper strips are used instead of pictures of candles, encourage the children to "light" the candles by dipping a finger into yellow paint and placing it at the top of the candlesticks.

Related books

Dreidel, Dreidel, Dreidel by HarperFestival
The Great Hanukkah Party by Suzy-Jane Tanner
Hanukkah Lights, Hanukkah Nights by Leslie Kimmelman
Winnie the Pooh and the Hanukkah Dreidel by Disney

❖ Sandra Nagel, White Lake, MI

Felt Board Christmas Tree

Materials

Green felt
Scissors
Small pictures of Christmas tree ornaments
Glue stick
Tagboard
Rubber cement
Felt
Flannel board
Recording of Christmas songs
Tape player

What to do

1. Cut out a Christmas tree shape from green felt.
2. Cut out small pictures of Christmas tree ornaments.
3. Glue the ornament pictures to tagboard using a glue stick. Cut out again.
4. Attach felt to the backs of the pictures using rubber cement.
5. Put the Christmas tree, ornaments, and flannel board in the Listening Center along with a recording of your choice of Christmas songs.
6. The children will enjoy decorating the felt tree and singing along to the music during free choice time.

More to do

Make Christmas trees for a craft project. Give the children a construction paper tree shape to decorate with colored Cheerios.

Related book

The Night Before Christmas by Clement Clarke Moore

♦♦ Jackie Wright, Enid, OK

Christmas Bell

Materials

Small jingle bells, two per child
Thin ribbon
Scissors
Small clear plastic cups, one per child
Small Christmas stickers

What to do

1. Give each child two jingle bells and a piece of ribbon, 6" to 8" (15 to 20 cm) long.
2. Show the children how to string the ribbon through the bells.
3. Poke a small hole in the middle of the bottom of each cup. Give one to each child.
4. Help the children double the ribbon and tie a knot so the bell is inside a little loop.

5. Help the children thread the two ends of the ribbon through the hole in the cup. Tie a knot for them.
6. Cut apart the sheets of stickers. Ask the children to pick out the stickers they want to use and stick them all over the cup.
7. Encourage the children to hold their "Christmas bells" by the ribbon and shake them to hear the jingle!

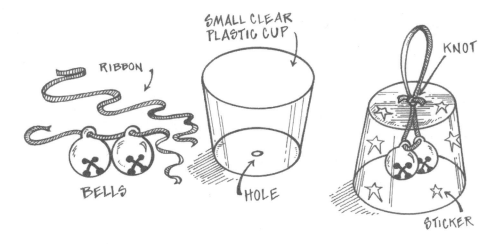

More to do

Put a variety of bells on a tray. Encourage the children to ring them and listen to the different sounds they make. Ask them questions, such as "Do you think this bell will have a loud or soft jingle? What does it sound like? Which one was the loudest? Softest?"

❖ Darleen Schaible, Stroudsburg, PA

Kwanzaa Hat

Materials

White crayon or white or yellow chalk
Yellow, red, and green construction or tissue paper
Black construction paper
Child scissors
Marker
Stapler
Glue stick or glue

What to do

1. Trace the lines of a hat onto a piece of black construction paper using crayon or chalk. Do this for each child.
2. Help the children cut out their hats. Ask the children to save a smaller piece of black scrap paper to use later.
3. Tear yellow, red, and green construction or tissue paper into pieces. Encourage the children to glue the pieces of paper all over one side of their hats.
4. Print the child's name on the hat.
5. Take the smaller piece of black paper and staple it to the edge of the hat to extend the width of the hat. Measure it to fit the child's head and staple the piece to the other side of the hat. Take the high part that is standing up and bend it to the back part of the hat. Staple it to the back area to keep it bent.
6. Now the hat is ready to wear.

More to do

Have a holiday party and ask the children to wear their Kwanzaa hats.
Dramatic Play: Keep the hats in the Dramatic Play Center.

Related books

Celebrating Kwanzaa by Diane Hoyt-Goldsmith
Imani's Gift at Kwanzaa by Denise Burden-Patmon
A Kwanzaa Celebration by Nancy Williams (a pop-up book)

❖❖ Sandra Nagel, White Lake, MI

Kwanzaa Corn

Materials

Information about the Kwanzaa corn
Tagboard
Scissors
Yellow, orange, and green paint and brushes
Glue
Brown or black marker
Brown paper (torn construction paper or tissue paper)
String
Paper punch

What to do

1. *Munhundi* means corn. The corn represents the children of a family (one ear of corn for each child). The corn symbolizes the parents' wish for the child to grow up strong and happy.
2. Cut out corn shapes from tagboard.
3. Ask the children how many brothers and sisters they have. Give each child one "ear of corn" for each sibling he has.

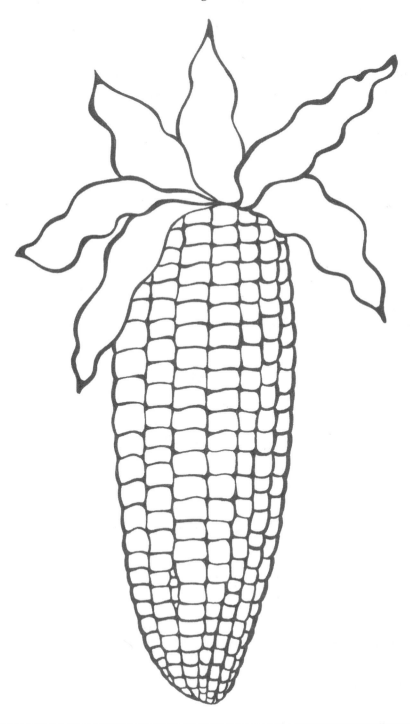

4. Encourage the children to paint their corn. When the corn is dry, encourage them to glue small pieces of brown paper to the top of each ear.

5. Give each child a piece of paper with information about Kwanzaa corn. Help them glue the information to the back of one ear of corn.

6. Write down the names of each child's siblings on a separate ear of corn.

7. Talk about what the corn symbolizes.

8. Punch a hole into each ear of corn and string them together. If you tie each ear if corn to the string, they will not overlap and lay on top of each other.

9. The child can take it home to be used as a door or wall hanging.

Related books

Celebrating Kwanzaa by Diane Hoyt-Goldsmith
Imani's Gift at Kwanzaa by Denise Burden-Patmon
A Kwanzaa Celebration by Nancy Williams

◆◆ Sandra Nagel, White Lake, MI

"W" Questions

Materials

None

What to do

1. Sit down with the children and have a discussion to help improve their language skills. Try to *really* listen to what they say.
2. Let them lead you where they want to go, but use the "W" questions when they need help going in a certain direction. *Who? What? When? Where? Why? How?* These words encourage open-ended conversation, no matter what age, even with adults.
3. The more you practice, the better you get at asking instead of telling. For example, if a child asks, "Where do you get grapes?" instead of saying, "From the store," ask leading questions. "Where do you think they came from? How do you think the grapes got to the store? What kind of truck do you think brought them to the store?"
4. Remember to repeat what the child asked by re-stating the question. If you allow the child to explore by asking and answering her own questions, she will expand her language skills and logical thought processes.

◆◆ Gail Whitney, Dameron, MD

Capturing Children's Thoughts

Materials

Large paper
Black marker

What to do

1. Ask the children questions, such as "If you were a butterfly and could fly anywhere in the world, where would you fly?"

2. Write down the children's exact words on a piece of paper.
3. Display on a wall, or put into portfolios for parents to see.

More to do

Literacy: Even three-year-olds can be introduced to writing activities. Set up a writing table with a variety of paper and different writing instruments, such as crayons, markers, rubber stamps, and chalk. Change them every week or so.

❖❖ Sue M. Myhre, Bremerton, WA

Pick a Spanish Word from the Piñata

Materials

Piñata
Small cards
Marker

What to do

1. Buy or make a piñata ahead of time.
2. On one side of each of the small cards, write simple Spanish words, such as *amigos, el professor, niño, muchacha,* and so on.
3. Write the English meaning of each word on the backs of the cards.
4. Cut a hole into the top of the piñata, big enough for a child's hand to reach inside.
5. Place a blindfold next to the piñata.
6. Each day before language, select a child to pick out the Spanish word for the day. Tie the blindfold around the child's head and help her reach into the piñata to remove a card. Make sure that every child gets a turn.

❖❖ Lisa Chichester, Parkersburg, WV

Felt and Flannel Fun

Materials

Assorted pieces of felt in a variety of colors
Cookie cutters in animal or shape patterns
Pen or marker
Scissors
Flannel board
Zipper-closure storage bag or basket

What to do

1. Trace animals or shapes onto pieces of felt and cut them out.
2. Gather the children into small groups or work with an individual child.
3. Ask the children to find specific felt pieces and place them on the flannel board. For example, say, "Place the white dog on the flannel board," or "Find the yellow circle and the blue triangle and put it on the board."

More to do

Add more shapes as the children become more aware of objects in their environment.
Math: Ask the children to count the number of shapes or animals on the flannel board.

❖❖ Margery A. Kranyik, Hyde Park, MA

Describe that Dinosaur

Materials

Large plastic dinosaurs, at least 4 different types
Paper
Marker
Magnifying glasses

What to do

1. Show the children a large plastic dinosaur and ask them to tell you about it. Encourage their input by asking questions such as "Is it big or small? What color is it? Does it have a short or long tail?"

2. Write the children's descriptions on a piece of paper.
3. Ask the children to describe a different dinosaur each day for four days, and continue the process of writing their descriptions for each dinosaur.
4. Display the children's descriptions in a prominent place in the classroom.
5. On the fifth day, hide the dinosaurs that the children have described.
6. During circle time, explain to the children that they are "dinosaur detectives" and they need to find the missing dinosaurs using the descriptions. Give them magnifying glasses to add to the fun.
7. Read the children's descriptions out loud and encourage the children to work together to find the missing dinosaur. Continue the process until they have found all four dinosaurs.

More to do

Dramatic Play: Ask the children how they could use descriptions to help find a lost pet. Hide a stuffed animal and ask the children describe what it looks like. They can make posters (with pictures and descriptions) that will help other classmates find the lost stuffed pet.

Related book

Whatever Happened to the Dinosaurs by Bernard Most

❖❖ Linda S. Andrews, Sonora, CA

Objects and Words of Comparison

Materials

Small bags or boxes, one for each child
Outdoor objects, such as stones, fallen leaves, wood, and old plastic items

What to do

1. Give the children small bags or boxes and go outside with them. Encourage them to collect items such as stones, fallen leaves, wood, and old plastic items. (Each child should collect more than one item.)
2. Back in the room, ask the children to sit in a circle on the floor and put their items in front of them.

3. Look at each one and talk about it with the children using comparative words. For example, "This stone is smooth. That stone is rough."

4. Encourage the children to touch each one and feel the difference as you say the words.

5. Other comparative words to use are *large, small; new, old; used, new; shiny, dull; thick, thin;* and *soft, hard.*

More to do

Art: Encourage the children to draw items that are large and small. Use materials that are rough or smooth to make collages.

Movement: Encourage the children to demonstrate with their hands and arms things that are large and small, thick and thin, and soft and hard. For example, ask if a house is big or little. Then ask them, "How big?" They will stretch their arms as wide as they can.

Snack: Ask the children to describe the food they eat (for example, *soft, hard, thick,* and *thin*).

Related book

Push, Pull, Empty, Full: A Book of Opposites by Tana Hoban

Original song

(Tune: "Three Blind Mice")
My house is big.
My house is big.
See how big!
See how big!
There's room for mom and dad and me,
And friends and all my family.
My house has everything I need to see.
My house is big.

This box is small.
This box is small.
See how small!
See how small!
There's only room for a little thing,
A pin, a paperclip, or ring.
This box is too small for me to fit,
I couldn't begin to live in it.
This box is small.

◆◆ Lucy Fuchs, Brandon, FL

Mystery Gift

Materials

Small unbreakable toy appropriate for a 3-year-old
Sturdy box
Wrapping paper and ribbon
Tape
Paper
Markers or crayons

What to do

1. Choose a small, inexpensive, non-fragile gift that a typical three-year-old would enjoy.
2. Put the gift in the box and wrap it, making sure it is free to move and "rattle" a little.
3. Introduce the wrapped gift to the children and explain that it is a "mystery gift" for the class. Explain that they will get to open it in a few days, but that until then they will get to guess what it is.
4. Let each child hold the box, shake it gently, and talk about what it might be.
5. Place the gift on a shelf near the paper and markers where the children are free to examine it as they did in the small group.
6. Ask the children to draw pictures of what the gift might be. Encourage each to tell you what they have drawn. Write down their dictated "guess" beside their picture. Children can make more than one drawing with different guesses if they wish.
7. After the allotted time has elapsed, assemble the children in a small group and look at the drawings of the guesses together, reading their dictated words aloud.
8. Open the gift so they can see what it really is. Explain that it belongs to everyone in the class and make it available for them to share and use.

More to do

If someone in the class is expecting a new baby in the family, wrap a baby gift such as a teething ring or a rattle using "baby" gift wrap. Encourage the child to guess what it could be. Let the child unwrap the gift and take it home as a gift from the school. This would be a good starting point for a discussion of what babies need, what they can and cannot do, and what to expect when the new baby arrives in the home.

Art: Invite the children to draw a picture of the gift they would most like to receive if they could have anything in the world. Write their verbal descriptions to go with the pictures. Then encourage them to draw a gift they would like to give to their mom, dad, or a friend if they could give anything in the world. Write their descriptions to go with the pictures.

Holidays: Wrap a gift suited to a special occasion, such as Christmas, Hanukkah, Valentine's Day, Easter, and so on. Even "Earth Day" could be included to encourage the children to think about what would be a good gift for the "Earth's" birthday (such as a package of seeds or a small bottle of water).

Related books

Happy Birthday, Moon by Frank Asch
Mr. Rabbit and the Lovely Present by Charlotte Zolotow
The Perfect Present by Michael Hague

❖❖ Susan Jones Jensen, Norman, OK

Tell the Doctor

Materials

Baby dolls
Old telephone or a plastic play phone

What to do

1. Give a baby doll to a child. Explain to the child that the baby is "sick" and that you would like her to call the doctor.
2. Give the child an old telephone or a play phone and ask her to pretend to call the doctor. An adult can pretend to be the doctor or another (very verbal) child can take the role.
3. Encourage the child who has the sick baby to describe the baby's symptoms to the doctor. The doctor can give the child some hints to help her along. For example, the doctor can ask, "Does your baby have a fever?" and "Does the baby have a stomachache?" If a child is playing the doctor role, give her some hints or words to repeat.
4. After the child has described the baby's symptoms, ask the child to take the baby to the hospital for treatment.
5. The objective of this activity is to encourage the children to be as verbal as possible and extend their vocabularies, so encourage lots of talking.

More to do

Dramatic Play: Set up an area that can serve as a hospital for the sick babies. Stock it with medical supplies such as gowns, masks, lab coats, play thermometers, blood pressure cuffs, empty pill bottles, fake syringes, phones, charts, and so on. Put a couple of baby doll cribs in the area for the sick patients and a small table designated as the exam table.

Related books

Doctor Shawn by Petronella Breinburg
Eric Needs Stitches by Barbara P. Marino
Island Baby by Holly Keller
My Doctor by Harlow Rockwell

❖❖ Virginia Jean Herrod, Columbia, SC

I Like to Say...

Materials

Pictures of (or real objects) with the sounds you want to practice

What to do

1. Decide what words you want the children to practice saying. Collect a bunch of pictures or objects illustrating the sound.
2. Introduce and practice the following song, inserting the words you want to practice. Use fun words such as *pickle, lollipop, Popsicle,* and *pizza.*

I Like to Say

> *I like to say lollipop, lollipop, lollipop.*
> *I like to say lollipop,*
> *Yes I do.*

3. Show the children pictures of the object or the object itself.
4. Encourage the children to choose the words they like to say.

More to do

Use fun sounds instead of words. For example, la la la la; zoom zoom; pop, pop, pop; buzzing; hissing; a raspberry sound; and farm animal sounds.
Books: Read fun and silly word play books to expand the children's ideas.

Games: Make it a game by putting paperclips on the pictures and using a string and a magnet to "fish" for sounds and words to sing.

❖❖ Sandra Nagel, White Lake, MI

Rhyme Time

Materials

Objects to represent pairs of rhyming words, such as block/sock, clock/rock, star/car, hat/cat, rope/soap, truck/duck, shell/bell, doll/ball, can/pan, and so on
Laundry basket (or plastic bin)
Pillowcase
Picture book with rhyming words, book of children's poems, or nursery rhymes
Blanket

What to do

1. Collect a bunch of objects to represent pairs of rhyming words. Separate the pairs of rhyming objects and place one set in a basket and the other in a pillowcase.
2. Ask the children to sit in a circle. Read the selected book or rhyme to the children. Read it again, pausing to allow the children to say each rhyming word before you have a chance to read it. Praise them for each correct rhyme.
3. Place the basket on a blanket in the center of the circle. Remove the set of objects from the pillowcase and scatter them on the blanket around the basket.
4. Invite each child to take a turn playing the "rhyme time game." Ask them to choose one object from the blanket and to look inside the basket to find its rhyming mate.
5. Encourage the rest of the children to offer hints to help each player as needed.

More to do

Music: Most popular children's songs have rhyming lyrics. Play a tape or CD and encourage children to identify the rhyming sounds they hear.

❖❖ Susan A. Sharkey, La Mesa, CA

I Love You

Materials

Construction paper and markers

What to do

1. Draw pictures of sign language for "I love you," "happy," "nice," and "friend."
2. Sing the following song to the tune of "Three Blind Mice" as you sign it.

The I Love You Song

I love you.
I love you.
You're happy, nice, and friendly,
You're happy, nice, and friendly,
I love you.
I love you.

3. Encourage the children to sing along and sign, "I love you."
4. After the children are doing well with signing, "I love you," practice the signs "happy," "nice," and "friend" separately until the children seem comfortable.
5. If the children are having trouble with "You're happy, nice, and friendly," shorten it by only signing the words, "Your happy friend."

The GIANT Encyclopedia of Preschool Activities for Three-Year-Olds

FRIEND

ME

LIKE

FATHER

MOTHER

More to do

Try the song silently, just using the signs.

Sing the song and try not to verbalize one word. Repeat the song, each time trying to verbalize one less word, yet sign them all.

❖❖ Sandra Nagel, White Lake, MI

Long Noses and Trunks

Materials

African fabric
Necklace
Flyswatter

What to do

1. Get the children's attention by placing a piece of fabric on the floor. Take time to smooth it out and fuss over it. Hold it up again so the children may see it. Then smooth it out again. When the children come over, don't say anything and continue fussing over the material. Point to where you want them to sit. Gently help a child to sit down to demonstrate what you want, but don't use any words!

2. After everyone is settled, take out two more pieces of material. Tie one piece around your waist and wrap the other piece around your head, turban style. Put on the necklace. Again, don't say anything. Sit on the first piece of fabric. Take out a flyswatter and start swatting with it.

3. Look at the children, one at a time. Start telling the following story. The story is based on an old folk tale.

Once a long time ago in the land of Africa, there once lived Brown Crocodile who liked to eat all kinds of animals. She ate fish. She ate frogs. She even ate birds. She would lay on the edge of the river and wait for her dinner to come down to the water to get a drink. Then SNAP! went her jaws on her dinner!

One day, a whole herd of elephants passed by the river where Brown Crocodile lived. In those days, elephants had small noses just like a pig. As the elephant family ate the tall grass, Baby Elephant went down to the river to get a drink. Baby Elephant did not remember that her mother said not to go to the river by herself. As she bent down to get her drink, Snap went Brown Crocodile on Baby Elephant's nose.

What a noise the two of them made! "Let my nose go!" yelled Baby Elephant.

"No!" cried Brown Crocodile. "I'm hungry!"

"Let my nose go!" yelled Baby Elephant again. And she dug her feet into the mud so she wouldn't fall in.

Now Brown Crocodile had lots and lots of trouble pulling Baby Elephant into the water. So she pulled even harder! As a matter of fact, Brown Crocodile pulled so hard that Baby Elephant's nose began to stretch and stretch and stretch!

Baby Elephant's mother heard the noise and ran down to the river to help her baby! She grabbed Baby Elephant's tail and yanked on it so hard that they both fell down. "Yea!" Baby Elephant said. "Brown Crocodile won't get me today!"

Brown Crocodile was so mad that she turned around and swam back into the river. When Baby Elephant joined the herd, everyone stared and stared at her new trunk. You see, Brown Crocodile had pulled and pulled on the elephant's nose so hard that her nose was now stretched out very long. And that's why all elephants today have long noses!

4. Be sure to end the story to allow the children to separate you from your "storyteller" role. Take off all of the props and start speaking the chant to transition to another area. For example:

Oh Mister Crocodile, don't bite me!
(Child's name) go wash your hands now.
One! Two! Three!

5. Ask one of the children to re-tell the story.

More to do

Literacy: Write down a story someone tells.

Related book

The Big Wide-Mouthed Frog by Ana Martin Larranaga

❖ Gail Whitney, Dameron, MD

Top It Off!

Materials

Story
Straw hat
Velcro stripping
Scissors
Magazines or assorted small items related to the story

What to do

1. Measure a strip of Velcro to reach around the brim of the chosen hat.
2. Attach it to the hat with the "sticky" side out.
3. Cut out magazine photos or choose small story items to match the story you are going to tell them.
4. Attach Velcro to the pictures or objects, again "sticky" side out.
5. Gather the children and tell a tale while placing the items on your story hat.

More to do

Make children's versions of the hat using sentence strips that have been measured to fit each child's individual head. Use Velcro for reusable story hats; use glue to create a permanent version.

❖❖ Charlene Woodham Peace, Semmes, AL

Story Bucket

Materials

Bucket
Small objects, such as toy cars, animals, and people
Easel
Easel paper
Marker or pen

What to do

1. Put small objects into the bucket.
2. Ask the children to sit in a circle. Explain to them that they are going to tell a story using their imaginations and the objects from the bucket.
3. Pass the bucket around and encourage each child to take out one object.
4. Pick one child to start the story.
5. Write down what the child says on easel paper.
6. Keep going until every child has a turn telling part of the story.
7. Read the story back to them. It doesn't matter if it makes sense the first time, the idea is to get them to realize that what they say turns into written words.
8. Hang it in the room so parents can read it.

More to do

Make copies of the stories and compile a classroom book of all the stories of the year or make a copy for each child to bring home at the end of the year.

❖ Darleen A. Schaible, Stroudsburg, PA

Letter Collages

Materials

Construction paper or poster board
Glue
Variety of items (see following page)

What to do

1. When introducing letters of the alphabet to three-year-olds, teachers often use a "letter of the week" format. Each week, you will make a "collage" shaped like each letter, decorated with something that starts with that letter (see below).

2. Depending on your preferences and the number of children in your class, you can give each child a cut-out letter to decorate or the children can work together to make a giant collage of each letter on poster board. As you progress from week to week, display one collage for each letter in the classroom.

3. Following are some suggested materials for each letter. You can vary them as you like, using whatever materials you have on hand that start with each letter.

A—acorn prints (acorn caps dipped in paint) or ants made from fingerprints

B—buttons, birdseed, beads

C—crayons (glue on the little stubby leftovers), confetti

D—doilies, dominoes (cheap set from the dollar store)

E—eggshell pieces (dyed, then crumbled up)

F—feathers, flowers (dried/pressed or artificial from craft store), felt pieces

G—glitter, gum wrappers (we chewed the sugar-free treat while we glued!)

H—hearts (stickers or cut from tissue paper or other colorful paper)

I—icicles (the shiny kind from a Christmas tree)

J—jingle bells (from craft store)

K—kisses (this is my favorite—the children put on lipstick and then kiss the paper!)

L—lace, leaves

M—play money, magnets

N—strips of newspaper, nickels

O—oak leaves, octagons and ovals (cut from paper), pictures of owls

P—pipe cleaners, "puff balls" (from craft store), pennies, paperclips

Q—"quilting" pieces (fabric cut into triangles and squares—try to make patterns), Q-tips

R—ribbon, rubber bands

S—stickers, stars (cut out or stickers), Silly String (from party store, comes in a squirt can)

T—tin foil (cut out shapes, watch for sharp edges), tape (the children love pulling pieces off the tape dispenser!), taffy

U—umbrella cutouts

V—Valentines (leftover), Velcro, velvet (scraps from a craft store)

W—watercolors

X—"X" marks the spot X's from our treasure hunt (see below)
Y—yellow yarn
Z—zippers (from craft store)

More to do

More Literacy: Once you have gone through the alphabet and all the letters are displayed on the wall, put a bunch of objects in a bag. Encourage the children to take turns pulling out an object and then running to the letter it starts with.
Art: When learning the letter Q, bring in quilts for the children to examine. Make a class quilt in which each child decorates a square (paper or fabric).
Games: For the letter X, have an "X marks the spot" Treasure Hunt. Hide some familiar classroom objects marked with a red X cut from construction paper. Give the children verbal clues or a map to find them. Save the X's to glue on that week's letter collage.

◆❖ Suzanne Pearson, Stephens City, VA

Alphabet Activities

Materials

Index cards
Markers
Variety of alphabet books with one to four illustrations per page
Basket

What to do

1. Choose a letter/sound you wish to focus on for a few days and write it on a large index card. Put a variety of alphabet books into a basket.
2. Form a group of no more than five children and invite each of them to choose a different alphabet book from the basket on the table.
3. Hold up the card containing the letter you wish to work on, and ask the children to name the letter. Then challenge them to try to find the letter in their books. You may simplify this step by locating the letter for the children and giving each one a chance to point and say the letter in their own book.
4. Go around the group and ask each child to identify a picture on his letter page. For example, for the letter "T," a picture in one child's book might be a toothbrush, the next child might have a tiger, and so on.

5. The others in the group repeat each word as it is identified by the child.

6. Now go around the group again, asking for another word that starts with "T" on their page.

7. After a while, children will notice that the beginning sound of each word is the same. There are many values to this activity. It promotes "reading" because the children get practice in handling the books, turning the pages, and "picture reading." In addition, the sound/symbol connection is being developed, which is the basis for phonemic awareness.

More to do

Set up an Alphabet Center in the classroom with books, alphabet puzzles, letter stamps and stamp pads, mini chalkboards and chalk, alphabet blocks, magnetic letters (metal cookie sheets make excellent individual boards for magnetic letters), primary pencils, and markers.

Art: Form alphabet letters using clay

Books: Make your own alphabet books using pictures from magazines, catalogues, or stickers.

Related song

What's The Sound That Starts This Word?
(Tune: "Old McDonald Had a Farm")

What's the sound that starts these words:
Baby, Ball, and Bat?
(wait for a response from the children)

/B/ is the sound that starts these words:
Baby, Ball, and Bat!

With a /B/, /B/ here, and a /B/, /B/ there
Here a /B/, there a /B/, everywhere a /B/, /B/.

/B/ is the sound that starts these words:
Baby, Ball, and Bat!

(Adapted from *The Reading Teacher*, May, 1992, Vol. 45, No. 9, p. 700 by Hallie Yopp.)

Related books

26 Letters and 99 Cents by Tana Hoban

ABC, A Chunky Shape Book by Jean Hirashima

Curious George's ABC's by H. A. & M. Rey

◆◆ Iris Rothstein, New Hyde Park, NY

Poetry Alphabet Search

Materials

Large piece of tag board

Marker

Laminate or clear contact paper

Dry erase marker

What to do

1. Choose any poem and write it in large letters on a large piece of tag board. Laminate the tag board or cover it with clear contact paper.
2. During morning group time, read the poem out loud. Select a child to help with circling one letter in the poem.
3. Vary the activity by asking one child to circle all of one specific letter, or ask the children to take turns circling letters.
4. Help the child count the letters.
5. When all the letters have been circled, hang the poem on the wall.
6. Repeat the activity using a new poem.

More to do

Type a poem on a piece of paper and make enough copies for each child. Give each child a copy to bring home so they can draw a picture to illustrate the poem. Make a class book of poetry using the drawings.

◆◆ Melissa Browning, Milwaukee, WI

Mr. And Mrs. Alphabet Puppets

Materials

Letter stencils
Felt in a variety of colors
Marker
Child scissors
Glue
Mitten, one for each child
Googly eyes, pompoms, and yarn

What to do

1. Give each child letter stencil and different colored felt.
2. Show the children how to trace and cut out felt letters.
3. Give each child a mitten. Help the children glue their letters on the mitten, along with moveable eyes and yarn for hair.
4. Use the puppets as props to sing the ABC song.

❖❖ Lisa Chichester, Parkersburg, WV

Your Name's the Game

Materials

Computer labels
Markers

What to do

1. Explain to the children that they will write their names on labels and that you will put their name labels on their artwork and belongings.
2. Help the children make nametags using markers and computer labels.

3. Learning the mechanics of writing is a process. At this age, children are experimenting with written language. Some children will be able to write letters and words, while others will express themselves with something that resembles scribbles, rather than distinguishable letters. Regardless of their stage of literacy, encourage the children to experiment with writing and praise their efforts.

More to do

More Literacy: Place paper and markers in various centers throughout the room, which the children can use to enhance their play. Model the use of writing in everyday experience, such as making lists, writing notes, and so on.

Transitions: Make nametags and use them as a transition from one activity to the next. Show the name tags to the children and ask them to pick their names.

Related book

Chicka Chicka Boom Boom by Bill Martin Jr. and John Archambault

◆❖ Linda Andrews, Sonora, CA

Beanbag Name Game

Materials

Beanbag
Alphabet chart

What to do

1. Ask the children to sit in a circle.
2. Toss the beanbag to a child and ask him to say, "My name is _____ and my name starts with _____." Then he goes to the front of the room and points to the first letter of his name on the alphabet chart.
3. Repeat this process until all the children have had a turn.
4. This is a great transition activity that incorporates movement and early literacy skills. Keep in mind that not all children are at the same developmental stage and some children will need help pointing to the letter that starts their name.

More to do

Write the letters of the alphabet on a large piece of poster board. Ask the children to toss a beanbag on the letters that are in their name.

Related book

Chicka Chicka Boom Boom by Bill Martin Jr. and John Archambault

❖❖ Linda Andrews, Sonora, CA

Name Recognition

Materials

Sturdy paper
Laminate or clear contact paper
Markers
Zipper-closure plastic bags
Wooden snap clothespins
Chart paper
Sturdy oaktag/cardboard

What to do

1. There are so many opportunities to use children's names in written form in the early childhood classroom. These are often the first words that a child learns to read. Following are some ways to use their written names.

2. Write the children's names on their cubbies, artwork, mailboxes, portfolios, job charts, bus lists, and so on.

3. Make each child a placemat using sturdy paper. Print the child's name and encourage him to decorate it. Laminate the mats or cover them with clear contact paper and store them in a zipper closure bag. Use the mats at snack time.

4. Give each child a wooden clothespin with his name printed on both sides. Use the pins to clip together boots, mittens, or unfinished paperwork.

5. The children can also use their pins as a "voting" device. Make a chart with two columns and encourage the children to vote for their favorite cookie, color, fruit, toy, and so on by clipping their pin on the appropriate side of the chart. Change the heading to reflect what is being voted for.

6. Make a name sign for each child in the class. Call upon children for their various activities by holding up their name sign. Of course if the child doesn't recognize his name, you should help him (perhaps with a special sticker next to the name). Before long the children will recognize not only their own names, but they will be able to read many of their classmates' names.

More to do

Art: Following are some art projects using names. The children can:
Write their name using glue and then sprinkle it with glitter or colored rice.
Make a collage of their name by rolling little balls of tissue paper and gluing them onto the name.
Form their name using clay, playdough, pipe cleaners, and so on.
Manipulatives: Make a name puzzle. Writing the child's name on a piece of paper and encourage him to decorate it. Cut it into as many pieces as you think appropriate, and see if the child can put it back together.

Related books

Chrysanthemum by Kevin Henkes
Rumpelstiltskin by Paul Zelinsky

❖❖ Iris Rothstein, New Hyde Park, NY

Vocabulary Wall

Materials

Flashcards, greeting cards, catalogs, and magazines
Sticky putty

What to do

1. Decide which words you want to focus on. Cut out pictures from greeting cards, magazines, and so on that depict these words.
2. Use sticky putty to attach the pictures on a wall where children congregate, making sure to place them at children's eye level.
3. When the children have to wait, ask them to stand next to a particular picture. For example, ask Sue to stand by the wagon, Billy next to the motorcycle, and so on.
4. After the children find the picture they are to stand next to, they can tell you something about the picture. For example, "My wagon has wheels" or "A motorcycle can go fast."

More to do

Language: Use the pictures as a natural stimulant for identification and description activities.

Math: Place a large variety of pictures on the wall and use them for other activities such as categorizing. For example, ask the children to point to two pictures of food; find something to wear when it is cold; point to something that is a toy; or find one object to use in the bathroom.

◆◆ Mary Volkman, Ottawa, IL

Putting Print in Their Play

Materials

See below

What to do

1. Adding print-related props to the Dramatic Play area provides opportunities for children to use print in situations that are meaningful, functional, and genuine.
2. Following are some suggested play themes with corresponding literacy props. Of course, you should also add other props appropriate for the situation.

Fine Dining

Easel chalkboard listing the daily specials
Menus
Paper and pens for writing food reviews
Pen and notepad for ordering
Sign with restaurant's name and hours

Grocery Store

Clean, empty food boxes
Clean, empty plastic food containers
Coupons
Newspaper flyers
Play money, credit cards, and checks
Price signs and daily specials
Receipts
Recipe cards
Sign displaying store name and hours

Travel Agency

Business cards for agents

Calendar

Magazines, brochures of various locales, travel posters

Maps

Pens, pencils and message pads

Sign displaying agency name and hours

Telephone and telephone book

Pizzeria

Coupons

Menus and daily specials

Pens, pencils, and order pads

Play money, credit cards, and checks

Rebus recipes for various types of pizzas

Receipts

Sign with restaurant's name and hours

Telephone and telephone book

TV Weather Studio

"On the Air" sign

Cardboard box cameras

Cue cards

Typewriter, pens/pencils, and paper*(for writing scripts)

Various maps

Automobile Repair Shop

Credit cards, play money, and checks

Magazines and newspapers (for waiting area)

Pens, pencils, and paper (for order forms and bills)

Receipts

Signs displaying shop name and hours

Telephone and telephone book

Theater

Marquis outside theater

Menu and price for concessions

Nametags for workers

Play money, credit cards, and checks

Playbill or programs

Posters advertising current show

Price list for tickets

Prop/costume boxes appropriately labeled

Scripts for short stories (including pictures and words)

Theater signs (Exit, No Smoking or Quiet Please)

Ticket window and tickets with numbers

Airline Ticket Counter

Credit cards, play money, and checks

Flight schedules

Luggage tags and stickers

Maps

Signs displaying name of airlines

Staples, paper clips, pens, and pencils (for making tickets and itineraries)

Car Dealership

Business cards for sales representatives

Dealership ads from newspaper

Magazines, brochures, posters

Mirror with wax pencil (for writing and changing prices)

Pens, pencils, and paper

Receipt pads and special order forms

Sign displaying agency name and hour

Window stickers

❖❖ Rebecca McMahen Giles, Mobile, AL

Clown Faces

Materials

Felt in assorted colors
Scissors
Flannel board

What to do

1. Cut out a large circle from felt. This will be the clown's face.
2. From other colors of felt, cut out several clown hats, eyes, noses, ears, mouths, and bows (for bow ties or hair bows).
3. Place the large circle on the flannel board. Put the other shapes in front of the board. Invite children to add features to the face to make a funny clown.
4. Encourage them to change the features to make other funny faces.

More to do

Art: Give each child a large paper circle. Provide glue sticks and a variety of pre-cut construction paper hats, eyes, ears, noses, mouths, and so on. Encourage the children to add features to their paper circles, forming clown faces.

Related book

Circus by Lois Ehlert

❖❖ Barbara Backer, Charleston, SC

Puzzles

Materials

Book covers
Glue
Heavy poster board
Shape stencils in different sizes
Marker
Exacto knife (adult only)
Clear contact paper
Zipper-closure storage bags

What to do

1. Glue a book cover on a piece of poster board.
2. Use the stencils to trace different shapes onto the book cover.
3. Cut out the shapes using an Exacto knife. Leave the traced lines to help the children. The leftover book cover will be the puzzle board.
4. Cover the cut-out shapes and the puzzle board with clear contact paper.
5. Repeat this process with other book covers.
6. Store the puzzles in zipper-closure bags.

Original song

(Tune "Are You Sleeping?")
This is a square, this is a square
How can you tell? How can you tell?
It has four sides, all the same size
It's a square, it's a square.

Related books

Can You Find It? by Bernard Most
Spot Looks at Shapes by Eric Hill
Squares by Mary Elizabeth Salzmann

◆◆ Liz Thomas, Hobart, IN

Simple Shape Puzzles

Materials

Wallpaper sample books
Scissors
Clear contact paper
Zipper-closure plastic bags

What to do

1. Cut out large shapes from wallpaper, such as a circle, triangle, square, heart, star, and tree.
2. Cover each shape with clear contact paper for durability. Trim away the excess clear paper.
3. Cut each shape into three or four simple pieces to make a puzzle.
4. Put each puzzle into a separate plastic zipper bag.
5. Show the children how to work the puzzles. Then put them where the children can use them.

More to do

For a variation of this activity, cut out pictures from wallpaper sample books. You may find teddy bears, dogs, balls, and other similar pictures in sample books of wallpaper for children's rooms. Cover these pictures with clear contact paper for durability, and then cut each into several puzzle pieces. Store them as above.

❖❖ Barbara Backer, Charleston, SC

Paper Plate Puzzles

Materials

Paper plates, two per puzzle
Crayons
Scissors

What to do

1. Give each child a paper plate. Ask them to draw a picture in the center of their plate.
2. Then cut the picture into three or four pieces.
3. Give the children the pieces of their drawing and an additional plate. Ask them to reassemble their pictures, using the second plate as a puzzle "tray."
4. As they are working, recite the following poem:

   I have a little puzzle.
   I took the pieces out.
   I put them back together,
   That's what it's all about!

More to do

Have a Puzzle Day, highlighting the classroom puzzles. Showcase any floor puzzles that are available. If possible, introduce new puzzles and encourage the children to try to reassemble a friend's drawing.
Art: Glue old jigsaw puzzle pieces to headbands to wear for Puzzle Day.

❖ Susan Oldham Hill, Lakeland, FL

Stickers and Chart Paper

Materials

Circle stickers or any other type of stickers, perhaps based on your theme or
season of the year (1" or less in diameter)
Chart paper with 1" squares

What to do

1. For three-year-olds, it is a good idea to cut the chart paper into 4" x 5" pieces.
2. Give one piece to each child, along with a sheet of stickers.
3. Encourage the children to put one sticker into each square of the paper to
   practice one-to-one correspondence.

More to do

Use bingo markers or stamp pads to fill in the squares.

◆❖ Linda N. Ford, Sacramento, CA

Sizing It Up

Materials

Blocks, balls, and toy cars, or cut-out shapes of different sizes
Basket

What to do

1. Discuss the words *big* and *little*.
2. Show the children a variety of objects or cut-out shapes and ask them to line
   up the items from big to little or little to big.
3. Ask the children to put as many small items as they can into a basket. Then, ask
   them to put as many big items as they can into the basket. Discuss the difference.

More to do

Line up the children in order of size.

◆❖ Melissa O. Markham, Huddleston, VA

What Size Is the Frog?

Materials

Plastic life-size frogs, or any other desired animal (If plastic ones are not available, make paper silhouettes of the animals.)

Ruler, optional

What to do

1. Ask the children to sit in a small group. Give each child a frog to hold.
2. Take time to explore the frog and talk about its characteristics.
3. Ask each child to find something in the room that is bigger than the frog and to bring it back to the group to check by comparing it to the frog.
5. Next, ask the children to find something smaller than the frog (or the same size).
6. Provide rulers if the children have an interest in measuring.

More to do

Art: Precut paper in the same shape as the animal. Encourage the children to paint them.

Sand and Water: Encourage the children to bring the animals to the water table to play.

Related books

Fish Is Fish by Leo Lionni

It's Mine by Leo Lionni

❖❖ Barbara Reynolds, Galloway Twp, NJ

Whale Measuring

Materials

Encyclopedia or book on whales

Long hallway

Masking tape

Tape measure

What to do

1. Beforehand, determine the lengths of the blue whale, humpback whale, gray whale, beluga whale, and killer whale. Go into a long hallway and put down a line of tape to represent each whale's length. For example, a blue whale is 100', so put down a piece of tape that measures 100'.
2. Then, during circle time when you are talking about whales, tell the children that they are going to measure how long whales are and how many children it would take to equal one blue whale, humpback whale, and so on.
3. Bring the children out into the hallway and ask them to lie down on the tape from head to toe. Once they do that, they will see they don't equal one blue whale. Then, you will need to go get another class. They will love this!
4. Leave the tape for parents to see.

More to do

Have a "whale day!" Put whales in the sensory table, paint whale shapes at the easel, read *Humphrey the Humpback Whale* by Ernest Callenbach, and sing "Baby Beluga."

❖❖ Holly Dzierzanowski, Brenham, TX

People Patterns

Materials

None

What to do

1. Ask the children to sit together in a circle.
2. Tell them, "Today we are going to make a people pattern. I will tell you where to stand to make the pattern."
3. Start by making a pattern, such as the first child stands, second child sits, third child stands, and so on.
4. As you direct the children to stand or sit, vocalize what you are doing. For example, "Robbie stands, Cherie sits, Jennifer stands," and so on.
5. After all of the children are in the pattern, walk behind each child and place your hand on their heads while saying, "Stand, sit, stand, sit," and so on.
6. Ask the children what the pattern is. Encourage them to say the pattern as you touch each child's head.

7. Repeat this process every day for a length of time, using a variety of patterns such as: front, back, front, back; hands up, hands down; or lay down, sit.

More to do

More Math: Prepare patterns on pieces of card stock using dots, shaped blocks, or other small items. Encourage the children to continue the pattern.

◆◆ Barbara Saul, Eureka, CA

Patterns, Patterns Everywhere!

Materials

See individual activities

What to do

The following activities reinforce the children's learning about patterns in different ways. Do one, or do them all, day in and day out!

1. **Cereal Patterns:** Arrange some decorative, yummy food bits, such as banana slices, raisins, and blueberries, in little custard cups to add to hot oatmeal. Encourage the children to add them one at a time, creating a pattern on the cereal. Then eat!

2. **Painting Patterns:**
   Fingerpainting: Pour a puddle of liquid starch on a piece of paper. Add a little tempera paint or food coloring. Encourage the children to draw patterns with all five fingers at once, dragging them through the paint to make designs.
   Feet Prints: Help each child step into a pan of paint with one bare foot, and then step onto a big sheet of paper. Encourage the child to make footprint patterns across the paper. Rinse foot in a tub of warm soapy water.

3. **Ladybug Patterns:** Look at a real ladybug or a picture of a ladybug. Now make Ladybug Prints! Cut a sponge into a circle and press it into red paint. Encourage the children to make a red circle print on a piece of paper, then make lots of red circles. Let dry briefly. Now they can dip a finger into black paint and make black dots on the ladybug's red back.

4. **Pattern Kabobs:** Make fruit kabobs or veggie kabobs on skewers with chunks of food. Make a pattern of colors or types of food. For example, pineapple/strawberry, pineapple/strawberry; or red/white/yellow (strawberry, banana, pineapple). Discover that some patterns have colors and tastes.

5. **Butterfly Toast:** Cut a slice of toasted bread in half from corner to corner. Now turn the halves around with points facing each other on the center of the plate. These are the butterfly's wings. Next, in small dishes mix some food coloring with milk. Make one color, or several colors. Encourage the children to use a small, clean paintbrush to paint symmetrical designs on the wings. For example, if you paint a yellow dot on the right wing, make a yellow dot on the left wing, too. Blue oval on the right wing? Blue oval on the left wing too. When done, look at the symmetry of the butterfly toast.

6. **Happy/Sad Cards:** One type of simple pattern that children recognize is the expression of happy and sad faces. Cut out magazine pictures of faces that are happy and faces that are sad and paste them on index cards. Ask the children to sort them into two piles—one for happy and one for sad.

7. **Nail Board Patterns:** Hammer broad-head nails around the border of a square of wood (8" x 8" works well), about 1" apart. Now take colored rubber bands and make stretchy patterns from one nail to another. Make plaid, stripes, diamonds, or other combinations. Encourage the children to discover how to create patterns that can be changed and rearranged using the same materials.

Original poem

ABC Patterns (by MaryAnn F. Kohl)

Pattern A, pattern A, all the kids love pattern A,
Clap, clap, clap and stamp, stamp, stamp
(make up patterns with clapping hands and stomping feet)
Pattern A is fun to play.

Pattern B, pattern B, all the kids love pattern B,
Clapitty, clap, clap and stamp and stamp,
Pattern B is fun to play.

Pattern C, pattern C, all the kids love C,
Clap, clap, stomp and clap, clap, stomp,
Pattern C is fun to play.

❖ MaryAnn F. Kohl, Bellingham, WA

Finding a Shape

Materials

Sandpaper
Scissors
Box or bag

What to do

1. Cut two of each of the following shapes from sandpaper: circle, square, triangle, rectangle, star, and oval.
2. Show them to the children, encouraging them to feel them.
3. Place them all into a box or bag. Ask the children to reach into the bag and feel the shapes without looking. Can they identify the shapes?
4. Ask a child to pull out a shape, without looking, and place it on the table.
5. Now challenge him to reach in and try to find a match by feeling for it.

More to do

Art: Encourage the children to use the sandpaper shapes to draw around, or to make a shape rubbing.

Related book

Shapes by Jan Pienkowski

❖ Sandra Hutchins Lucas, Cox's Creek, KY

Color Bags

Materials

Novelty paper bags in a variety of solid colors
Variety of objects in assorted colors or colorful pictures of objects

What to do

1. Encourage the children to put each item into its matching color bag. Encourage the use of color words as children make the matches.

2. When the children are ready, hide all the items, give each child a different bag, and encourage them to go on a "color hunt." Encourage them to find the items that match their assigned color. (Be sure to make putting the objects back part of the task.)
3. You can also use these bags at clean-up time. Encourage the children to use the bags to pick up all the play items of that particular color.

Note: To make this activity more durable, sew simple drawstring bags using colored fabrics.

More to do

Home-School Connection: Send the bags home with children to encourage them to look for things at home that are a particular color.

Literacy: Write or attach a label with the color word spelled out to encourage letter awareness.

◆◆ Bev Schumacher, Dayton, OH

People Sorting

Materials

None

What to do

1. Ask the children to sit together in a circle.
2. Tell them, "I am going to sort you by what color hair you have." Designate an area of the room for different hair colors. For example, say, "Frank, you have black hair—go stand by the bulletin board. Kaitlyn, you have red hair—go stand by the door." Repeat this with every child until they all have been sorted.
3. Go to each group and say, "Everyone in this group has red hair. Is this correct?" Let them talk about it, then move to the next group and continue, "Everyone in this group has blonde hair. Is that right?"
4. After each group has been identified, let them go back to their normal activity.
5. Repeat this process every day for a length of time. Each time you sort the children, use a different criteria, such as children wearing pants and children wearing dresses, children wearing boots and children wearing tie shoes or Velcro, eye color, and so on.

More to do

Take a photo of each child. Put them in a center and encourage the children to sort them in different ways. Ask them to tell you what categories they used.

❖❖ Barbara Saul, Eureka, CA

Sorting Colored Caps

Materials

Paper plates
Crayons or paint
Numerous colored caps from plastic milk cartons, juice cartons, and so on
Bowl

What to do

1. Paint or color three or four paper plates to match the colors on the caps.
2. Put all the caps into a bowl on the table.
3. Encourage the child to place one cap at a time on the matching colored paper plate.

More to do

Use small shapes, including circles, squares, and triangles instead of caps.

❖❖ Elaine Commins, Athens, GA

Sorting Small Items

Materials

Variety of small items such as buttons, paper clips, washers, coins, dried beans, hair clips, and so on
2 empty egg cartons, with lids removed

What to do

1. One or two children may play with this at a time.
2. Give each child an empty egg carton.
3. Encourage the child to sort the objects into the compartments of the egg carton.

❖❖ Elaine Commins, Athens, GA

Buried Treasure

Materials

Paper
Black marker
Sand table or bucket filled with sand
Items of different colors to bury in the sand, such as a red block, a blue car, and so on
Book about buried treasure

What to do

1. Before class, make the graph for the project. Divide the paper into columns—one for each color. Write the name of the color above each column.
2. Gather the items you want to bury in the sand for the children to find. Make sure you have more than one item for each color.
3. Before the children arrive, bury the objects in the sand table or the bucket.
4. During circle time, read a book about buried treasure. (See the book list below for ideas or go to your local library for books.) After reading the story, tell the children they are going to have a chance to look for buried treasure.
5. Take them to the sand table or bring out the bucket. If you are using a bucket, you may want to place it on a piece of newspaper or old tablecloth to catch spills.
6. Explain that each child will have a chance to dig in the sand and see what he can find.
7. As the children uncover the items in the sand, ask them what color the item is. Make a check on the graph for that color.
8. When they are finished finding their treasure, hold up the graph and ask, "How many red items did we find?" Count the items and make note of the number on the graph. Do this for each color. When you are finished, ask,

"Which color had the most items found?" Look at the graph and see which color had the most items buried.

9. This is a good way for children to learn their colors and to count. In addition, digging through the sand helps to develop their small muscles.

More to do

Do this activity using items that are different shapes.

Related Books

Amy's Eyes by Richard Kennedy
Benjamin's Treasure by Garth Williams
P. B. Bear's Treasure Hunt by Lee Davis
Sunken Treasure by Gail Gibbons
The Treasure Chest by Dominique Falda

❖❖ Sherri Lawrence, Louisville, KY

Sports Sorter

Materials

Common sports cards from a variety of sports (baseball, football, hockey, basketball, and so on)
Laminate or clear contact paper, optional
Small box, such as a shoebox
Graph paper and pencil

What to do

1. Collect a variety of sports cards. If desired, laminate them or cover them with clear contact paper for durability. Store them in a small box.
2. Ask the children to sort the cards according to sport. Ask questions such as: "How do we know this is a basketball player? What equipment is used to play baseball? Is football played inside or outside?"
3. Help the children count the cards in each sports category.
4. See if the children can sort the cards according to team (same hat, helmet, jersey, and so on).
5. With the children, graph the cards according to sport. Ask questions such as: "How many baseball cards do we have? Football cards? According to our graph, which sport has the most cards?"

Related song

Take Me Out to the Ball Game

Take me out to the ball game,
Take me out to the crowd.
Buy me some peanuts and Cracker Jack,
I don't care if I never get back,
Let me root, root, root for the home team,
If they don't win it's a shame.
For it's one, two, three strikes you're out,
At the old ball game.

◆❖ Jeannie Gunderson, Casper, WY

Holiday Graphing Lesson

Materials

Candy or food related to holiday (see below)
Copies of a graph you make
Pencils

What to do

1. Do this activity for any holiday, using candy or food related to the holiday. Following are some ideas:
   - Halloween: Mix up candy corn, candy pumpkins, and wrapped taffy.
   - Thanksgiving: Use some type of candy that comes in different colors, such as Skittles or jelly beans.
   - Christmas: Use Christmas kisses or M&Ms.
   - Valentine's Day: Use boxed Valentine hearts.
   - Saint Patrick's Day: Use Lucky Charms from the Lucky Charms cereal.
2. Be sure the children wash their hands before handling the food.
3. Give each child a copy of a graph with the appropriate boxes on it.
4. Give each child the box or bag of whatever candy they are using to graph.
5. Ask them to count out how many different colors of each candy are in their box. For example, count the pink hearts, green hearts, white hearts, and so on.
6. The children then color in the amount on their own graph, as shown on the next page.
7. Save the food for snack.

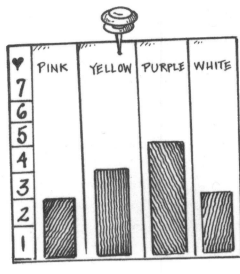

◆◆ Lisa Chichester, Parkersburg, WV

Sorting Buttons

Materials

Muffin tin
Buttons in a variety of colors

What to do

1. Place buttons in the top left cup of the muffin tin. The number of different colors and size of buttons will be determined by the child's attention span and manual dexterity. Larger buttons are easier to handle; small buttons are more challenging. Have a different number of buttons for each color (for example, three reds, two whites, one blue, and so on). To teach the concept of *equal*, two colors could be the same.

2. Encourage the child to work from left to right, placing a different color button into each cup, then finding others to match.

3. Keep the activity interesting by changing the items to be sorted. Try seashells, beads, swatches of cloth with different textures, and so on.

4. Help the child count the buttons in each cup. Which color has the most buttons? Which has the fewest? Are there more blue than red? How many buttons in all?

More to do

Art: Use buttons with other materials to create a collage.

Games: Play "Button, button, who has the button?" Ask the children to sit in a circle. Choose one child to be IT and ask him to leave the group. The other children hold out their hands in a "prayer" position. Hold your hands in the same position as the children, but put a button between your palms. Move from child to child, sliding your hands through the child's hand. Release the button to one child, who tries to avoid showing surprise. When all the children have been visited, the children say, "Button, button, who has the button?" IT returns and tries to guess who has the button. If he does not guess after three tries, the person who has the button reveals it and becomes the new IT.

Language: Emphasize the vocabulary words: *more, less, few, total,* and *equal.*

❖❖ Mary Jo Shannon, Roanoke, VA

Body Parts Match

Materials

Construction paper
Marker
Scissors
White poster board
Glue stick

What to do

1. Trace an outline of a body onto a piece of construction paper and cut it into individual body parts (e.g., head, arms, hands, torso, legs, feet).

2. Draw parts of a face (e.g., ears, eyes, nose, mouth) on a piece of construction paper and cut them out.

3. Divide a piece of white poster board in half by drawing a vertical line. Label one side with the heading: "I have 1 of these" and the other side with: "I have 2 of these." Place one dot above the numeral one and two dots above the numeral two to help the children recognize the amount represented by each numeral.

4. Place the poster board on the floor and arrange the cutout body part shapes next to it in the shape of a person. Place the cutout face parts on the head of the body shape.

5. Ask the children to sit in a semi-circle around the poster board and paper person.

6. Help the children identify and count the various body parts addressed in this lesson.

7. Read the poster headings to the children. Then, ask individual children to tell you the number of each body part that he or she has. For example, "John, these are eyes. (Point to your own eyes or the eyes on the paper face.) How many eyes do you have?"

8. Ask each body part is identified and counted, place glue on the corresponding paper part(s) and ask the child to attach it to the poster board under the appropriate heading.

9. Continue until the paper person has been disassembled and all the pieces are correctly glued onto the poster board.

More to do

Art: Show the children how to make handprints by dipping their hands into tempera paint and pressing them onto large pieces of construction paper. Make footprints too!

Science: Make an outline of a child's body by tracing around him or her on a large piece of butcher paper. Label each body part (e.g., hands, feet, arms, legs, head, eyes, ears, nose, mouth, and torso) on the outline. Then, cut the outline into pieces to make a floor puzzle.

Related songs

"Head, Shoulders, Knees, and Toes"
"Hokey Pokey"

Related books

Here Are My Hands by Bill Martin, Jr. and John Archambault
I'm Growing by Aliki

◆❖ Rebecca McMahen Giles

Planting a Paper Garden

Materials

Large sheet of brown roll paper, approximately 3' x 6'
Construction paper in vegetable colors, such as orange and green
Scissors
Crayons or markers
Glue

What to do

1. Cut out vegetable shapes from construction paper (or use reproducible vegetable pictures). Cut out a lot of them (or make a lot of copies).
2. Draw lines down the roll paper lengthwise to form a row for each kind of vegetable.
3. Encourage the children to color the vegetable and cut them out.
4. Help the children glue their vegetables onto the paper garden, making sure to keep one kind of vegetable in each row.
5. Ask the children count the number of vegetables in each row. Encourage the children to compare which row has the most and which has the least number of plants growing.
6. Ask the children to compare the colors of the vegetables and count how many are red, green, yellow, and so on.

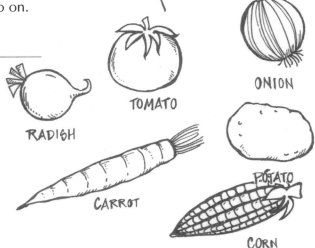

More to do

Dramatic Play: Put out toy gardening tools (hoes, rakes, shovels, and so on) so the children can pretend to take care of the garden.

❖ Sandra Suffeletto Ryan, Buffalo, NY

Baby Birds Nesting

Materials

Self-sticking tags
Marker
Bird stickers
5 berry baskets
Miniature plastic eggs
Craft birds
Basket

What to do

1. Beforehand, place one to five bird stickers onto five self-sticking nametags. For example, put one bird sticker on the first tag, then two birds on the second tag, and so on.
2. Stick each tag on a berry basket.
3. Place a plastic egg into each berry basket, corresponding with the number on the front of the basket. For example, put one egg into the first basket, two into the second, and so on.
4. Put small craft birds into a basket. Demonstrate how to open the egg and put one bird inside each egg.
5. Encourage the children to count birds all the way up to the number five and put them into the eggs.

More to do

Field trip: Go on a bird watching experience.

Related books

Baby Bird by Joyse Dunbar
Baby Bird by Judy Tuer
The Beak Book by Pamela Chanko
Birds by Susan Canizares and Pamela Chanko
Have You Seen Birds? by Joanne Oppenheim
The Things Birds Eat by Betsey Chessen
Where Do Birds Live? by Betsey Chessen

❖ Quazonia J. Quarles, Newark, DE

Which Egg Doesn't Belong?

Materials

5 egg cartons
Plastic eggs in assorted colors and sizes

What to do

1. Fill egg carton with about 10 eggs of similar colors. Add a couple of eggs that are a different color or size.
2. Ask the children the following questions: Which eggs do not belong? Why don't they belong? What makes them different?

❖❖ Quazonia J. Quarles, Newark, DE

Teddy Bear Counters

Materials

Cardboard or tagboard
Markers in the same color as the teddy bears
Teddy bear counters

What to do

1. Write a number on each piece of cardboard, from 1 – 10.
2. On each card, draw the number of circles as the number on the card. For example, draw one circle for the "1" card, two circles for "2," and so on.
3. Make cards for each color counter.
4. Encourage the children to use the cards to count each color of teddy bear.

More to do

More Math: Do simple addition problems with the counters and the cards.
Circle Time: Ask the children to bring in their teddy bears from home to share.
Outdoors: Combine this activity with a teddy bear picnic day!
Snack and Cooking: Eat teddy bear graham crackers for snack.

Related books

Corduroy by Don Freeman

Little Mouse, the Red Ripe Strawberry and the Big Hungry Bear by Don and Audrey Wood

A Pocket for Corduroy by Don Freeman

❖❖ Sandy L. Scott, Vancouver, WA

Sorting Stickers

Materials

Stickers in two or three different sizes, colors, or styles ("sticky dots" are good o use)

Construction paper or grid paper with 1" squares

Scissors

Dice, one die for each child, optional

Pencil

What to do

1. Cut the paper into a size manageable for the children in your class. (I usually start with one quarter of an 8 ½" x 11" piece of paper, but by the end of the year, the children are using the entire sheet.)

2. Encourage the children to put one sticker into each square to learn one-to-one correspondence.

3. Using a black marker, divide the paper into sections. Encourage the children to sort the stickers, such as all the blue ones on one section, all the yellow ones on another section, and so on.

4. Practice counting. Write the numbers 0-3 or 0-5 (whatever is appropriate for your children) down the left side of the paper. Ask the children to place the corresponding number of stickers next to the numbers.

5. For older children, cut the grid paper into strips six to seven blocks long. Then, ask the children to roll a die and place that many stickers onto their paper strip. Some children may be able to copy the numerals onto their papers.

More to do

Make a chart and ask the children to vote for their favorite color by placing a "sticky dot" of that color on the chart in the appropriate place.

Art: Make dot collages using leftover sticky dots, dot markers, circle cutouts, and so on. Talk about the circles.

Related books

Ten Black Dots by Donald Crews
What Comes in 2's, 3's and 4's? by Suzanne Aker

❖❖ Linda N. Ford, Sacramento, CA

Count the Cubes

Materials

Plastic ice cubes
5 plastic drinking cups
Marker
Ice cube tray
Tongs
Masking tape

What to do

1. In advance, freeze reusable plastic ice cubes and number the plastic drinking cups 1-5.
2. Place ice cubes into ice trays. Give each child tongs.
3. Encourage the children to remove the cubes from the tray and put the correct amount of cubes into each cup. Ask them to count out loud as they place the ice in each cup.

❖❖ Quazonia J. Quarles, Newark, DE

Counting Cups

Materials

Five (or ten) matching plastic tubs with lids (margarine tubs or whipped topping tubs work great)

Permanent marker

Scissors

Pegs, craft sticks, or straws

Items to count

What to do

1. Write the numbers 1-5 (or 1-10) on each lid and on the inside bottom of the tub. For example, write 1 on one tub and lid, 2 on the second, and so on.
2. Cut out a small hole in the lid corresponding to the number on the lid. For example, one hole on 1, two holes on 2, and so on. Make the holes big enough to hold a peg or craft stick.
3. Encourage the children to count items and put them into the appropriate tub. You can change whatever items the children count as often as desired.
4. As the children get to be better counters, remove the lids and just use the tubs.

❖❖ Catherine Shogren, Eagan, MN

Number Necklaces

Materials

Yarn

Scissors

Transparent tape

Drinking straws (preferably the kind with colorful stripes)

Construction paper tabs, about ½" x ½"

Hole punch

Blank paper tabs

Tray

Small baskets

What to do

1. Beforehand, cut yarn into 24" pieces, wrap transparent tape on one end of each piece, and knot the other end. Cut drinking straws into 1" pieces. Punch holes into one end of each construction paper tab and write the number you want to use on each one. (These can be all different colors or color-coded by number, such as pink for 3's, yellow for 4's, and so on.) Write the children's names on blank paper tabs slightly larger than the construction paper tabs. Punch a hole at the end of each one. Sort the items into small baskets.

2. Put the small baskets on a tray and bring out the activity.

3. Explain to the children that they will be making number necklaces. Choose a number, such as 3, and have the number 3 written on all the construction paper tabs.

4. Invite the children to select a piece of yarn. Show them how to start by putting their name tab on first, threading it all the way to the knotted end of the yarn.

5. Follow this with one of the number tabs, threading it all the way to the end, and then three straw pieces (or whatever number you are using), again threading them as far as they will go.

6. Add another number tab, then three more straw pieces.

7. Encourage the children to complete the necklace by adding more number tabs and sets of three straw pieces until the yarn is nearly full. Some children may prefer to remove the first sets of number tabs and straw pieces after they have been shown what to do so they can begin at the beginning and do it all themselves.

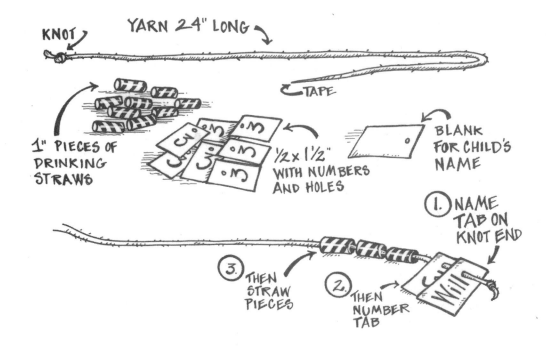

KNOT

YARN 24" LONG

TAPE

1" PIECES OF DRINKING STRAWS

½ x 1½" WITH NUMBERS AND HOLES

BLANK FOR CHILD'S NAME

1. NAME TAB ON KNOT END

2. THEN NUMBER TAB

3. THEN STRAW PIECES

8. Tie the two ends of yarn together to make a necklace and invite the children to wear their creation.

9. Make this activity available so the children can make necklaces whenever they want. Also, use different materials for stringing, such as pieces of straight pasta, to encourage the children to return to the activity.

10. Repeat the activity as desired using different numbers. For example, after having 3's available for a week or two, change to 4's.

More to do

As the children master the numbers one to five or higher, make a necklace of the numbers in sequence. For example, use the number 1 and one straw piece, then the number 2 and two pieces, and so on to the desired number, then begin again at 1 until the yarn is filled.

Holidays: Make number necklaces as gifts. These make great Mother's Day gifts!

Related books

Count and See by Tana Hoban
Over in the Meadow by John Langstaff
Ten Black Dots by Donald Crews
The Very Hungry Caterpillar by Eric Carle

◆◆ Susan Jones Jensen, Norman, OK

Clay Numbers

Materials

Package of oil clay, which is the kind of clay that won't harden
Scissors
Piece of paper
Marker

What to do

1. Form the numbers 0-9 using oil clay. Do this by rolling the clay between your palm and the table until it is a thin tube about ¼" (6 mm) thick. Cut the tube into 2" (5 cm) pieces and form the pieces into the numbers 0-9.

2. Write the numbers 0-9 on a sheet of paper and place the paper in front of a child.

3. Put three clay numbers on top of the paper, out of numerical order. Ask the child to place the clay numbers in the correct order from smallest to largest.

4. Start by using three numbers adjacent to each other, such as 4, 5, and 6. Place them in random order, such as 5, 4, and 6.

5. As they master their numbers, give them numbers such as 2, 7, and 9. You can also remove the number guide as they get more familiar with numbers.

❖❖ Richard Latta, Plainfield, IL

Circles and Dots Matching Game

Materials

Several large cardboard circles
Black, felt-tipped marker
Wooden, spring-type clothespin

What to do

1. Divide several cardboard circles into six equal sections. On each circle, draw black dots, from one dot to six dots.
2. Draw matching black dots on clothespins.
3. Give two, three, or more children cardboard circles. Demonstrate how to attach the proper clothespin with the matching section in the circle.

Note: Careful supervision is needed so children can learn to manipulate the clothespins without pinching their fingers.

More to do

More Math: To enforce number identification, use numerals instead of dots.

❖❖ Elaine Commins, Athens, GA

Paper Link Math

Materials

Construction paper in a variety of colors
Stapler or tape

What to do

1. Cut out strips of construction paper approximately 1 ½" in width and 8" long.

2. Choose the focus for a math lesson, such as counting patterns, more/less, or maybe even some simple addition or subtraction for very advanced three-year-olds.

3. Loop a paper strip and staple it to make a circle. Add more strips by looping them together and stapling them.

4. For a simple lesson in counting, ask the children to sit in a circle and count together as you add links. Ask the children, "How far do you think our chain can reach if we put 10 links on it?" Count as you add them, but then go back and re-count when you're done. Give each child a chance to come up and count them individually.

5. For a lesson in simple patterning, choose two colors and alternate the links three times each so that you have six links on the chain. Ask the children to tell you what color should come next. Say the colors out loud together as you point to them to help the children establish the pattern: "BLUE-RED-BLUE-RED-BLUE-?" If they are ready, try a three-color pattern.

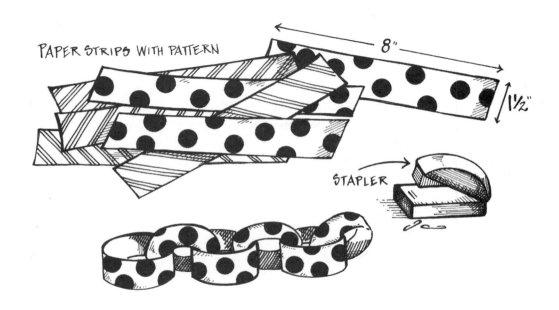

PAPER STRIPS WITH PATTERN   8"   1½"

STAPLER

6. For a lesson in more/less, divide the children into two or three groups, with an adult in each group. In a five-minute span, ask each group to make as long a chain as they can. Then hold them out next to each other. Whose chain has more? Whose has less? Count them to confirm your guess. (Three-year-olds will still be unsure which number is higher, so make it as visual as you can, showing the difference between the longer and shorter chains.)

7. For children who are ready to start seeing a little bit of basic addition and subtraction, ask two "teams" to each make a chain and count the links. Then link both chains together and see how many there are. For subtraction, start with a chain with five or ten links. Ask a child to come up and snip off a designated number of links. How many are left?

8. Don't be afraid to use words such as "add" and "subtract." Exposure to these terms will only help the children down the road.

More to do

Art: Encourage the children to decorate the paper before using them in a math lesson. They can decorate them according to the theme or just for fun.

Holidays: Make a link chain to designate how many days are left until a holiday or a special event in the classroom. Take a link off every day and recount. Or start a chain at the beginning of the year or particular month and add a link every day to see how many days they've been in school or to help calculate the date. For example, "There are eight days on our March chain—that means it is March 8th."

❖❖ Suzanne Pearson, Stephens City, VA

"Here I Am" Morning Activity

Materials

Camera and film
Copy machine
Scissors
Popsicle sticks
Glue
Attendance board with a place for the children's names

What to do

1. Take a picture of each child and get them developed.
2. Photocopy the pictures of the children and cut out their faces. Glue each face onto a Popsicle stick.
3. Attach a duplicate picture next to their name on the attendance board.

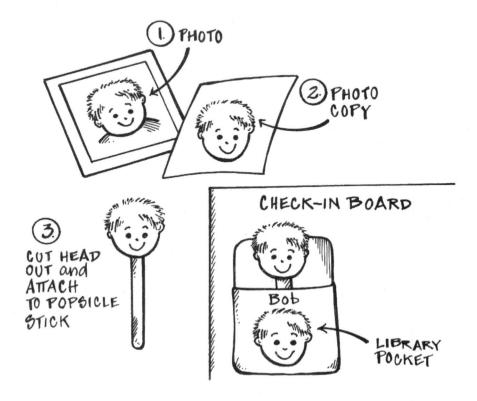

1. PHOTO
2. PHOTO COPY
3. CUT HEAD OUT and ATTACH TO POPSICLE STICK
CHECK-IN BOARD
Bob
LIBRARY POCKET

4. When children come in every morning, they grab their face stick and match it with their name/picture. This is a great way for the children to learn name recognition and a great way for the children to learn each other's names.

❖❖ Laurie Nied, Charlotte, NC

Calling All Soldiers

Materials

Camera and film
Small trumpet pattern
Pencil or marker
Paper
Scissors
Laminate or clear contact paper
Velcro
Pattern of a large solider and large trumpet

What to do

1. In advance, take a picture of each child in the class.
2. After the pictures are developed, trace a small trumpet onto paper, one for each child. Cut out each trumpet to fit the face of the child. (See illustration on following page.)
3. Glue each child's photo to a trumpet and write his name underneath.
4. Laminate the trumpets or cover them with clear contact paper. Place Velcro on the back of each trumpet.
5. Cut out a large soldier blowing on a large trumpet with a banner hanging down. Write the words, "Announcing the Arrival of…" at the top.
6. Attach Velcro to the banner.
7. Hang this on your classroom door. Ask the children to Velcro their trumpet to the banner when they arrive in the morning.
8. This is a great way to take attendance and acknowledge a child's presence.

❖❖ Quazonia J. Quarles, Newark, DE

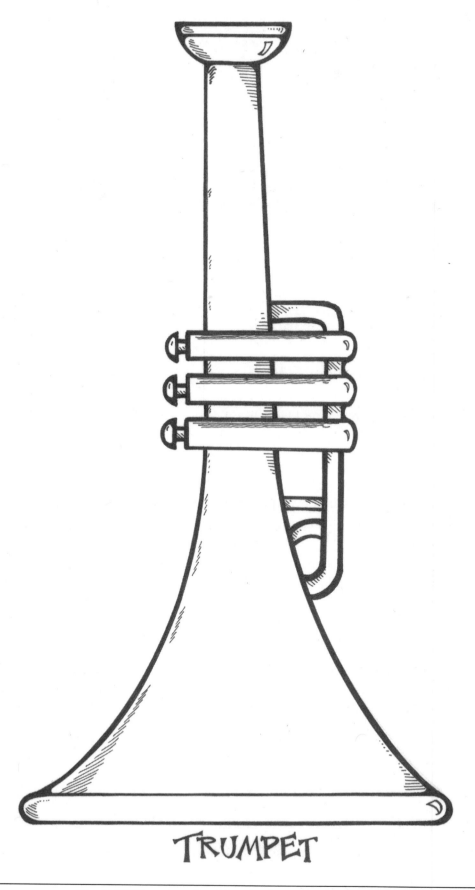

TRUMPET

Hello!

Materials

None

What to do

1. A fun way to welcome children to circle time in the morning is to sing the following song, using whatever tune suits you. Shake each child's hand as you sing:

   Hello, hello
   How are you?
   You're my friend and I like you!

2. Repeat for each child.

More to do

This song can be used at the snack or lunch table too.

❖❖ Sue M. Myhre, Bremerton, WA

Here We Are Together

Materials

Large paper
Markers and crayons

What to do

1. After all the children arrive in the morning, gather them together and join hands, forming a circle.

2. Swinging your hands back and forth, sing the following song to the tune of "Lassie."

   Oh here we are together, together, together.
   Oh here we are together at school today.

3. As each child's name is called, he pops to the floor like a piece of popcorn.

More to do

Art: Select a child to pick someone he wants to draw a picture with. Give the two children a large piece of paper, crayons, and markers to take to a designated area of the room to make a picture together. Repeat this until all of the children have a partner. If there are three children at the end, give them a larger piece of paper and all three will make a picture together.

❖ Carol Sargeant, Lynchburg, VA

This Is How I Feel Today

Materials

Paper plates
Markers
Nametags

What to do

1. On paper plates, draw faces showing different emotions, such as happy, sad, and so on. Write each child's name on a nametag.
2. Gather the children and discuss the different kinds of emotions. Show the children the paper plate faces and see if they can guess which emotion is being expressed. Ask, "Why would someone feel this way? What do you think happened to this person to make him feel this way?"
3. Explain to the children that when they come into the classroom every morning, they will put their nametag next to the face that resembles their feelings.
4. Be sure to put the faces at the children's level.
5. During circle time or group time, invite the children to share their feelings.

More to do

Math: Count how many children are next to each emotion. Compare the numbers and which face has the most names.

❖ Laurie Nied, Charlotte, NC

Sing, Sing, Sing!

Materials

None

What to do

Following are some reasons why singing with children is beneficial.

1. **Increases intellectual development.** Children learn many basic concepts through song lyrics and enhance their creativity by recognizing patterns, identifying rhyming words, adding motions, and creating original lyrics for favorite tunes.

2. **Provides opportunities to develop physical/motor skills.** Singing allows children to release excess energy through clapping, snapping, stomping, swaying, and other appropriate movements. In addition, they develop rhythm and coordination.

3. **Enhances perceptual awareness.** When singing and moving, young children refine their sense of spatial relationships and direction.

4. **Develops language and increases vocabulary.**

5. **Increases cultural awareness.** Music has long been a common link between mankind that can help us better understand the world and those who live in it. By introducing songs, instruments, and musical traditions of different cultures, teachers can expose children to the diversity that exists in our society.

6. **Gives opportunities to practice social skills.** Successful singing experiences build children's self-esteem while teaching them how to be a contributing member of a group.

7. When introducing a new song, sing the entire song through, rather than line-by-line. Children will attempt to join you in singing the songs they find appealing as early as the first time it is heard. If a song doesn't catch on, drop it. There are plenty of others to try.

8. Variations for singing include:
   - adding instruments,
   - omitting words,
   - adding motions,
   - singing at various levels (soft or laud) or at a different pace (fast or slow),
   - singing in different voices.

❖ Rebecca McMahen Giles, Mobile, AL

Ring Around the Rosie

Materials

None

What to do

1. Ask the children to stand in a circle and hold hands.
2. As the group sings "Ring Around the Rosie," the children go around in a circle. They fall to the ground at the cue.

   Ring around the rosie,
   Pocket full of posies,
   Ashes, ashes,
   We all fall down.

3. Repeat the song several times.

❖ Sandra Nagel, White Lake, MI

Row Your Boat

Materials

None

What to do

1. Ask the children to choose a partner.
2. Then ask each pair to sit across from each other with their legs crossed. The partners hold hands.
3. As the group sings "Row, Row, Row Your Boat," the children rock back and forth. They are working on pulling and pushing.

   Row, row, row your boat
   Gently down the stream,
   Merrily, merrily, merrily, merrily
   Life is but a dream.

4. Repeat the song several times.
5. This is a good activity to work on cooperation. It is also a good filler when there is extra time between planned tasks.

More to do

When children must sit and wait, this can break up the need for movement and curb the wiggling.

❖❖ Sandra Nagel, White Lake, MI

Teddy Bear Fun

Materials

Teddy bear

What to do

1. Introduce this activity by showing the children a teddy bear.
2. Discuss or review how bears move or might dance.
3. Teach or review the following traditional jump rope verse:
   Teddy bear, teddy bear, turn around, 'round, 'round,
   Teddy bear, teddy bear, touch the ground, ground, ground,
   Teddy bear, teddy bear, show your shoe, shoe, shoe,
   Teddy bear, teddy bear, skidoo, skidoo, kidoo.
4. Invite the children to do the motions. (Skidoo action can be running in place.)

More to do

Books: Read a bear story.
Social Development: Have a Teddy Bear Tea Party or picnic with the children's stuffed animals. Invite family members.
Transitions: Add new verses to transition to new activities. For example, "Teddy bear, teddy bear, go to snack, … your cubby," and so on.

❖❖ Margery A. Kranyik, Hyde Park, MA

Mother Goose Songs

Materials

Pictures of Mother Goose characters
Scissors
Felt
Rubber cement
Flannel board
Recording of Mother Goose songs
Tape player

What to do

1. Cut out pictures of Mother Goose characters.
2. Use rubber cement to glue the pictures to felt.
3. Put the pictures and flannel board in the Listening Center along with a recording of Mother Goose songs or verses to accompany the pictures.
4. Encourage the children to put up the appropriate Mother Goose character when they hear a song.

Related book

My Very First Mother Goose by Iona Opie

❖❖ Jackie Wright, Enid, OK

Grab Bag Music

Materials

Assorted small items
Drawstring cloth bag or paper lunch sack

What to do

1. Gather small items to represent favorite circle time songs, such as a dog for "Bingo," a smiley face for "If You are Happy and You Know It," and so on.
2. Put the items into a bag.

3. Encourage the children to take turns drawing an item from the bag.
4. Sing the song represented by the item.

❖❖ Charlene Woodham Peace, Semmes, AL

Color Walk

Materials

Construction paper in a variety of colors
Tape
Music

What to do

1. Tape construction paper to the floor in a circle where you will be playing the music.
2. Ask each child to stand on a color.
3. As you play music, the children will walk around the circle, stepping on the colors. When the music stops, each child will step on a color.
4. Select a color and ask," Who is standing on the color_____?"
5. The children standing on that color will say their names.

Related poem

Yellow is a star.
Yellow is the sun.
Yellow is the moon,
When the day is done.

Green means go
When driving, beep, beep!
And green lily pads
Are where the frogs sleep.

Blue is the ocean.
Blue is the sky.
Blue are the blueberries
I put into the pie.

Related books

Color! Color! Color! Color! by Ruth Heller
Colors by Pamela Schroeder
Is It Red? Is It Yellow? Is It Blue? by Tana Hoban
Of Colors and Things by Tana Hoban

❖❖ Liz Thomas, Hobart, IN

Musical "Washing"

Materials

Pieces of cloth, such as scarves
Music without words

What to do

1. Give each child a piece of cloth.
2. Play music and encourage the children to dance.
3. As the children dance, they can pretend to take a bath. Call out the names of the body part to "wash."
4. The children can use one hand to wash their elbows and arms, and hold each end of the scarf to wash their back or back of a leg.
5. Vary the speed of the music selections and encourage the children to speed up or slow down.

More to do

More Music: Sing songs that name body parts.
Science and Nature: Encourage the children to name the body parts on stuffed animals or puppets.

❖❖ Brenda Miller, Olean, NY

Bubble Break Dancing

Materials

Several jars of bubbles with wands
Music

What to do

1. Ask for some volunteers to blow bubbles at circle time.
2. Turn on the children's favorite music and encourage the children to break the bubbles as they dance to the music.
3. Change bubble blowers every so often.

More to do

Art: Make your own wands using thin string tied to a stick, plastic six-pack holders, and straws.
Outdoors: Put dishes of bubbles and a variety of wands outdoors during playground time.

❖❖ Ann Gudowski, Johnstown, PA

Mexican Hat Dance of Colors

Materials

Different colored scarves
Mexican sombrero
Mexican music

What to do

1. Ask the children to stand in a circle. Give each child a different colored scarf.
2. Place the sombrero in the center of the circle and explain what it is. Tell the children that they will be doing a Mexican hat dance.

3. As you play the music, they are to move in a circle waving the scarves. When you stop the music, yell out one color in Spanish. The children with that color scarf move to the center of the circle and sit around the hat.
4. Begin the music again and continue until all the colors are called.
5. Following are some Spanish words and their pronunciations for different colors:
   - rojo (roho)—red
   - verde (bearday)—green
   - negro (naygro)—black
   - morado (more-ah-doe)—purple
   - azul (azool)—blue
   - anaranjado (ah-nah-rahn-hadoe)—orange
   - amarillo (am-a-reeho)—yellow

❖ Lisa Chichester, Parkersburg, WV

Follow the Leader

Materials

Drum
Marching music, optional

What to do

1. Ask the children to stand in a line.
2. Explain or review the term *leader*.
3. Invite the children to follow you as you beat the drum and lead them around the room or outdoor area.
4. Vary your motions, having children tiptoe, march, baby step, giant step, and jump. Provide cues as needed.
5. Observe to see if the children can relate to the motion.
6. Let the children take turns being the leader.
7. If desired, play recorded march music and march around the area.

More to do

Language: Discuss the word *march*. Demonstrate, if necessary. Talk about parades.

Related songs

"March" from *The Nutcracker Suite* by Tschaikovsky

"March of the Children" by Prokofiev

"March of the Lions" from *Carnival of Animals* by Saint-Saens

"March of the Toys" by Victor Herbert

❖ Margery A. Kranyik, Hyde Park, MA

Get the Beat

Materials

Cylindrical coffee or oatmeal containers with covers, one for each child

Glue

Wrapping, construction, or contact paper

Markers

Drum beaters, if available

What to do

1. Give each child a cylindrical container. Help them cover their containers with paper.
2. Encourage the children to use markers to personalize their drums.
3. Ask the children to sit in a circle.
4. Encourage them to follow your lead and play their drum loud, soft, fast, slow, with one finger, two fingers, palms, and so on. Discuss vocabulary and demonstrate as needed.

Related book

Thump, Thump, Rat-a-tat-tat by Gene Baer

❖ Margery A. Kranyik, Hyde Park, MA

Drum Workshop Party

Materials

Many drum-shaped containers such as oatmeal canisters, cookie tins, and so on
Paper and pen or computer (for invitations)
Poster board
Cookies and tea
Construction paper in a variety of colors
Markers, crayons, and stickers
Scissors
Glue
Tape
Rice or pebbles, optional

What to do

1. Ask parents to save drum-shaped containers and bring them in. Collect enough so that each child has at least one (having two for each child is even better).
2. Two weeks before the date of your "Drum Workshop Party," design and send out invitations to all the parents. Make sure you include the fact that they will be helping their children make a drum.
3. Make several posters illustrating the steps of making a drum. Post these in the room the day before the party.
4. A day before the party, help the children make simple round cookies and tea to serve the parents.
5. On the day of the party, give each child a container and some construction paper. The children and their parents can work together to color and decorate the paper as they wish. Encourage the use of stickers or cut paper applied with glue.
6. Ask the parents to help the children fit the paper to the outside of their containers. Cut off the excess paper and tape in place.
7. If desired, put rice or pebbles in the containers before sealing. When the children shake or drum on the drum, it will make a neat sound.
8. Use tape to secure the lid to the container. You now have decorated drums for playing.
9. Play some music and drum along.

More to do

Make mallets to use with the drums. Ask the children to collect large sticks and bring them in. Cut scrap fabric into 6" squares. Place fiberfill on the fabric square and lay the stick on the fiberfill. Fold the fabric over the fiberfill and stick. Tie securely with yarn or string. Add tape as necessary to keep the pad from falling off the stick.

More Music: Make rainsticks to go along with the drums. Cover old potato chip or tennis ball containers in the same manner as described above. Crumple some aluminum foil and insert in the container. Add a few tablespoons of rice. Seal the top with tape. Shake the container or turn it over and over to listen to the musical sound of the "rain."

Outdoors: Take your drums outdoors and have a parade.

Related books

Dancing Drum by Gail Kredenser
Drummer Hoff by Barbara Emberley
Faraway Drums by Virginia Kroll
Mama Rocks, Papa Sings by Nancy van Laan

❖ Virginia Jean Herrod, Columbia, SC

Jingle Bells

Materials

Felt
Scissors
Large needle or sewing machine
Fishing line or metallic thread
Velcro
Fishing line or metallic thread
Small bells, five for each child

What to do

1. This is a good activity to involve the parents. Ask for parent volunteers to come in and help.
2. Cut felt into pieces ½" wide and long enough to go around a child's wrist.
3. Sew Velcro on the felt. Make sure that one side of the Velcro is on one end and the other side is on the opposite end.
4. Sew the bells to the felt, spacing them evenly, using fishing line or metallic thread.
5. When completed, the children can wear their bells on their wrists.

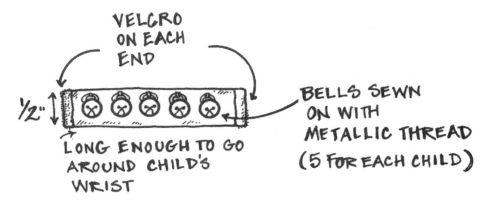

VELCRO ON EACH END

½"

LONG ENOUGH TO GO AROUND CHILD'S WRIST

BELLS SEWN ON WITH METALLIC THREAD (5 FOR EACH CHILD)

More to do

Play "Jingle Bells" and encourage the children to jingle to the music.

Related book

The Polar Express by Chris Van Allsburg

❖❖ Barbara Saul, Eureka, CA

Making Percussion Instruments

Materials

Empty containers (salad dressing or ketchup bottles work best because they are easier to grip)
Assortment of items, such as beans, rice, seeds, popcorn, rocks, sand, and so on

What to do

1. Discuss with the children that musicians are artists and that they play many kinds of instruments.
2. Explain that one type of instrument is a percussion instrument, which means that sound is made from something hitting against something else. Tell them that they can make percussion instruments with their hands by clapping.
3. Show the children how different substances in containers make different sounds. Ask them why they think this is so. For example, why does rice sound different from rocks?

4. Give each child an empty container. Encourage the children to pour a few spoonfuls or handfuls of various items into their containers. (You may want to encourage them to limit the variety of items they choose so that you have as many different sounding instruments as possible. You may also want to limit the amount they put into their containers because less "stuff" in the containers enhances the sound.)

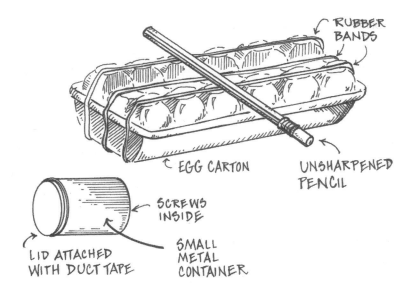

More to do

Put on marching music and encourage the children to dance or march with their instruments.

Dramatic Play: Set up an orchestra in the Dramatic Play area.

Games: Make pairs of identical containers to create many different sound-matching games.

Sorting: Make several pairs of containers ahead of time. Give one to a child and challenge him to find its mate.

Related books

Berlioz the Bear by Jan Brett
Orchestranimals by Vlasta Van Lampen
Zin! Zin! Zin! A Violin by Lloyd Moss and Marjorie Priceman

Related recording

"Old MacDonald Had a Band" by Raffi

◆◆ Shirley R. Salach, Northwood, NH

Making String Instruments

Materials

String instrument or triangle
Styrofoam trays
Rubber bands

What to do

1. Explain to the children that not all artists create artwork to look at and that some artists are musicians.

2. First, demonstrate how vibration causes sound. Strum strings on any string instrument or tap a musical triangle, but HOLD each instrument to prevent it from vibrating. (There are many things you can use to demonstrate this, such as symbols, a xylophone, a glass, and so on.)

3. Now release the strings or triangle so they are able to vibrate and make a sound.

4. Show the children how they can make a string instrument of their own by wrapping rubber bands around a Styrofoam tray. The rubber bands vibrate to cause sound.

5. Ask them to predict whether or not the sound will be higher or lower if you make a rubber band tighter. This is similar to what a musician must do to tune his string instrument.

6. Give the children rubber bands and Styrofoam trays and encourage them to create their own string instrument.

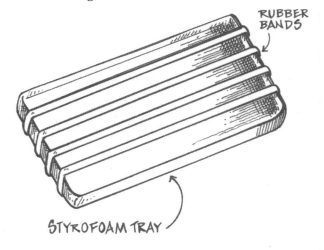

RUBBER BANDS

STYROFOAM TRAY

More to do

Put on marching music and encourage the children to dance or march with their instruments.

Make various string instruments by cutting out sections from cereal or pasta boxes, attaching a paper towel tube to one end, and adding rubber bands.
Dramatic Play: Set up an orchestra in the Dramatic Play Area.

Related books

Berlioz the Bear by Jan Brett
Orchestranimals by Vlasta Van Lampen
Zin! Zin! Zin! A Violin by Lloyd Moss and Marjorie Priceman

Related recording

"Old MacDonald Had a Band" by Raffi

◆◆ Shirley R. Salach, Northwood, NH

What Do I Hear?

Materials

Bell bracelet
Rhythm sticks
Triangle
Another adult, if possible

What to do

1. Get the children's attention by holding up a bell bracelet, shaking it, and saying, "What is this?"
2. Then pick up the rhythm sticks and do the same thing. Next pick up the triangle.
3. Be sure to make enough noise so that the children will hear you. Then ask if anyone would like to march around the room with you.
4. Give each child an instrument. Start singing a song, such as "The Ants Go Marching," and march around the room.
5. March around the centers, tables, or other areas in the room. Stop singing long enough to say, "Now let's march *around* this table." Hopefully, the children will follow in a parade line. (Another adult is very helpful if you have more than a few children to guide.)

6. After 5 to 10 minutes, it's time to transition to another activity. Use the song to sing, "When (Kyle) goes marching around the town, he puts his bells in the can and goes over to wash his hands. Boom! Boom! Boom! When Elisa goes marching…"

7. This activity helps children develop locomotor skills.

More to do

Outdoors: Do this outside and use kitchen utensils to make "music."

◆❖ Gail Whitney, Dameron, MD

The Recycle Band

Materials

Empty containers, such as oatmeal containers, cans with lids, empty water bottles, plastic containers, and film canisters

Small items to put into containers to make sounds, such as dried peas, rice, and beans

Empty paper towel rolls

Boxes

Tape and stapler

Rubber bands

Markers and crayons

Construction paper

Music with a fun beat

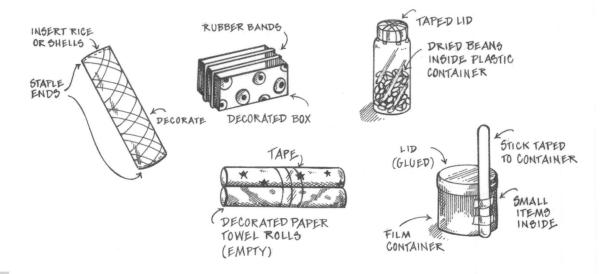

What to do

1. Encourage the children to create instruments using the materials that you wish to recycle.

2. Children can place small items, such as beans, inside plastic containers to make shakers. (NOTE: Know your group. You have to decide what small objects are safe and which might not be.) Tape the tops to avoid spilling.

3. Show the children how to tape the paper towel tubes together for sound. Tape or staple one end closed, put in some small objects, tape the other end closed, and you have a shaker or rain stick.

4. The children can use boxes as drums or put rubber bands around them and pluck the bands to make sounds.

5. Encourage the children to decorate the containers using markers, crayons, and construction paper. On the cans with lids, measure paper for the children to decorate and help them glue the paper to the can.

6. Play some fun music and encourage the children to use their "instruments" to practice beat and rhythm. March like a band to music.

7. Have fun and let your imagination go. Pretty soon, everything around the children could become an instrument.

More to do

Talk about what the instruments sound like. What sound does it make? Try to come up with labels for the sounds. Compare the sounds to traditional musical instruments.

Related book

The Happy Hedgehog Band by Martin Waddle

❖❖ Sandra Nagel, White Lake, MI

Parade

Materials

An assortment of household items and garage sale items, see below
Music

What to do

1. Gather a variety of items. (Garage sales are a great place to look.). Transform the items into rhythm band instruments.
2. Wrap the bowl end of a wooden spoon with a few rubber bands and show the children how to use it as a mallet to strike a pot lid.
3. Wrap a few rubber bands around a closed, empty Styrofoam egg carton. Show the children how to rub the side of an unsharpened pencil back and forth along the carton's "bumps" to make an unusual sound.
4. Put some metal nails or screws into a small metal tin and glue the top closed. For safety, secure the top with duct tape too. Show the children how to shake the tin to produce sounds.
5. Pour ¼ cup of unpopped corn or dried beans into a clean, empty half-gallon milk or juice carton. Glue on the top and secure it with duct tape. The children can hold the container by the handle and shake it to produce sounds.
6. Obtain two pot lids. Show the children how to strike them together, like cymbals, to produce sounds.
7. Make sure you have more instruments than children, then invite each child to choose an instrument to play.
8. Ask the children to form a circle. Then ask everyone to turn to the right. Play the music and encourage the children to march around in the circle for a parade. If possible, take the music outside and let children march around the play yard.
9. Let each child have a turn to lead the parade.

More to do

Dramatic Play: Encourage the children to present a parade of stuffed animals, dolls, or cars and trucks.

Related book

Parade by Donald Crews

❖❖ Barbara Backer, Charleston, SC

Treasure Bucket

Materials

Empty, well-washed gallon bleach bottles
One-hole paper punch
Plastic clothesline, 12" for each bucket
Permanent marker
Watercolor markers

What to do

1. Cut off the tops of each bleach bottle to make a bucket shape.
2. Use a hole punch to make a hole on each side of the bucket. (Be sure they are exactly opposite each other so the bucket will be balanced.)
3. Tie a plastic clothesline through the holes to make a handle.
4. Write the child's name on the bucket with the permanent marker.
5. Encourage the children to use watercolor markers to decorate their buckets.
6. The children can use their buckets to collect "treasures" outside.
7. Encourage the children to describe the objects they collect to enhance language skills.

More to do

Games: Line up several buckets and encourage the children to try to toss beanbags into them.

Math: In the sand box, use measuring cups to fill a bucket.

More Math: Count the objects collected. Arrange them in order of size from smallest to largest.

❖❖ Mary Jo Shannon, Roanoke, VA

Scavenger Hunt

Materials

Paper lunch bags
Marker
Glue or tape
Nature items, such as a leaf, grass, stick, feather, pinecone, acorn, and so on
Poster board
Easel

What to do

1. Label each bag with the child's name.
2. Glue or tape each nature item on a piece of poster board.
3. Put the poster board outside on an easel in your "hunting" area.
4. Give each child a bag. Encourage the children to collect nature items, such as the ones on the poster board.
5. Encourage the children to "show and tell" their collection.

More to do

Art: Make a collage on a paper plate using nature items.

Games: Have an indoor "hunt." Suggestions for items to find include colors, shapes, something with eyes, soft, hard, and so on. For example, say, "Look for something square."

❖❖ Anne Bonstead, New Hartford, NY

Blowing Bubbles

Materials

Plastic straws
Scissors
Mild dish detergent and water or commercial bubble mixture
Margarine tubs

What to do

1. This activity may be simple, but the children love it. It is a great outdoor activity, especially on a sunny, breezy day. It helps develop fine muscle coordination and breath control.
2. Cut plastic straws in half. Cut ½" slits in one end of each straw. This helps hold the liquid and identifies which end goes into the liquid.
3. Make a mixture of mild dish detergent and water (about 2 tablespoons of detergent to a cup of water). Pour the bubble mixture into margarine tubs (which makes sharing easier).
4. Go outside with the children and bring the straws and bubble mixture. First, check to see that children understand how to blow instead of suck through the straw. Explain that the uncut end goes between their lips. Ask them to blow and feel the air as it escapes.
5. Show the children how to dip the cut end into the liquid.
6. Encourage them to blow gently and watch the bubble form. Tell them to try not to burst the bubble, but if it bursts, try again.
7. What happens if they blow harder? Encourage them to try to make a very big bubble by blowing as gently as they can.

More to do

Science: Explain that air is inside the bubble, which comes from their breath. Explain that they take air into their lungs when they breathe in, and their bodies use the oxygen. Then they breathe out what their bodies don't need. Blowing forces the air out faster.

More Science: Encourage the children to observe the bubbles and notice the colors reflected. Explain that light has many colors but you can't see them unless something separates them. For example, moisture in the air after a rain causes a rainbow in the sky. A crystal or prism breaks the light into colors. The wet bubble breaks up the light and reflects the colors.

◆◆ Mary Jo Shannon, Roanoke, VA

Color Bubble Catch

Materials

Liquid soap
Water
Tempera paint
Plastic container
Bubble blowers
Construction paper

What to do

1. Pour liquid soap, water, and a small amount of tempera paint into a plastic container. Cover and shake well to mix.
2. This activity is best to do outdoors, so bring the children outside.
3. Demonstrate how to blow bubbles using a bubble blower and encourage the children to practice blowing bubbles.
4. Show the children how to catch the bubbles on a piece of paper. The bubbles will burst and leave an impression on the paper.

More to do

Make different-shaped bubble blowers by bending straws or coat hangers.

Related books

The Big Orange Splot by Daniel Manus Pinkwater
It Looked Like Spilt Milk by Charles G. Shaw

◆ Barbara Saul, Eureka, CA

Paint the Sidewalk

Materials

Several plastic buckets
Water
Old paintbrushes, about 2" (5 cm) wide

What to do

1. Take the children outside to a nearby sidewalk.
2. Pour water into each bucket.
3. Give the children paintbrushes and encourage them to "paint" the sidewalk!

Note: Although this seems very simple, children love to watch the color of the concrete change. They also are using large muscles and developing coordination and directionality, as they move from top to bottom and left to right.

More to do

Language: Discuss the meanings of *dry* and *wet*.
Science: Discuss the concept of evaporation as the children watch the water dry.

❖❖ Mary Jo Shannon, Roanoke, VA

Pitter Patter Painting

Materials

Outdoor area
Bulletin board paper or poster board
Tempera paint
Paper plates, two for each color of paint used
Washbasin with warm soapy water and towels

What to do

1. On a warm, sunny day, take the children outside and spread out a long piece of bulletin board paper or poster board.
2. Ask the children to take off their shoes.
3. Pour tempera paint onto paper plates. (Use liquid tempera paint because it is not as slippery as other paints, such as fingerpaint.)
4. One at a time, ask the children to come up and step into the paint.
5. Once the bottoms of their feet are covered sufficiently with paint, ask them to "pitter patter" across the paper.
6. For best results, encourage all the children to run across the paper using the same color, then go back and do it again using a different color.
7. Help the children wash their feet in the washbasin.
8. In the end you will have a really cute and colorful "collage" of footprints. And the children love it, too!

More to do

For a less messy and easier version of this activity, encourage the children to make footprints using plain water on a sidewalk.

Math: After the paint dries, use a ruler to measure the footprints. Who has the biggest foot? Who has the smallest foot? Can you count all five toes on each footprint? Can you tell if a print is from the left foot or the right?

Related book

The Foot Book by Dr. Seuss

❖❖ Suzanne Pearson, Stephens City, VA

Snow Colors

Materials

Snowy day
Empty spray bottles, one for each child
Food colors
Water
Plastic sand buckets, sand molds, and shovels

What to do

1. This is a good activity to do when there is snow on the ground.
2. On a snowy day, give each child an empty spray bottle.
3. Show the children how to fill their bottles with water. Then, ask them to choose a food color and add a few drops to the water.
4. Take the children outside with sand buckets, shovels, molds, and the spray bottles.
5. Have a snowy beach day! Encourage the children to make snow castles and other sand mold creatures, and then spray them with the colored spritz bottles.

❖❖ Lisa Chichester, Parkersburg, WV

Run and Stop

Materials

Large grassy area (a slight hill is nice) or asphalt area
Tape or rope, optional
Whistle or hand bell

What to do

1. Identify a starting line. This can be a piece of tape, a rope, a painted line, or even the shadow of a building or tree.
2. Ask the children to line up on the starting line.
3. Explain that each time you say, "Run!" they will run They will stop when you blow the whistle or ring the bell.
4. Vary the length of time between "run" and "stop." Make some times very short—almost instantaneous.
5. If desired, encourage the children to jump or hop instead of run.

More to do

You can do this activity indoors using the same rules, but instead of running, children can clap their hands, pat their thighs, stamp their feet, and so on.

❖❖ Mary Jo Shannon, Roanoke, VA

Sun and Moon, Where Should You Be?

Materials

Large poster of the sun and the moon
Poster board
Scissors

What to do

1. Cut out a large sun and moon from poster board.
2. During circle time, have a discussion with the children about things we do during the day and things that happen at night.

3. Go outside with the children. Hang the sun on one side of the playground and the moon on the other.

4. Explain to children that when you give them a clue, they should carefully run to where they think they should be, either under the sun or moon.

5. Following are some examples of clues. Ask, "Where should you be when...?"
   - Your parents are asleep?
   - You are eating lunch?
   - You have on your pajamas?
   - You are at preschool?
   - You need to turn on lights to see?

Related book

Goodnight Moon by Margaret Wise Brown

❖❖ Angela Williamson La Fon, Lynchburg, VA

May Pole

Materials

Carpet tube (check rug stores for tubes that rugs are rolled on)
White paint and paintbrush
Christmas tree stand
8 satin ribbons about 2" wide
   or crepe paper the same size
Duct tape

What to do

1. Paint the cardboard tube white. Put the tube in a Christmas tree stand.

2. Attach eight ribbons or pieces of crepe paper to the top of the tube using duct tape. The streamers should be the length of the tube.

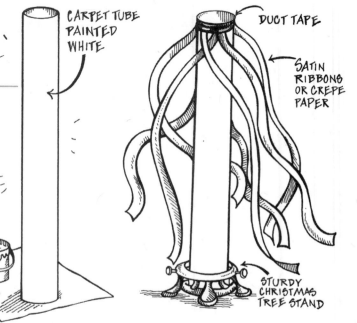

CARPET TUBE PAINTED WHITE

DUCT TAPE

SATIN RIBBONS OR CREPE PAPER

STURDY CHRISTMAS TREE STAND

3. Take the pole outdoors and encourage eight children at a time to grab a streamer and skip around the pole.

4. If desired, play Vivaldi's "Four Seasons" (Spring).

More to do

Paint the pole a different color and draw flowers on it. Decorate the ends of the streamers with crepe paper flowers.

❖❖ Jean Potter, Charleston, WV

Paper Bag Kite

Materials

Lunch bags, one for each child
Hole punch
Notebook reinforcers or tape
Yarn
Scissors
Crayons, markers, or paint
Ribbon and paper scraps
Glue

What to do

1. Open each lunch bag and punch a hole about 1" from the top on either side of the bag. (See illustration on following page.)

2. Put a notebook reinforcer on each hole. Or, place a piece of tape over the holes and punch a hole through the tape.

3. Give each child a bag. Encourage them to use crayons, markers, and paint to decorate their bags. They can glue ribbons to the bag.

4. After the bag is decorated, tie an 18" piece of yarn through the holes in the bag. Then tie a longer piece of yarn to the 18" piece.

5. Go outside with the children and encourage them to run with their "kites." As the children run, the bag will fly behind them.

6. These kites do not tear as easily as regular paper kites made by children.

Related book

Gilberto and the Wind by Marie Hall Ets

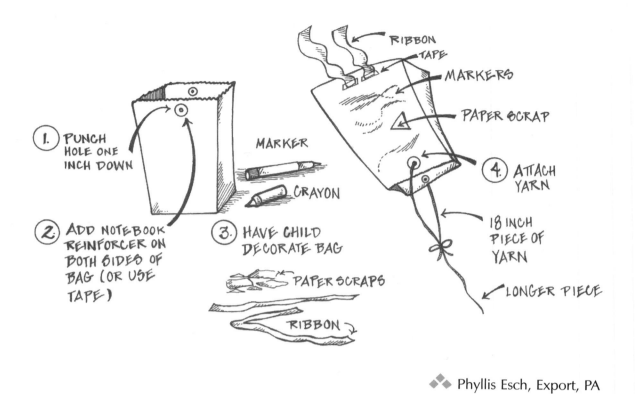

Diagram labels:
1. PUNCH HOLE ONE INCH DOWN
2. ADD NOTEBOOK REINFORCER ON BOTH SIDES OF BAG (OR USE TAPE)
3. HAVE CHILD DECORATE BAG
4. ATTACH YARN

MARKER
CRAYON
PAPER SCRAPS
RIBBON
RIBBON
TAPE
MARKERS
PAPER SCRAP
18 INCH PIECE OF YARN
LONGER PIECE

❖ Phyllis Esch, Export, PA

On the Go!

Materials

Outdoor space

What to do

1. When outside, encourage the children to notice different cars, trucks, trains, airplanes, or helicopters that pass by.
2. Encourage the children to pretend to be different vehicles. For example, as a vehicle passes by, ask the children what it is. Then encourage them to pretend to be that type of vehicle as you walk around the playground together.
3. Point out the vehicle again and say, "I wonder how many people are in there." Encourage the children to guess where the vehicle might be going. Encourage them to name places in the town or city in which they live, nearby cities, or other countries.
4. Say, "I wonder what they will do when they get there?" Let the children guess what the people might do when they reach their destination.

5. If the trucks you see have signs on them, ask the children what they think the signs mean. Encourage them to identify any letters, shapes, or numbers on the trucks.

6. When another interesting vehicle goes by, switch! Repeat steps 1 through 4.

7. Sing a song for each vehicle. Use any familiar tune you know or make one up. For example:

   (Tune: "My Bonnie Lies Over the Ocean")
   The airplanes are flying up in the sky,
   Flying from here to there.
   If I could fly up in the sky
   I'd be able to go anywhere.

More to do

Art: Create an "I can go anywhere" collage. Divide a large sheet of poster board into three sections: sky, water, and land. Ask the children to color the three sections and draw roads on the bottom section. Then ask them to cut out magazine pictures of airplanes, boats, cars, and trucks. Glue these in the appropriate places on the poster board. As the children do this, ask them to tell you where they would go if they could travel in an airplane, boat, or car. Record their answers and post them near the collage.

Blocks: In the block area, provide cars and trucks for the children to use. Create streets on the floor using masking tape or buy a rug with a street pattern on it. Encourage the children to drive their cars and trucks through the streets.

Language: Ask, "Where would you go if you could go anywhere in the world?" Record the children's answers. Make a poster with the headline: IF I COULD GO ANYWHERE. List the children's responses on it.

Related books

Elephants Aloft by Kathi Appelt
Freight Train by Donald Crews
Hey! Get Off Our Train by John Burningham
My Mom Travels a Lot by Caroline Feller Bauer
Night Driving by John Coy
The Travels of Babar (Le Voyage de Babar) by Jean de Brunhoff
Truck Song by Diane Siebert

❖ Virginia Jean Herrod, Columbia, SC

Bike Rodeo

Materials

Rope
Sidewalk chalk
Bikes or scooters
Streamers, colored masking tape, small pinwheels, bike noisemakers, balloons, and so on

What to do

1. The day before this activity, send a note home asking parents to let their children bring their bikes or scooters to school the next day.
2. Before the children arrive, rope off a portion of the parking lot.
3. Draw some obstacle courses with chalk for the children to follow. Make some "start" and "stop" areas.
4. When the children arrive, help them decorate their bikes and scooters using streamers, masking tape, pinwheels, and so on.
5. After all the bikes are decorated, take them outside for the "rodeo."
6. You may even have a bike inspection area to check tire inflation and brakes.

❖ Sandy L. Scott, Vancouver, WA

Traffic School

Materials

Sidewalk chalk
Poster board and markers
Outdoor riding toys such as tricycles, wagons, and scooters
Small, pocket-sized notebooks and pencils
Police officer hats, badges, or aprons, optional

What to do

1. Talk to the children about driving rules that adults use. Encourage them to brainstorm traffic safety rules they know.
2. Make traffic signs with the children.

3. Go outside with the children and set up the playground like a road. Encourage them to use sidewalk chalk to draw roads.

4. Encourage the children to take turns being the police officers and the drivers of the vehicles. The police officers can give out "tickets" to traffic offenders.

More to do

Field Trip: Take a field trip to a police station and ask a police officer to explain safety rules.

Related books

Curious George Rides a Bike by H.A. Rey
Follow that Bus by Reid
Franklin Rides a Bike by Bourgeois
Officer Buckle and Gloria by P. Ruth Mann

❖❖ Barbara Saul, Eureka, CA

It's a Good Day for a Car Wash

Materials

Poster board and markers, optional
Buckets
Soapy water
Sponges and rags
Hose
Old toothbrushes
Dirty bikes and trucks

What to do

1. Designate an area on the playground for a "car wash." Make posters for this area, if desired.

2. Fill buckets with soapy water and add rags or sponges.

3. Ask the children to bring their bikes and any toy trucks or cars you may have in your room to the car wash area.

4. Encourage the children to wash the dirt off the vehicles, even scrubbing the tires with toothbrushes.
5. Hose off the soap and let them be on their way!

More to do

Math: Encourage the children to count the "cars" in line.
More Math: Draw parking spaces for the waiting cars. Make sure to write numbers in the parking spots to help introduce/reinforce number recognition.

Original poem

Five little cars waiting in a line, one got washed and then there were four.
Four little cars waiting in a line, one got washed and then there were three.
Three little cars waiting in a line, one got washed and then there were two.
Two little cars waiting in a line, one got washed and then there were one.
One little car waiting in a line, it got washed and then there were none.

❖ Ann Gudowski, Johnstown, PA

Camping in the Schoolyard

Materials

Snack, such as animal crackers
Water bottles or juice packs
Picnic basket or bag
Mats
Books
Large blankets

What to do

1. On a nice day, plan a picnic on the playground.
2. Prepare a snack that travels easily, such as water in plastic bottles or individual juice packs and animal crackers or cheerios.
3. Ask the children to help gather mats, pack the snack in a basket or bag, and collect books to read.
4. Go to the playground and throw blankets over playground equipment, such as a slide or monkey bars. This will make a tent so the children can read in the shade.

5. Put the mats in a circle on the ground and eat the snack. Then tell stories and read books together.
6. Ask the children to help pick up.

More to do

Health and Safety: Talk about the preparation necessary to go camping or on a picnic and talk about the importance of cleaning up, dousing fires, and so on.
Literacy: Read stories about camping or taking care of the environment.

Related books

Amelia Bedelia Goes Camping by Peggy Parish
Bailey Goes Camping by Kevin Henkes
Just Camping Out by Mercer Mayer

❖❖ Melissa O. Markham, Huddleston, VA

Wash and Dry

Materials

Doll clothes
Washtubs
Clothespins
Clothesline
Soap and water

What to do

1. Set up a laundry area in the outdoor play area. Put out tubs of soapy water, hang clotheslines, and bring out doll clothes.
2. Encourage the children to wash the doll clothes in the soapy water, and then hang them on the clothesline with clothespins.

More to do

Dramatic Play: Fill the sink in the Dramatic Play area with a little soapy water and encourage the children to wash dishes. Add sponges and drying towels.

Original song

(Tune: "Row, Row, Row Your Boat")
Wash wash wash the clothes
Get them really clean.
Wash wash wash the clothes
And get them really clean.

Related song

This Is the Way We Wash Our Clothes
This is the way we wash our clothes,
Wash our clothes, wash our clothes.
This is the way we wash our clothes
So early in the morning!

❖❖ Sue M. Myhre, Bremerton, WA

Truck Day

Materials

Fliers
Trucks (see below)

What to do

1. Send a flier to parents asking if they know of anyone who could bring a large truck to the center on an appointed day. Make sure to clear this activity with the site supervisor and make sure there is a safe place where the trucks can park, such as a turn-around driveway. Try to get a vast assortment of trucks, such as dump truck, logging truck, hydraulic basket truck, utility trucks, humvees (call the local National Guard), fire truck, and so on.
2. Ask for parent volunteers for this day.
3. At the appointed place and time, take the children outside to see the trucks.
4. Ask the drivers to explain what each of the trucks do. If possible, ask the drivers to demonstrate what the trucks do.
5. Let the children take turns sitting in, on, and around the trucks.

More to do

Art: Put out precut geometric shapes and encourage the children to glue them on paper to make trucks.

More Art: Use a die-cut machine to cut outlines of various trucks. Encourage the children to glue them on paper to make a "Truck Day" collage. Also bring in magazines with pictures of trucks and help the children cut or tear them out to add to the collages.

Language: Brainstorm with the children words about the trucks. Write them down on a large white board or easel. Review them on the following day, adding more words.

❖ Barbara Saul, Eureka, CA

Outdoor Truck Counting

Materials

Large wood or plastic trucks
Small blocks

What to do

1. Bring toy trucks and small blocks outside. As the children are playing, encourage them to build something with the small blocks. Point out that they can use the large trucks to move the blocks to where they want to build.
2. Ask the children to put one block in the truck and deliver it to the construction site. Count out loud with them as they load the block.
3. When they return, ask them to put two blocks in the truck and deliver it. Count out loud with them as they load the blocks.
4. Continue in this manner, adding one block on each trip until you reach a total of five blocks in each truck. Remember to count out loud with them each time.
5. Accompany the children to the construction site and help them build a large house or any other structure they want.

More to do

Math: As you help the children build, count the number of blocks used.

More Math: Make a large block graph on the sidewalk with chalk. Draw a graph six squares high and five squares long. In the bottom row of squares, print the numbers 1 through 5 (both numerically and alphabetically). Ask the children to place one block in the first column, two in the second column, and so on until the graph is filled. Count each block as they are laid in each column, starting at one each time. When the graph is finished, count all the blocks in it.

Related books

1 Is One by Tasha Tudor
Aaron and Gayla's Counting Book by Eloise Greenfield
Anno's Counting House by Mitsumasa Anno
Count! by Denise Fleming
Let's Count It Out, Jesse Bear by Nancy White Carlstrom
One Gorilla: A Counting Book by Atsuko Morozumi
Ten, Nine, Eight by Molly Bang

❖❖ Virginia Jean Herrod, Columbia, SC

How to Build a House

Materials

Large hollow wooden blocks (set of 25 or more)
Camera and film
Large outdoor area with a flat surface
Paper and pencil
Large oaktag or tagboard (9" x 12" or larger)
Glue or tape
Hole punch
Yarn or heavy string

What to do

1. Put hollow wooden blocks in your outdoor space and encourage the children to build a house with them.
2. Photograph the children as they build the house. Be sure to get at least one photo of each stage as the house develops. Include the children who are working on the house in each photo.

3. Get the photos developed and view them with the children who helped build the house. Ask them to tell you what they were doing or thinking in each photo. Record their answers making sure to keep the comments with the photo they match.

4. Explain to the children that they will be making a book. Ask them to choose a photo for the cover and glue or tape it in the center of a piece of oaktag or tagboard.

5. Help the children choose several photos that accurately chronicle the building of the house. Arrange them in order.

6. Encourage the children to glue or tape each photo to a large sheet of oaktag or tagboard. Make sure they position the photos so they will be on the outside edge of each page after the book is put together. Also make sure they leave enough space below the photo to add the text.

7. Review the photos and the notes taken during the children's interviews. Paraphrase the children's comments and create text for each photo. For example, the first photo may show several children as they gather the wooden blocks into one place. The text might read, "Get everything you need together in one place." The second photo may show a few children stacking blocks to make a wall of the house. The text might read, "Stack some blocks to make the walls." Continue in this manner until all photos are in order and have a descriptive text.

8. Help the children think of a title for the book. Print this on the cover page.

9. Stack the pages together (remember to include the front and back cover) and punch three holes in the left edge of each page. Bind with yarn or heavy string.

10. Encourage the children to take turns reading the book to each other. They can also take them home to share with parents.

More to do

Ask the children to notice buildings under construction as they travel in the car. Encourage them to share what they have seen.

Related books

Babar the King by Jean de Brunhoff
The Block Book by Susan Arkin Couture
Changes, Changes by Pat Hutchins
Lazy Lion by Mwenye Hadithi
The Little House by Virginia Lee Burton
Machines at Work by Bryon Barton
Raising the Roof by Ronald Kidd
The Three Little Pigs by Paul Galdone

❖ Virginia Jean Herrod, Columbia, SC

Sand City

Materials

Outdoor sand area
Empty, sturdy plastic containers and wax milk cartons
Shovels or garden trowels
Pebbles, seashells, twigs, acorns, and other natural items
Toy cars, trucks, and so on
Whiskbrooms

What to do

1. Wet the sand in your outdoor sand area. Squeeze a clump of it in your hand, and then open your hand to see if the sand will hold a shape. Add more water until the sand holds a shape but is not soggy.
2. Show the children how to fill a container with wet sand, then turn it over to un-mold the container.
3. Encourage the children to build a "sand city" with the structures they make. Remind them that shells, pebbles, and so on make fine windows and doors.
4. Let them bring small cars, trucks, dolls and other washable classroom items into their city.
5. Provide whiskbrooms for brushing sand off of clothes before the children go inside.

More to do

Home-School Connection: Take digital pictures of the sand city to send home in your class's newsletter.
Math: Encourage the children to make and un-mold shapes in order from smallest to largest.
Science: On another day, don't wet the sand. Let the children attempt to make and un-mold shapes with dry sand. Discuss the results. Guide the children to discover why the sand won't hold its shape. Support their efforts to solve the problem by adding water.
Snack and Cooking: Serve gelatin that was prepared with juice in place of half of the water. Make this in small molds. Let each child un-mold her own snack.

Related books

At the Beach by Anne F. Rockwell
Beach Play by Marsha Hayles
Sand Cake by Frank Asch (This book is out of print but may be available at your
    public library.)

❖❖ Barbara Backer, Charleston, SC

Playground Map

Materials

Outdoor playground or designated play area
Poster board or large paper
Markers

What to do

1. Go outside and bring the children to a spot with a good vantage point to see the whole play area. Ask them to sit down.

2. Explain that they will try to make a map of the playground so visitors can see what the playground is like.

3. Begin by drawing a red circle to show where you and the children are sitting. Then draw an item or two to help them get an idea of the layout. (For example, "Here is where the swings are, and the slide is over here.")

4. Now ask the children to tell you where to draw the rest of the items on the playground. Be sure to include trees and other natural landmarks. Use lots of good "position" words as you describe where to draw things. (For example, "The see-saw is between the tree and the sidewalk.")

5. Once the map is complete, play a game where you point to a spot on the map, and one or two children run to that spot on the playground. Ask the rest of the children to decide if they have gone to the right spot. Start out with easy directions, such as pointing directly to the slide or swings. Then make it more challenging by pointing to an area near certain landmarks.

6. Hide an object somewhere on the playground and give clues using the map and encourage the children to go find it.

More to do

Make a map of the classroom using the same techniques.

Home-School Connection: Ask the children and their parents or older siblings to make a map of their home or bedroom.

◆◆ Suzanne Pearson, Stephens City, VA

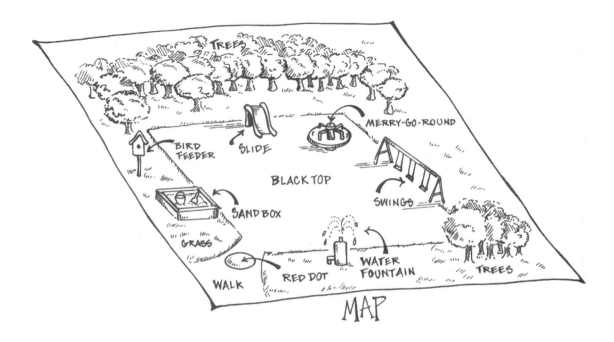

It's Time for Nap

Materials

Quiet music
Sheets

What to do

1. Put all the mats, blankets, and stuffed animals in place before the children enter the room. (Make sure the children rest in the same place every day so they won't have to scurry around looking for their mats.)
2. Before the children enter, cover all the toys and other distractions with sheets and turn off the lights (or dim them).
3. Have quiet music playing as the children enter and continue playing it during rest time. Children enjoy classical music and also find environmental sounds (such as ocean waves, bird calls, and rain showers) to be soothing. These set a calming mood for rest time.
4. Use a quiet, calming voice to give instructions to the children. If you need to speak to one child, walk over to that child and speak quietly. Calling across the room stimulates all of the children.

◆◆ Barbara Backer, Charleston, SC

Calming Lotion

Materials

Mild, unscented hand lotion

What to do

1. Ask the children to wash their hands just before rest time or naptime.
2. Put a small dab of hand lotion in each child's outstretched hands.
3. Encourage them to slowly and gently rub the lotion into their hands. If they desire, they can also gently massage some into their forearms too. Remind them to go slower and slower.
4. This activity calms children and helps them relax.

◆◆ Barbara Backer, Charleston, SC

A Restful Ride

Materials

Soft, instrumental music or environmental sounds tapes
Tape recorder

What to do

1. Ahead of time, decide on an object that the children can imagine their mats are during naptime. Choose something that they can imagine is gently carrying them while they sleep, such as a boat, cloud, hot air balloon, swinging hammock, and so on.
2. Choose music or a meditation tape that will match the chosen item (such as a babbling brook sound if they are going to imagine their mat is a boat).
3. As the children are settling down for nap, introduce the "Restful Ride" of the day or week. Give it a clever name such as "soaring sleepers," "float your boat," "cling to your cloud," "hanging in your hammock," and so on.
4. Begin the music or tape and encourage the children to let their imaginations go!

More to do

Art: For non-nappers or early risers, have paper and markers available. Encourage them to draw a picture of where they will go on their "Restful Ride." When they are finished, they can dictate a story as you write it down. Share the stories with the class and display them.

❖❖ Ann Gudowski, Johnstown, PA

The Silent Game

Materials

None

What to do

1. Play this game at rest time while the children are sitting on their mats. This activity helps develop listening skills as the children experience silence.

2. Turn off the lights and ask the children to lie very still and close their eyes. Ask them to listen carefully to any sounds they hear. Explain that when you say a child's name, he may tell you what sound he heard.

3. As the children become quite, make a sound, such as clapping your hands, whistling, walking, or writing on the chalkboard.

4. After each sound, whisper one child's name and let that child name the sound.

More to do

Transitions: Whisper children's names when it's time to get in line.

◆◆ Mary Jo Shannon, Roanoke, VA

Telling Naptime Stories

Materials

None

What to do

1. After the children get settled on their mats or cots, explain that you are going to tell them a story.

2. Tell them that in order to hear the story, they must lie quietly on their cots and make the pictures in their heads by closing their eyes.

3. Start the story with the "Student of the Week" as the main character. Add the other children in the group to the story as you continue. If desired, make the children animal characters (for example, "Sally Seagull") or plants (for example, "Tracy Tree"). Children are very interested in hearing their own names and will often stay quiet to do so.

4. Speak in a quiet, low voice with little animation. Continue quietly about the almost boring adventures of the characters in your story.

5. Continue telling the story until all the children are asleep. Stories can continue from day to day, or you can start them over each day or each week.

More to do

Play quiet music in the background, such as lullabies or classical music.

◆◆ Linda Ford, Sacramento, CA

Naptime Books

Materials

Children's books or old magazines
Large basket

What to do

1. While preparing for naptime, encourage the children to select a book or magazine from the basket. They can read their own naptime story until they fall asleep.
2. Collect the books when the children fall asleep.
3. Change the books at least monthly.

More to do

Art: As the children wake up, ask them to draw pictures about their story and share them during circle time.

◆◆ Nicole Sparks, Miami, FL

"Naptime, Naptime"

Materials

None

What to do

1. Familiarize the children with the words to the following song. Encourage them to sing it as you transition to naptime.

Naptime, Naptime
(Tune: "Are You Sleeping?")
It is naptime, it is naptime,
What are we to do? What are we to do?
Everyone is napping, everyone is napping.
And so should you, and so should you!

More to do

Transitions: Change the words to the song for anytime during the day. For example:

It is lunchtime, …everyone is eating…
It is work time, …everyone is working…
It is story time, …everyone is listening…

◆◆ Nicole Sparks, Miami, FL

Time to Take a Rest

Materials

None

What to do

1. As the children gather on their mats for rest time, quietly sing the following song to the tune of the "Farmer in the Dell." Sing each verse more slowly and more quietly.

    It's time to take a rest.
    It's time to take a rest.
    It's the time that we like best.
    It's time to take a rest.

    I lie down on my mat.
    I lie down on my mat.
    I close my eyes and take a rest.
    I lie down on my mat.

    I close my eyes and dream.
    I close my eyes and dream.
    I dream of happy, happy things.
    I close my eyes and dream.

◆◆ Barbara Backer, Charleston, SC

Quiet "Stuff" for Naptime

Materials

Shoebox
Markers, crayons, construction paper, and glue
Small toys or books from home

What to do

1. Give each child a shoebox and encourage him to decorate it.
2. Ask parents to send in a small toy, book, or quiet activity. Put the item into the child's decorated shoeboxes and store it in the child's cubby until rest time.
3. Since some children don't nap or begin to outgrow the nap as they approach the age of four, the little box of "stuff" gives them something to do during the quiet time.

More to do

More Rest or Nap: Instead of playing typical lullaby tapes, try playing environmental sounds such as summer rain, ocean sounds, or sounds of the forest. The Homedic machines that are available at bed and bath stores are great! You can set the machine to play for a certain length of time automatically. (The children in my class particularly enjoyed the cricket sound, and after we read *The Very Quiet Cricket* by Eric Carle, they felt like they KNEW the cricket! One little boy would ask for me to "play the crickets" when he got sleepy. He went to sleep every time!)

❖❖ Tracie O'Hara, Charlotte, NC

Rest Time Boxes

Materials

Small plastic school boxes or small shoeboxes
Quiet items and toys, such as flannel pieces, puzzles, etch-a-sketch, paper and markers, miniature books, and so on

What to do

1. Put small quiet items and toys into plastic school boxes or shoeboxes to make "rest time boxes."
2. During naptime, make sure all the children rest quietly for a period of time on their mats.
3. After this period of time is up, let the children that are not napping get a naptime box to work with quietly on their rest mats.
4. This activity allows the children who do not nap an activity to work on independently.

More to do

Science: Make shoebox activities for other areas of the room, such as the Science area. Put magnets, items to look at with magnifying glasses, and color paddles with paper and markers into shoeboxes.

❖❖ Melissa Browning, Milwaukee, WI

Pillow Pals

Materials

Inexpensive washcloths, two for each child
Large needle and thread
Large movable eyes
Glue
Yarn
Fabric scraps
Cotton stuffing

What to do

1. Give each child two washcloths. Demonstrate how to lay them flat.
2. Help the children sew the two washcloths together, leaving a space to add stuffing later.
3. Encourage the children to decorate their pillows by gluing on eyes, yarn (to make hair), and fabric scraps.
4. Stuff the pillow and sew it closed. Use these as "naptime pals."

❖❖ Lisa Chichester, Parkersburg, WV

Pompom Table

Materials

Sand and water table
Two large bags of pompoms in assorted sizes
Appropriate toys such as scoops, little bowls, plastic spoons, and plastic animals

What to do

1. As a way of introducing the sand and water table to the children, fill it with pompoms. This is a great introduction because it's quiet, not messy, and easy to establish the table's guidelines.
2. Encourage the children to play with the pompoms, scoop them up, and hide toys.

More to do

Use other items to fill the sand and water table, such as Styrofoam "peanuts," large buttons, teddy bear counters, and so on.

Health: Keep in mind that germs are shared more easily at the sand and water table, so avoid it during peak cold and flu season. Get the children in the habit of washing their hands before and after using the table.

◆ Nancy DeSteno, Andover, MN

Gooey Sticky-ooooo!

Materials

Sand and water table
Packing peanuts made of cornstarch
Spray bottles
Water
Food colors

What to do

1. Add packing peanuts to the sand and water table for the children to explore.
2. Fill spray bottles with colored water and give them to the children to squirt.
3. The water will make the packing peanuts sticky and allow them to stick together.

◆ Sandy L. Scott, Vancouver, WA

Rice and Marbles

Materials

Sand and water table or large tub
Large bag of uncooked rice (or sand or birdseed)
Scoops and cups
Marbles

What to do

1. Fill the sand table or a large tub with uncooked rice. (Big bags can usually be found at club stores.) You can substitute sand or birdseed, but children really like the texture of rice.
2. Playing in the rice with scoops and cups is great fun for three-year-olds, but to spice things up a bit, add a bunch of marbles to the mix.
3. Play "marble hunt" by burying all the marbles in the rice while the children close their eyes. Then when all the marbles are out of sight, ask the children to use their hands to dig through and pull out the marbles and put them in a cup. Let the children each take a turn hiding the marbles for the others to find.
4. Another game is to see how many marbles a child can scoop into her cup before it fills with rice. The rule is you can't dump out any rice if it "sneaks" in.
5. Encourage imaginative play using the marbles. For example, a child can pretend she is stirring "cookie dough" (the rice), and then stir in some "chocolate chips" (marbles). Or she can fill muffin tins with rice to make "cupcakes" and then decorate them with the marbles for cherries.

Note: Supervise closely, especially if children still put objects into their mouths.

More to do

Art: Make rice collages. Also, write the child's name with glue on a piece of paper and encourage her to sprinkle the rice over it.
Snack and Cooking: Cook rice in a microwave and eat for a snack with a touch of butter.

Related book

Chicken Soup with Rice by Maurice Sendak

❖❖ Suzanne Pearson, Stephens City, VA

Mix It Up for Fun!

Materials

Sand and water table or kitty litter-size tubs
Variety of items (see below)

What to do

1. Instead of adding water and sand to the water and sand table, try adding some of the following fun things:
   - Birdseed
   - Corks
   - Cornmeal
   - Dirt
   - Ice cubes
   - Popcorn (un-popped)
   - Shaving cream
   - Styrofoam packing pieces
   - Wet sand

2. Depending on your current theme, you can turn the sand and water table into an ocean, a pond, a baby doll bath tub, an arctic zone, a dinosaur landscape, and so on. Just use your imagination, or ask the children for their ideas.

3. Following are some other ways to extend sand and water play:

   Water:
   - Add bubbles to the water.
   - Add a drop of food coloring.
   - Bring out doll babies and sponges.
   - Wash dishes.
   - Add different sizes of plastic boats.
   - Add fish and other sea life, shells, and sand.
   - Add pond life, such as plastic frogs, lily pads, fishnets, and so on.

   Sand and other ingredients:
   - Add scooping cups and containers.
   - Add cars and trucks.
   - Add plastic wild and farm animals.

◆◆ Sue M. Myhre, Bremerton, WA

50 Ways to Change Your Table

Materials

See below

What to do

1. Adding any of the following items to your sand and water table will result in new opportunities for discovery and learning while linking this center to your current unit of study.

Acorns	Food coloring	Rocks or pebbles
Baby dolls (to wash)	Funnels	Salt
Basters	Glitter	Sand
Biodegradable peanuts	Gravel	Sawdust
Boats	Hay	Seashells and seaweed
Birdseed	Ice	Seeds
Blocks	Keys	Silverware
Bubbles and wands	Large buttons	Sponges
Buckets and bowls	Large wooden beads	Snow
Confetti	Leaves	Squirt bottles
Dinosaurs	Liquid starch	Styrofoam peanuts
Dishes (to wash)	Marbles	Teddy bear counters
Eggshells	Measuring cups and spoons	Wood shavings
Farm animals	Nuts (in the shell)	Yarn
Fish	Nets	Zoo animals
Foam letters or numbers	Ocean creatures	
	Pitchers and cups	
	Plastic foods	
	Pompoms	

❖❖ Rebecca McMahen Giles, Mobile, AL

Fingerpainting with Snow

Materials

Measuring cups
Water
Ivory soap flakes
Dish tubs

What to do

1. Mix ½ cup water with 1 cup Ivory flakes. Pour the mixture into dish tubs.
2. Encourage the children explore by scooping, piling, and drawing in the "snow."

More to do

Art: Mix ½ cup water with ½ cup Epsom salts. Encourage the children to use paintbrushes to create snow pictures on constriction paper.

Dramatic Play: Encourage the children to build "snow forts" with white shoeboxes.

Outdoors: Go outside on a snowy day and play "Follow the Leader" by stepping on footprints in the snow.

Science and Nature: Discuss how some animals hibernate or migrate in the winter.

❖ Barb Lindsay, Mason City, IA

Gathering Eggs

Materials

Sand and water table
Yellow, orange, and brown shredded paper strips
20 white plastic eggs
Laminate or clear contact paper
4 hen patterns
Tape
4 baskets

What to do

1. Do this activity with four children.
2. Fill the sand and water table with yellow, orange, and brown shredded paper strips to represent hay.
3. Hide the white plastic eggs in the "hay."
4. Laminate four hen patterns or cover them with clear contact paper. Tape them to the insides of the four inner walls of the sand and water table. This will indicate to the children where they should stand.
5. Give one basket to each child. Encourage the four children to look for five eggs each.
6. After they have found them, hide the eggs in the "hay" again and ask four different children to play.

Related books

Barnyard Banter by Denise Fleming
Little Red Hen illustrated by Lucinda McQueen

❖❖ Quazonia J. Quarles, Newark, DE

The Very Hungry Caterpillar Meets the Sensory Table

Materials

Sand and water table or large sweater box
Plastic Easter grass
Plastic foods
Very Hungry Caterpillar puppet (homemade or purchased)

What to do

1. Fill the sand and water table or a large sweater box with plastic Easter grass.
2. Add some plastic foods and representations of the foods the caterpillar eats in the book by Eric Carle.

3. Reenact the story using the puppet. Have the puppet search through the plastic grass to find the foods.
4. *The Very Hungry Caterpillar* is a favorite for three-year-olds. The children love to act it out over and over.

More to do

Go to Eric Carle's website for ideas, pictures, and information. (The children in my class especially enjoy looking at photos of Eric Carle working in his studio.)

❖❖ Tracie O'Hara, Charlotte, NC

Bug Dig

Materials

Sand and water table
Dirt or sand
Variety of plastic bugs
Shovels and brushes

What to do

1. Fill the sand and water table with either sand or dirt.
2. Hide small plastic bugs in the dirt.
3. Give the children small shovels and brushes to uncover the bugs.

❖❖ Sandy Scott, Vancouver, WA

The Great Cover Up

Materials

Assorted colors of contact paper
Seashell patterns
Pencil
Scissors
Sand
Sand and water table
Shovels and buckets

What to do

1. In advance, trace seashell patterns onto contact paper.
2. Cut out the seashell shapes from the contact paper. Remove the shapes from the protective adhesive.
3. Stick the shapes on the bottom of the sand and water table.
4. Fill the sand table half full with sand, covering all the shapes.
5. Add shovels and buckets and encourage the children to dig until they uncover all the seashells.
6. As each group finishes digging, dump the sand back into the table.

More to do

Field Trip: Visit a small beach area and collect many interesting shells.
Science: Provide seashells for children to look at and touch. Show them how to hold shells to their ear to listen for sounds.

Related books

At the Beach by Anne Rockwell
At the Beach by Huy Voun Lee

❖❖ Quazonia J. Quarles, Newark, DE

Tide Pool

Materials

Books and pictures about tide pools
Dishpans
Sand
Variety of shells
Plastic sea animals
Water
Sequins, optional

What to do

1. Read the children books about tide pools. Have a discussion about tide pools and show them pictures.
2. Fill dishpans with a shallow layer of sand.
3. Place shells and plastic sea animals on top of the sand. Add enough water to cover the items.
4. If desired, add sequins to the water for extra sparkle.
5. Place the dishpans on tables accessible to children and encourage them to explore.

More to do

Display collections of shells in the room.

Literacy: Encourage the children to dictate stories about what they would do if they could go to the beach to see a real tide pool. Encourage them to illustrate their dictated stories.

◆❖ Linda S. Andrews, Sonora, CA

Treasure Hunt

Materials

Sand and water table
Shells and colored rocks
Large marbles
Plastic dinosaurs
Any kind of plastic toy or jewelry
Paper and markers
Small plastic utensils

What to do

1. Plan a Treasure Hunt for the children. Before the children arrive, hide plastic toys, jewelry, dinosaurs, shells, and marbles underneath the sand in the sand and water table.
2. Draw a map of the room and write about five clues on pieces of paper. Each clue should lead the children to the next clue. Put the clues where they belong before the children arrive.
3. When the children arrive, explain that they are going to use a map and clues to find "buried treasure."
4. Encourage the children to follow the clues. For example, the first clue might tell them to go to the hallway, where the second clue is hidden. The second clue might tell them to go to the piano, where the third clue is hidden.
5. The last clue should lead them to the sand and water table, where the "buried treasure" is.
6. Ask the children to guess what might be hidden in the sand before they begin digging. Give them small plastic utensils to dig with.
7. Make sure that each child discovers at least one item.

More to do

Dramatic Play: Put pirate and explorer clothes in the Dramatic Play center for the children to play with.
Literacy: Ask the children to dictate a story about the object they discovered. They can make up a story about the object and what it does, where it lives, and so on.
Math: Sort objects and graph them using tally marks or stickers.

◆◆ Sheryl Smith, Jonesborough, TN

Water Play with a Baster

Materials

Water
Plastic baster
At least two containers

What to do

1. Pour water into one of the containers.
2. Demonstrate how to squeeze the bulb on the baster to take up water. Then, show the children that when you release the bulb, water remains in the tube.
3. Demonstrate how to transfer the water to the other container by squeezing the bulb.
4. Encourage the children to practice the same procedure. They may transfer the water from one container to the other indefinitely.

More to do

Add food color to the water. Use several containers of colored water and encourage the children to observe what happens when two colors are blended. Use eyedroppers and small containers.

Art: Make drip paintings using eyedroppers and colored water on coffee filters.

Language: Build vocabulary using words such as *squeeze, bubble, drip*, and *pour*.

Science: Explain how squeezing the air out of the baster creates a vacuum and picks up the water.

❖ Mary Jo Shannon, Roanoke, VA

Water Fun

Materials

Sand and water table or dish tub
Plastic tubing or small sections of garden hose and funnels
Variety of plastic bottles
Toy boats
Small plastic pitchers and spoons
Raincoats or plastic aprons for the children, optional

What to do

1. If possible, do this activity outdoors in small groups.
2. Fill the sand and water table or a large dish tub with water.
3. Put out plastic tubing, funnels, plastic bottles, boats, pitchers, spoons, and so on and encourage the children to experiment with the materials. Invite the children to find things in the room or outdoors to experiment with.
4. If desired, ask the children to wear raincoats or plastic aprons.
5. Encourage the children to discuss what they are doing (to help develop their language skills).

❖ Barbara Saul, Eureka, CA

Will It Float?

Materials

Sand and water table or dish tub
Water
Objects to dip in water, such as a rock, piece of wood, pencil, jar lid, sponge, leaf, crayon, paper, piece of plastic, aluminum foil, toy dishes, and so on
Two cookie sheets labeled "yes" and "no"

What to do

1. Fill the sand and water table or a dish tub with water.
2. Show the children the objects, one at a time. Ask the group to decide whether the object will float or sink.
3. Encourage them to experiment with the objects to see if they sink or float.
4. Help them put the objects that float on the "yes" cookie sheet and those that don't on the "no" sheet.

More to do

Encourage the children to find things in the room or outdoors to experiment with.

❖ Barbara Saul, Eureka, CA

Floating Targets

Materials

Sand and water table
Water
Plastic rings
Food coloring
Squirt bottles

What to do

1. If possible, bring the sand and water table outside. Fill it about ½ full.
2. Put the floating rings in the water.
3. Fill squirt bottles with water and add a drop of food color to each one.
4. Give each child a squirt bottle. Encourage them to aim for the rings and try to squirt color into them. This will signify that they hit the target.

Related books

Little Blue and Little Yellow by Leo Lionni
Mouse Paint by Ellen Stoll Walsh

❖❖ Quazonia J. Quarles, Newark, DE

Science Is "Tray" Cool!

Materials

Medium-sized trays
Various science items and experiments

What to do

1. Collect a variety of science items and place them on individual trays.
2. Place the trays on the table so that the children can use the items in a specific area. Putting the trays on one table allows the teacher better supervision and direction with the use of the materials.
3. Suggestions for the tray include:
   - Sink and float items with a small plastic container of water.
   - Magnets and items that are magnetic and nonmagnetic.
   - Color paddles and watercolor paints.
   - Small plastic cups with red, blue, and yellow water and eyedroppers for color mixing and exploration.
   - A bucket balance and items to be weighed with another item that serves as a weight measure (such as teddy bear counters).
   - Items for visual exploration, such as binoculars, kaleidoscope, and so on.

❖ Melissa Browning, Milwaukee, WI

Mirror Mirror

Materials

Old compact disks
Decorative adhesive paper

What to do

1. Collect old compact disks, such as the free ones that come in the mail from Internet service providers. Cover the label side of each disk with decorative adhesive paper, leaving the reflective side of the disk completely uncovered.
2. You now have little mirrors that the children can use in a variety of ways. They are safe because they have no sharp edges and are virtually unbreakable.

3. When the sun is shining through a window, show the children how to hold the mirror in the beam and reflect it throughout the room.

4. Use the mirrors when doing self-esteem activities. Give the children a mirror and ask them to describe who they see. Record their thoughts and post them in the room.

5. Encourage the children to use their imaginations to discover the many uses of mirrors.

More to do

Art: Use the mirrors to make a decorative and reflective wall hanging. String several disks together in a row. Hang in the room in a sunny spot.

More Art: Encourage the children to look at their reflections and draw self-portraits.

Social Development: Use the mirrors as tools to help the children learn about emotions. When a child is angry, happy, or discouraged, ask him to get a mirror so he can look at his face. Encourage him to notice the clues in his facial expression that show his emotions. For example, say, "See, Jamal, your mouth is all turned down at the corners. This shows me that you are sad or upset."

Original poem

"Mirror Mirror"

Mirror mirror! Look at me! (hold mirror up to reflect own image)
I look so fine as you can see! (smile broadly at self in mirror)
I have two eyes, two ears, two cheeks,
One nose, one mouth with many teeth (touch each part as it is mentioned)
I'm looking good! I'm looking grand! (make a "thumbs up" gesture with free hand)
Look at me in the mirror in my hand. (point to self in mirror)

Related books

The Rooster's Gift by Pam Conrad
Stranger in the Mirror by Allen Say
When the Sun Rose by Barbara Helen Berger

◆◆ Virginia Jean Herrod, Columbia, SC

Shadows

Materials

Flashlights

What to do

1. When the sun is shining brightly, take the children outside on a "shadow hunt." Encourage them to look for shadows of each other and large objects, such as trees and buildings.
2. On a cloudy day, go outside again and look for shadows. Discuss the sun as the missing factor in shadow formation and how the clouds prevent them from occurring.
3. Give each child a flashlight. In a darkened area, show the children how to make shadows of objects in the room using a flashlight. Then let them experiment using flashlights to make shadows.

More to do

Art: Use a lamp or overhead projector in a darkened room to make head silhouettes of each child. Cut them out and mount on paper. Display them in the room or give them to parents as gifts.

❖❖ Barbara Lindsay, Mason City, IA

Snowflake Catching

Materials

Snowy day
Black construction paper

What to do

1. Go outside with the children while it is snowing and catch snowflakes on black construction paper.
2. Encourage the children to look at the designs and shapes the snowflakes make as they fall on the paper.
3. Back inside, talk about snowflakes.

More to do

Take the paper outside on a rainy day and catch raindrops.

◆◆ Jean Potter, Charleston, WV

Box Deserts

Materials

Pictures and books about deserts
Shoeboxes, one for each child
Sand
Sticks and rocks
Paper
Markers and crayons
Glue

What to do

1. Talk about deserts with the children. Read a story about deserts and show them pictures.
2. Give each child a shoebox. Help the children fill the bottom of their box with sand.
3. Encourage the children to put sticks and rocks inside the box.
4. Give the children paper, markers, and crayons. Encourage them to draw things found in deserts, such as snakes and cacti.
5. Help them glue the drawing to the bottom and sides inside the box.

◆◆ Lisa Chichester, Parkersburg, WV

Underground Days

Materials

Earthworms and dirt
"Dirt cake" ingredients (see below)
Plastic or chocolate coins
Rocks
Gold spray paint
Books about gold
Artificial diamonds and gems
Jars and bugs
Ant farm

What to do

1. Explore things that are found under the ground. Explain to the children that many creatures live underground and that many valuable minerals can be found underground, too. Following are some ideas.
   - Study worms. Bring in earthworms and put them on a dirt-filled table for children to explore. Make "Dirt Cake" with chocolate pudding, Oreo cookies, and gummy worms.
   - Learn about gold. Have a treasure hunt to find a hidden bag of "gold" (plastic coins or wrapped chocolate candy coins). Find rocks outside and spray paint them gold. Read a book about gold.
   - Learn about diamonds and gems. Show the children artificial diamonds and gems (from a craft store). Read or watch "Snow White" (the seven dwarfs worked in a mine).
   - Study bugs that live underground. Go outside on a bug hunt and catch bugs to bring back and observe in the room. Have a class ant farm.

More to do

Books: Read a *Winnie the Pooh* book that has the character, Gopher, in it. Gopher's grandpa dreamed of making an aboveground underground city.
Outdoors: Go outdoors and dig tunnels.

◆◆ Lynn Reihl, Lynchburg, VA

Let's Investigate Bugs!

Materials

Insects
Paper
Crayons

What to do

1. Take the children outside to look for bugs ("potato" bugs are easy to find). A good place to look is under rocks in the shade. Watch out for spiders!
2. Encourage the children to draw a picture of their bug.
3. Ask the children, "How many legs and antennae does your bug have? What does your bug do when you touch it? Why do you think it does that?"
4. Encourage the children to draw pictures of their bugs in their natural environment, such as under rocks, and so on.

More to do

Invite an entomologist to come in and talk to the children.
More Science: Discuss different plants and how they attract certain bugs, such as butterflies. Explain why some bugs are good for the garden and some are not.
Books: Read books about bugs. (The library is a great resource.)
Field Trip: Go to a museum of natural history and visit the bug section.

❖❖ Christine I. Waugh, Littleton, CO

Brick Homes

Materials

Several bricks
Gardening gloves, one pair for each child

What to do

1. Go outside with the children. Choose two areas to place the bricks—one should be a sunny spot and the other in the shade. Place a few bricks in each spot.
2. After a few days, give each child a pair of gardening gloves to wear. Go outside and demonstrate how to pick up a brick gently to see what is underneath.

3. Encourage the children to explore underneath each brick without touching anything. Discuss what they see. For example, "Who lives under this brick house?"
4. Gently replace the bricks to cover the tiny animals living there.
5. Repeat with all of the bricks. Ask, "Are more animals under the bricks in the shade or the bricks in the sun?"
6. Let the children visit the critters each day. Remind them to wear the gloves and not to touch the bugs. Remind them also to move the bricks gently so they don't hurt the animals.

More to do

Dramatic Play: Provide a sheet that the children can hide under to pretend that they are living under a brick.

Gross Motor: Ask the children to watch how the small animals move. Encourage them to move in a similar manner.

◆◆ Barbara Backer, Charleston, SC

Worms!

Materials

Paper plates, one for each child
Rubber gloves, one pair for each child
Earthworms
Magnifying glasses

What to do

1. Give each child a paper plate and rubber gloves.
2. Place earthworms on each child's plate. Encourage the children to touch and explore the worms. Remind them to be gentle.
3. Encourage them to use magnifying glasses to observe the worms more closely.

More to do

Music and Movement: Give each child a piece of yarn about 6" long to use as their worm. Play "Walter the Waltzing Worm" by Hap Palmer and follow the directions in the song.

◆◆ Sue M. Myhre, Bremerton WA

Work, Worms, Work!

Materials

Large, clear plastic bucket with lid

Potting soil

Leaves and composted material

Live worms (look outdoors in a garden or compost area or purchase them at a
pet store or bait shop)

Black cloth or construction paper

Shredded paper, lettuce, carrot peelings, raw potato peelings, and so on

What to do

1. Discuss composting. Explain how worms turn organic matter into soil.
2. Create a compost pile in a large, clear plastic storage bucket. Fill the bucket
   half full with loose potting soil. Add leaves or composted material to improve
   the soil.
3. Add worms to the soil. If you place a log or stone in the bottom center of the
   bucket, the worms will move closer to the sides of the bucket, making them
   more visible from the outside.
4. Make a black removable cover for the bucket using cloth or construction
   paper (worms like to live in darkness).
5. Encourage the children to feed the worms vegetable scraps and other organic
   matter. The worms will turn the garbage into soil.
6. Keep the bucket moist (but not wet) and in a cool place. Young children love
   to feed the worms as well as dig for them and observe them.

More to do

More Science: Remove a worm from the bucket and observe it more closely.
Outdoors: Encourage the children to dig outside and discover worms in the
ground.

◆◆ Kathleen Wallace, Columbia, MO

The Life of a Butterfly

Materials

Books and videos about butterflies
Cotton swabs
Scissors
Glue
Construction paper leaves
Packing peanuts, pipe cleaners, and cotton balls
Craft sticks
Yarn
Glitter and tissue paper pieces
Zipper-closure plastic bags

What to do

1. Study butterflies. Read books about butterflies to the children and show them videos. If possible, show them real butterflies.
2. Talk about the life cycle of a butterfly. Explain that butterflies go through four stages: egg, caterpillar, cocoon, and butterfly.
3. Help the children make their own representations of a butterfly life cycle. Begin by cutting off the tips of cotton swabs (these will be eggs). Help the children glue the "eggs" onto paper leaves.
4. Make caterpillars using colored packing peanuts, pipe cleaners, and cotton balls.
5. Show the children how to glue or tape a craft stick to their caterpillar and then wrap yarn around it to make a cocoon.
6. Make butterflies. Put glitter and scraps of tissue paper into a zipper-closure bag and spray water into it to mix the colors. Pull it together in the middle with a pipe cleaner or clothespin to create the body and wings.
7. Give each child a large zipper-closure bag to store each part of the life cycle.

❖❖ Lynn Reihl, Lynchburg, VA

Apple Disk Bird Feeders

Materials

5 large red apples
Sharp knife
String
Scissors
Peanut butter
Plastic or wooden spoons
Birdseed

What to do

1. Talk about birds and what they like to eat. Explain that they are going to make bird feeders.
2. Slice the apples horizontally into 1" thick round disks (adult only). Do not peel the apples because the red peeling will attract birds. Then use the knife to poke a hole into each disk (adult only).
3. Give each child an apple disk. Help the children thread a 12" piece of string through the hole and tie the two ends together in a knot.
4. Encourage the children to spread peanut butter on one side of the disk using spoons.
5. Next, the children can sprinkle birdseed on the peanut butter.
6. Help the children hang the apple disks from a tree or a shrub so they can watch the birds enjoy their treat.

SLICE HORIZONTALLY

LEAVE THE RED

STRING THROUGH HOLE

HOLE

PEANUT BUTTER

BIRD SEED

7. Observe the birds that come to eat. Use *The Audubon Society Field Guide to North American Birds* to identify each bird.
8. Talk about the other foods birds might like to eat and try them out too. Possibilities include breadcrumbs, sunflower seeds, thistle seeds, fruit, sugar water for hummingbirds, and worms.

❖❖ Melissa O. Markham, Huddleston, VA

Pinecone Investigations

Materials

Pinecones, one for each child
Paper plates

What to do

1. Give each child a pinecone and a paper plate. Encourage the children to pull off the petals of the pinecone.
2. Encourage the children to investigate the seeds from the pinecones. Explain that squirrels eat the seeds.
3. Experiment by putting pinecones in water. When wet, the petals close. When dry, the petals open.

More to do

Art: Use pinecones to make nature prints. Show the children how to dip pinecones into shallow pans of poster paint. Encourage the children to dab cones on paper, tissue paper, or wrapping paper.
Math: Count the pinecones. Help the children organize them from smallest to largest.

Related book

In the Woods: Who's Been Here? by Lindsay Barrett George

❖❖ Jill Putnam, Wellfleet, MA

Analyzing Annuals

Materials

Assortment of dried flowers
Empty sand and water table or trays
Tweezers
Clean, empty margarine tubs

What to do

1. Fill the sand and water table with a variety of dried flowers. (Roses with the thorns removed, bachelor buttons, sunflowers, and black-eyed Susans are good for analyzing.) For individual exploration, use trays instead of the water table.
2. Add tweezers and margarine tubs.
3. Encourage the children to analyze the parts of the flowers by picking them apart with their hands or tweezers.
4. The children can use margarine tubs to collect the pieces they would like to keep.

More to do

Art: Encourage the children to bring their margarine tubs filled with flower parts to the art table and use the flowers to make a collage.

Related book

Counting Wildflowers by Bruce McMillan

❖❖ Ann Gudowski, Johnstown, PA

How Trees Change During the Seasons

Materials

Trees
Camera and film
Clear contact paper or laminate

What to do

1. Select an area outside that has several trees, including both deciduous and coniferous (evergreen) trees.
2. Visit the trees with the children in early September. Ask them to each pick a tree to "adopt" and observe. Ask them to explore everything they can about the trees, such as feeling the bark, examining the leaves or needles, looking for seeds, pinecones, nuts, and so on. Ask them to compare leaves with needles and note the differences.
3. Take a photo of each child next to his tree. (The children's clothing will provide additional clues about what season it is.) As the deciduous trees begin to show signs of change, take another photo and ask the children how their trees look different. Take photos as the trees with leaves change color and then lose leaves. Ask the children if the evergreen trees have changed. If so, how?
4. Continue checking on the trees with the children throughout the year. Take photos in the spring when the trees are budding and when they have all their leaves in June.
5. Laminate the photos or cover them with clear contact paper and spread them on a table. With the children, discuss the seasonal changes. This provides a sequencing lesson based upon the children's own experience during the year.

More to do

Art: Show the children how to sponge paint the way trees look at different times of the year.
Movement: Encourage the children to act out the changes a tree goes through from season to season. They can be the bud unfolding, the leaves and branches swaying in the wind, the leaves falling to the ground, and the tree "resting" in the wintertime.

Related book

The True Book of Seasons by Illa Podendorf

◆◆ Bea Chawla, Vincentown, NJ

Spring Planting

Materials

Plastic children's swimming pool
Potting soil
Seeds
Seed packets, optional
Rulers, optional

What to do

1. Place a plastic swimming pool in an outside area where sunlight will reach it. Fill it about half full with potting soil.
2. Encourage the children to plant seeds in the "garden." If desired, place seed packets over the ends of rulers and place them in the dirt to mark the rows of seeds.
3. Choose a "farmer" daily or weekly to water the garden. Watch it grow!

More to do

Extensions to this activity are endless and extend across all aspects of curriculum. You can connect farming, planting, the parts of flowers and vegetables, weather, measurement, sorting, patterning, and many other topics to this activity.

Related song

"The Farmer in the Dell"

Related books

The Carrot Seed by Ruth Krauss
Planting a Rainbow by Lois Ehlert

◆◆ Julie Hoffman, Olean, NY

Indoor Mini-Gardens

Materials

Newspapers

Smocks

Clear glass containers with wide opening, such as a goldfish bowl

Colorful aquarium rocks or other small gravel

Potting soil

Variety of small plants (Ivy and asparagus ferns are hearty and usually fare well; good floral plants to use are pansies, petunias, miniature roses, and African violets. Any dwarf or miniature flower should work well.)

What to do

1. This is a messy activity, so spread old newspaper over the work area. Ask the children to put on smocks.
2. Give each child a glass container. Encourage the children to fill their containers about ⅓ full with colorful rocks or gravel.
3. Help the children use a measuring cup to scoop potting soil into the container, filling it about another ⅓ full.
4. Show the children how to remove the plants from their plastic containers.
5. Encourage them to arrange the plants in their glass containers any way they want. They can use their hands to "smoosh" down the potting soil around the roots. If needed, add a small amount of potting soil to keep the plants in place.
6. For cleanup, scoop up excess potting soil with the old newspaper.
7. Place the indoor mini-gardens in a sunny window and water them with about ¼ cup of water about twice a week. The children will need you to remind them to do this, but they will enjoy watering them.

❖❖ Jayne Morrison, Magna, UT

Grass Shape Sponges

Materials

Sponges
Scissors
Water
Foam tray
Grass seed
Sunlight
Squirt bottle

What to do

1. Cut sponges into shapes that correspond to your current theme, such as dinosaur shapes when discussing dinosaurs or umbrella shapes when discussing rain.
2. Give each child a sponge. Help them moisten their sponges with water.
3. Place each sponge on a foam tray.
4. Encourage the children to sprinkle their sponges generously with grass seed.
5. Place them in a sunny area. Squirt the sponges with water every day.
6. In a couple of days, the seeds will begin to sprout!

More to do

Art: Encourage the children to make collages using grass seed.
Sand and Water Table: Add grass seed to the sensory table.

❖ Sandy L. Scott, Vancouver, WA

Wheels on the Bus

Materials

Variety of objects that roll, such as wheels on small toys, Lego wheels, a ball, a hula hoop, and so on
Variety of objects that do not roll, such as blocks, pieces of wood, puzzle pieces, a beanbag, and so on

What to do

1. Set up an area in the room where the children can explore all the objects.
2. After everyone has finished exploring, guide the children in a discussion. Which objects rolled? Why do they roll? Does a ball roll? Why? Does a square block roll? Why not?
3. Encourage the children to find objects in the room to explore. Make two labels: "Objects That Roll" and "Objects That Do Not Roll." Help the children sort the objects into the correct categories.

More to do

Outdoors: Go outside and look for things that roll.

Related song

"The Wheels on the Bus"

❖❖ Barbara Saul, Eureka, CA

Metal Mining

Materials

Play sand
Washtubs or sandbox
Several bar magnets
Trays
Magnifying glasses

What to do

1. Pour sand into washtubs or use a sandbox for this activity.
2. Give each child a bar magnet. Ask them if they know what will happen if they rub the magnet in the sand.
3. Encourage the children to rub their magnets in the sand and observe what happens. They will probably see black fuzzy things sticking to the magnet (these are metal filings).
4. Explain that some rocks are made of metal and that sand comes from rocks that wear down (this may be a good time to introduce the concept of erosion).
5. Ask the children to rub the metal filings into a container for later exploration in the classroom.

6. Place the metal filings from the sand on trays. Encourage them to experiment by moving the magnets in a circular movement over the filings.

Caution: Make sure that children do not use magnets near computers.

More to do

More Science: Ask the children to find other objects that stick to the magnets. You may want to plant a few objects around the room or set out a tray of objects that the magnets will attract.

❖ Linda S. Andrew, Sonora, CA

Magnetic Motors

Materials

Box, approximately 2' x 1' x 6"
Scissors
Construction paper
Glue
Markers
Clear contact paper
Large paper clips
Magnet wand

6"
1'
2'

CUT ONE SIDE OUT

COVER WITH CLEAN CONTACT PAPER

CAR

HAND GOES INSIDE BOX TO MOVE VEHICLES

3 PIECES OF PAPER

3"
1"
2 INCHES
1 INCHES
FOLD

PAPERCLIP INSIDE

What to do

1. Place the box flat on a table and cut off one of the long sides so that a child can reach inside.
2. Cover one large, flat side of the box with construction paper. Use markers to draw a street scene. Make roads, buildings, street signs, and so on.
3. Cover the scene with clear contact paper.
4. Cut three pieces of paper into 3" x 1" rectangles.
5. Crease the paper so that one side is 2" long and the other side is 1" long.
6. Draw a vehicle on the side that is 2" long.
7. Put a paper clip on the 1" side. Fold the paper in the crease so that the paper clip can rest on the box and the vehicle stands up perpendicular to the box.
8. Encourage the children to move the vehicles across the street scene on the box by holding the magnet wand inside the box and moving it across the top of the box. The paper clip on the vehicle will move along with the magnet wand and the children will be able to move the vehicles around the roads on the box.

Related books

Little Red Plane by Ken Wilson-Max
Planes by Byron Barton
Richard Scarry's Cars and Trucks from A to Z by Richard Scarry
Trains by Byron Barton
Trucks by Byron Barton

❖❖ Ann Gudowski, Johnstown, PA

Making Colors

Materials

White paper towels
Construction paper
Glue
Mouse Paint by Ellen Stoll Walsh
Containers of water
Food coloring
Paintbrushes

What to do

1. Glue a white paper towel to a piece of colored construction paper so that the towel is "framed" by the construction paper. Make one for each child.
2. Read *Mouse Paint* to the children. Discuss how the mice mix colors to make completely different colors.
3. Give each child a construction paper/paper towel frame.
4. Put out three containers of water. Place several drops of red food coloring into the first container, several drops of yellow into the second container, and several drops of blue into the third container. Put paintbrushes into each cup.
5. Encourage the children to "paint" on the paper towel with the colored water and observe how the colors blend into each other, making the same colors that the mice in the story made.

Related book

Little Blue and Little Yellow by Leo Lionni

◆❖ *Diane Angus, Kittery Point, ME*

Luscious Lemonade

Materials

Lemons, one for each child
Knife (adult only)
Small cups, one for each child
Plastic spoons
A faucet or pitcher of water
Small bowls of sugar
Measuring spoons
Crackers or cookies, optional

What to do

1. Talk about the sense of taste and how some things are bitter and some things are sweet. Explain to the children that they are going to make lemonade.
2. Give each child a lemon and a small cup. Cut the lemons into quarters (adult only).
3. Encourage the children to squeeze the quarters of lemon into their cups.
4. Ask them to sip a bit of the lemon juice and describe how it tastes.

5. Help the children fill the cup with water and stir with a spoon. Again, ask the children to try it and describe the taste.
6. Brainstorm with the group how to make the drink sweeter.
7. Demonstrate how to measure sugar into their drinks until it tastes just right.
8. Ask the children what happens to the sugar when stirred in the water.
9. Drink the lemonade with crackers or cookies, if desired.

Related book

The Empty Pot by Demi

❖❖ Barbara Saul, Eureka, CA

Nice Ice

Materials

Paper cups, two for each child
Marker
Refrigerator or freezer
Water
Small pie pans, two for each child

What to do

1. Write each child's name on two cups.
2. Give the children their two cups and help them pour water into each one about ¾ full. Put one cup into the freezer and leave the other in the room.
3. The next day, remove the cups from the freezer.
4. Give each child his cup from the freezer and the cup left at room temperature.
5. Encourage them to compare what happened to the two cups of water. Ask them why it happened.
6. Give each child two pie pans. Ask them to pour the cup of water into one pan and the ice from the other cup into the second pan. Encourage them to compare and contrast the water forms.
7. Put both pans outside and encourage the children to compare what happens to the ice and water.

More to do

Snack: Make small Popsicles by pouring flavored, colored water into ice trays. Put a toothpick into each compartment. Freeze overnight.

Related book

Angelina Ice Skates by Katherine Holabird

❖❖ Barbara Saul, Eureka, CA

Wax to the Max

Materials

Small glass containers
Candles, any scent and color (If desired, match them to the season. For example, use black and orange pumpkin-scented candles for Halloween.)
Wax paper

What to do

CAUTION: This activity involves hot wax and lit candles. Supervise CLOSELY at all times.

1. Discuss solids and liquids and what happens when something changes temperatures.
2. Give each child a small glass container and a candle. Ask the children to put their candles inside their glass container.
3. An adult lights each candle. Instruct the children not to touch but to watch what happens as the candle burns.
4. After each child has observed a solid heating up and turning to liquid (wax melting), ask the children to blow out the candles.
5. At this point, an adult goes to each child and helps him pour his liquefied wax onto wax paper.
6. Talk to the children about the liquid wax cooling and hardening once again.

❖❖ Lisa Chichester, Parkersburg, WV

Washing Hands

Materials

Vegetable oil
Cinnamon
Soap and water
Towels

What to do

1. Talk about germs and explain that they are invisible. Discuss the importance of washing hands before eating and after toileting.
2. Put a couple drops of oil onto each child's hand and sprinkle cinnamon on top of the oil. Ask the children to rub their hands together. Explain that these are pretend "germs" that they can see.
3. Ask the children to wash their hands. If they wash their hands using only cold water and no soap, the cinnamon and oil will remain on their hands. However, if they add soap and wash their hands really well, the cinnamon and oil will disappear.
4. Have a hand inspection and explain what is necessary to get hands clean.

❖❖ Phyllis Esch, Export, PA

Classroom Cooking

Materials

None

What to do

1. Following are some general tips for cooking with children.
2. Begin by preparing the work area and the children. This involves washing the utensils and work surface, as well as gathering all necessary materials, ingredients, and equipment. Be sure that all the children wash and dry their hands and put on aprons or smocks.
3. Show the children the recipe, utensils, and ingredients. Begin by reading the recipe in its entirety. Rebus/picture recipes are wonderful to use with young children and can be found in many books, such as Cook and Learn: Pictorial Single Portion Recipes by Beverly Veitch and Thelma Harms.
4. Explain the procedure. Take time to talk to each child about her part and answer any questions that may arise. Be sure to mention when and how food will be eaten.
5. Ask the children to assist in the cleanup.

❖ Rebecca McMahen Giles, Mobile, AL

Colorful Conversations

Materials

None

What to do

1. During snack or mealtime, have a discussion about the different colors found in everyone's food.
2. Count how many red foods the children see, how many green they see, and so on.
3. Play "I Spy." For example, "I spy something green. It is a vegetable."

More to do

Transitions: As a transition from circle time to free play, chart the color of everyone's favorite food. Ask the children to name some colors and write them on a large sheet of paper. Go around the circle and ask each child what her favorite food is. Then ask what color it is and write it under the appropriate color. After a child names her favorite food, she may go to free play. At the next circle time, count each color's list of food and discuss what color foods the group likes more and what color they like the least.

❖❖ Ann Gudowski, Johnstown, PA

Alphabet Activities

Materials

Different foods and materials for each letter of the alphabet (see below)

What to do

1. For each letter of the alphabet (such as "letter of the week"), fix a fun snack and/or do a fun activity. Parents can help out by sending in snacks.
   FOODS AND ACTIVITIES:
   A– Eat applesauce, apricots, apple muffins, apple juice, or apple cereal; make apple prints.
   B– Eat blueberry muffins, bananas, or blueberries; have a "Balloons and Bubbles" day; sing "Baby Bumblebee."
   C– Eat cantaloupe, celery, or carrots; draw pictures using crayons and chalk.
   D– Eat dried fruit or dill pickles; draw dogs and dinosaurs.
   E– Eat egg salad sandwiches on English muffins; dye eggs.
   F– Eat fruit or figs; play with Frisbees.
   G– Eat anything green!
   H– Eat honey and peanut butter crackers; have "Hat Day"; give lots of hugs.
   J– Eat Jell-O or jelly sandwiches; read *Giant Jam Sandwich* by John Vernon Lord and Janet Burroway.
   K– Eat Kix cereal; fly kites.
   L– Eat lima beans, lemonade, or lentils.
   M– Eat melons, mangos, or muffins; read *Mooncake* by Frank Asch.
   N– Eat noodles and cheese or nuts (check for allergies!).
   O– Eat oranges or orange juice; learn about the ocean.

P– Eat pickles, pizza, peaches, or pineapples; make puppets out of a paper bag.

Q–Eat "quackers" and peanut butter; visit a duck pond.

R– Eat radishes or raisins; draw or paint a rainbow.

S– Eat soup and sandwiches; make sock puppets; play with sand and seashells.

T– Eat turkey or tuna sandwiches; draw a turtle; have "Teddy Bear Day."

U–Eat sandwiches cut into "U" shapes or umbrella shapes.

V– Eat vegetables; make Valentines.

W–Eat waffles; practice whistling.

X– Eat sandwiches cut into X's; have a treasure hunt—X marks the spot!

Y– Eat yogurt or yellow bananas; make yellow yarn pictures.

Z– Eat spaghetti noodles and ask the children to put them into "Z" shapes; draw zigzags.

More to do

Books: Make an ABC book with the children. For each letter of the alphabet, write a giant letter on a piece of paper. Encourage the children to glue related objects on the letter. For example, for the letter "B," color it blue and glue blue construction paper circles on it. For "D," glue small dog biscuits to it, and so on.

Literacy: Encourage the children to think of their own recipes they could use beginning with the letter of the week. Write the child's recipe on a piece of paper and ask her to illustrate it.

Related books

Aardvarks Disembark! by Ann Jonas
The Popcorn Book by Tomie dePaola

❖ Sheryl Smith, Jonesborough, TN

Winter Picnic

Materials

Blankets
Picnic food (hot dogs, cookies, chips, drinks, fruit, and so on)
Paper plates, plastic bowls, cups, and so on
Picnic basket
S'mores (graham crackers, marshmallows, and chocolate)

Hot chocolate
The Snowy Day by Ezra Jack Keats
Old newspaper

What to do

1. This is a great activity for a cold winter day. Explain to the children that they will be having a picnic! Of course, it will have to be indoors.
2. Find a place other than your classroom to have the picnic, if possible. Spread blankets on the floor.
3. Encourage the children to help prepare food for the picnic. Put chips into a bowl, set out cups, and so on. An adult will boil hot dogs (or ask a parent to volunteer to grill outdoors). Let the children fix their hot dogs and get the food they want. Drink hot chocolate.
4. Sit on the blankets while you eat.
5. After eating, sing a few "campfire" songs and recite some fingerplays.
6. Make s'mores for dessert! (Put chocolate squares and marshmallows between two graham crackers and melt.) While eating dessert, read *The Snowy Day* by Ezra Jack Keats.
7. Let the children make pretend snow angels like Peter does in the story. Pretend to make footprints in the snow.
8. Have a "snowball fight" using wadded newspaper.

More to do

Art: Encourage the children to draw a winter scene. Or make a class mural of a winter scene. Use paint, torn construction paper, and so on.
More Art: Make paper snowflakes.

◆◆ Sheryl Smith, Jonesborough, TN

Tickle Your Tastebuds

Materials

Different foods that represent each category of taste (see below)

What to do

1. Beforehand, gather a variety of foods that represent each of the four categories of taste. For example:

- sweet (a grape, an orange, candy, jelly)
- sour (a lemon, warhead candy)
- salty (chips, popcorn)
- bitter (baking chocolate, grapefruit, cinnamon without sugar)

2. Explain to the children that their tongues are sensitive to four types of taste: salty, sweet, bitter, and sour. Tell them that they are going to have a taste test.
3. Put out one sample for each taste group. Encourage the children to taste each food. Discuss each flavor as they try it.
4. Put out four more samples, one from each group, for the children to taste. Ask them to identify the taste and which group it belongs in.

More to do

Math: Graph which flavor the children like best.

Related books

Blueberries for Sal by Robert McCloskey
Bread and Jam for Frances by Russell Hoban
Eating the Alphabet by Lois Ehlert

Related songs

"Do You Know the Muffin Man?"
"Who Stole the Cookie?"

❖ Vickie Whitehead, Citronelle, AL

Crazy, Mixed-Up Snack Attack

Materials

Snacks from home
Large plastic bowl
Wooden spoon
Zipper-closure plastic bags

What to do

1. Ask the children to bring in their favorite snack.
2. Sit in a circle with the children (and their snacks).
3. Put a large plastic bowl in the middle of the circle. Each child takes a turn dumping her snack in the bowl.
4. Ask each child to take a turn stirring the snacks in the bowl.
5. Pour the "Silly Snack" into small plastic bags and give one to each child. Then eat the snack!
6. This activity promotes taking turns and sharing.

❖❖ Lynn Reihl, Lynchburg, VA

Friendship Mix

Materials

Trail mix ingredients (see below)
Zipper-closure plastic bags

What to do

1. Send a note home to parents asking them to bring in an ingredient to make trail mix. Each child should bring in a different ingredient. **Note:** Check for allergies. Some ideas are:
   - Cheerios
   - Pretzels
   - M & M's
   - Raisins
   - Peanuts
   - Dried fruit
   - Mini-marshmallows
   - Chocolate chips
   - Banana chips
   - Mini teddy grahams and sandwich cookies
2. Ask the children to sit in a circle. Give each child a plastic bag.
3. Pass around the ingredients one at a time. Encourage the children to put a little bit of each ingredient into their baggies. This way, they can choose what they like and pass on what they don't like.
4. Eat the "Friendship Mix" together!

❖❖ Sue M. Myhre, Bremerton, WA

Peanut Butter Playdough

Materials

1 cup (320 g) peanut butter
1 cup (360 g) honey or corn syrup
1 cup (125 g) powdered milk
1 cup (90 g) oatmeal
Bowl
Measuring cup
Heavy large spoon
Coconut or powdered sugar, optional

What to do

1. This activity is a great opportunity to make something good to eat and fun to play with at the same time. It is a great fine motor and sensory experience.
2. Help the children measure 1 cup peanut butter, 1 cup honey, 1 cup powdered milk, and 1 cup oatmeal. Mix the ingredients together in a large bowl, pointing out how the ingredients are changing.
3. Once the mixture is dough-like, spoon out some dough for each child.
4. Encourage the children to mix it some more using their hands and fingers. If it is sticky, add small amounts of oatmeal and powdered milk.
5. Encourage the children to explore this edible playdough. If desired, the children can make "snowballs" by rolling a rounded ball of dough in coconut or powder sugar.
6. Explain to the children that this is the one time that it is okay to eat playdough.
Note: Check for allergies.

◆◆ Sandra Nagel, White Lake, MI

Following Directions

Materials

Large chart paper
Markers
Bread, peanut butter, and jelly
Plastic knives

What to do

1. Explain to the children that there are five steps for making peanut butter and jelly sandwiches. Write the following words on a large sheet of chart paper. Demonstrate each step as you write the words on the chart.

    BREAD: Pick up two pieces of bread.

    PEANUT BUTTER: Spread the peanut butter on one slice.

    JELLY: Spread the jelly on the other slice.

    PUT TOGETHER: Put the two pieces together.

    EAT.

2. Go over the words again. Ask the children to repeat the five steps, counting them out on their fingers.

3. Make sandwiches with the children, using the chart.

4. Use this technique whenever you are demonstrating anything that has more than one step in it. It will introduce the children to some simple words, as well as give them initial training in putting items in order and following directions.

More to do

Clean-Up: Before leaving for the day, help the children to remember what they need to do: Put toys and books away, straighten up the room, get their sweaters, and so on.

Outdoors: Before outdoor play, depending on the weather, ask the children to remember what they need to put on (for example, coats, boots, caps, gloves).

Original song

Almost any activity can be put to the tune of "Here We Go 'Round the Mulberry Bush." For example:

Here we put our toys away,
Toys away, toys away.
Here we put our toys away,
Before we go home today.

Here we get ready to take a nap,
Take a nap, take a nap.
Here we get ready to take a nap,
Before we go to sleep.

Here we get into a nice circle...
Here we find our place for work...
Here we get ready to go outside.....

◆◆ Lucy Fuchs, Brandon, FL

Cookie Cutter PBJ's

Materials

Bread
Cookie cutters in desired shapes
Peanut butter
Jelly
Plastic knives and spoons

What to do

1. Give each child two pieces of bread. Show them how to use cookie cutters to cut out shapes from the bread. (Smaller ones work well, but larger ones can be used if no bigger than a slice of bread.)
2. Next, encourage the children to spread peanut butter and jelly on the bread to make a sandwich.
3. Use the sandwiches for a tea party or picnic lunch or just a fun snack.

More to do

Holidays: Use holiday-shaped cookie cutters and have a party.

◆◆ Lisa Chichester, Parkersburg, WV

Peanut Butter and Jelly Swirls

Materials

Bread
Serrated knife (adult only)
Rolling pin
Creamy peanut butter
Grape or strawberry jelly
Plastic knife

What to do

1. Cut off the crusts of the bread using a serrated knife (adult only).
2. Give each child a slice of crustless bread.
3. Demonstrate how to use a rolling pin to roll the bread flat.
4. Encourage the children to use a plastic knife to spread a thin layer of peanut butter on the bread, followed by a thin layer of jelly.
5. Help the child roll up the bread, jelly roll style. Use the serrated knife to cut each child's roll into approximately five slices (adult only).
6. Enjoy at snack time.

◆◆ Vicki L. Schneider, Oshkosh, WI

Peanut Butter and Jelly Burritos

Materials

Tortilla shells, one for each child
Peanut butter
Jelly
Plastic knives
Microwave oven (adult only)

What to do

1. Give each child a tortilla. Show them how to spread peanut butter and then jelly onto it.
2. Next, show them how to wrap it up to make a burrito.
3. Put each child's burrito into a microwave for about 15 seconds.
4. Eat and enjoy this simple, tasty, and fun snack.

❖❖ Lisa Chichester, Parkersburg, WV

Making Peanut Butter and Honey Sandwiches

Materials

Plastic container
Plastic spatula
Peanut butter
Honey
Bread

What to do

1. Pour a generous amount of peanut butter and honey into a plastic container.
2. Encourage the children to stir the contents together with a spatula.
3. Then ask them to spread the peanut butter and honey mixture onto a piece of bread to make a sandwich.
4. It's easy to save any leftover mixture for later because it's already in a plastic container!

❖❖ Jayne Morrison, Magna, UT

Pita Pocket Food

Materials

Variety of sandwich fixings, such as hot dog slices, sandwich meats, shredded
cheese, peanut butter, jelly, pieces of fruit, tomatoes, butter, ketchup, mustard,
and mayonnaise
Small bowls
Plastic spoons and knives
Pita pockets

What to do

1. Put the sandwich fixings into small bowls and put out plastic knives and
   spoons.
2. Give each child half of a pita pocket.
3. Encourage the children to fill their pockets with whatever fixings they want.
4. Eat and enjoy.

More to do

Bulletin Board: Give each child a paper pocket to fill with pretend items. Ask
the children to talk about her "Pita Pocket." Write down what the child says. This
makes a great bulletin board display.

❖❖ Sandra Nagel, White Lake, MI

Bagel and Cream Cheese

Materials

Cream cheese
Strawberry jam
Mini-bagels, ½ for each child
Plates
Plastic knives and spoons

What to do

1. Mix strawberry jam with the cream cheese to give it a slight color and flavor.
   Children enjoy watching the color change.

2. Give each child a plastic knife and half of a mini-bagel.
3. Put a small amount of cream cheese on top of each bagel half and ask the children to spread it.
4. With a spoon, let each child put a small dollop of strawberry jam in the center of the bagel.

More to do

Mix dill with the cream cheese instead of using jam. Top with a slice of cucumber.

❖❖ Sandy L. Scott, Vancouver, WA

Cinnamon Toast

Materials

½ cup (125 g) sugar
½ cup (75 g) cinnamon
Measuring cup
Spoons
Bowl
Bread
Plastic knives or butter knives
Soft butter or margarine
Cookie sheets
Wax paper or foil
Oven (adult only)

What to do

1. Help the children measure ½ cup sugar and ½ cup cinnamon and mix them together in a bowl.
2. Give each child a piece of bread. Demonstrate how to spread butter on it.
3. Encourage the children to sprinkle the sugar and cinnamon mixture on top of the butter, until the surface of the bread is thinly covered.
4. Place the bread on a cookie sheet covered with foil or wax paper. Bake in the oven (adult only) for about 10 minutes or until bubbly (adult only).
5. Let them cool away from the children. Eat them when cool.

❖❖ Sandra Nagel, White Lake, MI

Cinnamon Bears

Materials

Bread
Toaster (adult only)
Bear-shaped cookie cutter
Butter and plastic knives
Cinnamon
Sugar
Small bowl
Raisins

What to do

1. Make toast with the children. Put bread into a toaster (one slice for each child).

CAUTION: Supervise closely. An adult should put the bread into the toaster and remove it when it's ready. Make sure the children do not touch the hot toaster.

2. Next, demonstrate how to use the bear-shaped cookie cutter to cut out a "toast teddy."
3. Ask the children to spread butter on their toast.
4. Mix cinnamon and sugar together in a small bowl. Encourage the children to sprinkle the mixture on top of the butter.
5. Finally, add raisin eyes and buttons.

❖❖ Lisa Chichester, Parkersburg, WV

Sugar Cinnamon Shapes

Materials

Refrigerated can of biscuits
Sugar
Bowl
Melted butter
Clean paintbrush

Plates
Cinnamon
Cookie sheet
Oven (adult only)

What to do

1. After discussing shapes, explain to the children that they are going to make and then eat their favorite shapes.
2. Give each child a plate and a slice of biscuit dough.
3. Show the children how to roll out their dough into long "snake" shapes. Ask, "How does the dough feel?"
4. Encourage them to form their favorite shapes.
5. Mix cinnamon and sugar together in a bowl. Encourage the children to brush melted butter on top of their shape, and then sprinkle with sugar and cinnamon.
6. Place the biscuit shapes on a cookie sheet. Bake according to the directions on the package.

Related books

Shapes by Jan Pienkowski
Shapes, Shapes, Shapes by Tana Hoban

◆❖ Sandra Hutchins Lucas, Cox's Creek, KY

Glazed Circle Cookies

Materials

Refrigerated sugar cookie dough
Blunt knife
Egg whites
Food coloring
Water
Bowls
Clean paintbrushes
Baking sheet
Oven (adult only)

What to do

1. Cut a roll of refrigerated sugar cookie dough into slices.
2. As you give each child a slice, talk about circles. Ask, "What else can you eat that is shaped like a circle?"

3. Mix egg whites, water, and food coloring together into bowls to make different colors.
4. Encourage the children to brush on their favorite color.
5. Put the cookies on a baking sheet. Bake as directed on the package.

More to do

Art: Put out a variety of round objects, such as cups, glasses, plates, pan tops, and cookie cutters. Encourage the children to trace around the objects to make different-sized circles.

❖❖ Sandra Hutchins Lucas, Cox's Creek, KY

Bread Dough Critters

Materials

Books and pictures of animals
Frozen bread dough
Tape measure
Paper and markers
Bowl
Towel
Pretzel sticks, raisins, chocolate sprinkles, coconut, frosting, and so on
Cookie sheet
Wax paper
Permanent marker
Oven (adult only)

What to do

1. This is a great activity to do during a woodland animal unit or some type of animal studies. Show the children books and pictures of animals.
2. Show the children the hard, frozen bread dough. Measure it with a tape measure and record the measurements, tracing its size on the paper.
3. Follow the thawing directions on the package.
4. After the children wash their hands, encourage them to knead the dough on a clean surface.
5. Put the dough into a bowl, cover it with a towel, and put it in a warm area to rise.

6. After the dough has risen, re-measure it. Compare and contrast the changes in the dough.

7. Give each child a handful of dough. Encourage them to knead the dough and shape it into an animal form.

8. They can add pretzel sticks to make a porcupine, coconut to make a polar bear, raisins for eyes, and so on.

9. Place the critters on a cookie sheet covered with wax paper. Print the child's name by her critter with a permanent marker.

10. Bake the critters in the oven (adult only), for a little less time than directed. Take them out when they are slightly brown. Let them cool and eat!

More to do

Books: Read stories about animals.

❖❖ Sandra Nagel, White Lake, MI

Bugs on a Log

Materials

Celery sticks
Peanut butter
Plastic knives
Raisins

What to do

1. Give each child a stick of celery.
2. Help the children fill their celery with peanut butter.
3. Encourage them to put raisins on the peanut butter. Now they can eat their "bugs on the log."

More to do

Science: Fill clear cups with water and two drops of food coloring. Put a celery stick into each color and watch the celery turn that color.

◆◆ Barbara Saul, Eureka, CA

Let's Eat a Bird Nest

Materials

Carrots
Grater
Chow mien noodles
Mayonnaise
Spoon and plate
Grapes

What to do

1. Show the children how to grate carrots. Explain that the little grater holes are very sharp, so they must be very careful. You may need to help them at first, but they will catch on quickly and love doing it.
2. For each child, mix together one half of a grated carrot and about ¼ cup chow mien noodles.

3. Ask them to stir in enough mayonnaise to moisten the carrots and noodles.
4. Show the children how to use a spoon to push it down to form a "nest."
5. Then the children can add grapes for their eggs.

❖❖ Sandra Hutchins Lucas, Cox's Creek, KY

B Is for Butterflies

Materials

Bananas
Plastic utensils
Peanut butter
Plates
Round wafer-type cookies

What to do

1. Peel the bananas (with the children's help, if desired).
2. Cut each banana in half lengthwise. Place each banana half on a plate, flat side down. Give one to each child.
3. Ask the children to spread peanut butter on the banana.
4. Give each child four round, wafer-style cookies. Demonstrate how to place two cookies on each side to make wings.

PEANUT BUTTER

PEEL and SLICE LENGTHWISE

ROUND COOKIES

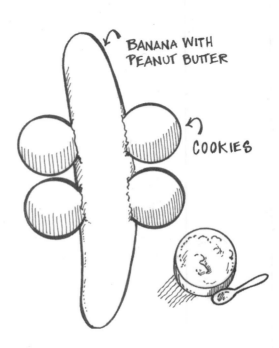

BANANA WITH PEANUT BUTTER

COOKIES

5. Eat your butterflies!

Related book

The Butterfly Alphabet Book by Brian Cassie

❖❖ Charlene Woodham Peace, Semmes, AL

Cupcake Cones

Materials

Cake mix
Large bowl
Mixing spoon
Flat-bottom ice cream cones
Cookie sheet
Oven (adult only)
Frosting (store-bought or homemade)
Plastic knives
Sprinkles

What to do

1. With the children's help, make cupcake batter according to package directions.
2. Spoon the mixture into cones, about ⅔ full.
3. Bake following the same directions as you would for cupcakes.
4. After the cupcakes cool, help the children frost them using plastic knives. Then they can dip the frosting end of the cone into sprinkles.

More to do

Turn the cupcakes into "teddy bear" cupcakes by sticking a mini cocktail umbrella into each one and a few gummy bears or mini teddy bear graham crackers on top of the frosting.

Holidays: At Hannukah, make an edible menorah by lining up nine cupcake cones next to one another and putting a candle into each one (adult only).

❖❖ Audrey F. Kanoff, Allentown, PA

Pizza Shop

Materials

Pizza sauce
Hot dog slices
Pepperoni
Shredded cheese
Green pepper
Bowls
Spoons
English muffins or hamburger buns, ½ for each child
Cookie sheets
Wax paper
Oven (adult only)
Marker

What to do

1. Put pizza sauce, hot dog slices, pepperoni, shredded cheese, and green pepper slices into bowls with spoons.
2. Give each child ½ of an English muffin or hamburger bun.
3. Demonstrate how to put a scoop of sauce on it and spread it around.
4. Encourage the children to sprinkle cheese on top of the sauce. Then they can choose other ingredients to put on top of their pizzas.
5. Put wax paper on the cookie sheet and place the pizzas on the wax paper. Write the child's name next to her pizza
6. Bake for 10 to 15 minutes—until the cheese is melted. Let cool and serve.

More to do

Make "Pizza Faces" by using the toppings to create hair, eyes, a nose, and a mouth.
Holidays: Make "Pizza Monsters" for Halloween.

Related book

Pete's Pizza by William Steig

◆◆ Sandra Nagel, White Lake, MI

Purple Giggles

Materials

3 packages of unflavored gelatin
1½ cups hot water
12 oz. can of frozen grape juice (thawed)
Mixing spoon
9" x 13" pan, greased
Refrigerator

What to do

1. After discussing the color purple, ask the children if they would like to eat something purple.
2. Pour three packages of unflavored gelatin into 1½ cups of hot water.
3. Stir in the grape juice.
4. Pour the mixture into a greased 9" x 13" pan and put it into the refrigerator to chill.
5. When the mixture is firm, remove it from the refrigerator and cut into strips.

More to do

Outdoors: Go on a "purple walk." Go outside (or walk around the room) and encourage the children to find things that are purple.
Science: You could use this activity as a little science lesson. Talk about other things that start out as a liquid but can turn into a solid, such as water into ice.

Related book

Harold and the Purple Crayon by Crockett Johnson

❖ Sandra Hutchins Lucas, Cox's Creek, KY

Applesauce

Materials

Apples
Sharp knife (adult only)
Plastic knives
Paper plates
Microwave-safe bowl
Mixing spoon
Cinnamon
Sugar
Measuring spoons
Potato mashers

What to do

1. Ask the children to wash the apples.
2. Peel, core, and slice the apples (adult only).
3. Place the apple slices on plates and ask the children to cut them into small pieces using plastic knives. (Make sure the children have washed their hands well through all stages of the activity.)
4. Put the small pieces into the bowl and place it in the microwave.
5. Remove the bowl from the microwave every two minutes to stir.
6. The second time, after stirring, ask the children to pour some sugar and cinnamon into the bowl. Start with a teaspoon of cinnamon and a tablespoon of sugar, then add as needed during the stirring process. The amount you add will depend on the amount of apples you use and individual preference.
7. Once the apples are mushy, show the children how to use potato mashers to mush it up more.
8. Serve the applesauce on top of favorite foods, such as pancakes, waffles, yogurt, or ice cream.

More to do

This is a great activity when you are doing a unit on apples (perhaps in the fall).

Related books

My Apple Tree by Harriet Ziefert
The Seasons of Arnold's Apple Tree by Gail Gibbons
Ten Apples Up on Top! by Theo LeStieg

❖❖ Sandra Nagel, White Lake, MI

Drinking Snowballs

Materials

Cups
Spoons
Milk
Vanilla ice cream
Shredded coconut or white sprinkles

What to do

1. Discuss snow with the children. Ask them if they know what snow tastes like. Then ask them if they would like to drink snowballs.
2. Explain that they are going to make snowball shakes. Make sure they understand that they won't be using real snow.
3. Give each child a cup. Help each child pour milk into her cup about ½ full.
4. Then help them spoon a round "snowball" scoop of ice cream into the milk.
5. Encourage the children to sprinkle shredded coconut or white sprinkles on top of the ice cream.
6. While the children drink their snowballs, talk about what they think would be fun to do in the snow.

More to do

Sand and Water Table: Use shaving cream instead of sand in the sand and water table, sandbox, or even on the tabletops. (It's a great way to clean your tables!) White packing foam is another fun "snow" to use.

Related books

Snowballs by Lois Ehlert
Snowman by Raymond Briggs
The Snowy Day by Ezra Jack Keats
White Wonderful Winter! by Elaine W. Good

❖❖ Sandra Hutchins Lucas, Cox's Creek, KY

Lemon Time

Materials

Large bag of lemons, approximately 3 per child
Sturdy plastic knives
Hand juicer or hand-operated lever-type juicer
Small strainer
Clear, unbreakable pitcher
Sugar
Water
Large mixing spoon
Measuring cups
Ice shavings or crushed ice
Plastic cups
Red food coloring, optional

What to do

1. Ahead of time, score lemons across the middle for easier cutting (adult only).
2. Ask the children to help cut the lemons in half. Supervise closely.
3. Place a lemon on the juicer and show the children how to squeeze the juice by twisting the half of the lemon on the juicer. Pull the lever if using that type of juicer.
4. Remove the rind and seeds using a strainer.
5. Pour the juice into a pitcher.
6. Now you are ready to make lemonade. Measure and add sugar and water to the juice in the pitcher. Use approximately ½ cup of sugar and 4 cups of water for every 3 lemons, or to taste. Stir thoroughly.
7. Chill and add safe-size ice shavings or crushed ice and serve. Adding a drop of red food coloring will make it pink lemonade.

More to do

Art: Snip the rind and note the aroma. Encourage the children to glue the lemon snippings to poster board to make a yellow collage.
Dramatic Play: Set up a lemonade stand in the Dramatic Play area and serve the drinks.
Math: Before the lemons are cut and squeezed, ask the children to count them and sort them by size.
More Math: Save the lemon seeds and use them as a counting activity.

◆❖ Maxine Della Fave, Raleigh, NC

Fruit Smoothies

Materials

Berries, bananas, oranges, cantaloupe, and other favorite fruits
2 or 3 small colanders
Plastic knives and spoons
Vanilla yogurt
Ice cream scoop
Blender
Cups

What to do

1. Put the fruit on a table. Encourage the children to explore it. Talk about the way it feels and smells.
2. Ask some volunteers to put the fruit that needs washed into colanders and wash it under running water.
3. Ask the other children to peel the bananas and cut them into small pieces. Do the same with the oranges and cantaloupe.
4. Put two scoops of yogurt into the blender and ask three children to put a handful (make sure their hands are clean) of their favorite fruit into the blender.
5. Blend for approximately 1 minute and pour into cups.
6. The children can drink it or eat it with a spoon.
7. Continue until all the children have had a smoothie.

Original song

(Tune: "Here We Go 'Round the Mulberry Bush")

This is the way we wash our fruit,
Wash our fruit, wash our fruit,
This is the way we wash our fruit
All day long.

This is the way we peel our fruit…
This is the way we cut our fruit…
This is the way we blend our fruit…
This is the way we eat our fruit…

◆◆ Ann Gudowski, Johnstown, PA

My Own Fruit Juice Smoothie

Materials

Clean, empty baby food jars with lids

Sherbet to match the fruit

Small ice cream scoop

Fruit, any kind (banana, pineapple, orange, strawberries)

Frozen fruit juice

What to do

1. Give each child a baby food jar. Help the children scoop their favorite sherbet into their jar.
2. Add frozen juice.
3. Give the children cut-up fruit to add to the jar as well.
4. Ask the children to put on the lids and shake.
5. Open and enjoy. This is a great way to make individual fruit smoothies because there's no mess!

❖ Lisa Chichester, Parkersburg, WV

Pasketti Soup

Materials

Red and white checkered tablecloth, optional

10 ¾ oz. can condensed tomato soup

15 oz. can of spaghetti with tomato sauce (or other pasta shapes)

Pitcher of water

Electric kettle or soup pot with hot plate

Ladle

Can opener

Rubber scraper

8 4-oz. Styrofoam cups and plastic spoons

Storybook about spaghetti, such as:

Cloudy with a Chance of Meatballs by Judi Barrett
Daddy Makes the Best Spaghetti by Anna Grossnickle Hines
Strega Nona by Tomie dePaola
Wednesday Is Spaghetti Day by Maryann Cocca-Leffler

What to do

1. Put the materials and ingredients on a table in view of the children. If desired, cover the table with a red and white checkered tablecloth.
2. Say, "Today we will each have a delicious bowl of something that can be hard to say. Some people call it 'Pasketti Soup' because 'Spaghetti' can be a very, very hard word to pronounce. Why don't you try saying it?"
3. Now tell the children that they will make the soup. Say and do each of the following steps:

    "First I open the cans.
    Then I pour the pasta with sauce into the pot.
    Next I pour the tomato soup into the pot.
    Now I'll add a can of water.
    Then I'll stir it all together.
    Last, I'll put on the lid and turn on the heat."

    (This recipe makes eight four-ounce servings. Increase ingredients as needed.)
4. Warn the children that the pot will soon be HOT. Ask them to stay away from the soup as it cooks.
5. Read one of the stories as the soup cooks. It simply needs to be heated to a simmering temperature to blend the ingredients. If the soup heats to a full boil, be sure to let it cool before serving.
6. Check the soup when you finish the story. Ladle the soup into cups when it's ready to serve.
7. Excuse the children to wash their hands and then gather at the table for tasting.
8. Sing the ever-popular "On Top of Spaghetti" song to conclude this activity.

❖❖ Susan A. Sharkey, La Mesa, CA

Graham Cracker Houses

Materials

Graham crackers
Small bowls, plastic knives, and spoons
Frosting
Fruit cereal, marshmallows, and candies
Shredded coconut
Food coloring

What to do

1. This is a great activity to do when children are learning about construction and building. Explain how mortar is used to hold bricks together, and that they will use frosting to hold their "snack building" together.
2. Give each child four or five graham crackers. Put out bowls of frosting, colored shredded coconut (for grass and roofing), fruit cereal, marshmallows, and candy.
3. Demonstrate how to spread frosting on the graham crackers and put them together to form a "house." Encourage them to decorate the houses as desired.
4. Take pictures of the children's finished products. Have fun eating them!

More to do

More Snack: Create a house built out of gingerbread using the same process as above.
Blocks: Encourage the children to use large Legos and blocks to create a structure. It can be a building, a house, school, or whatever the children desire.

Related books

Hammers, Nails, Planks, and Paint: How a House Is Built by Thomas Campbell Jackson
Mom Can Fix Anything by Kimberlee Graves
My Very First Book of Tools by Eric Carle

❖ Cookie Zingarelli, Columbus, OH

Funny Face Sandwiches

Materials

Foods to use as facial features (see activity below)
Bowls
Tub of whipped cream cheese
Creamy peanut butter
Small paper plates
Markers
English muffins, ½ for each child
Plastic knives
Food containers and spoons
Hand mirror, optional

What to do

1. Put a variety of foods into bowls for the children to use as facial features. Be creative and offer a variety of choices. (HINT: Go to a market where you can see and choose small quantities from bulk bins.) Following are some examples:

   EYES: green grapes, black olives (cut in halves), gumdrops, circular cereal
   NOSES: almonds, dried apricots, miniature marshmallows
   MOUTHS: tomato wedges, pieces of red "shoestring" licorice or fruit leather
   EARS: banana chips, pickle pieces, cheese curls
   HAIR: alfalfa sprouts, shredded carrots, coconut flakes (can be dyed yellow with food coloring)

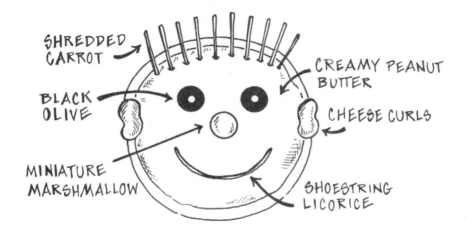

2. Put out a tub of whipped cream cheese and a bowl of creamy peanut butter for the children to use as "skin."

3. Use a marker and a paper plate for each step of the recipe as shown in the illustration:
   a. skin
   b. eyes
   c. nose
   d. mouth
   e. ears
   f. hair
   g. face

4. Put the recipe plates and ingredients on a table in chronological order. If the table is a rectangle, go from left to right. If it's a circle, go counter-clockwise.

5. Introduce the activity by reviewing the parts of the face. Ask, "Where is your hair? How many eyes do you have? How many ears? Is your skin light or dark?" Pass around a hand mirror, if desired.

6. Say, "We're going to make 'Funny Face' sandwiches for our snack today. First we'll spread the skin and make two eyes. Next we'll add a nose and mouth. Then two ears. Last we'll add the hair. You can make your face as funny as you want. Have a good laugh and then gobble it up!"

7. Guide each child along in following the steps in the process. Proceed to the giggle-and-gobble stage!

More to do

Social Development: This activity supports positive self-image, lends itself well to talking about physical differences among people, and relates to clowns/circus themes.

❖❖ Susan A. Sharkey, La Mesa, CA

Saying "Good Morning!"

Materials

None

What to do

1. Invite the children to join you in a seated circle.
2. Discuss how you and your co-workers greet each other in the morning when you arrive by saying, "Good morning, (name)."
3. Explain that when they arrive in the morning, it is courteous for the teachers and children to greet each other.
4. Invite one of the children to act out his arrival in the morning. Say, "Good morning" using his name and prompt the child to answer back using yours.
5. Switch roles with the child—you pretend to be the arriving child and he pretends to be the teacher. Act out the morning greeting as before.
6. Invite the rest of the children, two at a time, to act out the morning greeting, giving both of them an opportunity to assume the roles of both child and teacher.
7. Follow through as the children arrive on the days after the lesson by greeting each one by name and giving them the opportunity to greet you in return. Some may need to be prompted to do this at first, but usually it isn't long before each child walks in anticipating the morning greeting with the teacher.

More to do

Practice saying good-bye in an appropriate way at the end of the day.

More Social Development: Use this practice to reinforce learning each other's names at the beginning of the year and the names of new children joining the group at mid-year.

Diversity: Ask parents of children with diverse ethnic backgrounds to teach you how to say "Good morning" in their native language. Then encourage the children to practice the greetings to help celebrate the diversity of the class.

Social Studies: Learn to say "Good morning" in other languages when learning about other countries. For example, teach the children to say, "Buenos dias" when learning about South America or Spain.

❖❖ Susan Jones Jensen, Norman, OK

Block Family

Materials

Pictures of each child and child's family
Small individual cereal boxes
Scissors
Glue
Clear contact paper

What to do

1. This is a great activity to do at the beginning of the year.
2. Ask the children to bring in a picture of themselves and a picture of their families. Make sure the parents know that the photos will be cut up and glued.
3. Give each child a small cereal box. Help them glue a photo of themselves on one side of the box and the photo of their family on the other side.
4. Help them cover the boxes with clear contact paper.
5. Encourage the children to share information about themselves and their family during circle time.
6. Add the new blocks to the block area. This will encourage the children to incorporate their family and friends into their playtime with the blocks.

❖❖ Sandy L. Scott, Vancouver, WA

Here I Am!

Materials

Copies of the template (see illustration)
Photographs of the child's family
Old magazines
Glue
Crayons and markers

What to do

1. Give each child a copy of the template and attach the following note:

Dear parents,
Your child is a special individual. Please fill out this paper with your child and send it back with your child to share with the rest of the children.
From,
Your child's teacher

2. Encourage the children to glue photos to the template or use pictures from magazines. They can also draw pictures on it.
3. Choose one child per week to do this family activity. Create a special bulletin board with all the pictures.

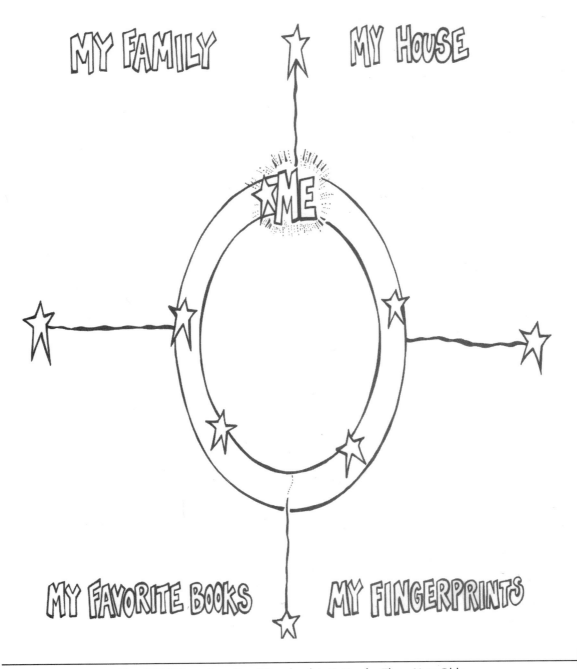

More to do

Put up all the pictures for parent visit time.

Books: Make a class book with the pictures.

Related books

Amazing Grace by Mary Hoffman
Leo the Late Bloomer by Robert Kraus
The Mixed-Up Chameleon by Eric Carle

❖ Barbara Saul, Eureka, CA

Family TV Stars

Materials

Large cardboard television (see illustration)
Star stickers
Photo (that can be cut up) of families

What to do

1. When talking about families, set up a "Star of the Week" (or month) on a bulletin board with the cardboard television as shown.
2. Ask each child to bring in a family photo when it's his turn. Make sure the child's parents know that the photo will be cut up.

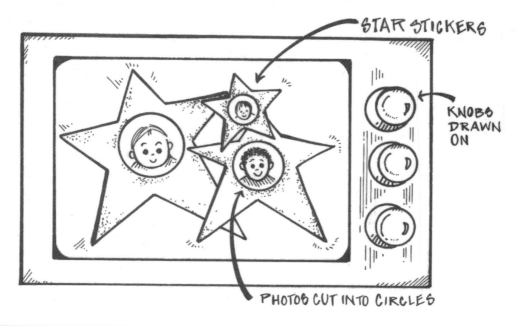

STAR STICKERS

KNOBS DRAWN ON

PHOTOS CUT INTO CIRCLES

3. Help the child cut out the faces of his family members into small circles. Then ask him to place the pictures inside the television screen with star stickers.
4. Encourage the child to talk about his family television stars!

❖❖ Lisa Chichester, Parkersburg, WV

Funny Faces

Materials

A few large mirrors or one small mirror for each child

What to do

1. Show the children how you use your face to express a variety of emotions: sad, happy, surprise, anger, puzzlement, grumpy, worried, scared, sorry, sleepy, shy, and silly.
2. Encourage the children to practice making a variety of faces in the mirrors.
3. This activity is fun for children because they enjoy making the different faces. You can further aid their understanding of these feelings by talking about each emotion. For example, "I feel sad when Amanda won't play with me," or "I feel happy when Ethan shares a toy."

❖❖ Melissa O. Markham, Huddleston, VA

Circle of Friends

Materials

Small shatterproof mirrors
Paper plates, one for each child
Markers or crayons
Buttons
Yarn in a variety of colors
Miscellaneous art supplies

What to do

1. At circle time, pass around some mirrors and ask the children to look at their faces. Talk about eye color and hair color. Encourage them to smile in the mirror and make different faces. Talk about how all of us are very special and unique.

2. Give each child a paper plate and a variety of art supplies. Ask them to draw their faces on the plate.

3. They can use yarn to make hair and a mouth, and buttons for eyes and a nose. But any way they want to create their face is fine.

4. Hang all of the paper plate faces in a circle on a bulletin board. In the middle of the circle, write the words "Circle of Friends."

5. Children love to see if they can guess which face belongs to which friend. It's also great at the beginning of the year or for Open House.

❖ Gail D. Morris, Kemah, TX

Friendship Necklace

Materials

Colored or striped plastic straws
Scissors
18" pieces of yarn
Construction paper
Photo of each child in class
Clear tape or clear contact paper
Hole punch

What to do

1. Cut plastic straws into 1" pieces.

2. Tape one end of each piece of yarn to make it like a "needle" for stringing. Tie a straw segment to the other end of each yarn piece.

3. Cut construction paper into circles with 3" diameters. Use clear tape or contact paper to attach each child's photo to a paper circle. Trim them to fit.

4. Punch two holes at the top of each photo circle.

5. Give each child a piece of yarn. Demonstrate how to string straw segments onto the yarn by threading the straw through the taped end of the yarn.

6. When the yarn is almost full, add the child's photo to the necklace and tie it off for wearing.

7. After all the children have completed their necklaces, encourage them to trade them with their friends so that everyone has a necklace with a picture of a friend on it.

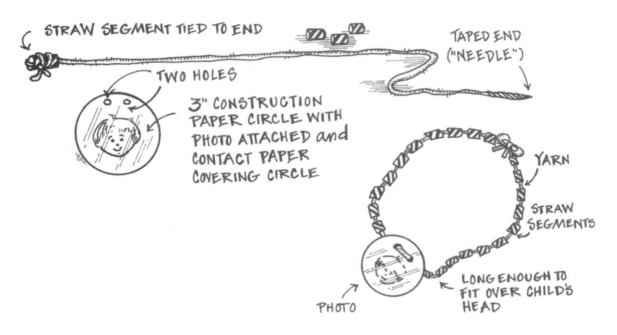

More to do

Books: Read stories about friendship.
Music: Sing songs about friendship.

Related song

The More We Get Together

The more we get together,
Together, together.
The more we get together
The happier we'll be.

'Cause your friends are my friends,
And my friends are your friends.
The more we get together
The happier we'll be.

Related books

Friends at School by Rochelle Bunnett
Making Friends by Fred Rogers

❖❖ Christine Maiorano, Duxbury, MA

friendship Quilt

Materials

Construction paper
Washable paint
Glue
Wallpaper scraps
Colored butcher paper
Markers

What to do

1. Give each child a sheet of construction paper. Help them press their hands into the paint and make handprints on their paper.
2. Help each child write his name next to his handprint.
3. After the handprints are dry, help the children glue wallpaper scraps on the corners of their paper.
4. Glue all of the handprint "quilt" pieces to a sheet of large butcher paper in a quilt-like fashion.
5. In the spaces between the quilt squares, write words such as "fun," "friends," "love," "play," and so on.
6. Hang the "quilt" on the wall or a bulletin board. At the top, write "In Friendship We Are One."
7. This is great for end-of-the-year celebrations.

◆❖ Sandy L. Scott, Vancouver, WA

Class Quilt

Materials

Construction paper in a variety of colors
Scissors

What to do

1. Cut construction paper into 8" x 8" squares.
2. Send home a construction paper square with each child, along with a note instructing the child and his family to decorate the square as a group project. Encourage them to be creative.

3. When the children bring in their completed squares, encourage them to share their squares with the rest of the children. Then put all the squares together to look like a real quilt.

4. Hang the "quilt" in the room. This makes a nice display to be enjoyed all year long.

More to do

Send home a note asking the children to bring in a real quilt from home. Ask the parent to write information about the quilt and send it in. For example, where the quilt came from, who made it, and for what occasion it was received. You will probably get some wonderful stories and it makes a very nice Show and Tell.

❖❖ Gail D. Morris, Kemah, TX

Sharing

Materials

Trays

What to do

1. When there are manipulatives to be shared, it can be hard to just dump them into a pile and expect the children to share without a squabble. Instead of putting them all together in a pile, place some onto separate trays and give one to each child. Each tray is a boundary for "ownership."

2. Another idea for sharing is to teach the children to ask, "What can I have?" when they want to share someone else's toys. For example, if a child wants to play with something that another child is playing with (such as Legos), he can ask, "What can I have?" This gives the other child a chance to select what he will share, and given the chance to be generous, the child usually does well.

Related book

We Share Everything by Robert Munsch

❖❖ Tracie O'Hara, Charlotte, NC

Share Puzzles

Materials

Puzzles appropriate for the children's skill level (typically 6 to 12 pieces for three-year-olds)

What to do

1. The first few times you do this activity, adults will have to assist. Ask the children to group into pairs ("teams"). Each pair of children chooses a puzzle and takes it to their work spot.

2. Ask the children to take turns removing a piece of the puzzle, until the puzzle frame is empty. (If they do each puzzle twice, the person that went second the first time goes first the next time they choose pieces.)

3. Then encourage the children to take turns putting in one of their pieces until the puzzle is complete.

4. Ask the teams to return their puzzle and choose another one. Repeat the turn-taking activity.

5. Two puzzles are good to begin with. The children can increase the amount they do as they get better at working together. Soon the children can be more independent forming their teams, choosing the puzzles, and taking turns.

More to do

Form teams randomly so the children can work with a variety of people. For example, draw names from a hat, pick teams by clothing items, and so on.

More Social Development: Practice doing other things in "teams." For example, ask the children to walk in pairs when going places. Encourage the children to practice teamwork by helping each other and working together.

Books: Read stories about sharing, such as *Rainbow Fish* by Marcus Pfister.

Language: Take photos of teams working together and make a "Cooperation Poster" of the class. Talk about the photos and teamwork.

❖❖ Sandra Nagel, White Lake, MI

The "I Want" Monster

Materials

Paper plate
Markers, yarn, or other suitable mask-making materials

What to do

1. This idea is designed to help turn those not-so-polite "I want" statements into more appropriate "May I please…" requests.
2. In advance, make a silly monster mask (not too scary!) using a paper plate.
3. Discuss with the children how some words and phrases are polite and some are not. Make a chart with two columns and list some polite words and some "monster" words.
4. Whenever you hear an "I want" statement from one of the children, say, "What was that? I thought I heard the 'I want' monster! Yes, I did! Uh, oh, here he comes!" Put on the mask and tickle the child or make a silly monster noise. Keep it light and the children will think this is funny. The hitch, though, is that the request will not be granted until the child rephrases by using a "May I please…" statement to scare the "I want" monster away.
5. At first, the children may use an "I want" statement on purpose to elicit an appearance from the monster, but soon they will realize that to get whatever it is they want, they need to skip the silliness and use a polite request instead.
6. Adapt the monster's name as needed. He is also widely known as "Gimme!"

More to do

Art: Make "I want" monster masks with the children.

❖❖ Suzanne Pearson, Winchester, VA

"I CAN" Shirts

Materials

White T-shirts, one for each child in one size larger than the child normally wears
Heavy cardboard or shirt board
Fabric paints
Paper plates
Fabric pen

What to do

1. As the children go about their daily routine in your class, notice and point out to them the things they can do. For example, when a child gets a drink of water on his own, say, "That's great how you took care of yourself. You were thirsty and wanted a drink and you did it all by yourself." When two children solve a dispute with little or no help, comment on that. You might say, "You two worked out that problem without any help. I'll bet that makes you both feel great."

2. Ask the children to tell you some things that they know how to do. Make sure you record at least thee things each child says.

3. Give each child a t-shirt. Insert a piece of cardboard or shirt board into the shirt.

4. Pour three colors of fabric paint onto three paper plates.

5. Ask each child to dip one hand into the first color and press it on the back of his shirt. Repeat for each of the other colors, changing hands as the child wishes. Make sure the children wash their hands thoroughly between each color to keep from mixing them.

6. Let the shirts dry for at least one day.

7. Use the fabric pen to print one thing each child said he could do on each handprint. Let dry.

8. Print "I CAN" on the front of the shirt using the fabric pen or create a stencil that says "I CAN" and use the fabric paints to sponge paint the words on the front of the shirt.

9. Let dry.

10. The children can wear their "I CAN" shirts with pride!

Note: Never put personal information such as the child's name on anything easily seen by others.

More to do

Buy some white or tan totes (available at any craft store). Encourage the children to design an "I CAN" tote bag using the same method as described in the activity.

Related book

Howie Helps Himself by Joan Fassler

❖❖ Virginia Jean Herrod, Columbia, SC

Practicing Good Hygiene

Materials

Small squares of paper
White paper plates, one for each child
Brown, yellow, red, and black pieces of yarn (cut into 2" pieces)
Glue
Scissors
Construction paper, in blue, green, brown, and gray colors
Fine-tip black markers
Flesh color construction paper
Facial tissues

What to do

1. Introduce the subject of practicing good hygiene. Talk about covering our mouths when coughing and sneezing, using a tissue for our noses, and so on. Explain to the children that it is also polite to cover their mouths and noses when they sneeze or cough.
2. Ask the children to practice coughing, sneezing, and wiping their nose into tissues and then disposing the tissues into the proper receptacle. Tell the children that if no tissue is available, they should cough and sneeze into their forearms rather than their hands, which readily spreads germs to anything they touch thereafter.
3. Beforehand, type the following poem onto squares of paper:
   When you cough
   And when you sneeze,
   Cover your mouth,
   If you please.

4. Read the poem to the children. Then give each child a paper plate and explain that they will be making a paper plate face that looks like them, covering their mouth with a tissue.

5. Encourage the children to glue on yarn for hair and draw in the outlines of eyebrows, a nose, and eyes with a fine-tip marker.

6. Cut colored construction paper into two small circles for the child's own eye color and glue them inside the eye outlines.

7. Trace hands onto "flesh" colored paper and cut them out. Glue them over the mouth area to hold the tissue in place.

8. Finally, glue the "When you cough" poem to the bottom edge of the plate.

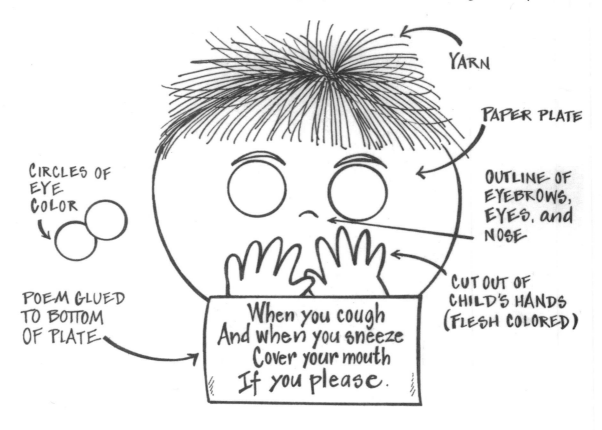

CIRCLES OF EYE COLOR

POEM GLUED TO BOTTOM OF PLATE

When you cough
And when you sneeze
Cover your mouth
If you please.

YARN

PAPER PLATE

OUTLINE OF EYEBROWS, EYES, and NOSE

CUT OUT OF CHILD'S HANDS (FLESH COLORED)

More to do

Health: Practice proper hand washing technique at the sink using water, soap, and paper towels.

Original song

Sing the following song to the tune of "Here We Go 'Round the Mulberry Bush." Pantomime the actions while singing it.

This is the way we wash our hands
Wash our hands, wash our hands.
This is the way we wash our hands
So early in the morning.

This is the way we wash our face…
This is the way we brush our teeth…

Related books

Body Battles by Rita Golden Gelman
Those Mean, Nasty, Dirty, Downright Disgusting But…Invisible Germs by Judith
   Anne Rice
What Makes You Ill by Mike Unwin and Kate Woodward

◆❖ Linda Becker, Rochester, MN

Teach Me to Tie

Materials

Paper
Copy machine
Scissors
Crayons
Glue
Styrofoam tray
Clear contact paper
Hole punch
Shoelace or long piece of yarn

What to do

1. Photocopy the shoe (see illustration) and cut it out. If desired, color it with crayons.
2. Glue the paper shape to a Styrofoam tray. Cover it with clear contact paper and cut it out.
3. Use a hole punch to make two rows of holes down the center of the "shoe."
4. Demonstrate how to lace a shoelace through the holes and criss-cross in and out.

5. Before long, the children will catch on and will love to practice over and over. Tell the children they can take their "shoe" home and practice with their parents.

❖❖ Sandra Hutchins Lucas, Cox's Creek, KY

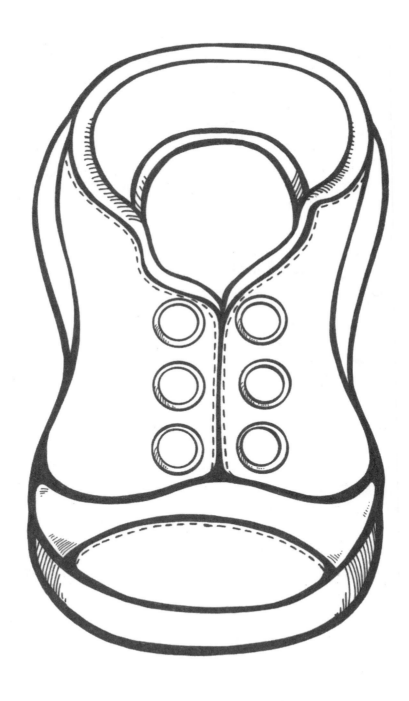

Tell Them with Tape

Materials

Colored plastic tape

What to do

1. Young children need anchors to help them with spatial organization. Put a piece of tape on the floor where children are to form a line. This will help make transitions more orderly.
2. Put a piece of tape a few feet from the water fountain. Children waiting for a drink will stand on the tape until the fountain is free.

❖ Mary Jo Shannon, Roanoke, VA

Color Cube

Materials

2 clean, ½ gallon cardboard milk cartons
6 3" x 3" squares of construction paper, each a different color
Clear tape or clear contact paper

What to do

1. Measure 4" up from the bottom of the milk cartons. Mark the 4" point around both cartons and cut off what remains above the 4" line.
2. Slide the two cartons together, open ends facing each other, until you have formed a cube.
3. Cover each side of the cube with a different color construction paper square.
4. Cover the entire cube with clear tape or clear contact paper.
5. At transition time, roll the cube and say, "All the children wearing (color) can go to free play."

More to do

Games: Use the cube for color games, Bingo, and so on.

Related books

Color Surprises: A Pop-Up Book by Chuck Murphy (artist)
Color Zoo by Lois Ehlert
Little Blue and Little Yellow by Leo Lionni
My Many Colored Days by Dr. Seuss
Snappy Little Colors by Kate Lee

❖❖ Ann Gudowski, Johnstown, PA

Transition Schedules

Materials

Old catalogs and magazines
Camera and film, optional
Scissors
3" x 5" or 4" x 6" cards
Wide tape, clear contact paper, or glue
Chart paper
Markers
Clothespin

What to do

1. Make a "Transition Schedule" showing photos and symbols of the day's activities. To include the children in the process, ask them to look through catalogs and magazines to find pictures or symbols of different activities they do throughout the day.
2. Cut out the pictures together. If you have a camera, take pictures of the children doing various activities, such as washing hands, listening to a story, sitting at the table, eating snack, and so on.
3. Use contact paper, wide clear tape, or glue to attach each picture to a card.
4. Make a chart using the photos or symbols of the day's activities. Attach each picture to the chart sequentially.
5. Clip a clothespin to the photo that shows what is happening now.
6. Five minutes before the transition, say, "In five minutes we will be stopping _____ and it will be time to_____.

7. When it is time to stop and transition, go to the schedule and state, "It's time to stop _____. It is now time to _____." As you state this, unclip the clothespin and clip it to the new picture.

8. If desired, draw an arrow on the clothespin so that it points directly to the card depicting what is presently occurring on the day's schedule.

9. This gives the children a visual schedule of what will happen next. Providing the sequence of the day often assists children who may have difficulty with transitions.

10. For children having difficulty with transitions, include them more in the process. For example, show them the picture before you announce the change to the group; ask the child to move the clothespin to the new picture; or before the day starts, preview the day's schedule with the child using the chart.

WASHING HANDS

EATING

More to do

If you do not have a chart, use a clothesline with clothespins.

Literacy: Display the photos or symbols of the day's activities on the chart left to right. This can help with pre-reading skills.

❖ Sandra Nagel, White Lake, MI

Ring that Bell!

Materials

Medium-size dinner bell

What to do

1. This is a great transition technique to use to notify the children when it's time to do something, such as come inside from outdoor play or to clean up.
2. Each day during outdoor time, choose a child to ring the special bell.
3. Give the bell to the chosen child when it's time to go in and ask her to ring it. The child that gets to ring the bell will be so excited and proud to have her turn.
4. Make sure that each child gets a turn ringing the bell.

◆◆ Sue M. Myhre, Bremerton, WA

Transition Tunes

Materials

Tape player
Tape of classical music (or other calming tunes)

What to do

1. About two minutes before one activity will end and another will begin, turn on a calming piece of classical music, a lullaby, or a "bedtime" tape. Keep the volume fairly low, but loud enough so that the children can hear it over the noise of their play. You may choose to tell the children that this indicates two minutes more of play, or you may want to wait and let them adjust to this as the transition routine.
2. After the two minutes are over, stop the tape and give the children the instruction for the new activity. You will find that after a few days of this, the music will start to clue the children that a change is coming, but it is not an abrupt stimulus so it is less likely to wind them up or cause anxiety.
3. If the activity that is ending requires cleanup, you may want to create a tape that plays a two-minute classical "warning" and then loops right into your clean-up song.

4. If you have a child who has particular trouble with transitions, ask her to start and stop the tape. The more control the child has over the transitions, the easier that transition will be for her.

More to do

Three-year-olds benefit from both auditory and visual stimuli. You may want to pair the "transition tune" with a homemade poster or sign that you hold up to show that there are two minutes left, or to indicate what activity will come next. **Math:** Using classical music during math lessons has been shown to increase learning of mathematical reasoning and concepts.

◆◆ Suzanne Pearson, Stephens City, VA

Five-Minute Warning

Materials

None

What to do

1. Even three-year-olds need a verbal warning before a transition. Give the children "five-minute warnings" for transitions during the day, such as cleanup, outdoor time, naptime, and circle time.
2. For example, tell the children, "Five minutes until clean-up time. Now is the time to finish working on what you are doing because in five minutes, it's time to clean."
3. You can set a timer for five minutes, or you can just give another gentle reminder at the end of the five minutes. For example, "Time to begin cleaning up—it's been five minutes."
4. Sing your favorite clean-up song while everyone helps. Young children need time to be able to finish up and prepare for what comes next.

Original song

Clean Up, Clean Up (Tune: "Mary Had a Little Lamb")
Everybody everywhere
Clean up clean up
Everybody do your share.

Come on everybody
Let's clean up, let's clean up.
Come on everybody, let's clean up
Everybody let's clean up!

Time to put the toys away
Toys away, toys away.
Time to put the toys away,
Everybody help clean up.

❖ Sue M. Myhre, Bremerton, WA

It's Cleanup Time

Materials

Labels
Photos of children putting toys away or catalogs
Scissors
Clear contact paper or clear tape

What to do

1. When it is almost clean-up time, announce, "Five more minutes left to play."
2. When five minutes are up, say, "It's time to clean up." Then sing the following song to the tune of "Skip to My Lou, My Darling" (or chant it).

Five more minutes left to play,
Five more minutes left to play,
Five more minutes left to play,
Five more minutes to play.

Clean up, clean up the room,
Clean up, clean up the room,
Clean up, clean up the room,
Clean up the room together.

3. Place labels, photos, or pictures cut from catalogs on shelves and areas where the materials are to be placed. Encourage the children to look through catalogs and find the items with you. Cut out the pictures and use clear contact paper or wide clear tape to mount them where materials are to be placed. Or use photos of the children putting away the materials.

More to do

More Transitions: Make a chart with photos or symbols of the day's activities. Clip a clothespin on the photo showing what is happening now. This gives the children a visual schedule of what will happen next. Providing the sequence of the day often assists children who may have difficulty with transitions.

◆◆ Sandra Nagel, White Lake, MI

Hi-Ho and Off We Go

Materials

None

What to do

1. Familiarize the children with the words to the following song. Sing it during transition times.
2. Sing the song to the tune of "Hi-Ho, Hi-Ho, It's Off to Work We Go."

   Hi-ho, hi-ho,
   To center time I go.
   I'm all cleaned up and ready to go,
   Hi ho, hi ho, hi ho.

3. Change the song for various transition times.

◆◆ Nicole Sparks, Miami, FL

Clean Up Song

Materials

None

What to do

1. When asking the children to help clean up, sing this fun song to the tune of "Frère Jacques." Children love hearing their names!

   I see Conner, I see Conner.
   He is picking up toys.
   I see Conner, I see Conner.
   He is picking up toys.

2. Continue until you have sung the names of all the children who are helping.
3. To personalize the song, you can sing the name of the toy the child is busy picking up. For example, "Conner is picking up the Legos," or "Conner is putting away the clothes."
4. Individual recognition is always good for small children. Those children who are not helping will often join in just for a chance to hear their names sung.

Related books

Clean Your Room, Harvey Moon! by Pat Cummings
Jonathan Cleaned Up, Then He Heard a Sound by Robert Munsch
Old Henry by Joan W. Blos
Pigs Aplenty, Pigs Galore! by David McPhail
Pigsty by Mark Teague
When the Fly Flew In by Lisa Westberg Peters

❖❖ Virginia Jean Herrod, Columbia, SC

We're Waiting

Materials

None

What to do

1. As much as we try to avoid it, there are inevitably times when the children will be required to wait for an anticipated activity or event to begin.
2. Before beginning this song, explain why they are being asked to wait and tell them you are going to sing a song together to make the waiting time go faster.
3. Ask the children to clasp their hands together, interlinking fingers.
4. Show them how to roll one thumb around the other in the typical "waiting" gesture. While the children are rolling their thumbs, sing this simple song to any tune you choose.

   We're waiting, we're waiting,
   We're waiting, we're waiting,
   We're waiting, we're waiting
   For (insert activity name here) to begin.

5. Change the song as necessary to reflect the situation. For example, if the children are waiting for the ice cream truck to show up, you might change the last line to "for the ice cream truck to come."
6. Play silly "mind" games. Ask the children to close their eyes and think about the anticipated activity. Guide them in their thoughts much as a meditation guru would guide those participating in meditation. If the activity becomes available while the children are meditating, you can tell them that their good thoughts helped to make the activity happen!

More to do

Games: If your anticipated activity seems to be endlessly delayed and you cannot move on to another activity, play some simple and fun games that require little or no equipment. For example, grab some small toys and play a "What's Missing?" game.

Original poem

I Don't Like Waiting! (begin with everyone standing)

I don't like waiting, no I don't! (shake head)
Not a tiny bit! (waggle index finger in air)
I don't like waiting, no I don't! (shake head)
I don't like to sit! (sit down suddenly)
But when I really have to wait, (pout)
It helps if I can find (hold both hands out, palms up)
Something to do with my hands (clasp hands together, fingers interlinking)
And occupy my mind. (nod head)

◆◆ Virginia Jean Herrod, Columbia, SC

Tap and Clap

Materials

None

What to do

1. When moving from one activity to another, use this transitional song.
2. Ask the children to sit on the floor with you. Encourage them to follow your motions as you demonstrate how to tap and clap.
3. Tap your thighs with open hands and say, "Tap." Clap your hands and say, "Clap." Repeat this rhythm and encourage the children to follow along.
4. When the children seem familiar with the rhythm, begin to sing the following song as they continue to tap and clap. Sing it to the tune of "If You're Happy and You Know It."

   If your name is (child's name), wash your hands.
   If your name is (child's name), wash your hands.
   If your name is (child's name), if your name is (child's name),
   If your name is (child's name), wash your hands.

5. Change the song according to the activity the children are heading toward. In this example, the children are washing hands in preparation for lunchtime.
6. You can use this song any time you ask a larger group of children to move from one activity to another. For example, when going outdoors sing, "If your name is (child's name), get your coat."

7. If you need to insert some waiting time in the song, such as when children are washing hands for lunch, sing the following verse while tapping and clapping:

We are waiting for friends to wash their hands.
We are waiting for friends to wash their hands.
We are waiting for friends, we are waiting for friends,
We are waiting for friends to wash their hands.

Related books

A Boy Went Out to Gather Pears by Maryann Kovalski
First Pink Light by Eloise Greenfield
Something Good by Robert Munsch
Wait and See by Robert Munsch
Will It Ever Be My Birthday? by Dorothy Corey

❖❖ Virginia Jean Herrod, Columbia, SC

Smooth Moves

Materials

None

What to do

1. Following are some ideas for smooth transitions with a large group of children.
2. When it is time for the whole group to go to the bathroom and the room has already been tidied, bring the children to the library or quiet center. Let the children use any item in this center and remind them to stay within its confines.
3. Ideas for putting jackets on a lot of children for outdoor play:
   - Put some quiet items in the area where coats are being zipped and buttoned by teachers. This helps to avoid rough play while each child waits her turn being dressed.
   - Make a "train" of masking tape or chairs for children to wait on.
   - Put a square of carpet in the area for children to sit on while waiting.
   - Sing songs to keep their minds off waiting.

❖❖ Carol Sargeant, Lynchburg, VA

A Hand on a Hip and a Hand on a Lip

Materials

None

What to do

1. When the children need to walk silently through a common area or the library, or when moving to different areas of the room, ask them to walk with one hand placed on a hip and the other hand's forefinger placed on their lips.
2. This simple phrase helps them to remember to walk quietly and to not touch their friends.

❖❖ Nancy M. Lotzer, Farmers Branch, TX

Move Like the Animals

Materials

None

What to do

1. When the children need to move to a new location, suggest that they pretend to be an animal while they walk. For example, they can:
   - slither like a snake
   - move as quietly as a mouse
   - fly like a butterfly
   - hop like a rabbit
   - move like an elephant (side to side with hands as trunk)
2. If desired, match the animal with your current theme.

More to do

Ask the children to imagine moving like a leaf falling to the ground or like a cloud through the sky.

◆◆ Sandy L. Scott, Vancouver, WA

"On the Lookout" Walk

Materials

Construction paper and scissors, or real shapes or objects related to the theme

What to do

1. Cut out different shapes, objects, and other items related to your theme from construction paper. Or use real objects.
2. Place the cutouts or real objects in the classroom, in the hallways, or on the walls ahead of time.
3. During a transitional time, ask the children to look for a specific item you've "hidden."
4. You can use this technique on the way outdoors or to another area in the center, in the classroom on rainy days, as a group time game, after naptime, and so on.

More to do

Ask the children to find items outdoors in conjunction with a unit on community helpers, birds, animals, gardening, or seasons.

◆◆ Tina R. Durham-Woehler, Lebanon, TN

Whose Lunch Box?

Materials

Children's lunch boxes
Masking tape

What to do

1. Place a strip of masking tape on the floor, long enough to place everyone's lunch box on top.
2. At the end of group time and before lunch, ask the children to sit in a large circle around the strip of masking tape.
3. Bring the children's lunch boxes to the circle and line them up on top of the tape.
4. Starting with the first lunch box, ask each child, one by one, to pick up a lunch box and match it to its owner. Then the child hands it to its owner. If they don't know who it belongs to, they can ask, "Whose lunch box?" Young children delight in this activity, especially at the beginning of the school year.
5. The children can either wait until everyone has their lunch box or go wash their hands as they get their lunch box.

More to do

Literacy: As the year progresses, the children can begin to match written name cards to the lunch boxes.
Math: Depending on the variety of lunch boxes, you could make a graph showing the quantity and types, such as hard and soft, colors, and so on.

Related book

Will I Have a Friend? by Miriam Cohen

❖ Barbara Reynolds, Galloway Twp, NJ

Glitter Bottles

Materials

Empty 20 oz. or 1-liter plastic soda bottles with caps

Filler items, such as glitter, sequins, plastic metallic confetti, small buttons, and so on

Baby oil or mineral oil

Super glue or hot glue gun (adult only)

What to do

1. These bottles are great to use for transitions because they have a calming, soothing effect on children. Whenever it's time for children to calm down, bring out the glitter bottles for children to manipulate and enjoy.

2. To make them, rinse out the bottles and allow them to dry.

3. Pour some of the filler ingredients into the bottom of the empty bottle. Add baby oil or mineral oil until almost completely full, leaving only a small margin at the top. If desired, change the concept a little and add something special for the children to find, such as one small button among lots of confetti.

4. Run a bead of super glue or hot glue around the neck of the bottle and replace the cap.

5. The children can tip the bottle from side to side to see the glitter move through the oil.

More to do

For a different effect, fill the bottle only partially with oil, and replace the rest with water. Food coloring can also be added.

Holidays: For a seasonal glitter bottle, use confetti with a holiday theme. At Halloween, it's fun to add black food coloring, plastic spiders, and wiggly eyes.

Science: Experiment with different kinds of oil. Some are denser than others and have different effects on the fillers you use.

❖❖ Vicki L. Schneider, Oshkosh, WI

Index

J

Jars, 45, 77, 126, 240, 475, 533
  baby food, 21, 578
  lids, 158, 240, 350, 527
Jelly, 556, 558, 560–561, 563
  sandwiches, 553
Jewelry, 117, 227, 305, 389, 419,
    458–459, 483
  boxes, 52, 227
  homemade, 41–42
  necklaces, 305, 410, 458–460
  plastic, 525
Jewels, 347
  "diamonds," 533
Jingle bells, 404, 424
  homemade, 479–480
Juice, 506, 553, 573, 578
  cans, 59, 378
  cartons, 486
  lids, 446
  packs, 500
July Fourth. See Fourth of July
Jump rings, 103, 109

K

Kaleidoscopes, 529
Ketchup, 563
  bottles, 480
Key rings, 129
Keyboards, 226
Keys, 238, 356, 519
Kisses, 424
  candy, 449
Kitchen utensils, 305, 484
  colanders, 577
  graters, 153, 569
  juicers, 576
  knives, 378, 400, 538, 548,
    561, 564, 566, 574
  ladles, 154, 305, 578
  meat forks, 305
  plastic, 154, 200, 225, 400,
    525, 558, 560–561,
    563–565, 569–571, 574,
    576–577, 580–581
  potato mashers, 29, 63, 574
  scoops, 220, 356, 516–518,
    577–578
  sieves, 158
  spatulas, 562
  spoons, 19, 21, 27, 48, 50,
    55, 125, 148, 154, 356,
    382, 486, 538, 556, 558,
    564, 569, 571–576,
    581–382
  strainers, 356, 576
  tongs, 24, 242, 457

whisks, 63
Kites, 553
  homemade, 495
Knives, 378, 400, 538, 548
  blunt, 566
  butter, 564
  Exacto, 43, 378, 436
  matte, 216–217, 219
  plastic, 154, 200, 225, 400,
    558, 560–561, 563–565,
    569–571, 574, 576–577,
    580–581
  serrated, 561
  sharp, 574
  utility, 215
Kwanzaa, 405–408

L

Labels, 54, 78, 95, 101, 181, 222,
    326, 342, 604
  address, 44
  computer, 428
Lace, 80, 424
Lacing cards, 243
Ladles, 154, 305, 578
Laminate, 61, 94, 109–110, 112,
    136, 206, 208–209, 238, 243,
    248, 301, 303, 333, 344, 384,
    388, 427, 430, 448, 465, 520,
    541
Language skills, 15–16, 53, 55, 76,
    88, 104, 154, 159, 187–188,
    191, 231, 237, 258–259, 286,
    289, 341, 368, 372, 377, 385,
    391, 394, 409–422, 431, 451,
    469, 476, 491, 497, 503, 526,
    592
  Spanish, 410, 475–476, 583
Large muscle skills. See Gross
    motor skills
Latkes, 153
Laundromat, 219–220
Laundry baskets, 219, 417
Leashes, 186, 222
Leaves, 40, 59, 63, 159, 270, 295,
    358, 412, 424, 488, 519, 527,
    536
  artificial, 211
  oak, 424
  paper, 380, 537
Lemonade, 548, 553
Lemons, 548, 556, 576
Letters, 107, 223, 297, 354,
    423–425 (see also Alphabet)
  foam, 519
  plastic, 63
  stamps, 426

stencils, 428
Libraries, 226
  books, 355
  pockets, 333, 354
License plates, 356
Lids, 87, 126, 230, 356, 484
  bottle caps, 19, 65, 288
  box, 212
  coffee can, 65
  copper, 388
  jar, 240, 350, 527
  juice cartons, 446
  liquid detergent, 29
  milk jug, 350, 446
  pan, 567
  plastic, 87, 230, 290, 356,
    458, 479
  pot, 486
Liquid detergent lids, 29
Liquid soap, 280, 315, 490
Liquid starch, 31, 50, 442, 519
Literacy skills, 15, 38, 77, 81,
    95–175, 177, 214, 289, 291,
    302, 410, 420, 445, 500,
    524–525, 554, 601, 612
Luggage tags, 434
Lunch bags, 286, 472, 488, 495
Lunchboxes, 612
  trees, 335

M

M&M candies, 449, 557
  counting books, 95, 168
Magazines, 51, 54, 76, 79, 107,
    117, 138, 219, 221, 223, 227,
    267, 299–300, 303, 347, 356,
    421, 426, 431, 433–434, 443,
    497, 503, 512, 584, 600
  teacher resource, 361
Magnetic tape, 268
Magnets, 297, 417, 424, 515, 529
  apple, 268
  bar, 545
  letters, 426
  squares, 57
  strips, 143
  wands, 546
Magnifying glasses, 126, 145, 181,
    411, 515, 535, 545
  homemade, 66–67
Manila folders, 328
Manila paper, 19, 123, 194
Manipulatives, 97, 158, 431,
    435–438
Maps, 433–434
  homemade, 507–508
  Ireland, 388

Children's Book Index